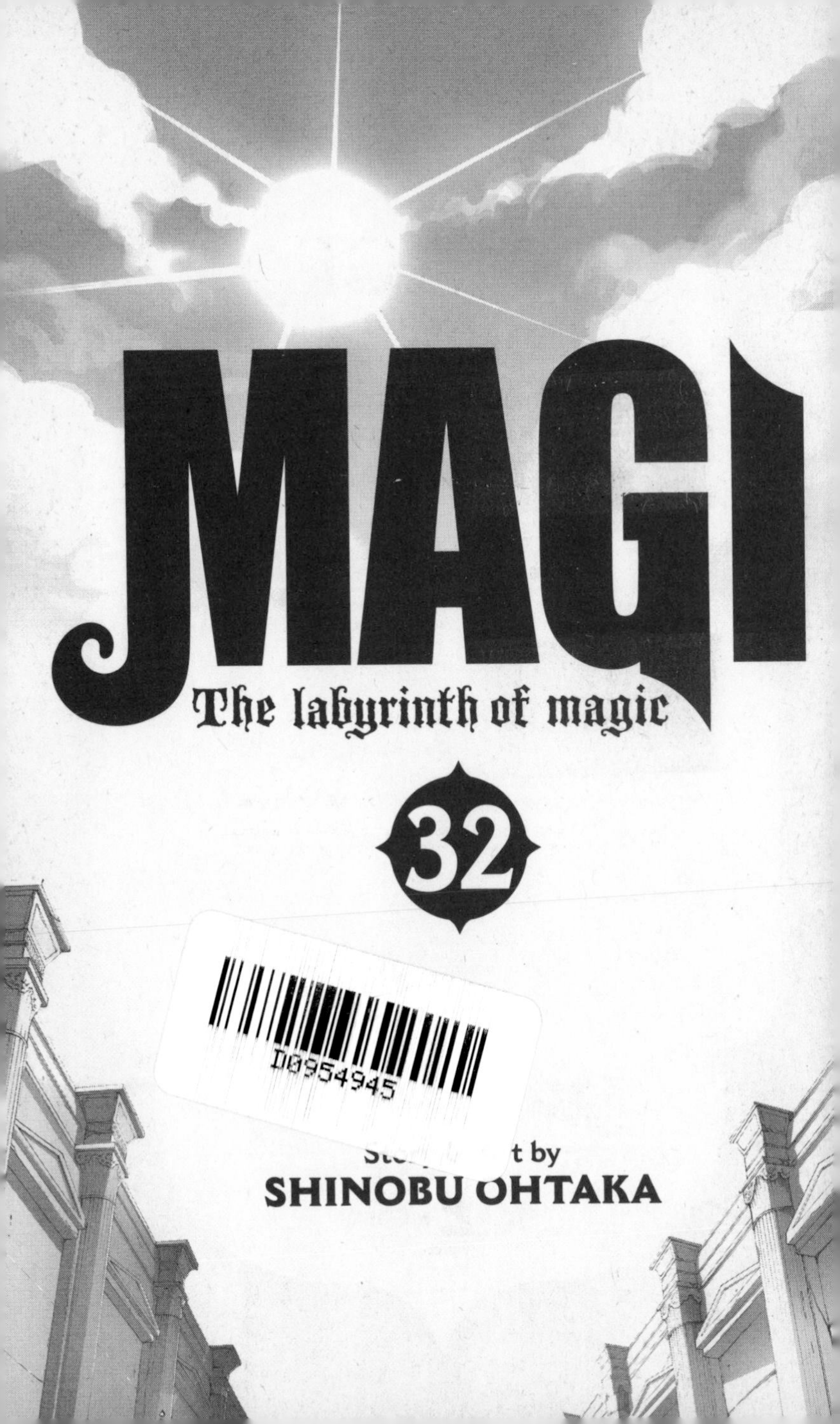

MAGI

The labyrinth of magic

32

Sto[illegible]t by

SHINOBU OHTAKA

MAGI
The labyrinth of magic

CONTENTS

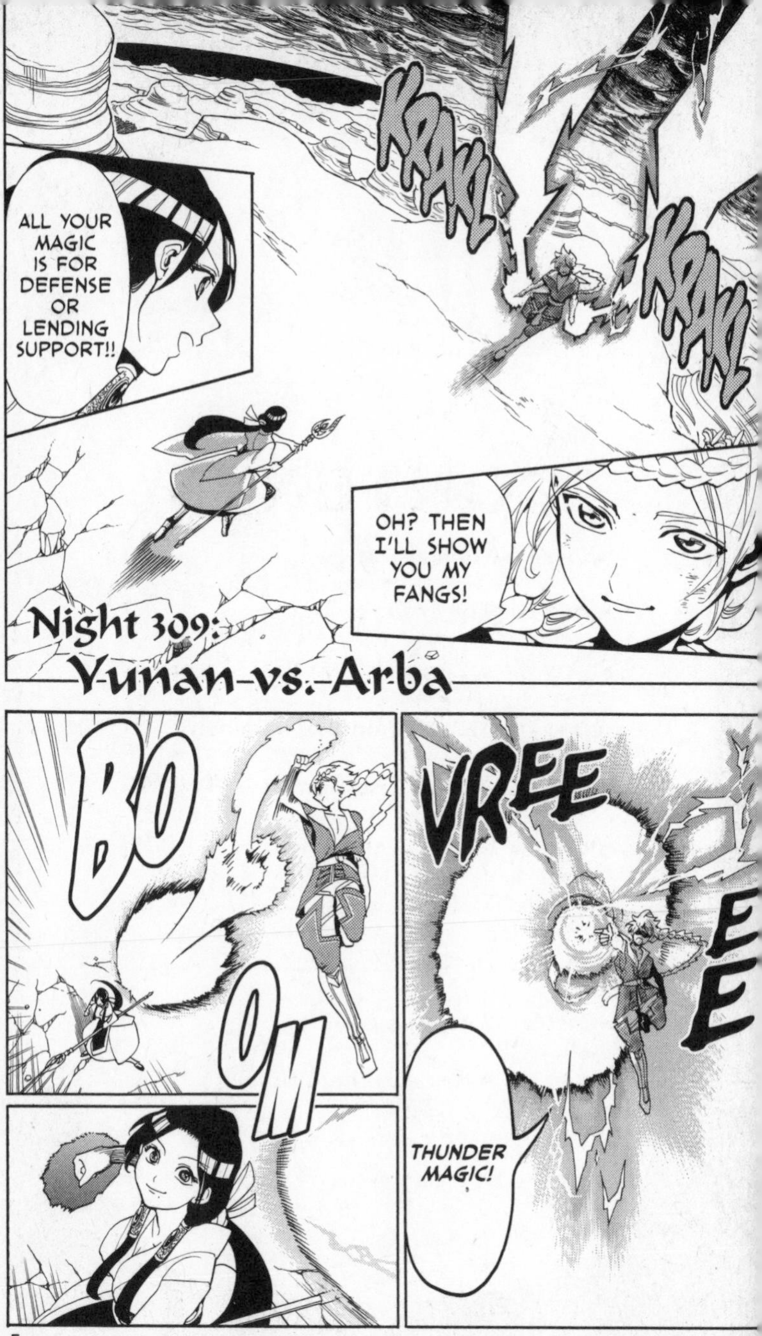
KRAKL
KRAKL
ALL YOUR MAGIC IS FOR DEFENSE OR LENDING SUPPORT!!
OH? THEN I'LL SHOW YOU MY FANGS!
Night 309: Yunan vs. Arba
VREEEE
THUNDER MAGIC!
BOOM

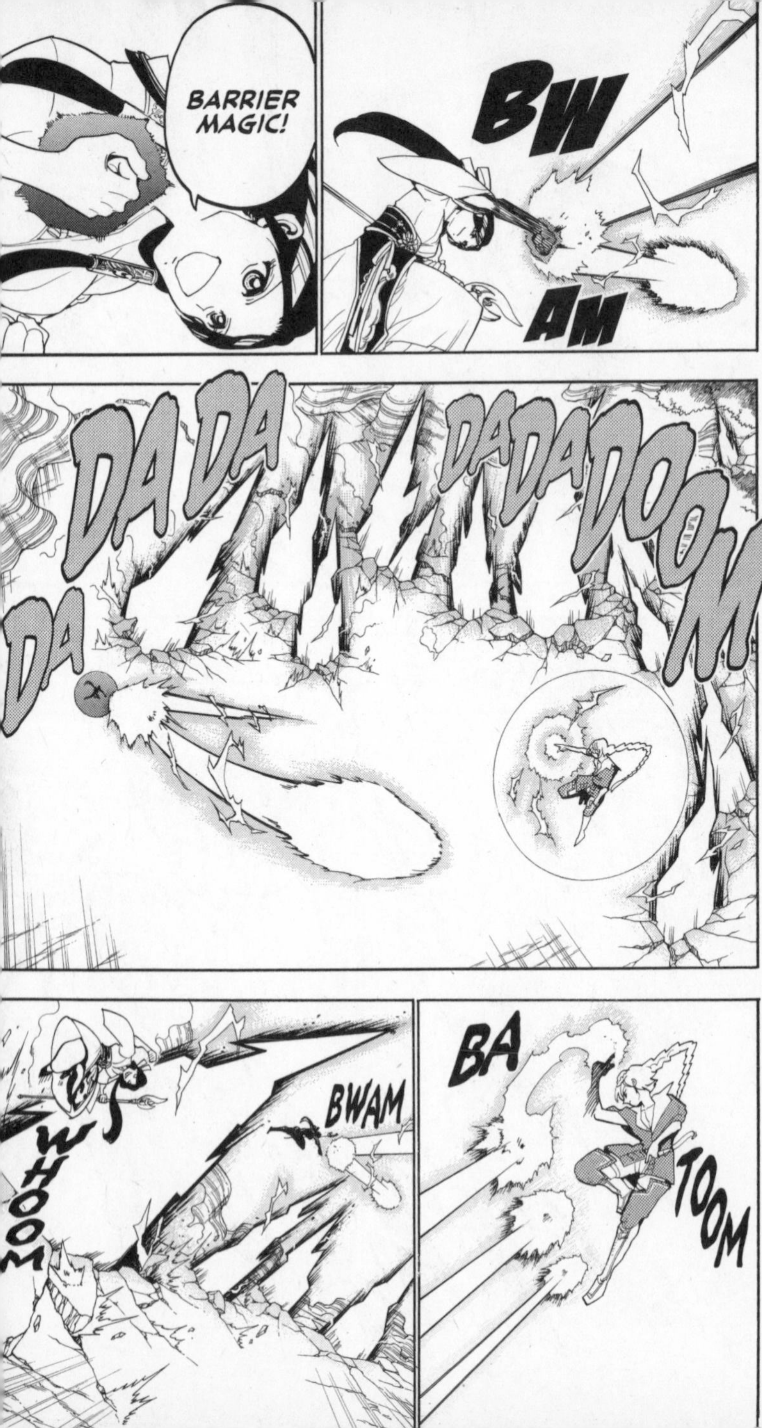
BW
AM
BARRIER MAGIC!
DADADOOM
DA DA DA
BA
TOOM
BWAM
WHOOOM

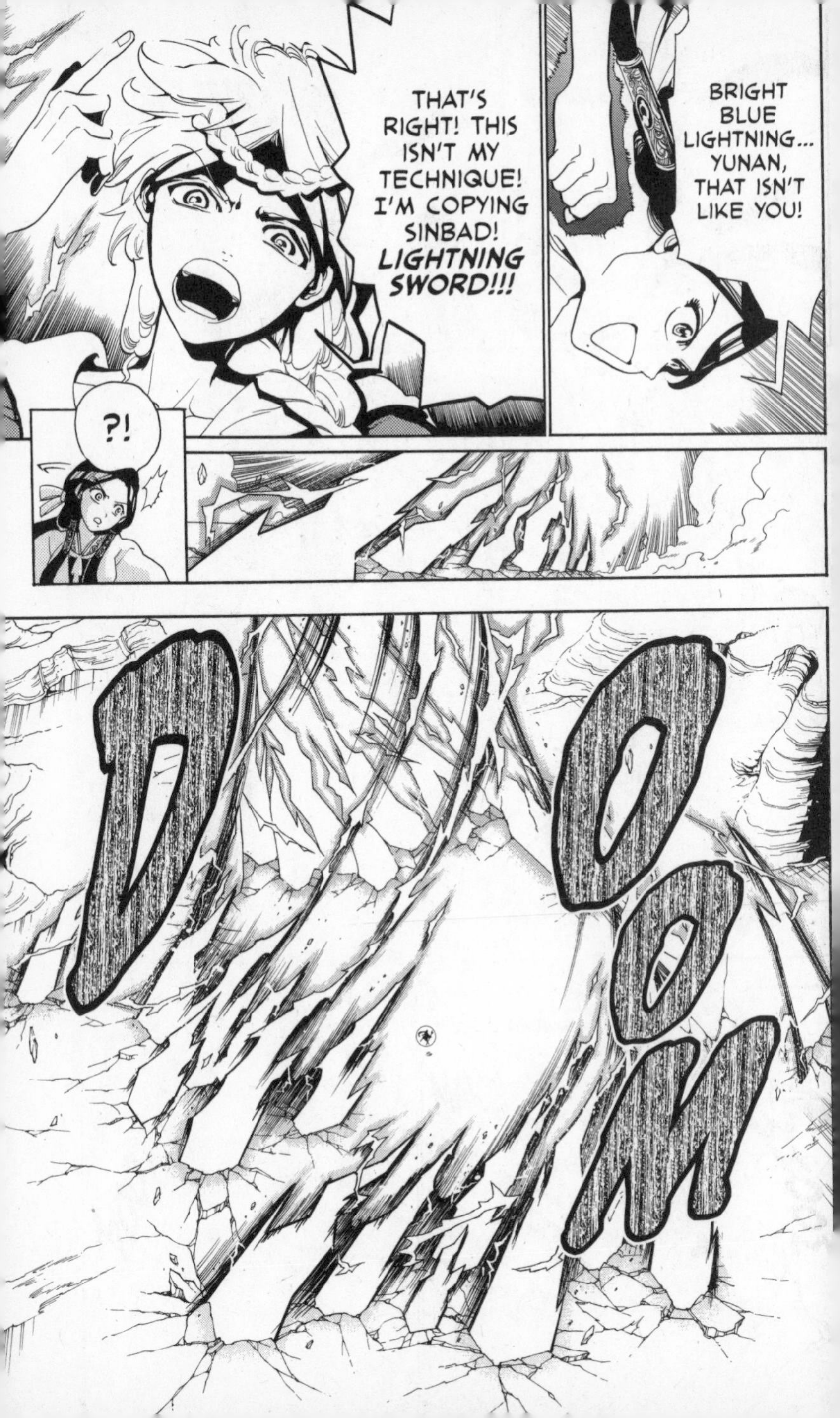
BRIGHT BLUE LIGHTNING... YUNAN, THAT ISN'T LIKE YOU!
THAT'S RIGHT! THIS ISN'T MY TECHNIQUE! I'M COPYING SINBAD! LIGHTNING SWORD!!!
?!
DOOM

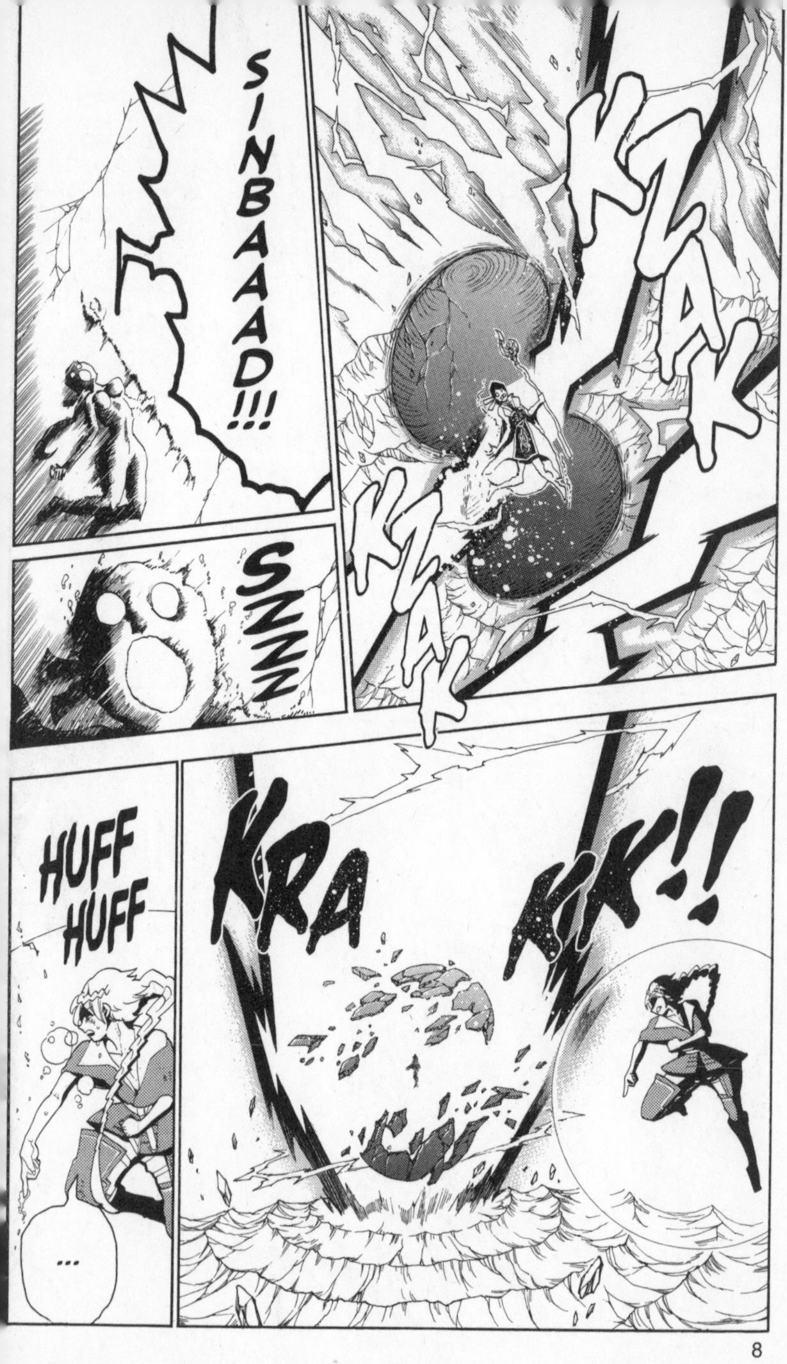
KZAK
KZAK
SINBAAAD!!!
SZZZZ
KRA KKK!!
HUFF HUFF
...

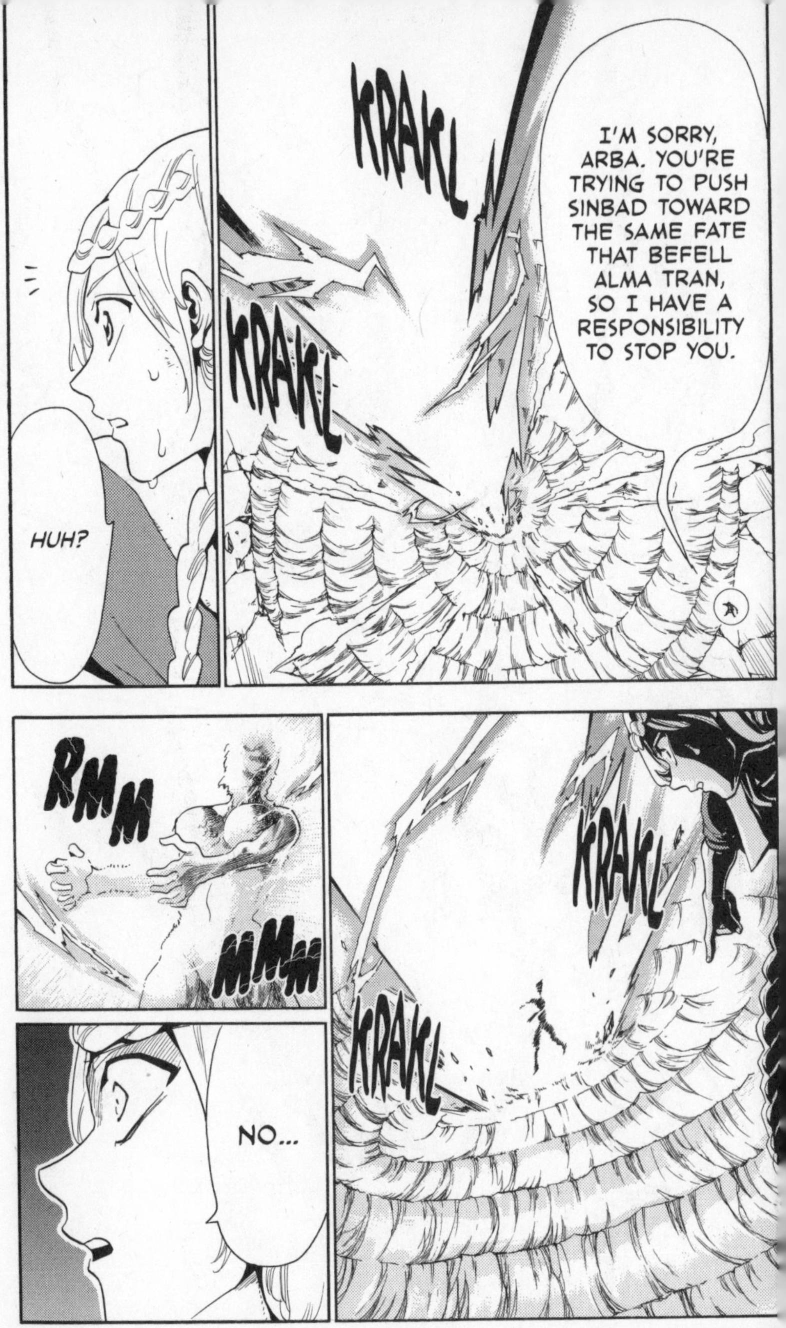

I'M SORRY, ARBA. YOU'RE TRYING TO PUSH SINBAD TOWARD THE SAME FATE THAT BEFELL ALMA TRAN, SO I HAVE A RESPONSIBILITY TO STOP YOU.
KRAKL
KRAKL
HUH?
KRAKL
KRAKL
RMM
MMM
NO...

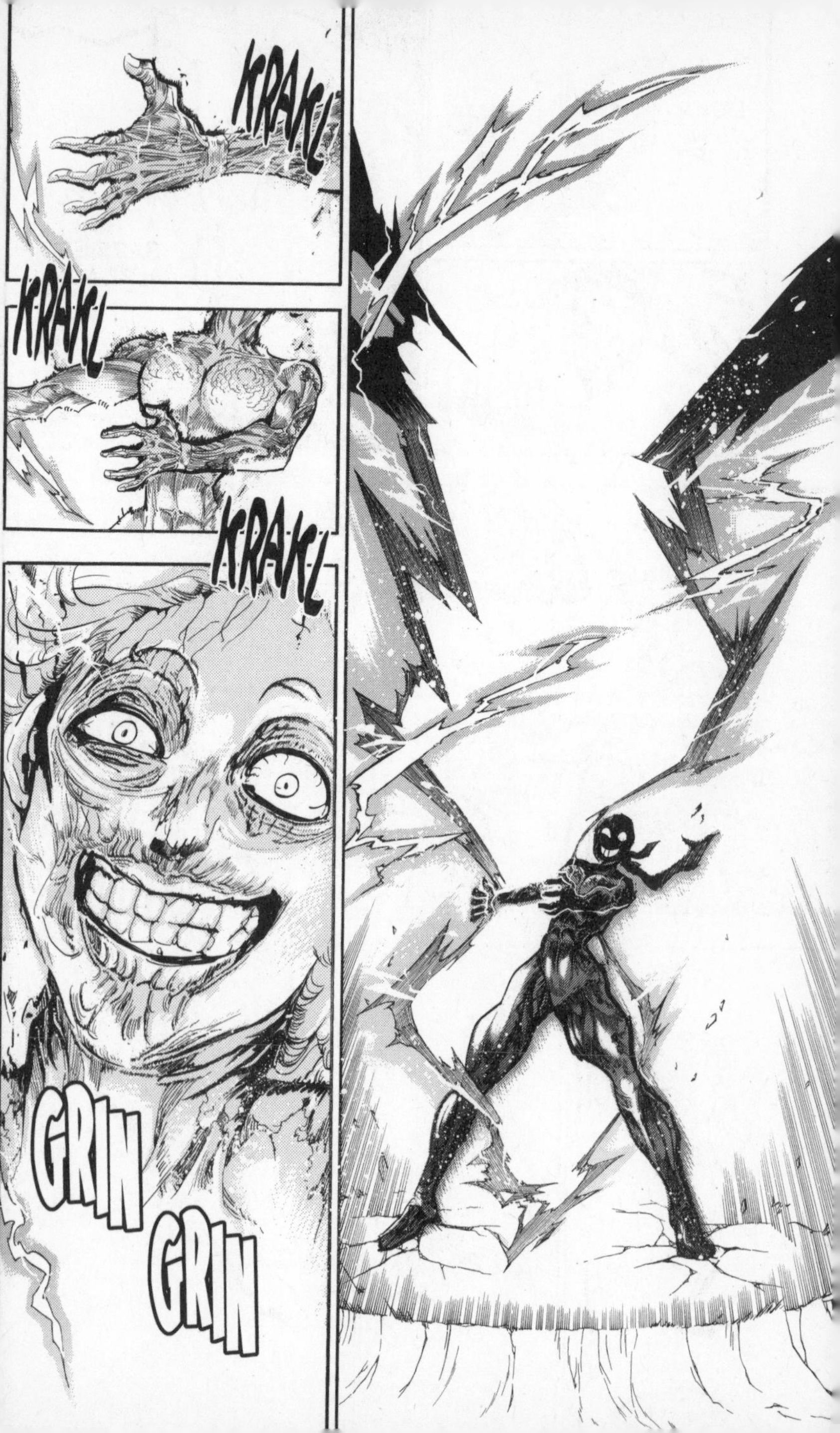
KRAKL
KRAKL
KRAKL
GRIN
GRIN

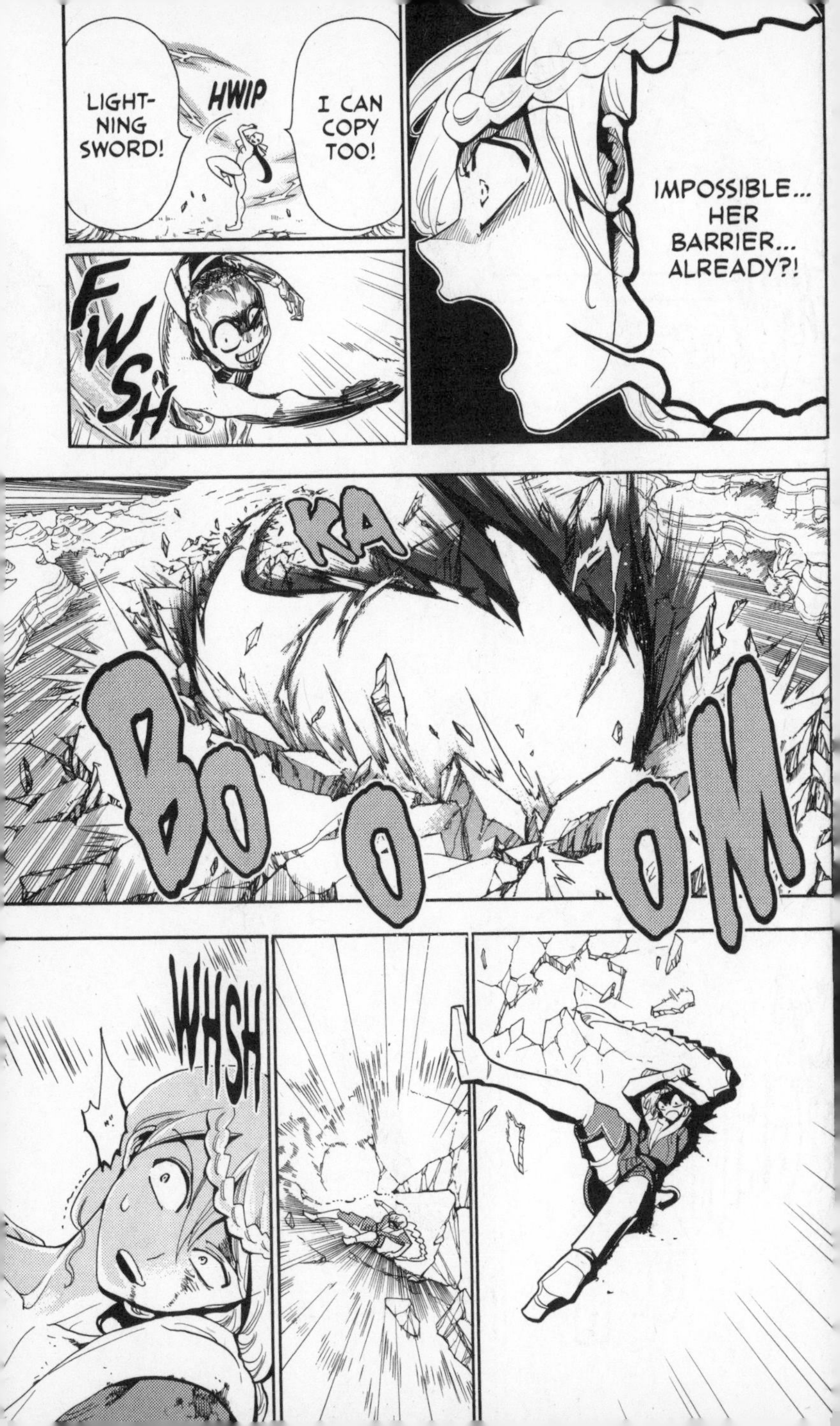
IMPOSSIBLE... HER BARRIER... ALREADY?!
I CAN COPY TOO!
HWIP
LIGHT-NING SWORD!
FWSH
KA
BOOOOM
WHSH

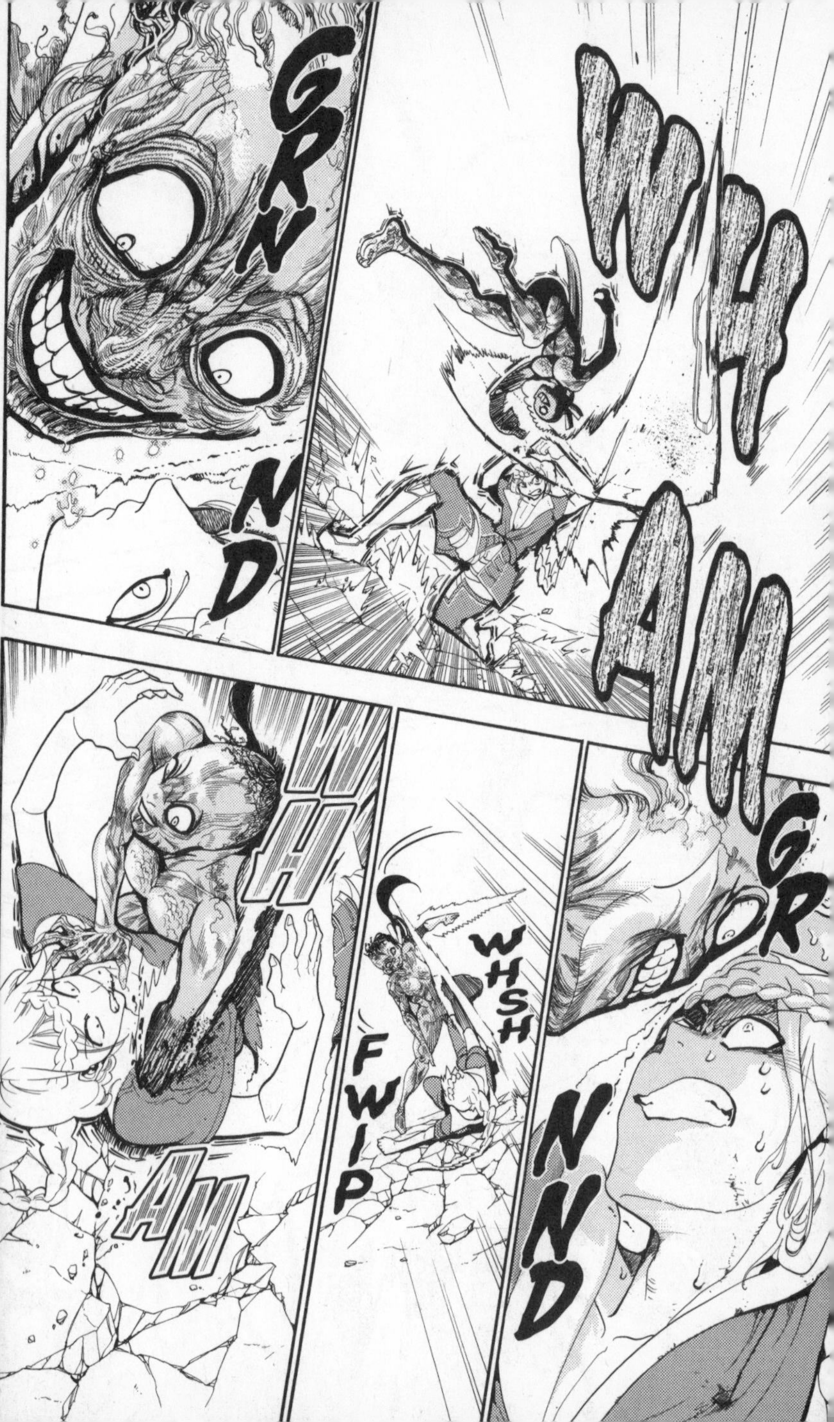
WHAM
GRN
ND
GR
NND
WHSH
FWIP
WH
AM

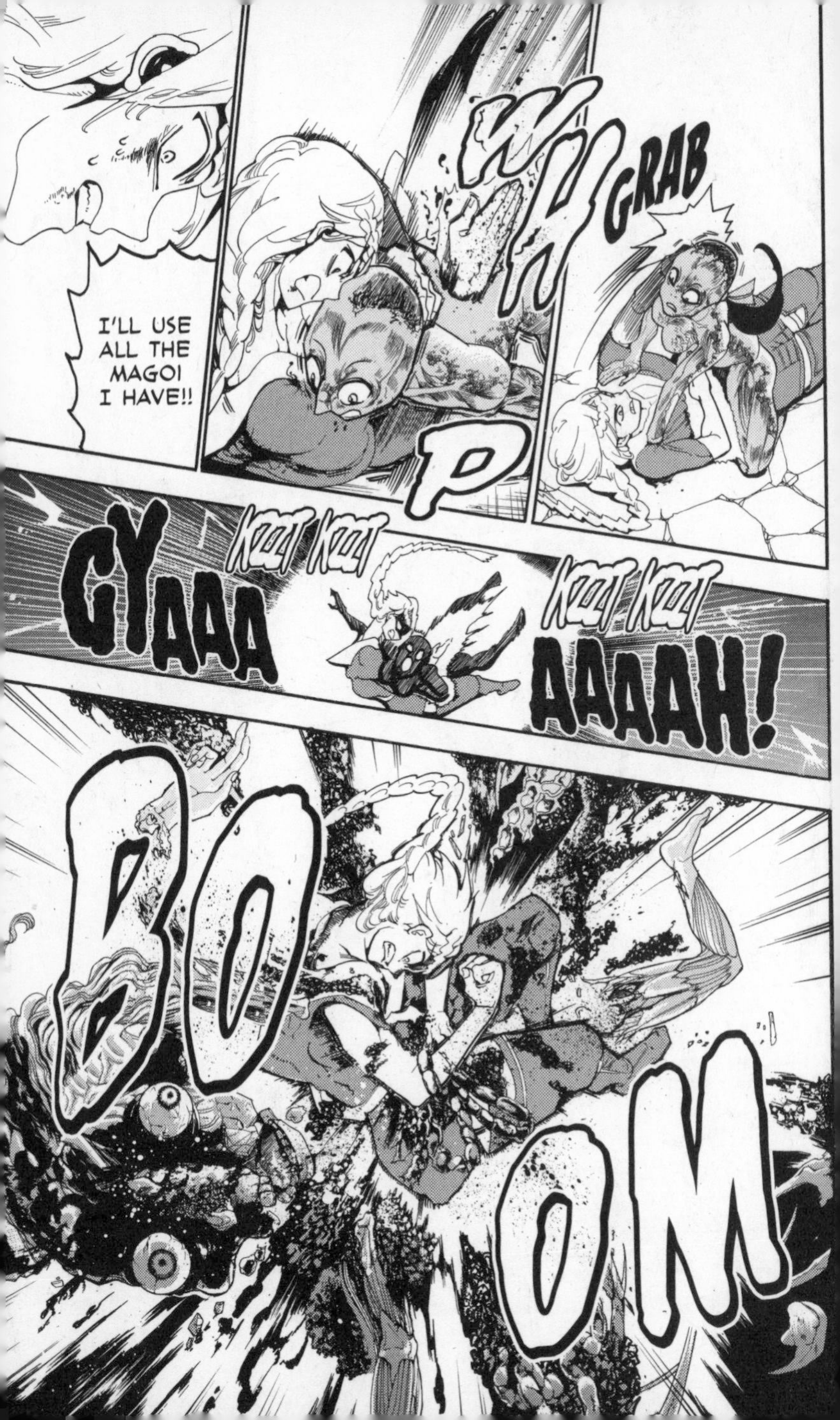
GRAB
WHAP
I'LL USE ALL THE MAGOI I HAVE!!
KZZT KZZT
KZZT KZZT
GYAAAAAAAH!
BOOM

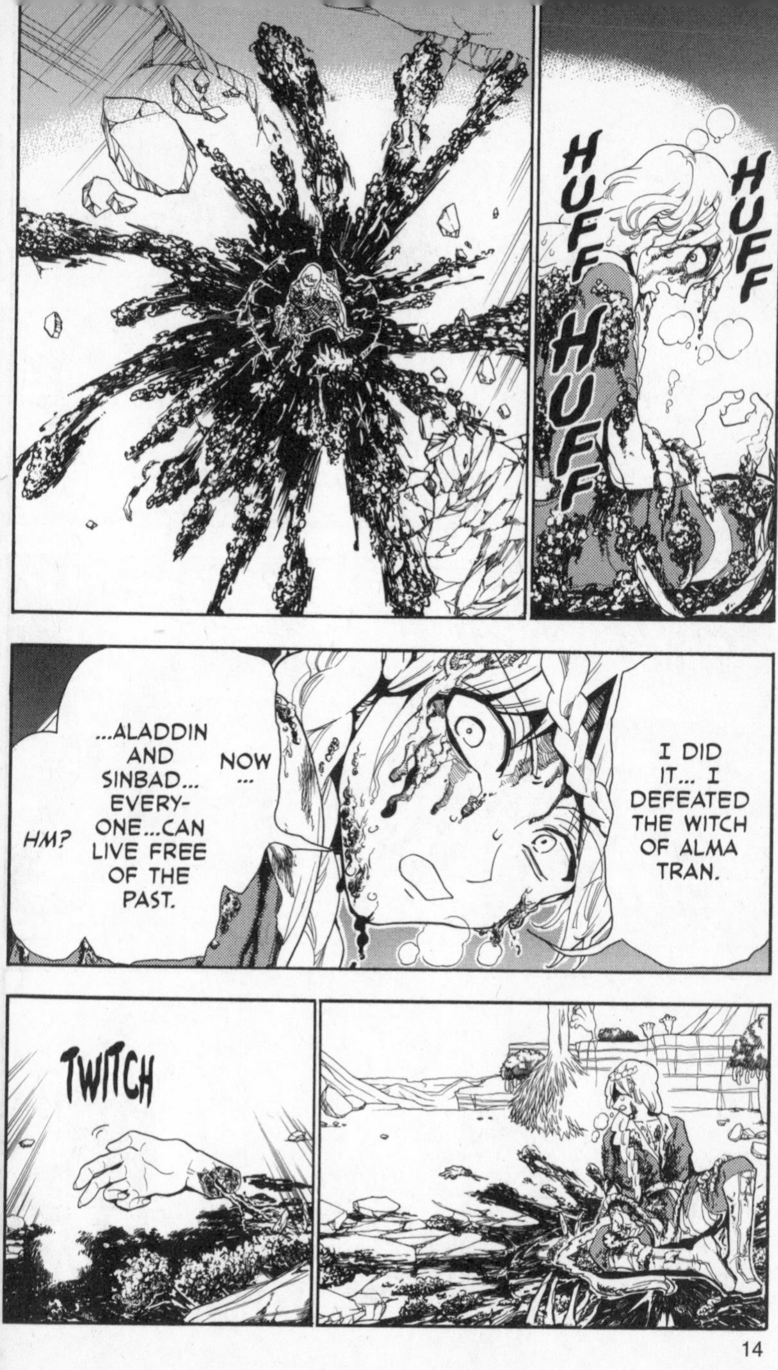
HUFF
HUFF
HUFF
I DID IT... I DEFEATED THE WITCH OF ALMA TRAN.
NOW...
...ALADDIN AND SINBAD... EVERYONE...CAN LIVE FREE OF THE PAST.
HM?
TWITCH

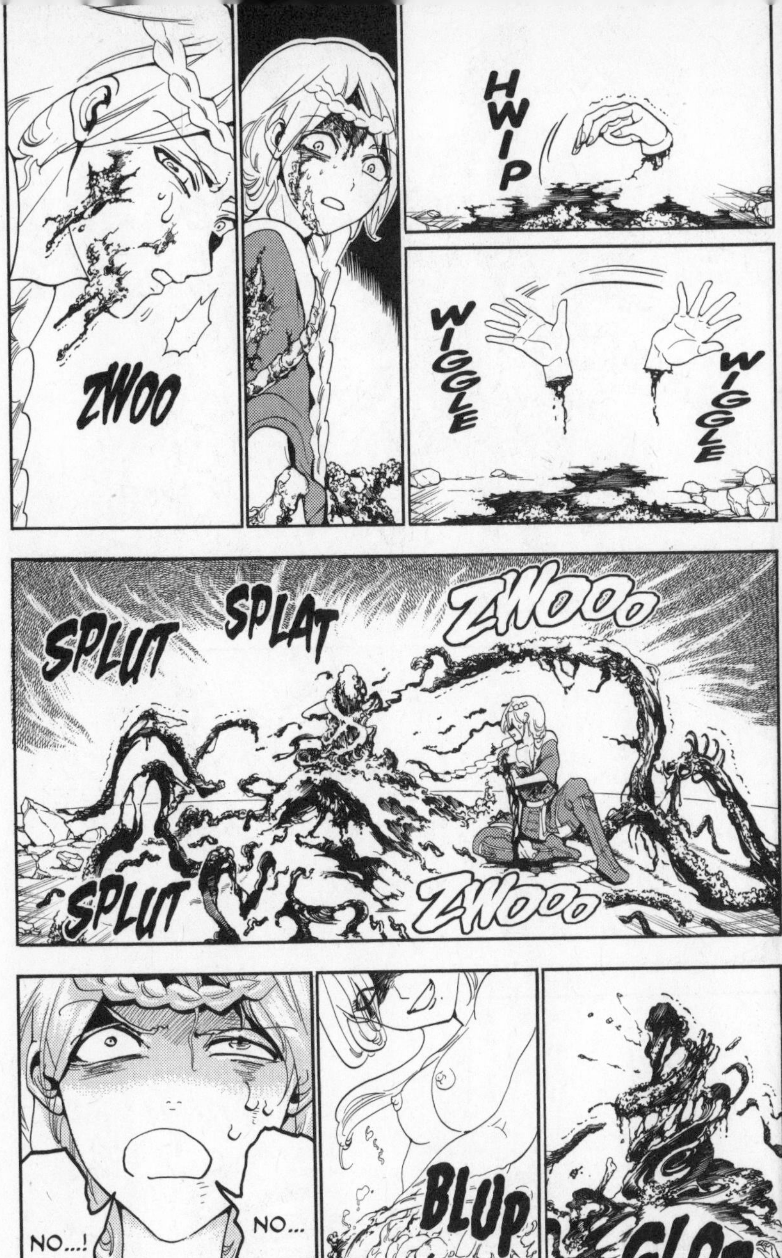
HWIP
WIGGLE
WIGGLE
ZWOO
ZWOOO
SPLAT
SPLUT
ZWOOO
SPLUT
GLOP
BLUP
NO...
NO...!

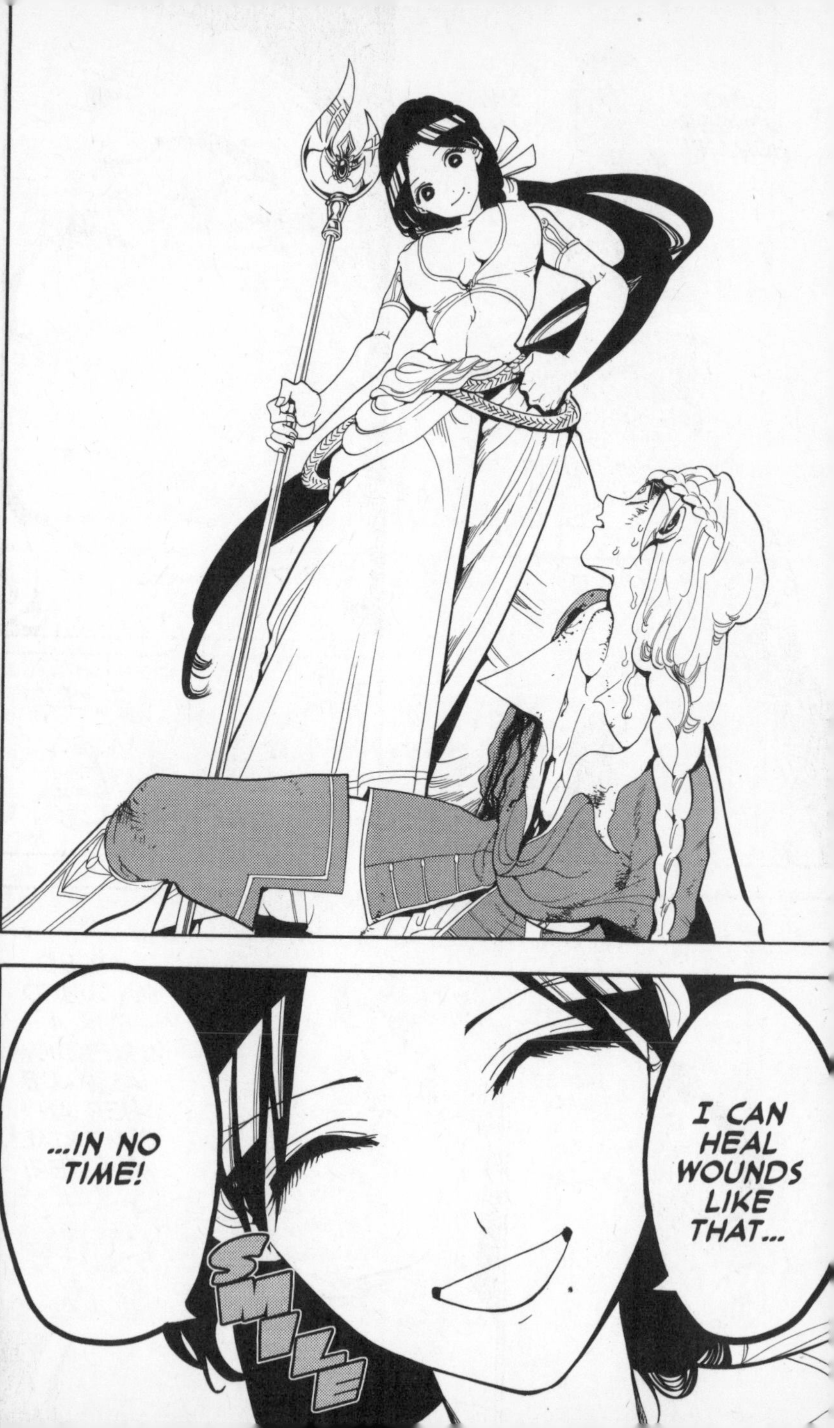
I CAN HEAL WOUNDS LIKE THAT...
...IN NO TIME!
SMILE

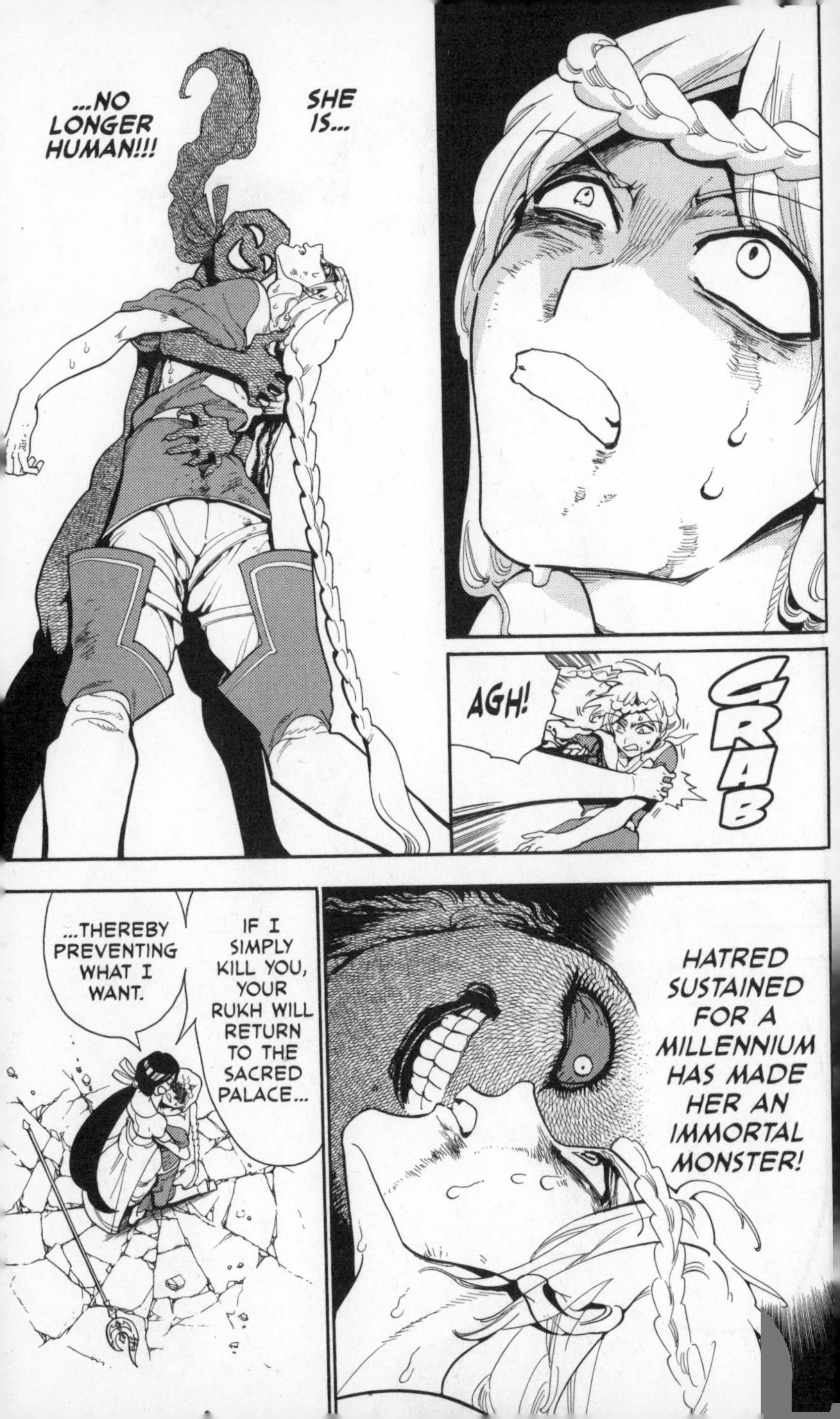
GRAB
AGH!
SHE IS...
...NO LONGER HUMAN!!!
HATRED SUSTAINED FOR A MILLENNIUM HAS MADE HER AN IMMORTAL MONSTER!
IF I SIMPLY KILL YOU, YOUR RUKH WILL RETURN TO THE SACRED PALACE...
...THEREBY PREVENTING WHAT I WANT.

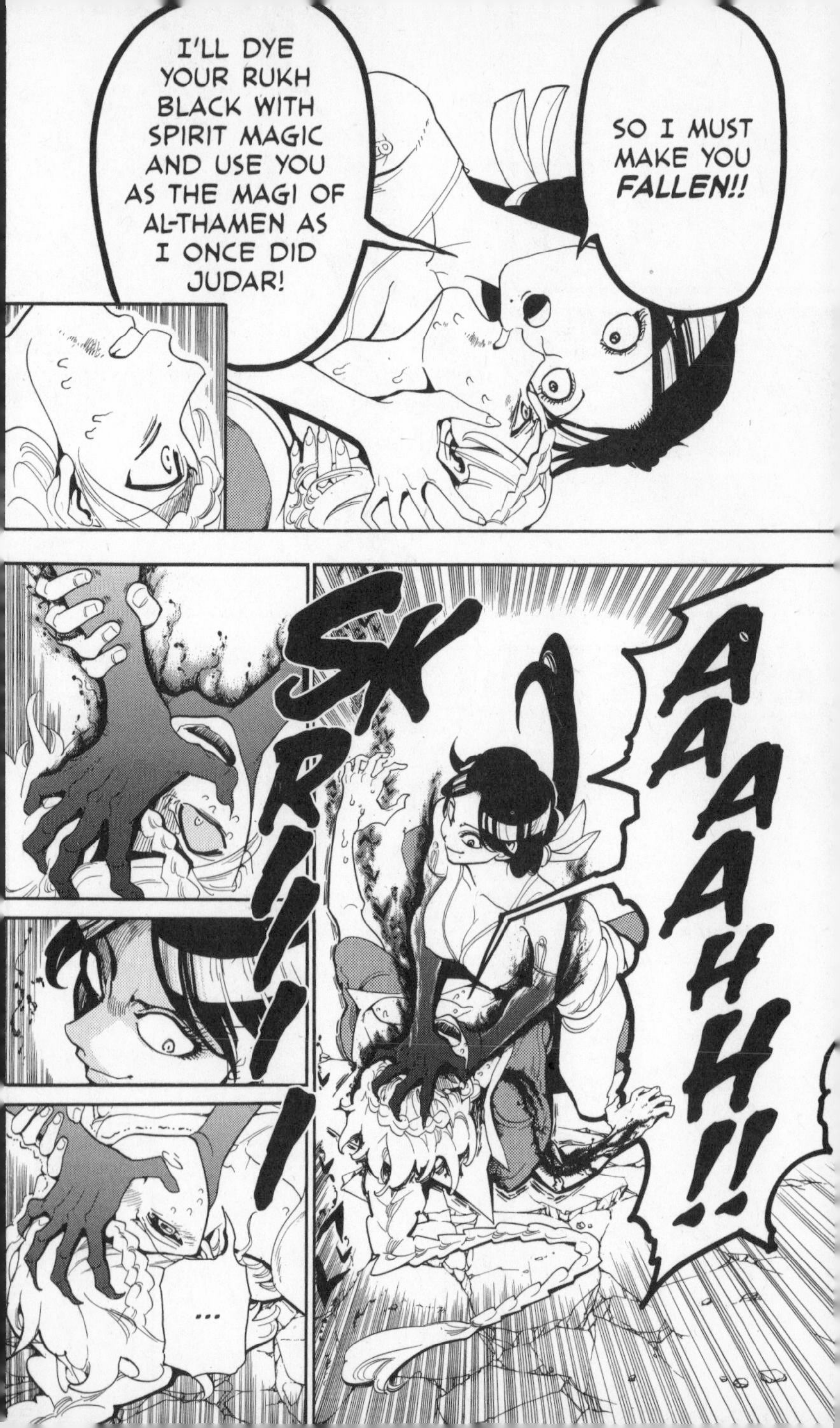
SO I MUST MAKE YOU *FALLEN!!*
I'LL DYE YOUR RUKH BLACK WITH SPIRIT MAGIC AND USE YOU AS THE MAGI OF AL-THAMEN AS I ONCE DID JUDAR!
AAAAAHH!!
SKRII!!
...

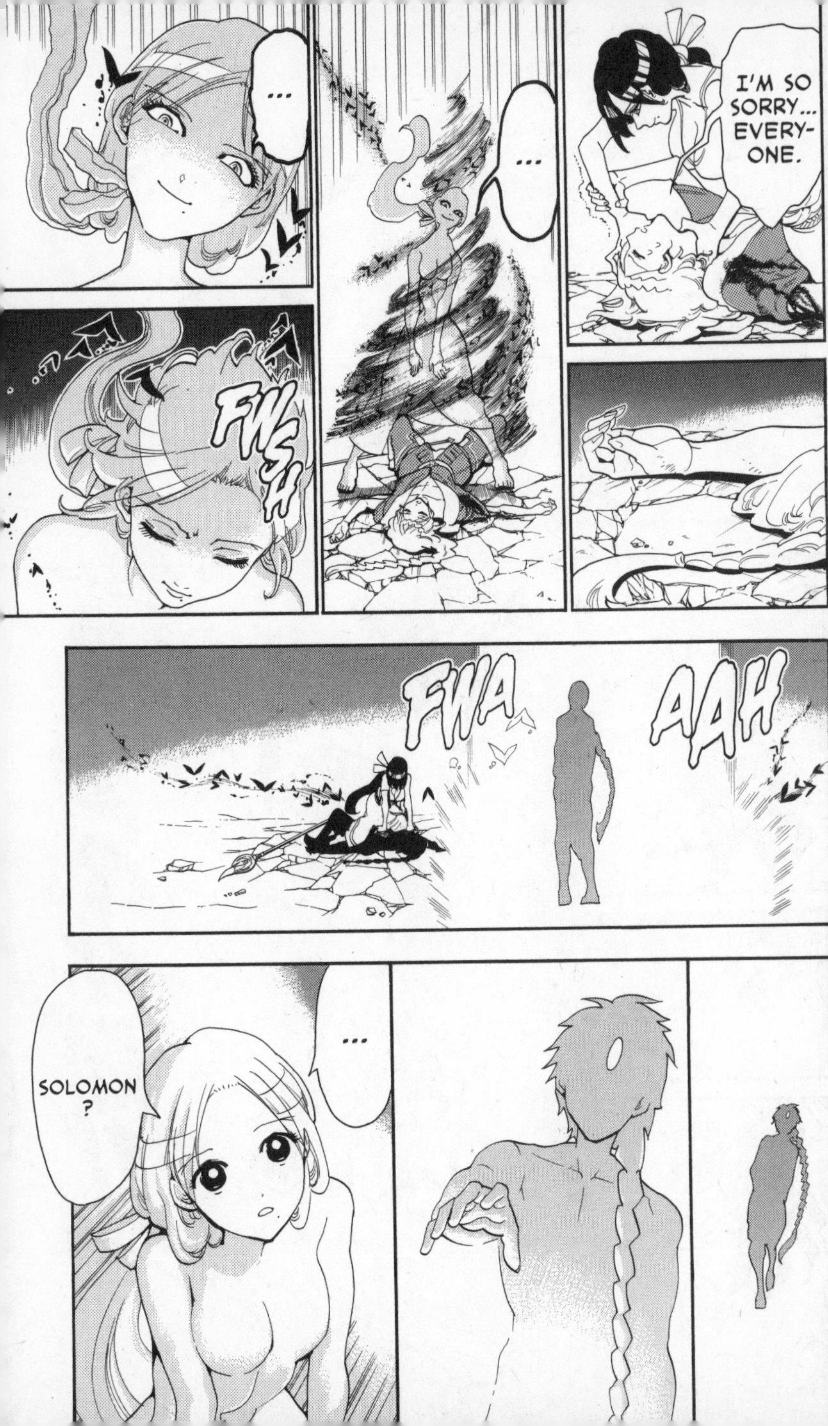
I'M SO SORRY... EVERYONE.
...
...
FWSH
FWA AAH
...
SOLOMON?

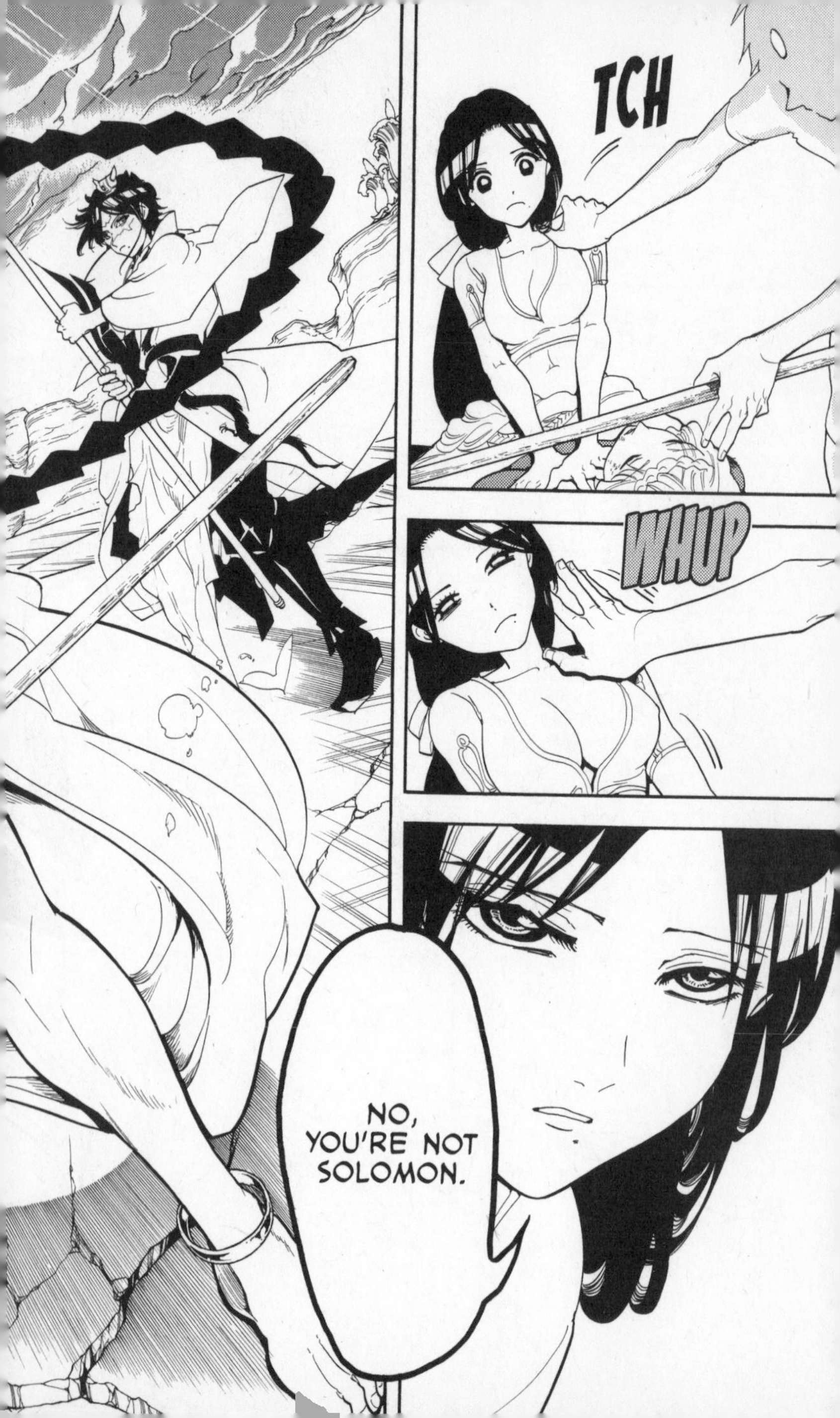
TCH
WHUP
NO, YOU'RE NOT SOLOMON.

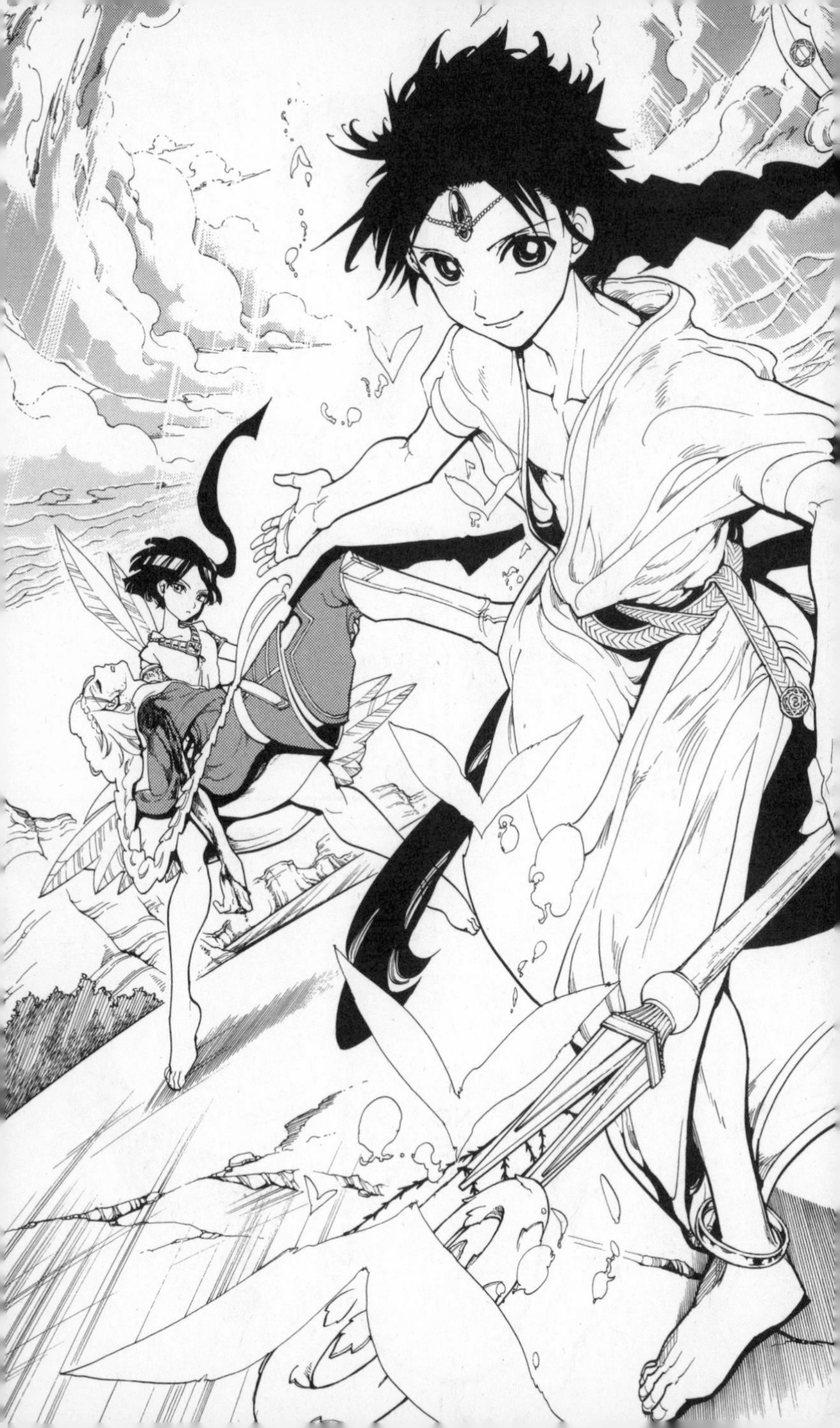

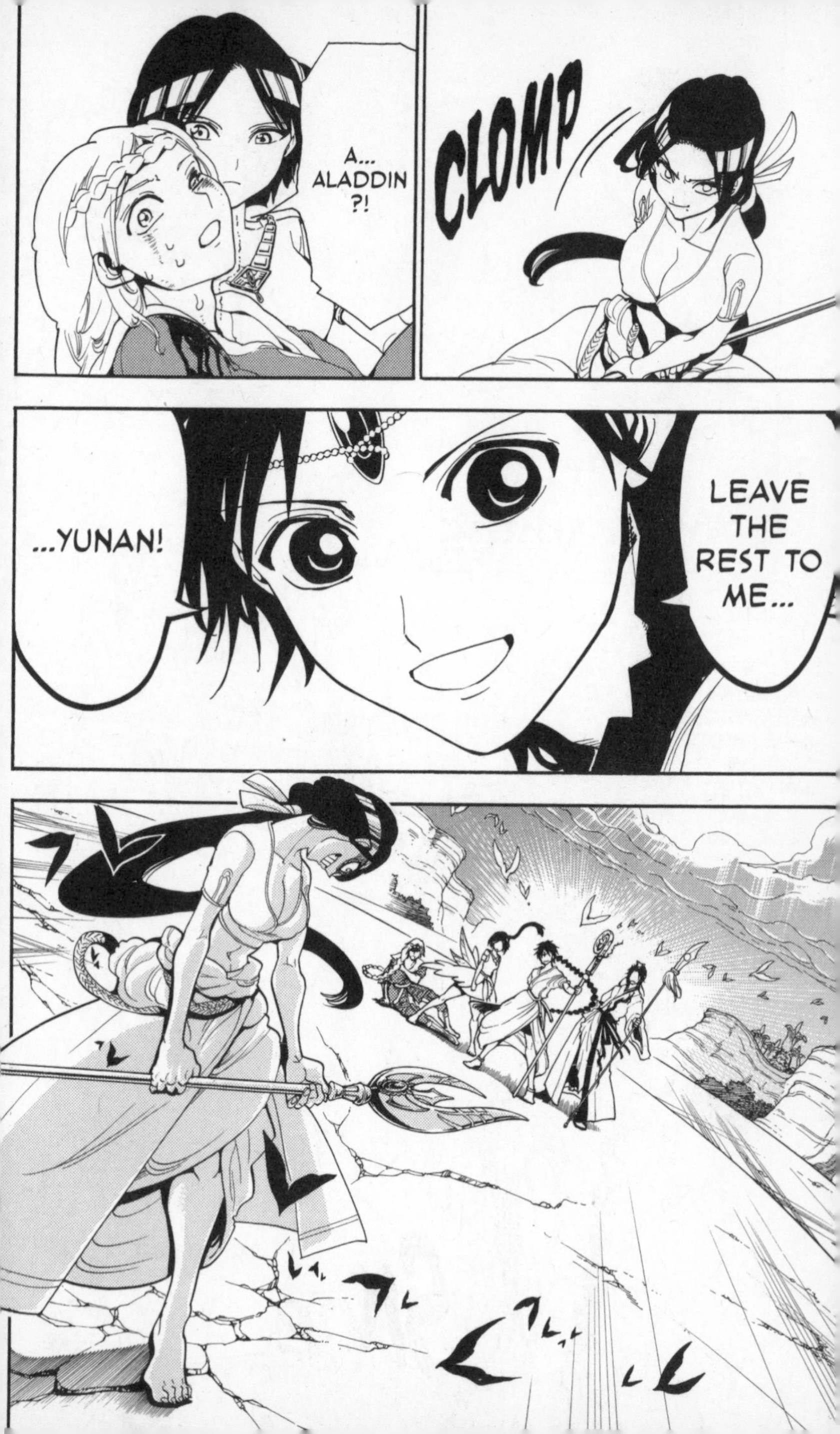
CLOMP
A... ALADDIN ?!
LEAVE THE REST TO ME...
...YUNAN!

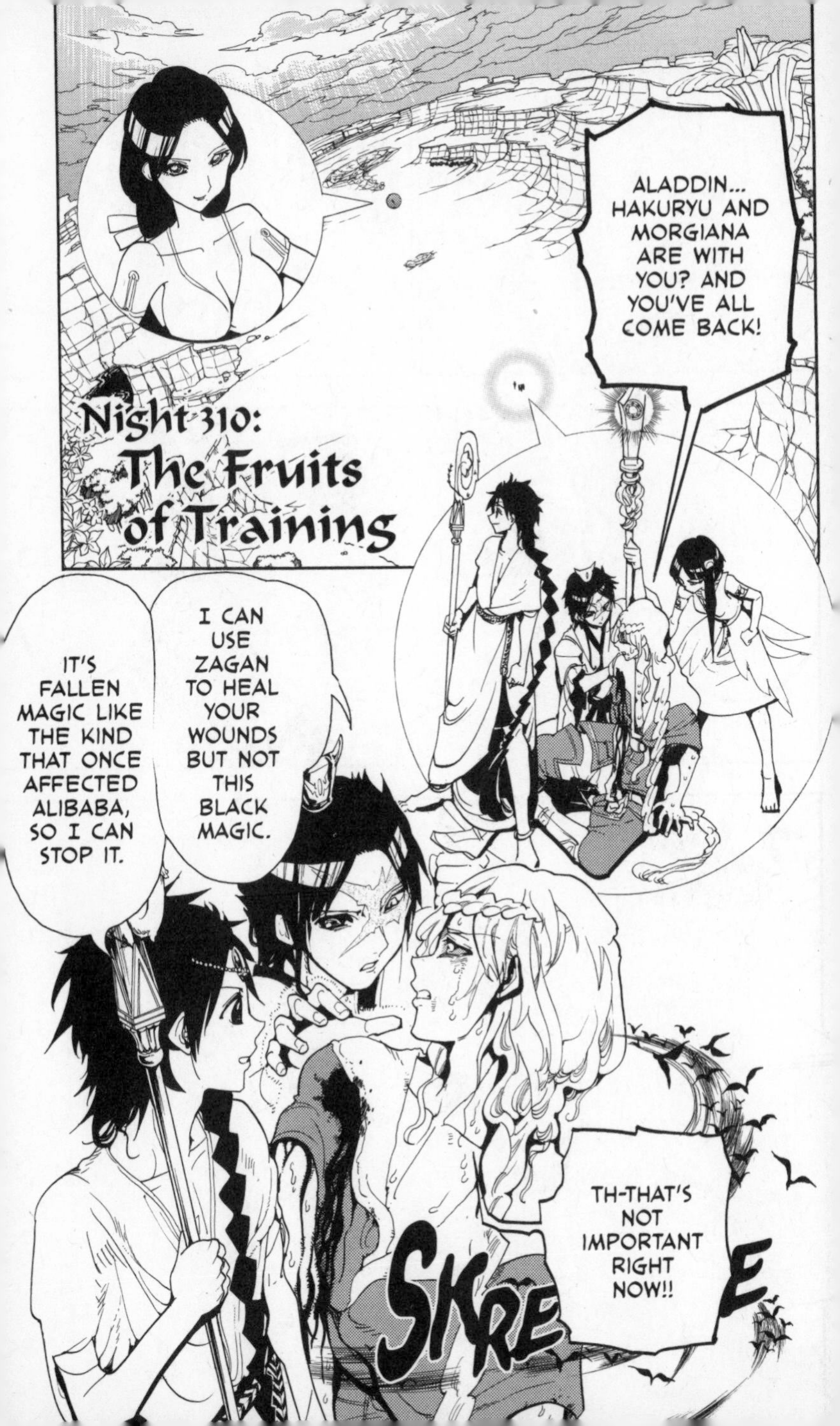
ALADDIN... HAKURYU AND MORGIANA ARE WITH YOU? AND YOU'VE ALL COME BACK!
Night 310: The Fruits of Training
I CAN USE ZAGAN TO HEAL YOUR WOUNDS BUT NOT THIS BLACK MAGIC.
IT'S FALLEN MAGIC LIKE THE KIND THAT ONCE AFFECTED ALIBABA, SO I CAN STOP IT.
TH-THAT'S NOT IMPORTANT RIGHT NOW!!
SKREE

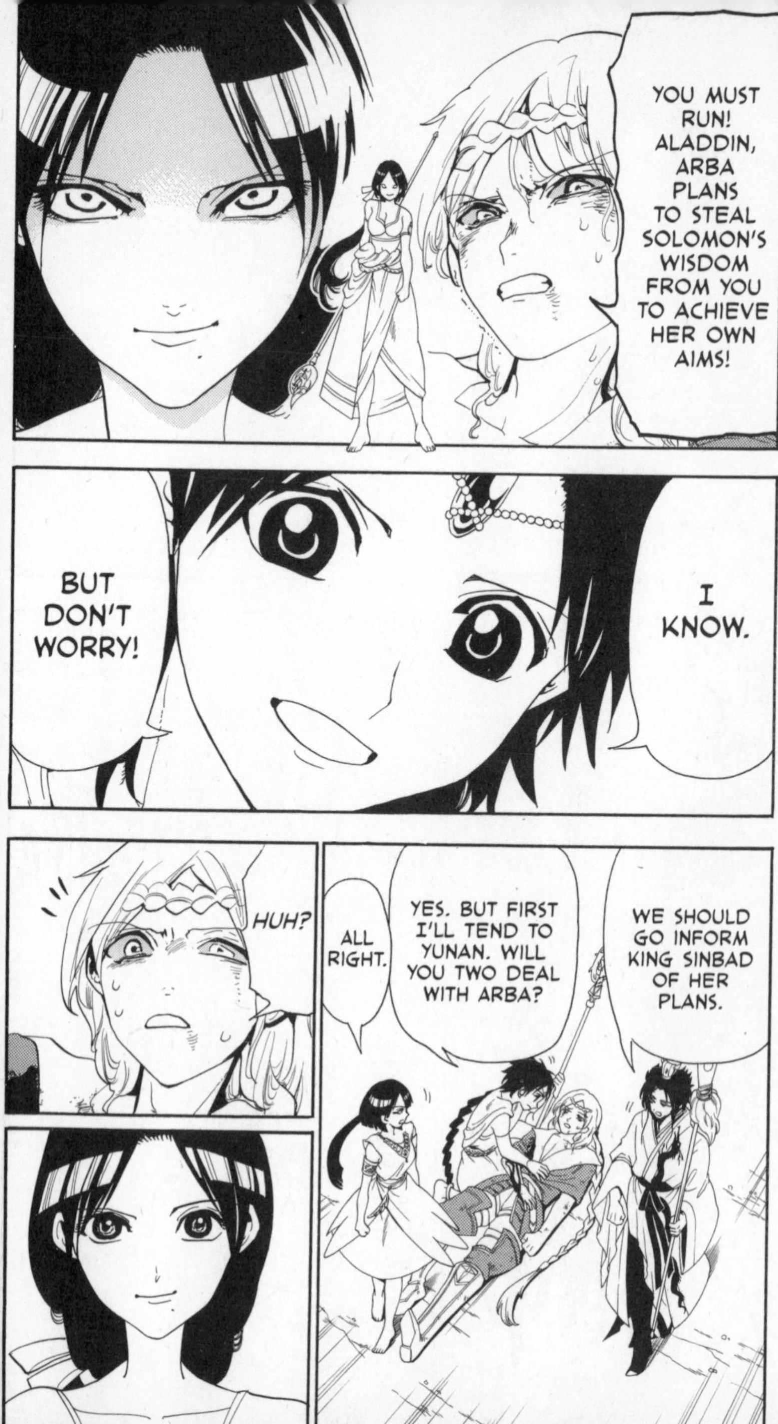
YOU MUST RUN! ALADDIN, ARBA PLANS TO STEAL SOLOMON'S WISDOM FROM YOU TO ACHIEVE HER OWN AIMS!
I KNOW.
BUT DON'T WORRY!
WE SHOULD GO INFORM KING SINBAD OF HER PLANS.
YES. BUT FIRST I'LL TEND TO YUNAN. WILL YOU TWO DEAL WITH ARBA?
ALL RIGHT.
HUH?

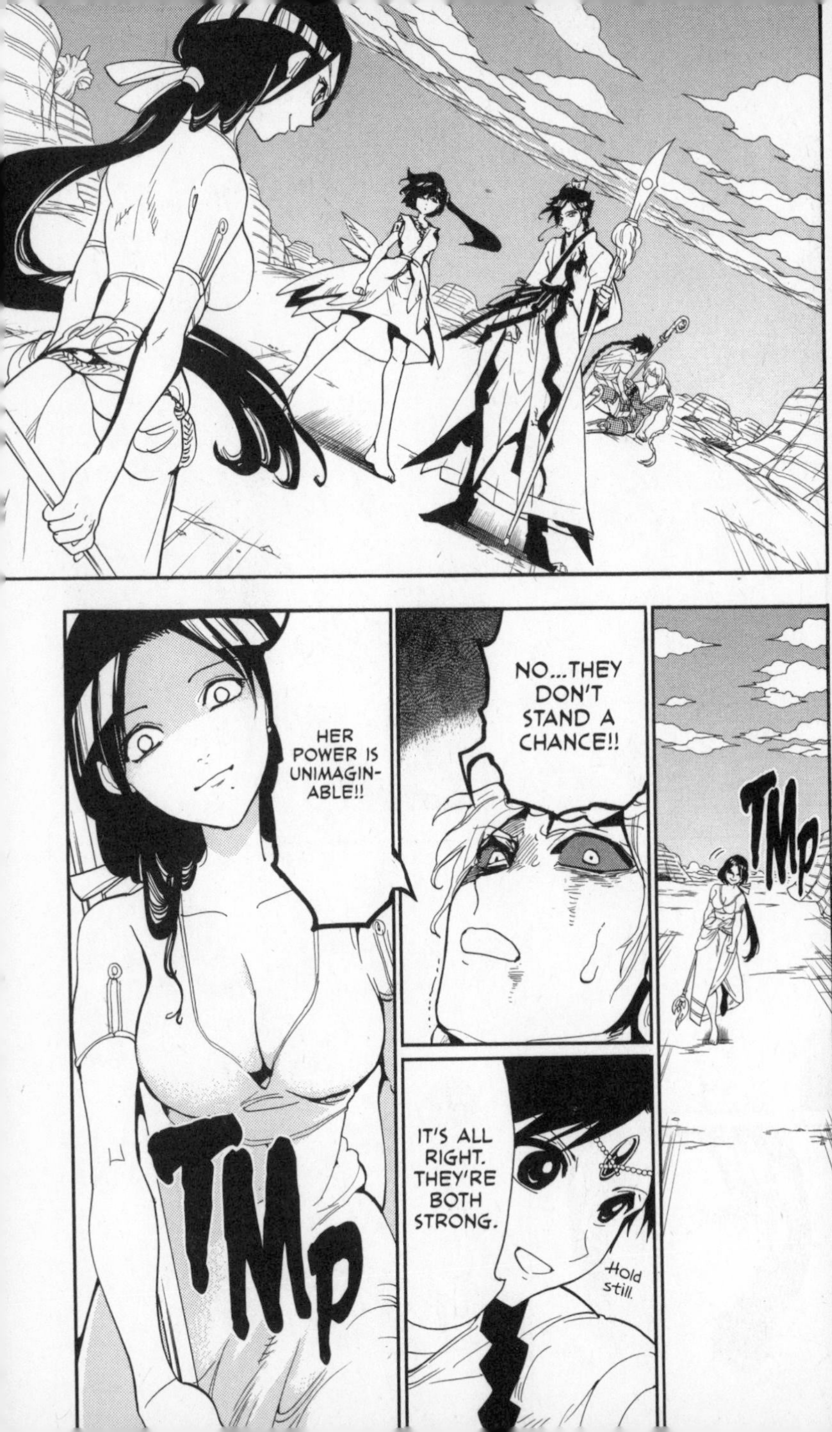
TMp
NO...THEY DON'T STAND A CHANCE!!
IT'S ALL RIGHT. THEY'RE BOTH STRONG.
Hold still.
HER POWER IS UNIMAGINABLE!!
TMp

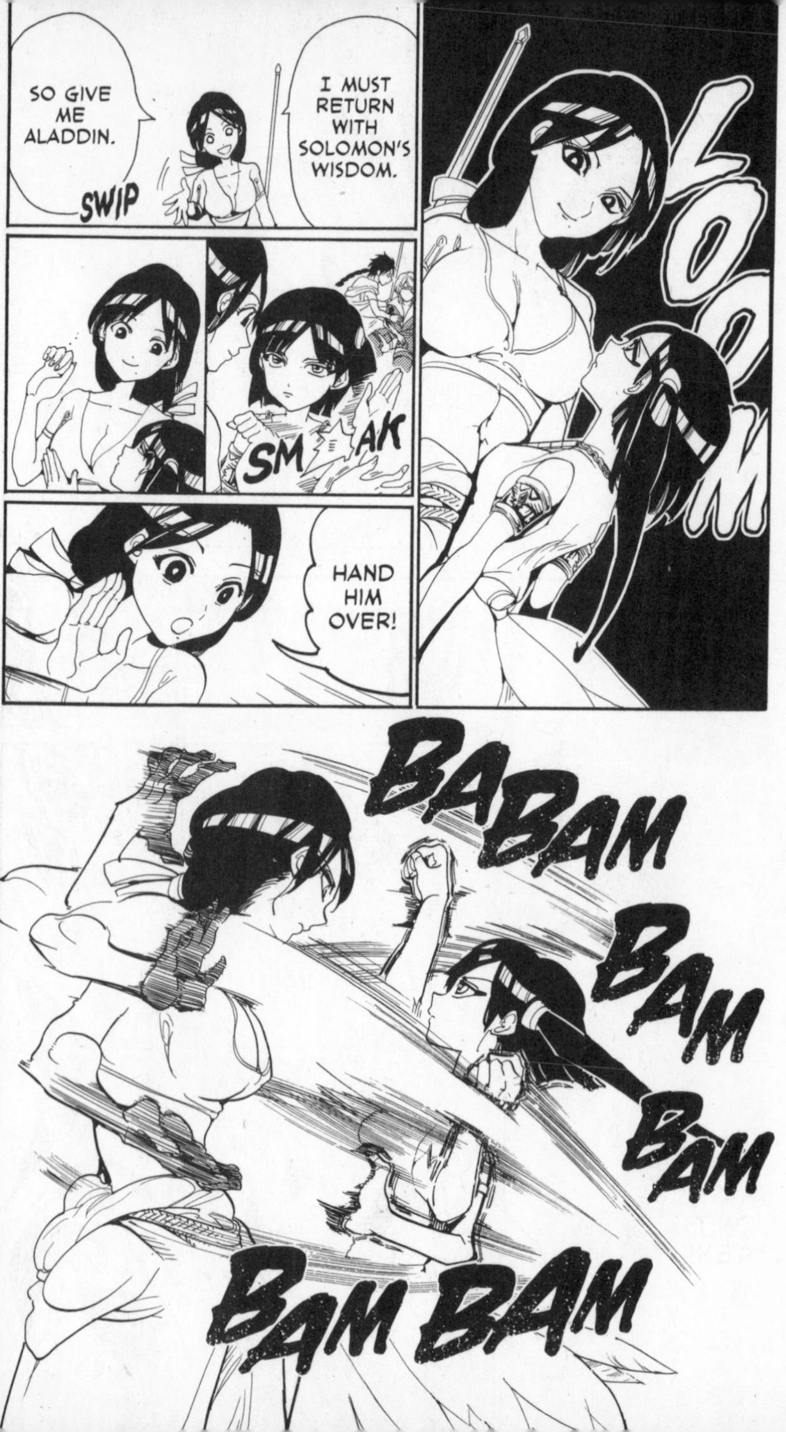
LOOM
I MUST RETURN WITH SOLOMON'S WISDOM.
SO GIVE ME ALADDIN.
SWIP
SMAK
HAND HIM OVER!
BABAM
BAM
BAM
BAM BAM

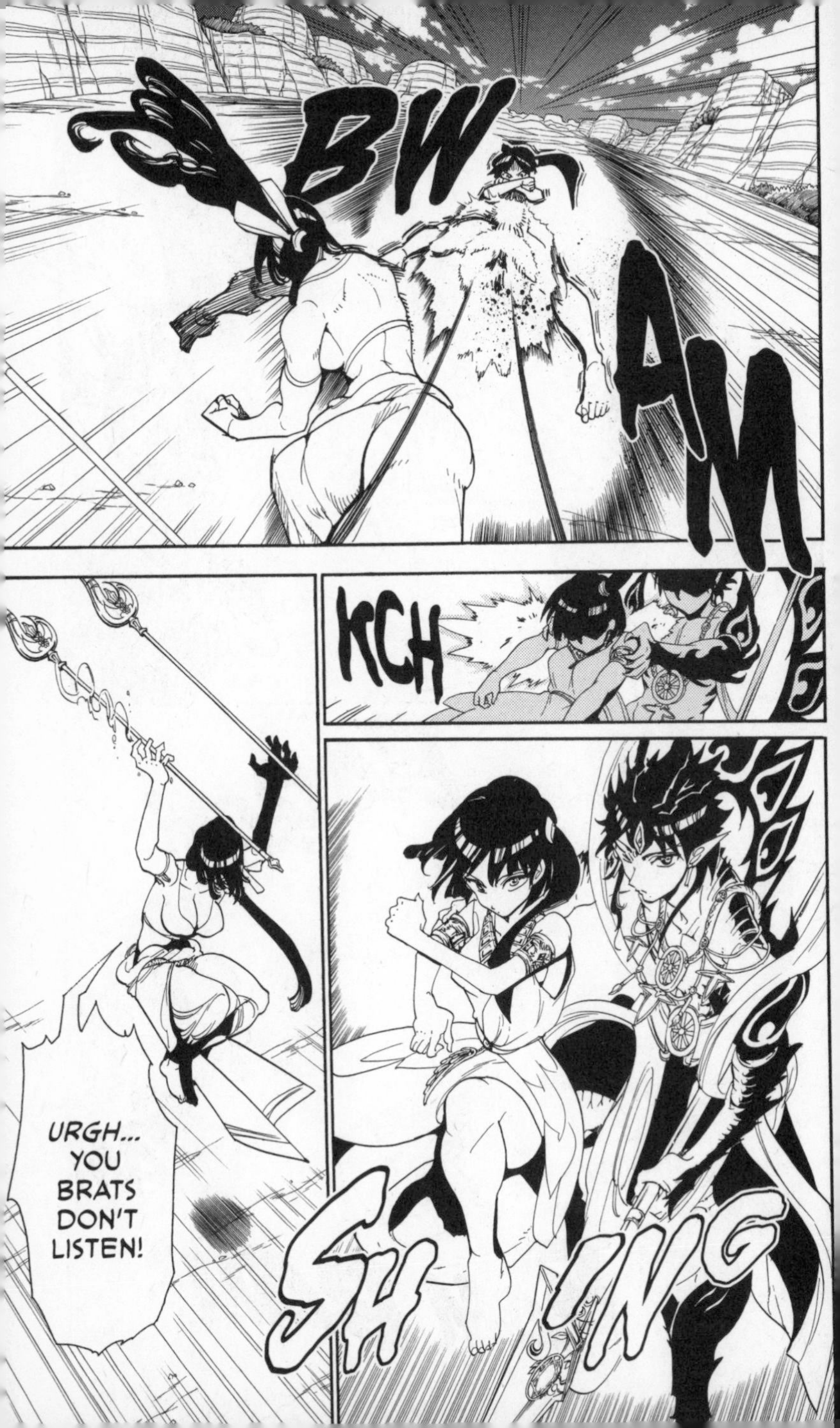
BWAM
KCH
SHING
URGH... YOU BRATS DON'T LISTEN!

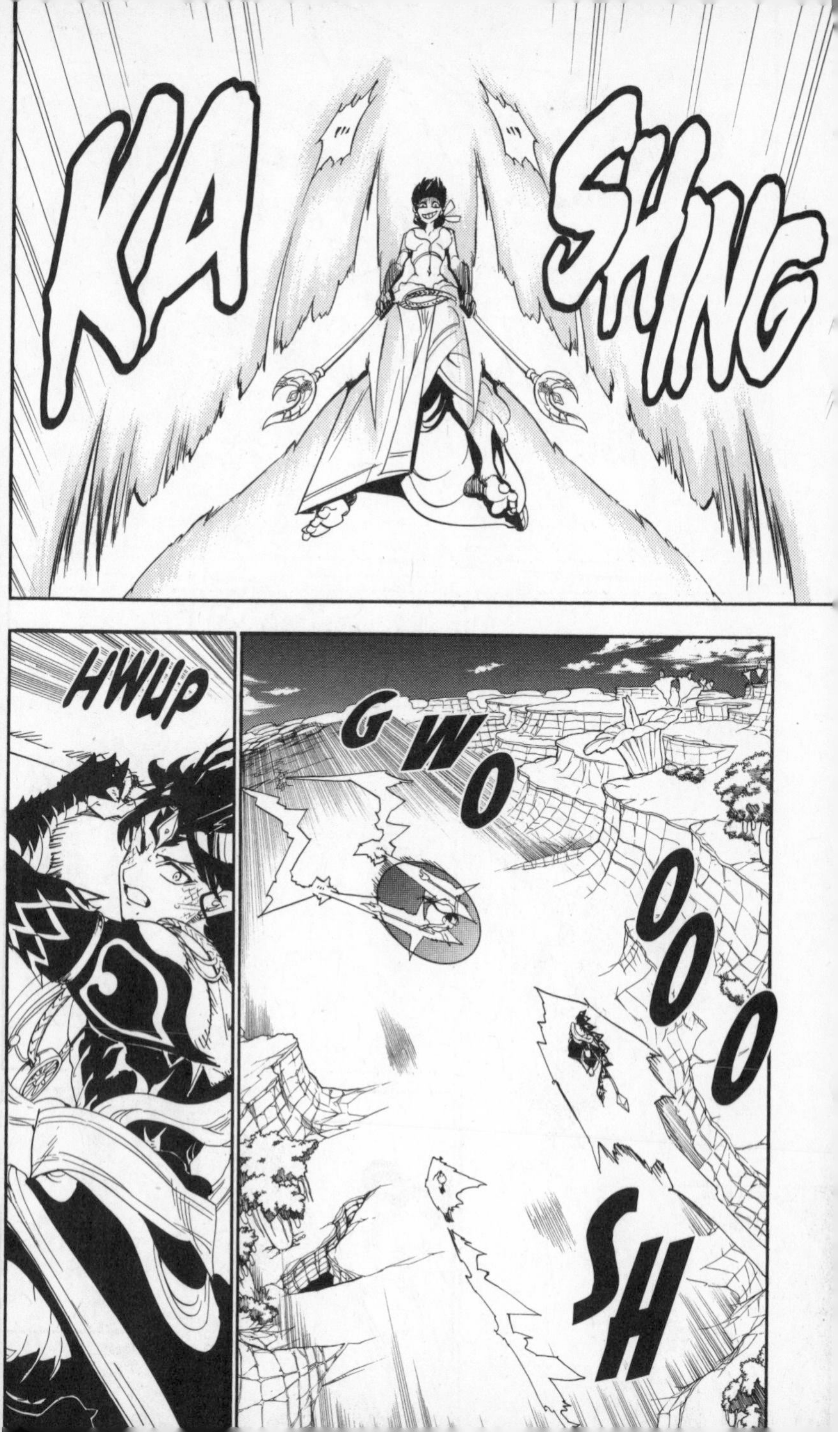
KA SHING
GWOOOOSH
HWUP

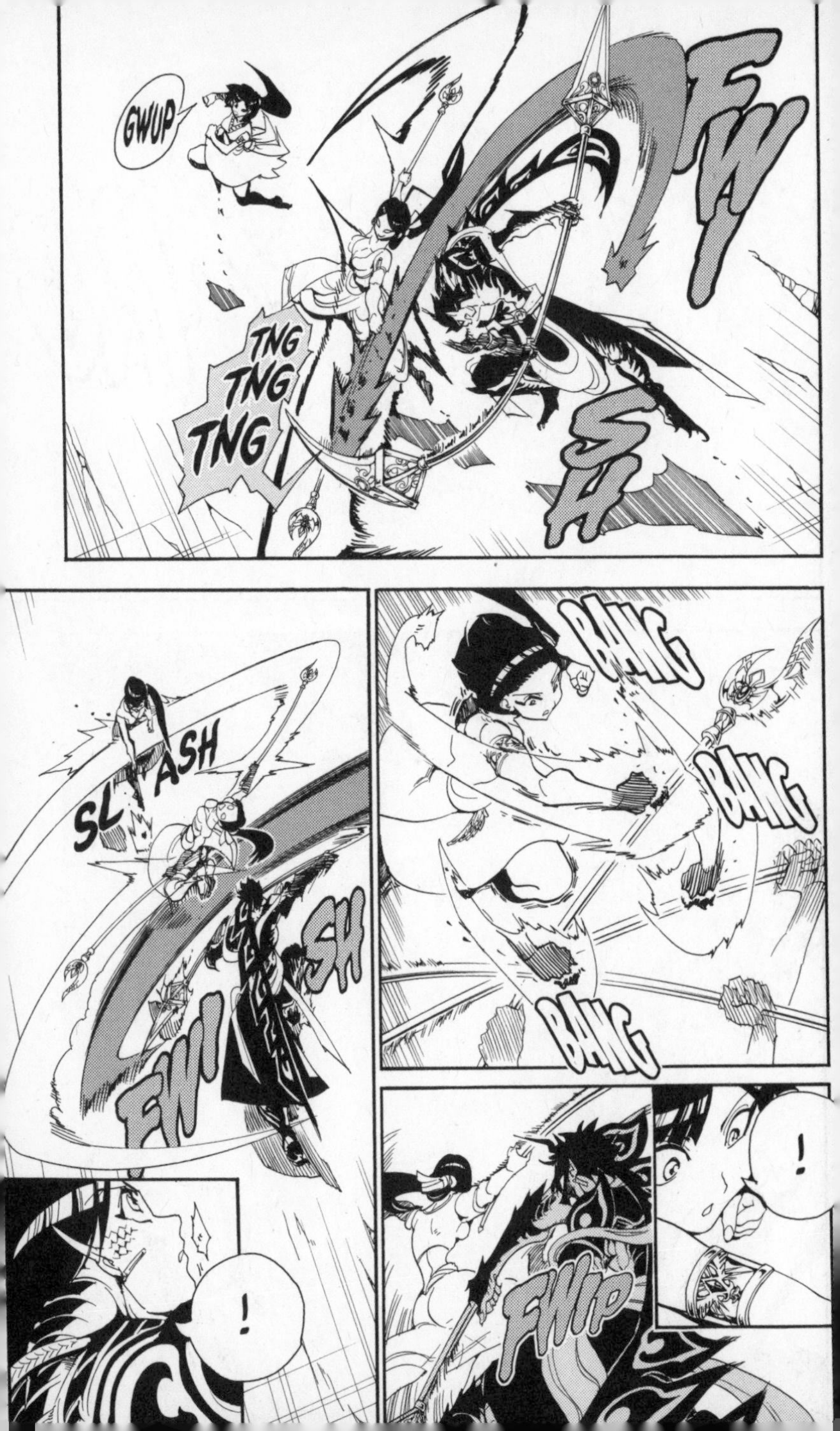
FWN
GWUP
SH
TNG TNG TNG
BANG
BANG
BANG
!
FWIP
SLASH
FWISH
!

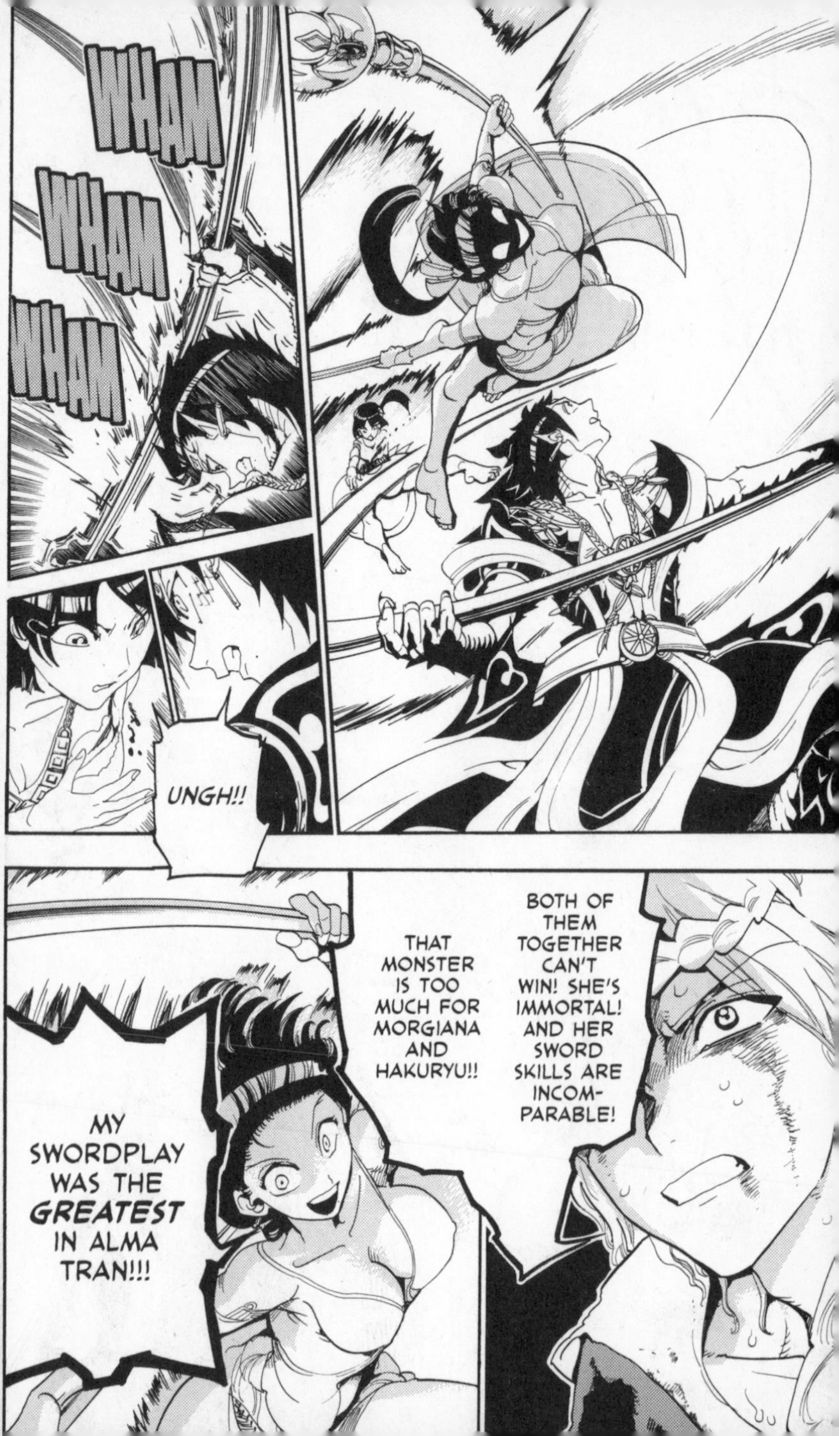
WHAM
WHAM
WHAM
UNGH!!
BOTH OF THEM TOGETHER CAN'T WIN! SHE'S IMMORTAL! AND HER SWORD SKILLS ARE INCOM-PARABLE!
THAT MONSTER IS TOO MUCH FOR MORGIANA AND HAKURYU!!
MY SWORDPLAY WAS THE GREATEST IN ALMA TRAN!!!

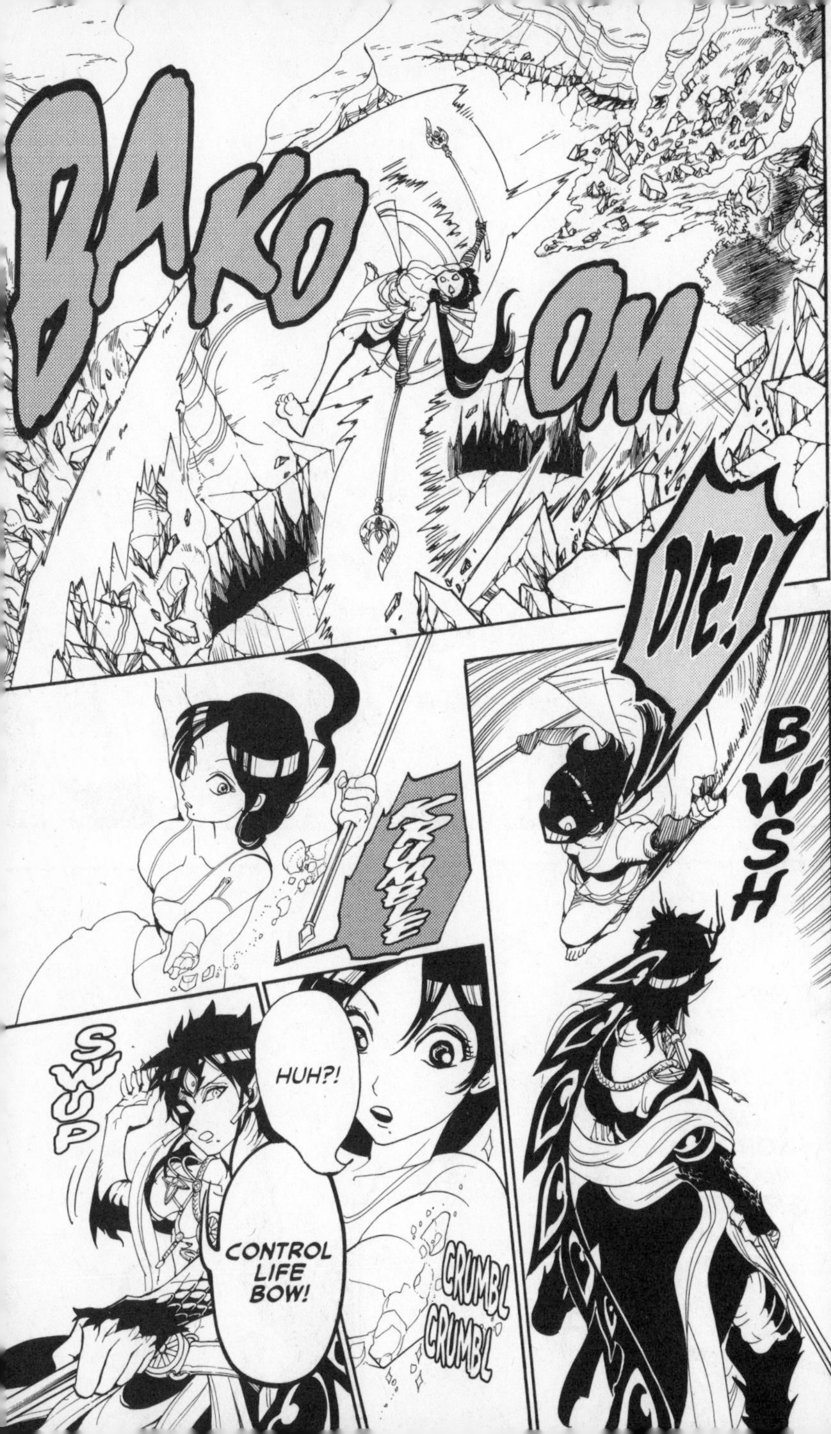
BAKOOOM
DIE!
BWSH
FUMBLE
HUH?!
CONTROL LIFE BOW!
CRUMBL CRUMBL
SWUP

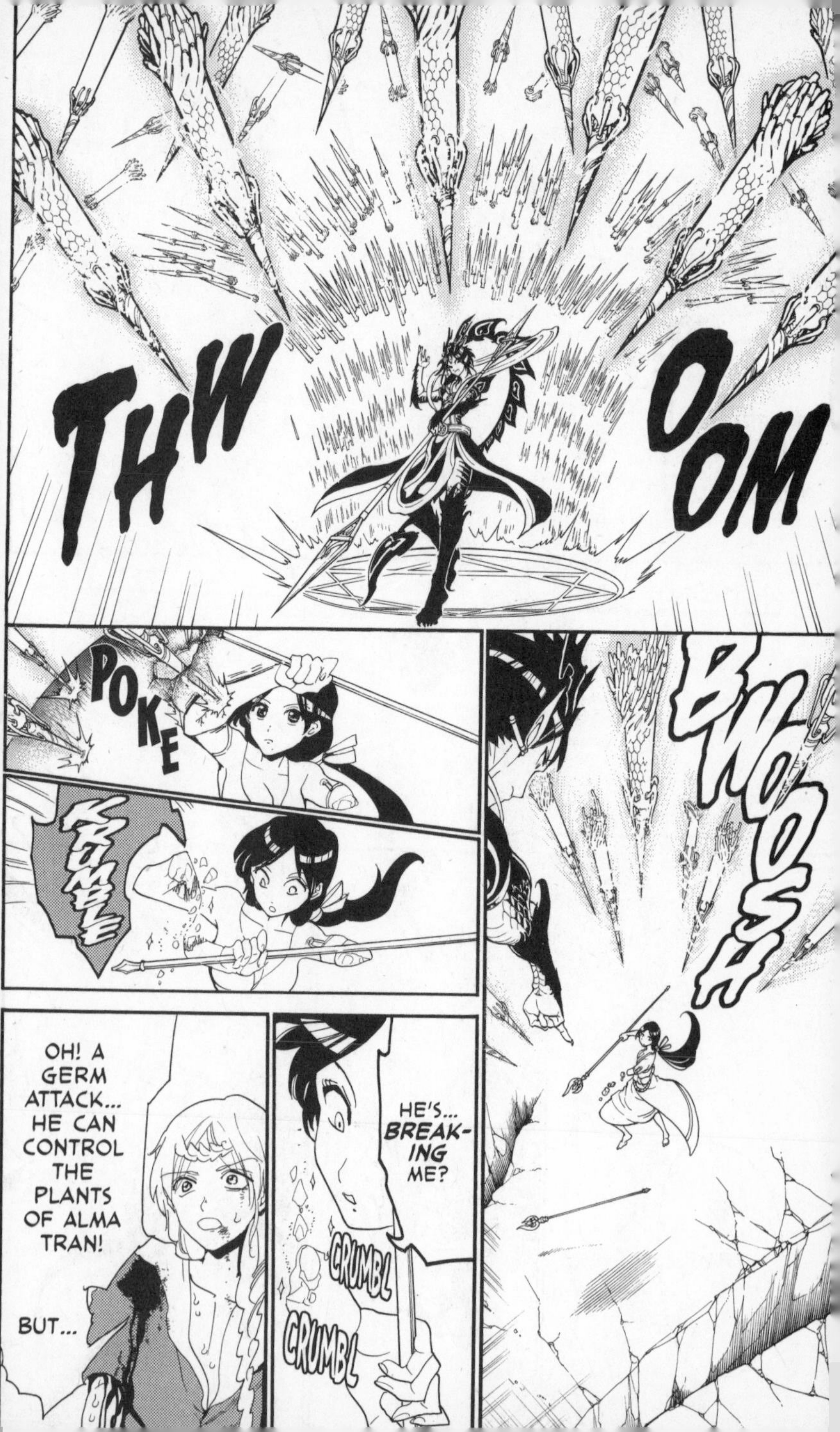
THWOOM
BWOOSH
POKE
KRUMBLE
HE'S... BREAKING ME?
CRUMBL
CRUMBL
OH! A GERM ATTACK... HE CAN CONTROL THE PLANTS OF ALMA TRAN!
BUT...

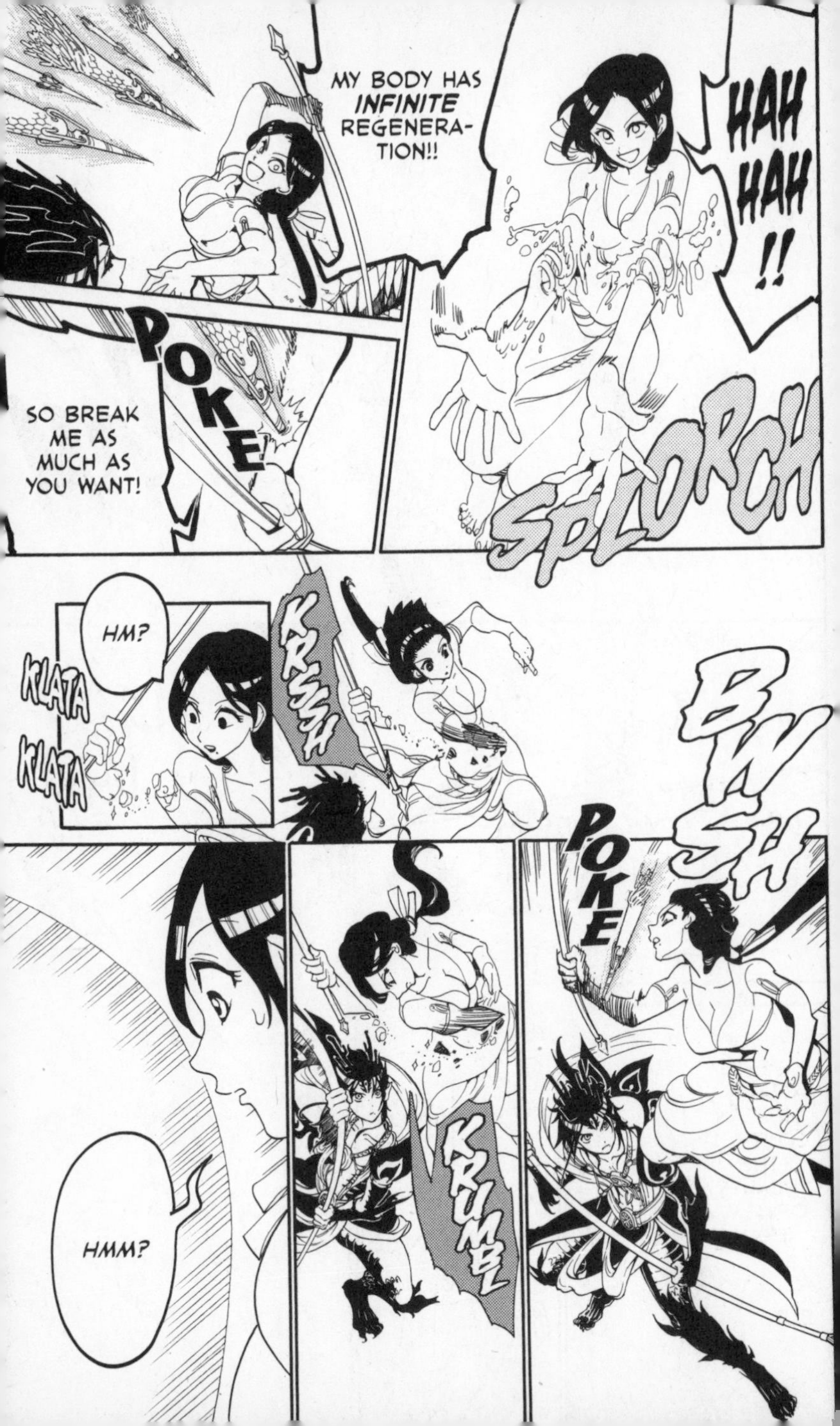
HAH HAH!!
SPLORCH
MY BODY HAS *INFINITE* REGENERATION!!
POKE
SO BREAK ME AS MUCH AS YOU WANT!
KRSSH
HM?
KLATA KLATA
BWSH
POKE
KRUMBL
HMM?

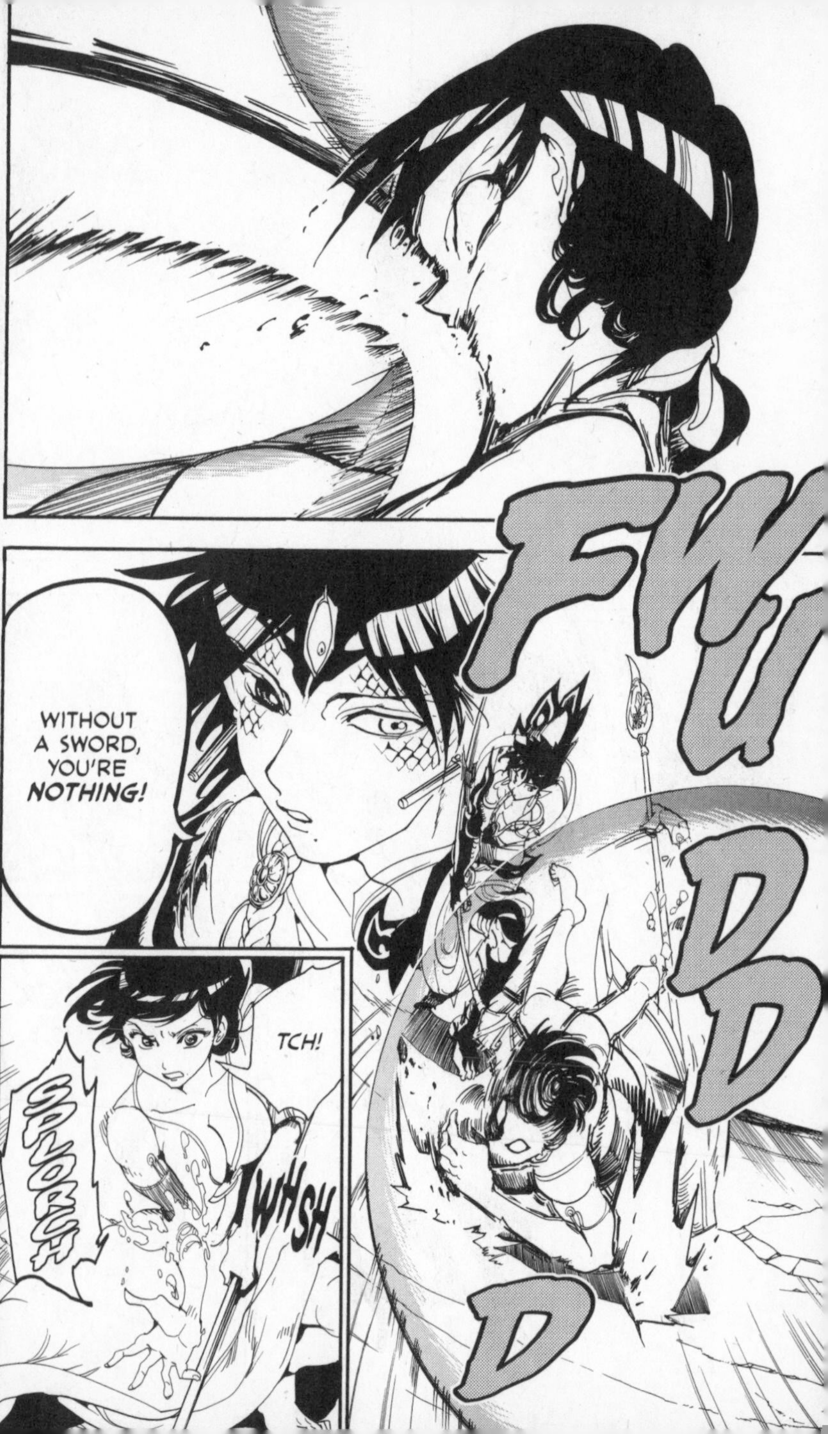
WITHOUT A SWORD, YOU'RE ***NOTHING!***
FWUDDD
TCH!
WHSH
SPLOOSH

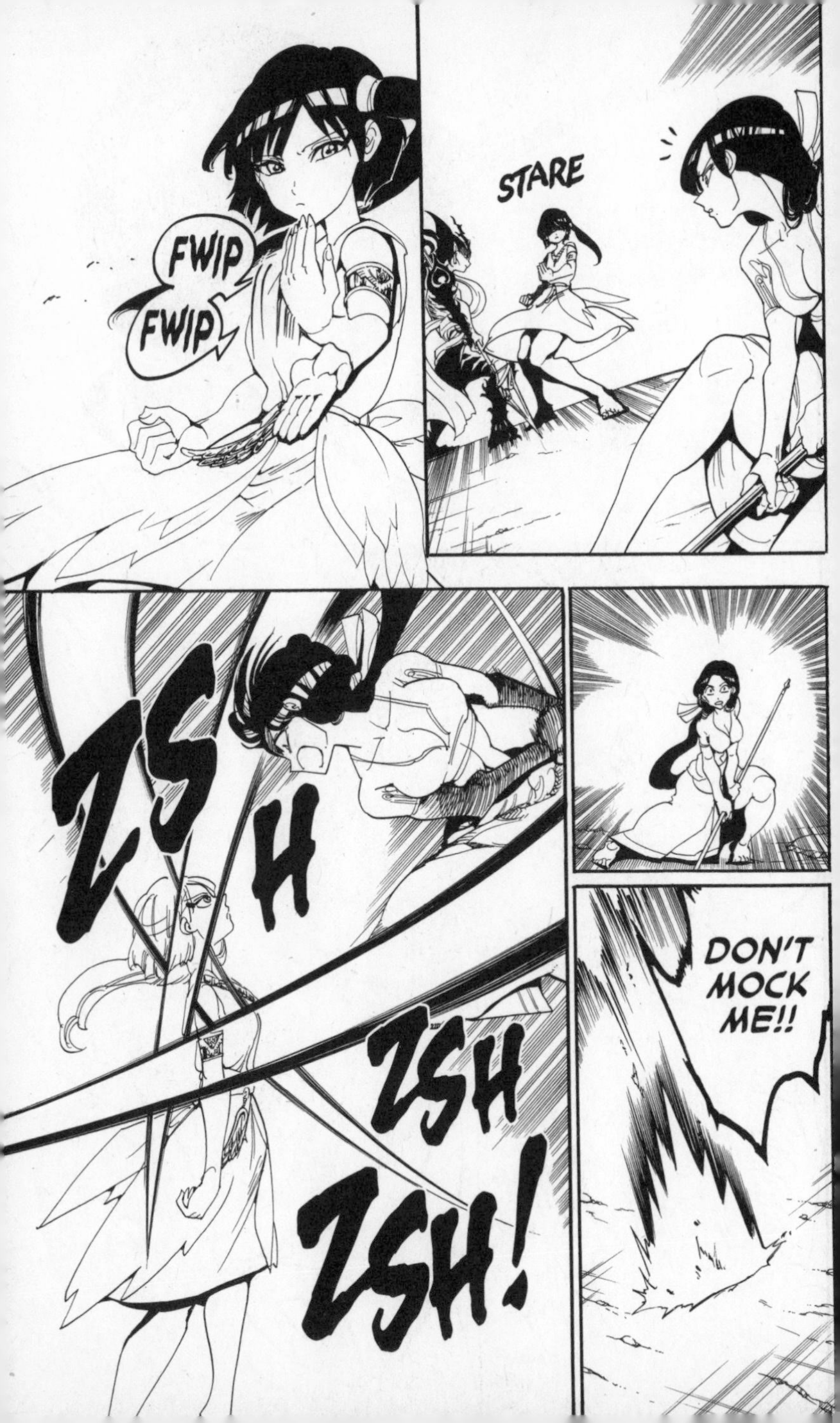
STARE
FWIP
FWIP
DON'T MOCK ME!!
ZSH
ZSH
ZSH!

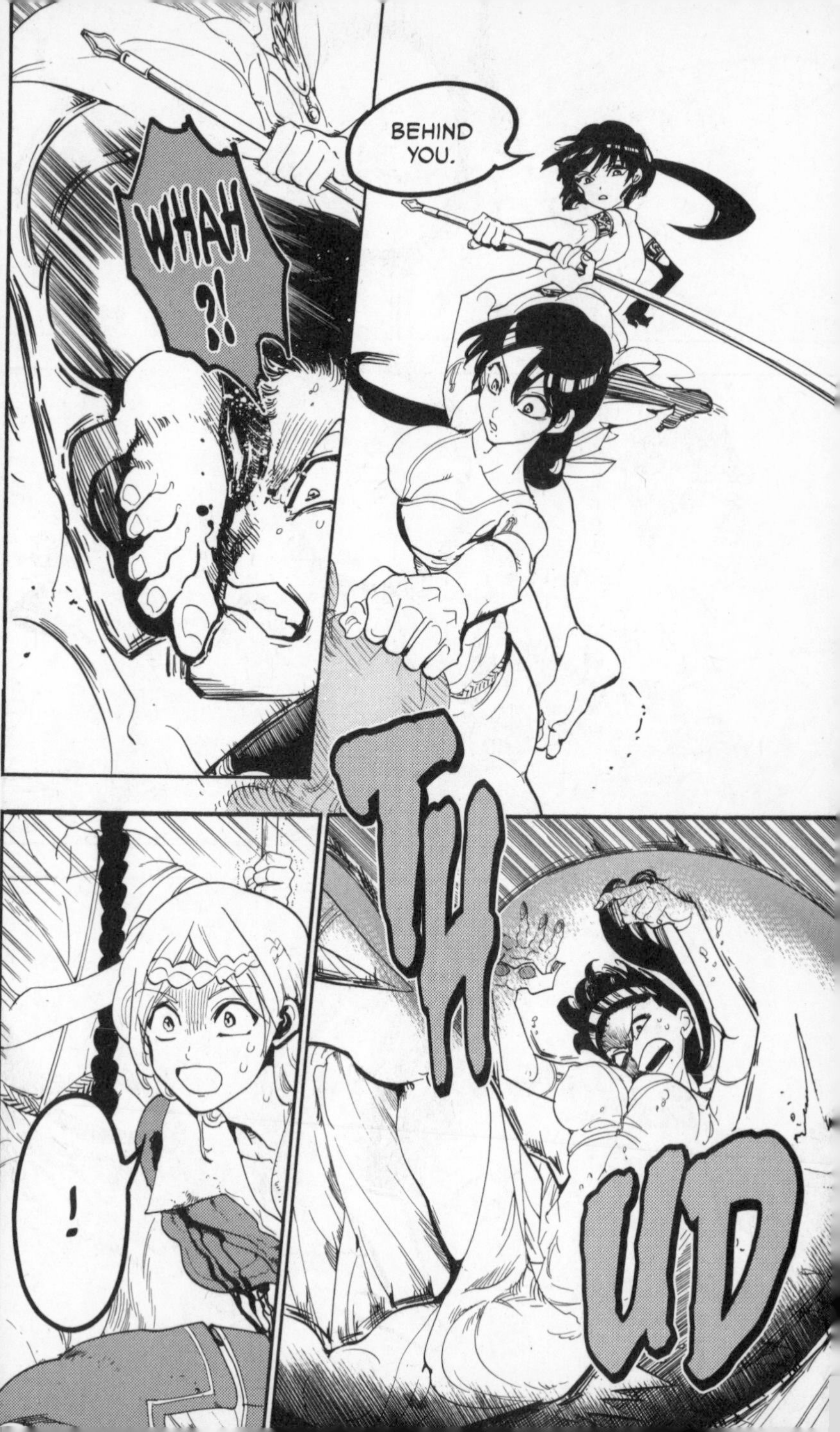
BEHIND YOU.
WHAH ?!
THUD
!

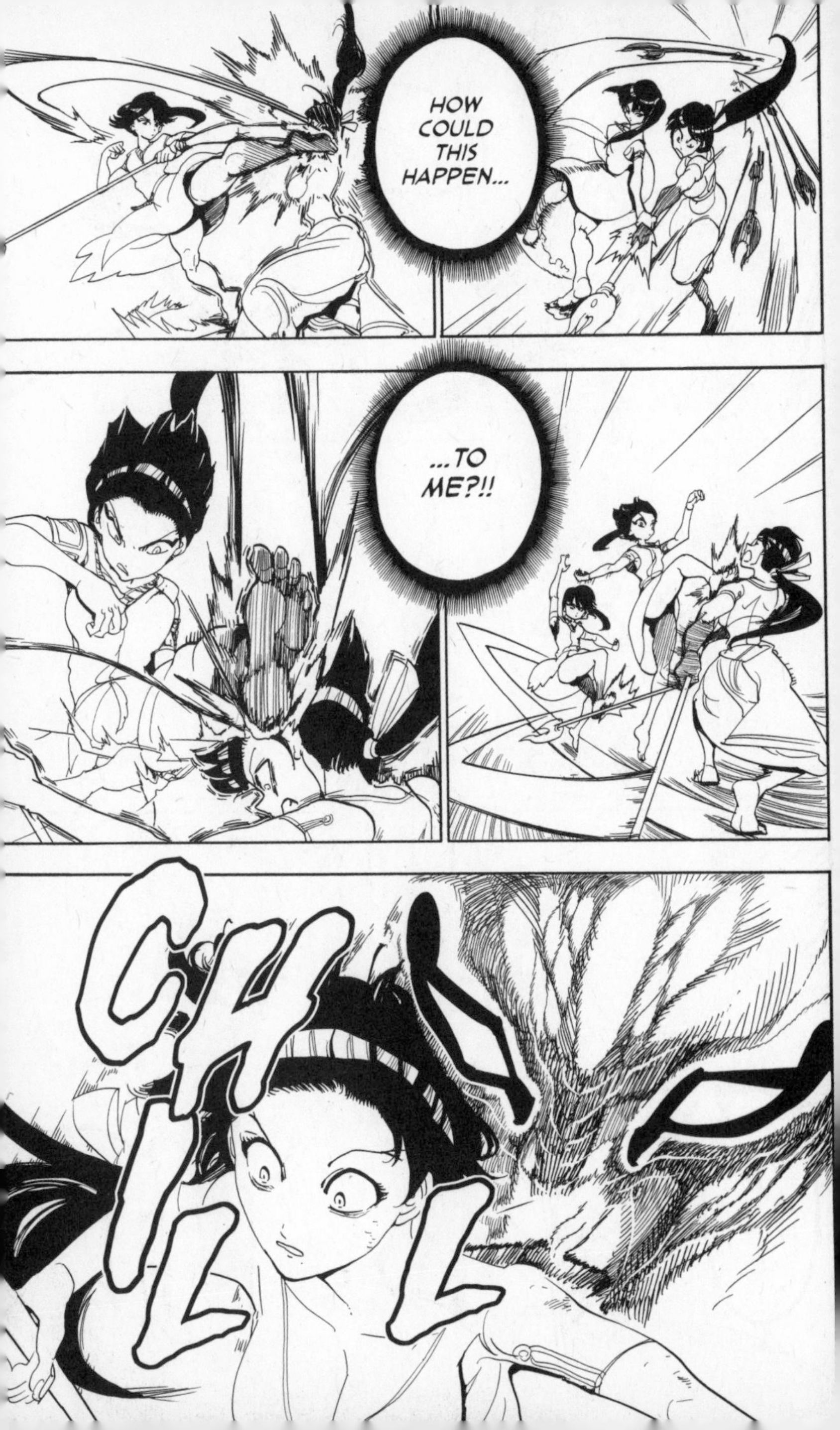
HOW COULD THIS HAPPEN...
...TO ME?!!
CHILL

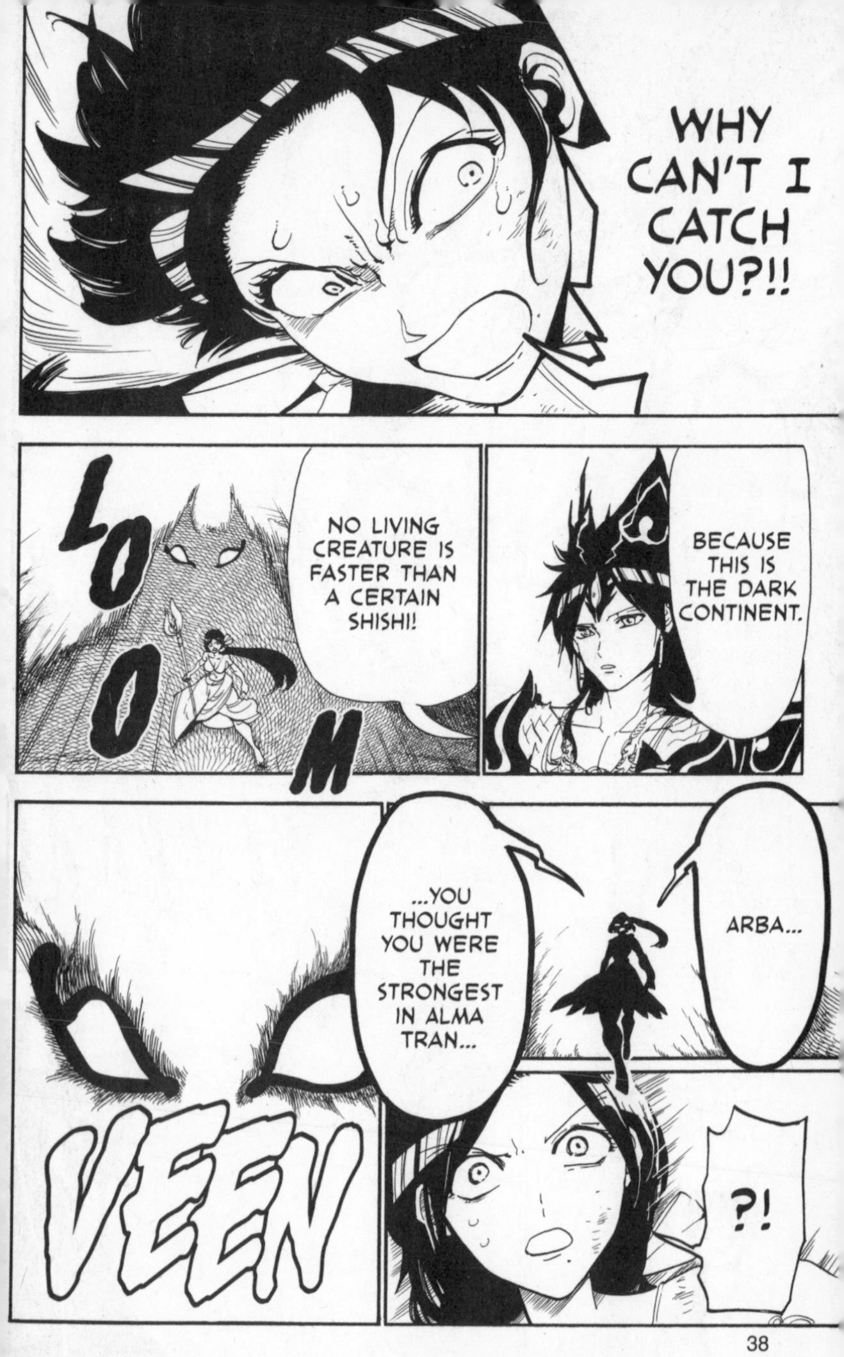

WHY CAN'T I CATCH YOU?!!
BECAUSE THIS IS THE DARK CONTINENT.
NO LIVING CREATURE IS FASTER THAN A CERTAIN SHISHI!
LOOM
ARBA...
...YOU THOUGHT YOU WERE THE STRONGEST IN ALMA TRAN...
?!
VEEN

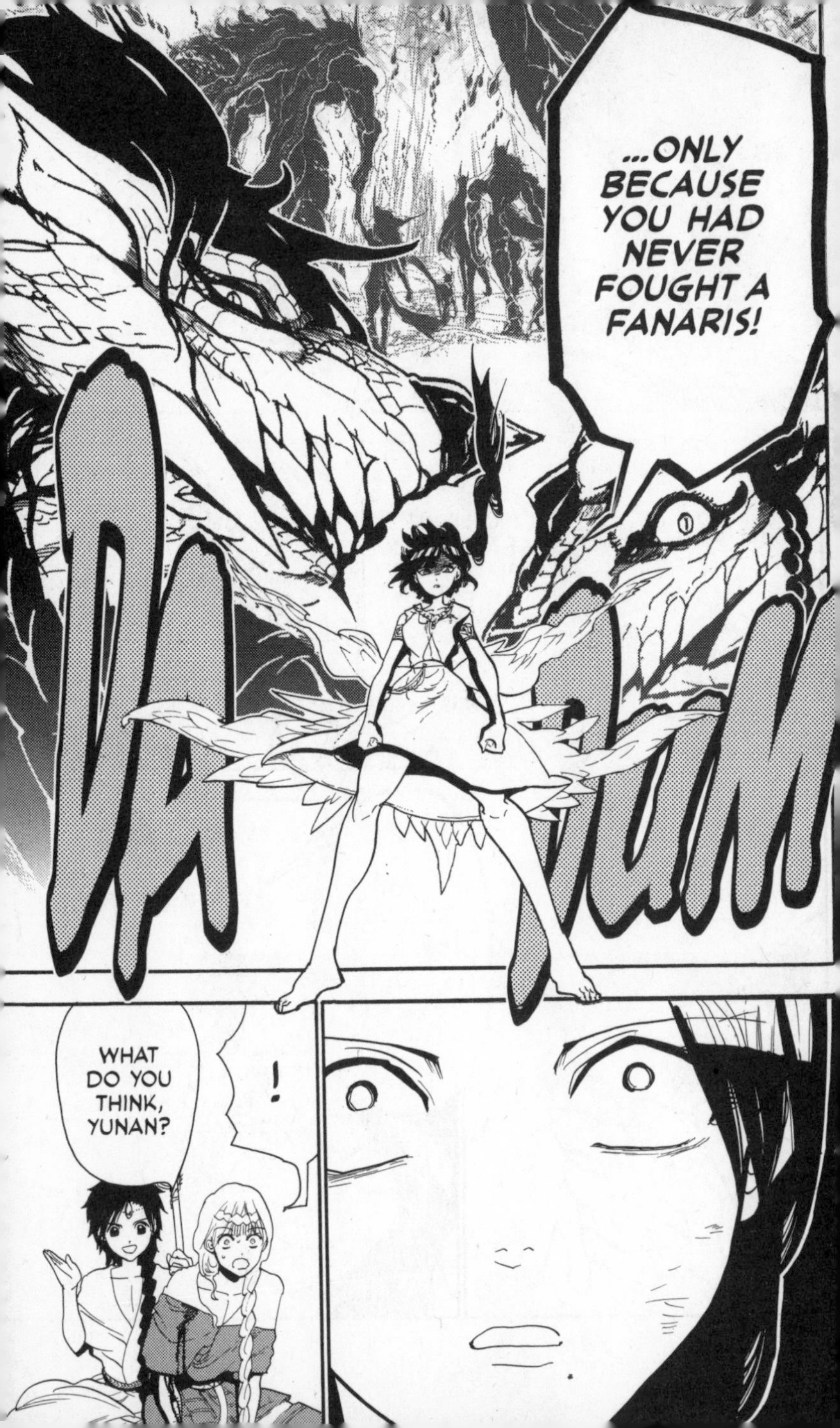
...ONLY BECAUSE YOU HAD NEVER FOUGHT A FANARIS!
WHAT DO YOU THINK, YUNAN?
!

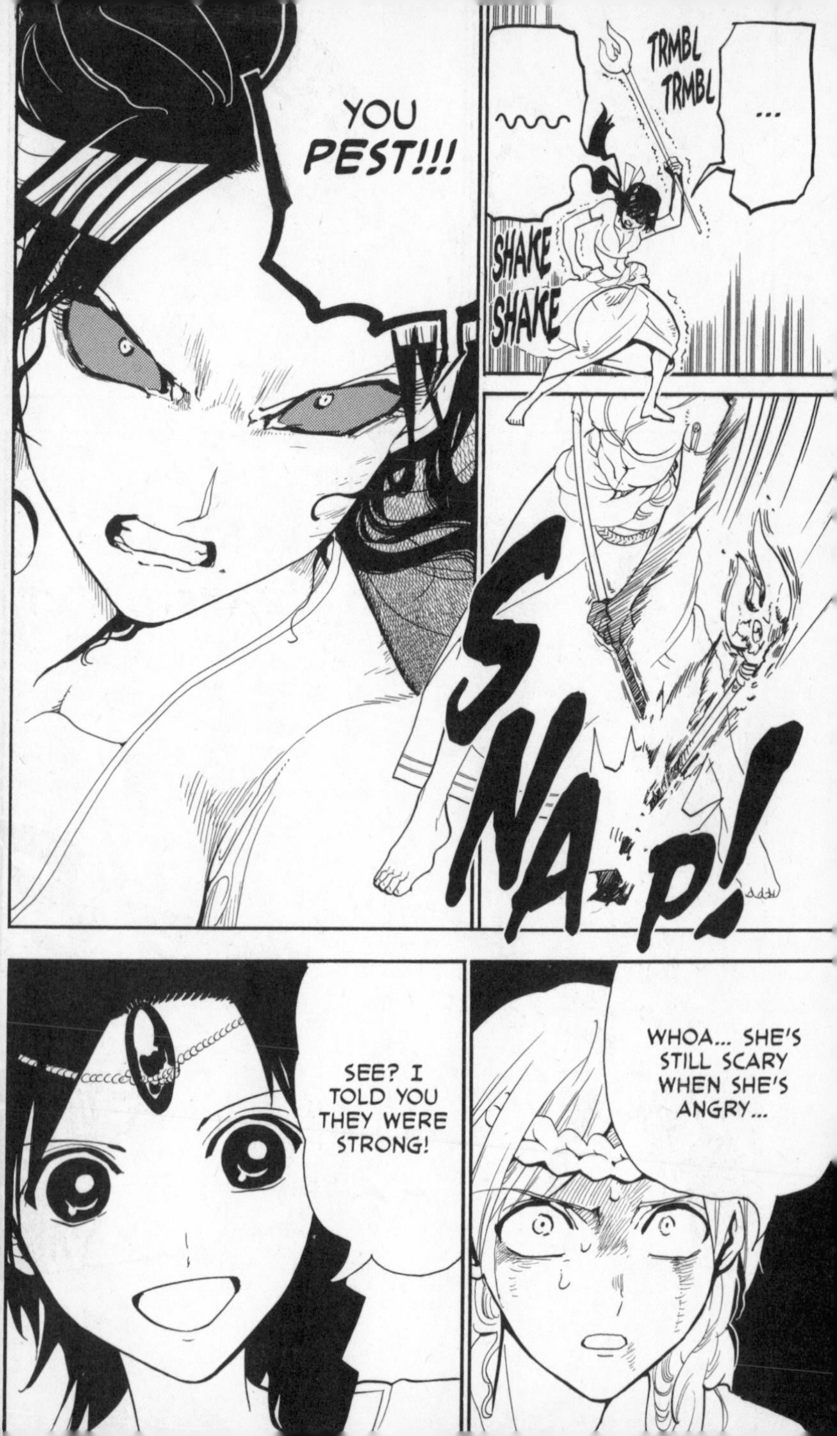
...
TRMBL TRMBL
~~~
SHAKE SHAKE
SNAP!
YOU PEST!!!
WHOA... SHE'S STILL SCARY WHEN SHE'S ANGRY...
SEE? I TOLD YOU THEY WERE STRONG!
~~~

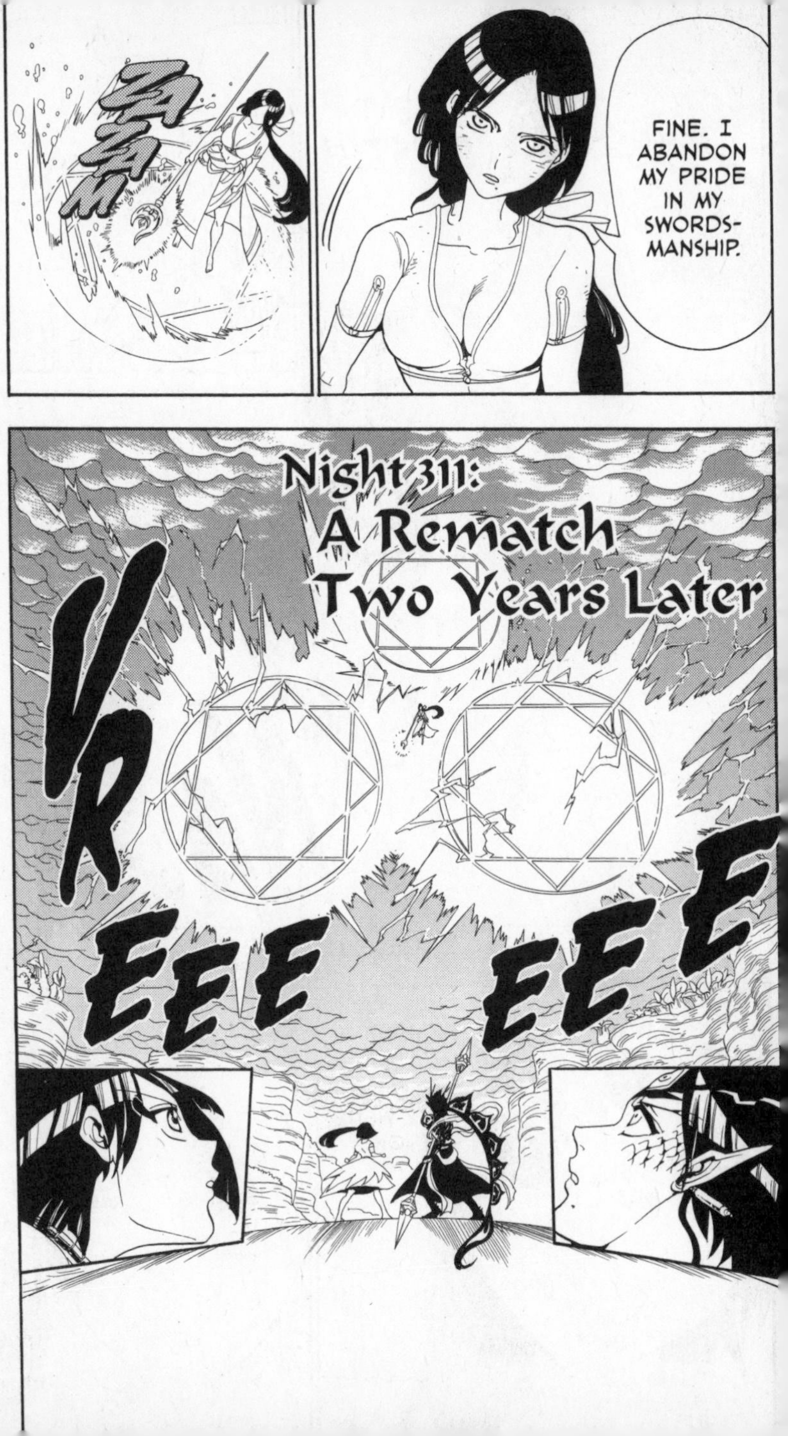
FINE. I ABANDON MY PRIDE IN MY SWORDS-MANSHIP.
Night 311: A Rematch Two Years Later

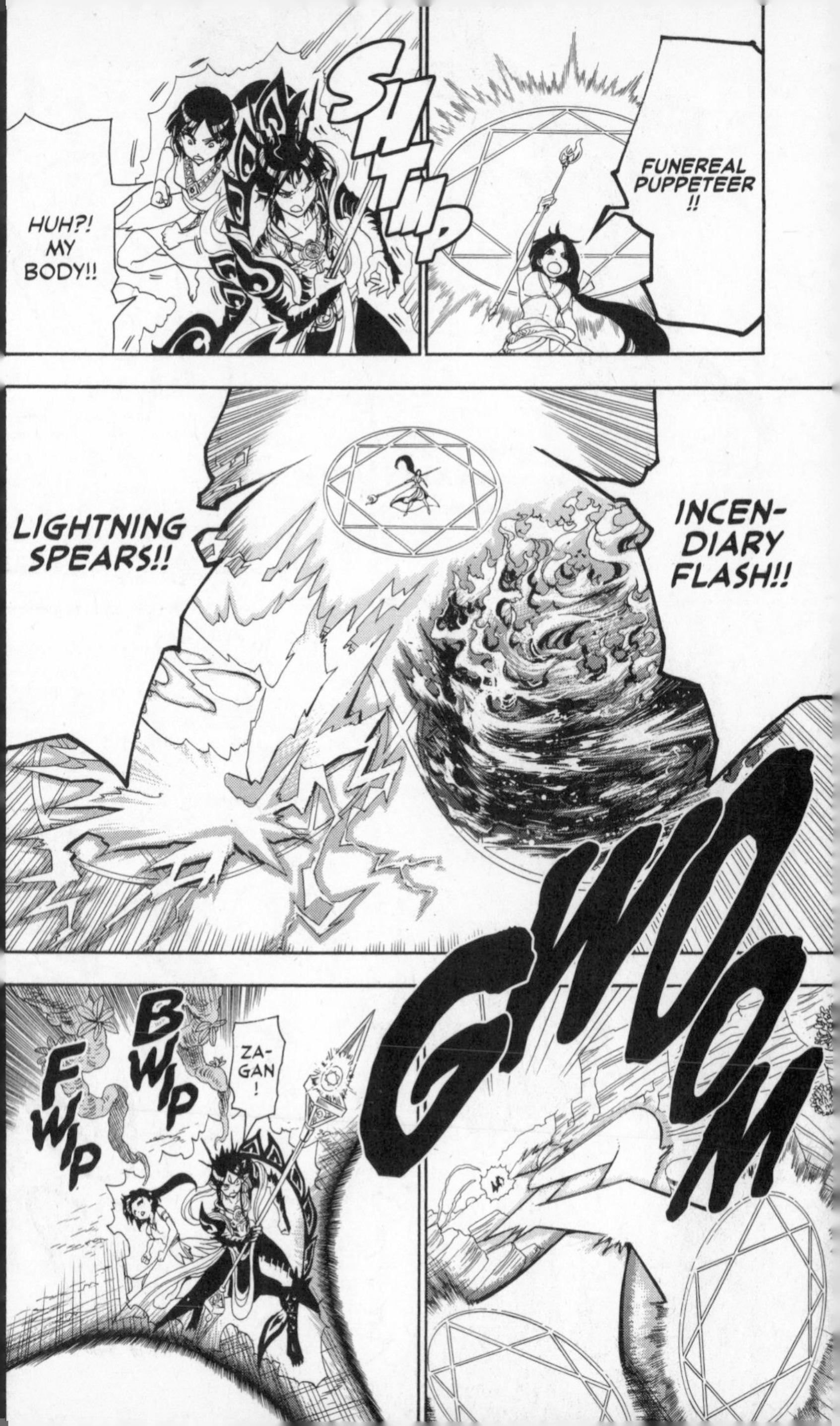
FUNEREAL PUPPETEER !!
SHTMP
HUH?! MY BODY!!
INCEN-DIARY FLASH!!
LIGHTNING SPEARS!!
GWOOM
ZA-GAN!
BWIP
FWIP

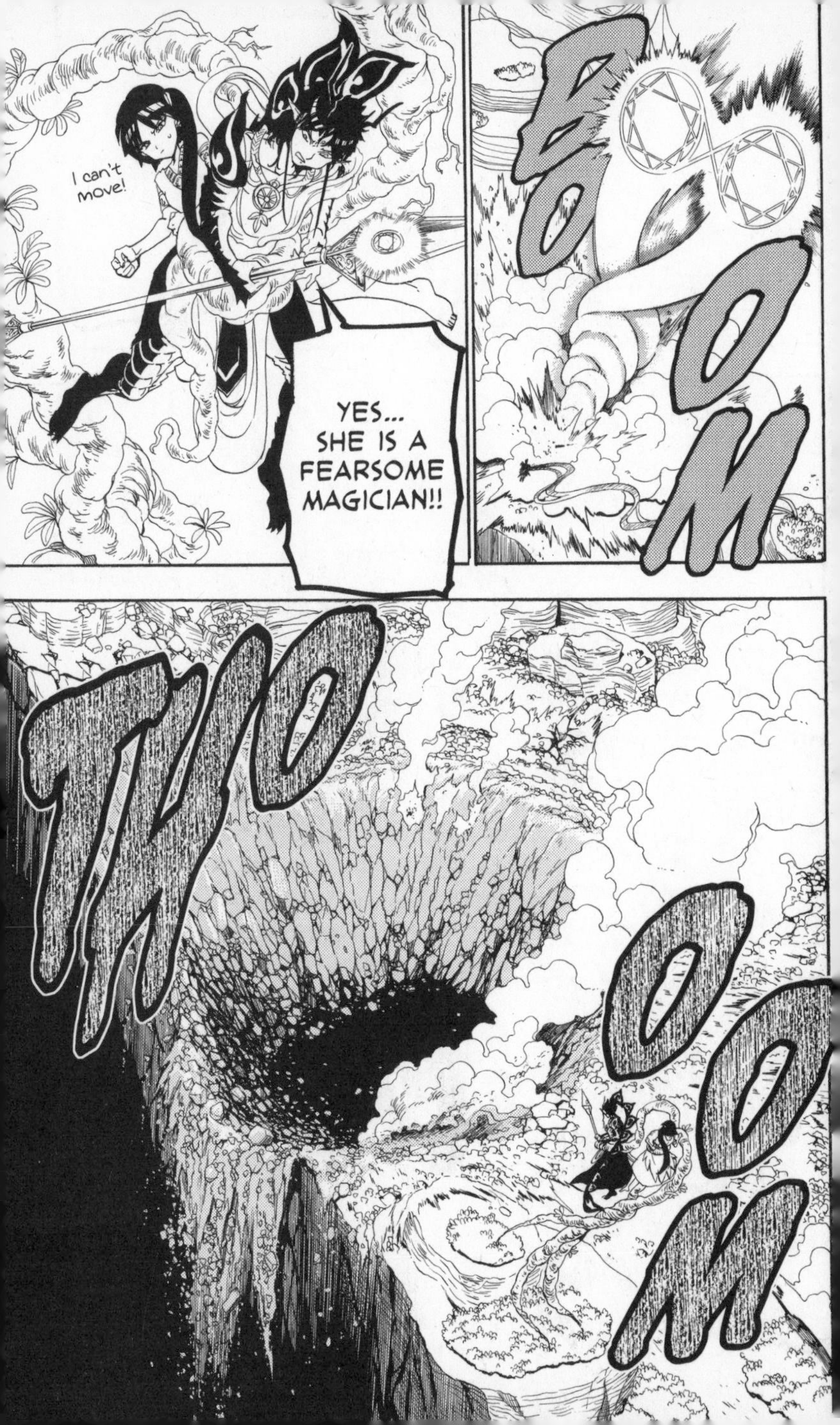
BOOM
YES... SHE IS A FEARSOME MAGICIAN!!
I can't move!
THOOOM

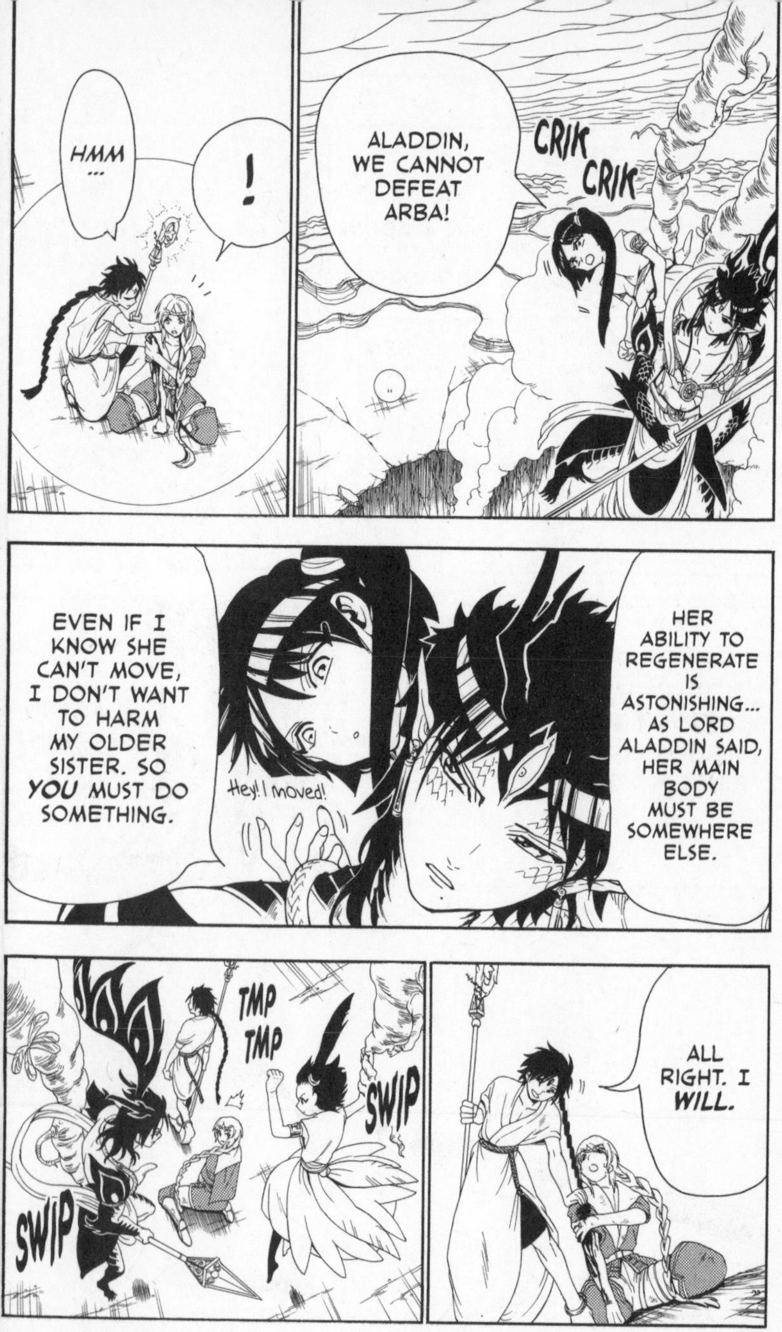
ALADDIN, WE CANNOT DEFEAT ARBA!
CRIK
CRIK
HMM...
!
HER ABILITY TO REGENERATE IS ASTONISHING... AS LORD ALADDIN SAID, HER MAIN BODY MUST BE SOMEWHERE ELSE.
Hey! I moved!
EVEN IF I KNOW SHE CAN'T MOVE, I DON'T WANT TO HARM MY OLDER SISTER. SO *YOU* MUST DO SOMETHING.
ALL RIGHT. I *WILL.*
SWIP
TMP
TMP
SWIP

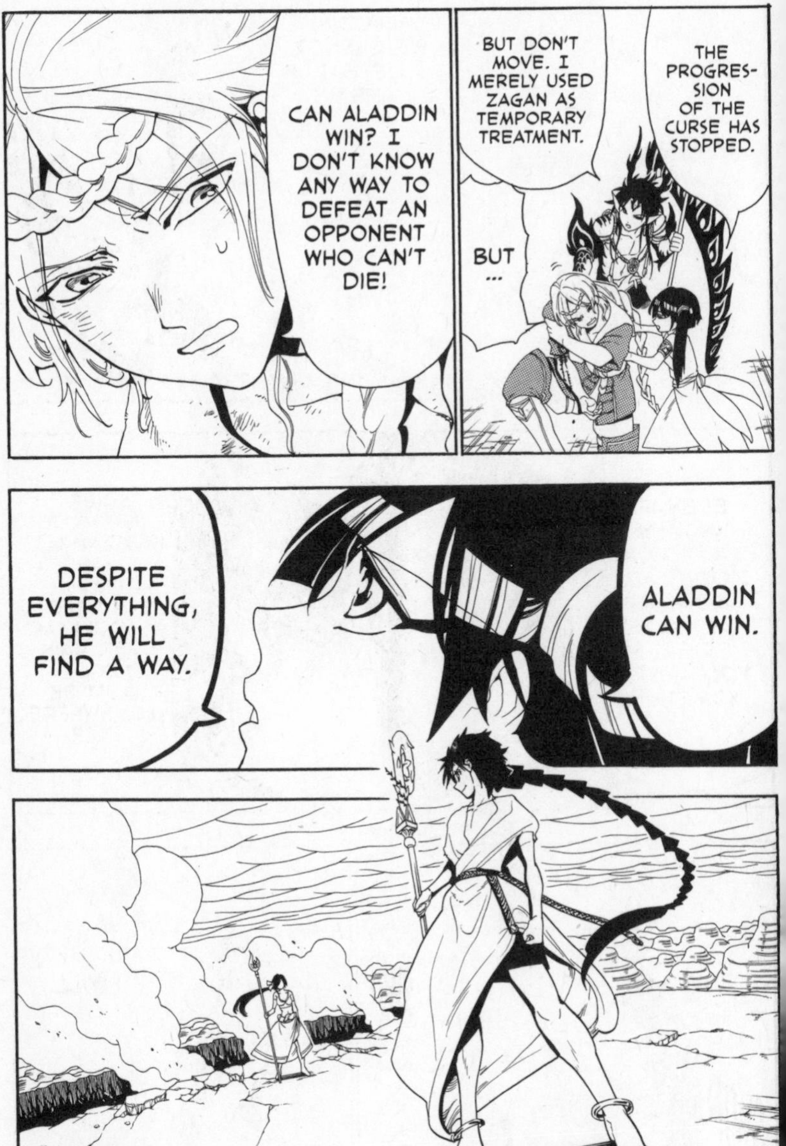
THE PROGRES-SION OF THE CURSE HAS STOPPED.
BUT DON'T MOVE. I MERELY USED ZAGAN AS TEMPORARY TREATMENT.
BUT ...
CAN ALADDIN WIN? I DON'T KNOW ANY WAY TO DEFEAT AN OPPONENT WHO CAN'T DIE!
ALADDIN CAN WIN.
DESPITE EVERYTHING, HE WILL FIND A WAY.

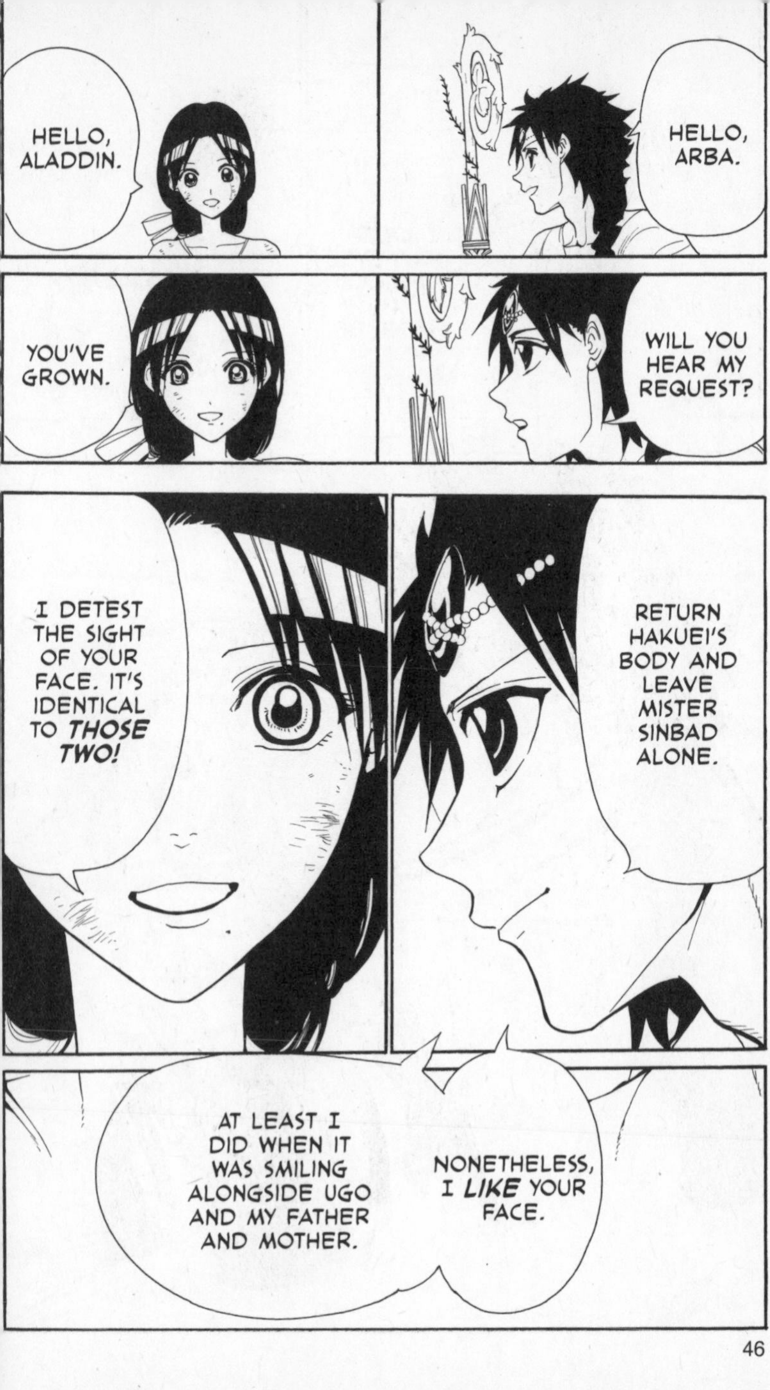
HELLO, ARBA.
HELLO, ALADDIN.
WILL YOU HEAR MY REQUEST?
YOU'VE GROWN.
RETURN HAKUEI'S BODY AND LEAVE MISTER SINBAD ALONE.
I DETEST THE SIGHT OF YOUR FACE. IT'S IDENTICAL TO ***THOSE TWO!***
NONETHELESS, I ***LIKE*** YOUR FACE.
AT LEAST I DID WHEN IT WAS SMILING ALONGSIDE UGO AND MY FATHER AND MOTHER.

GIVE ME SOLOMON'S WISDOM.
I CAN'T DO THAT.
OUR FATHER... GRANT ME POWER!
SWUP
KRAK
KOOM

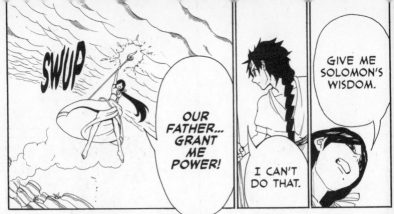

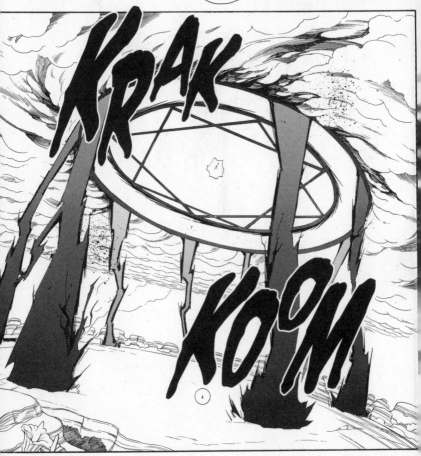

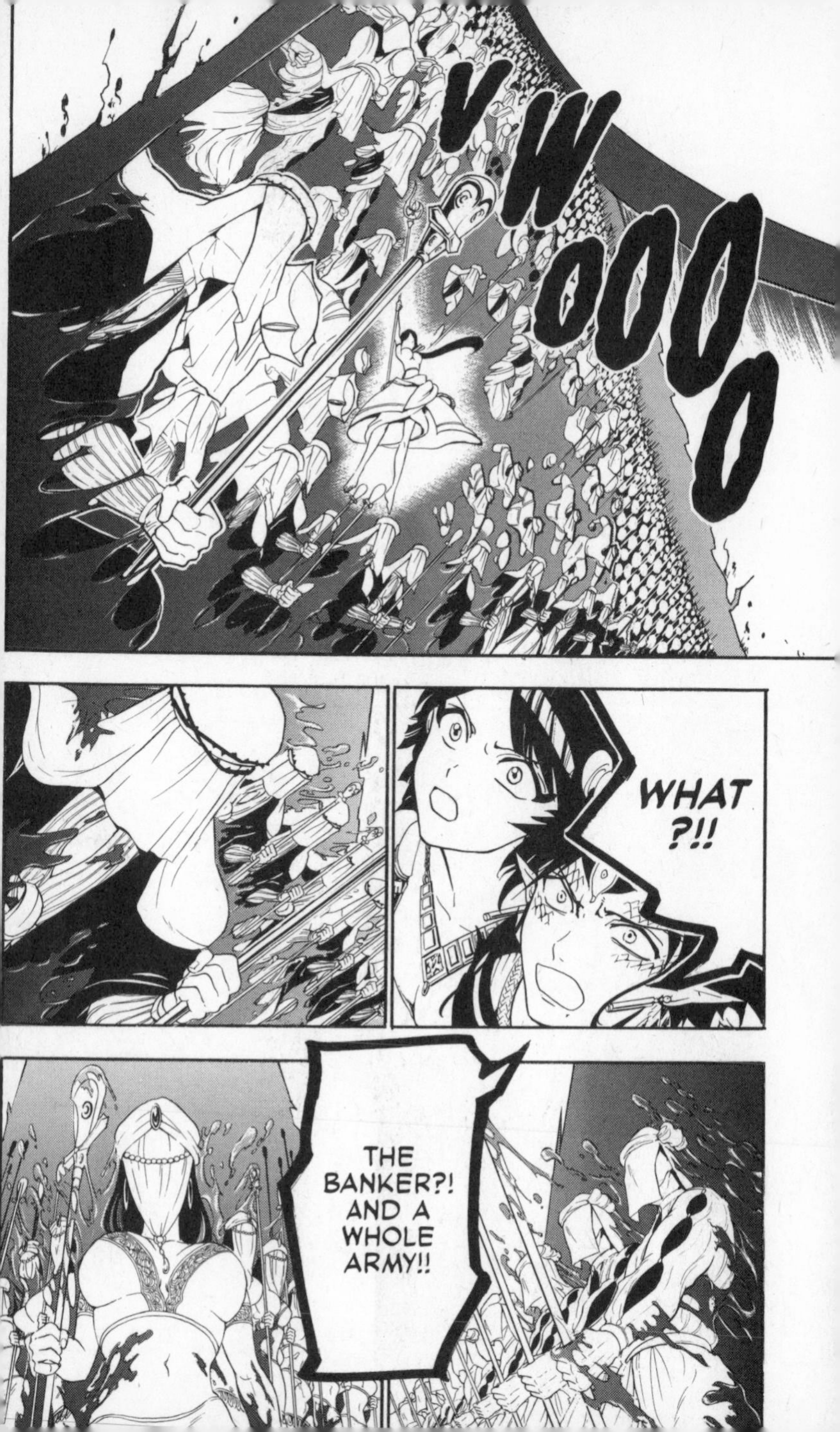
VWOOOO
WHAT ?!!
THE BANKER?! AND A WHOLE ARMY!!

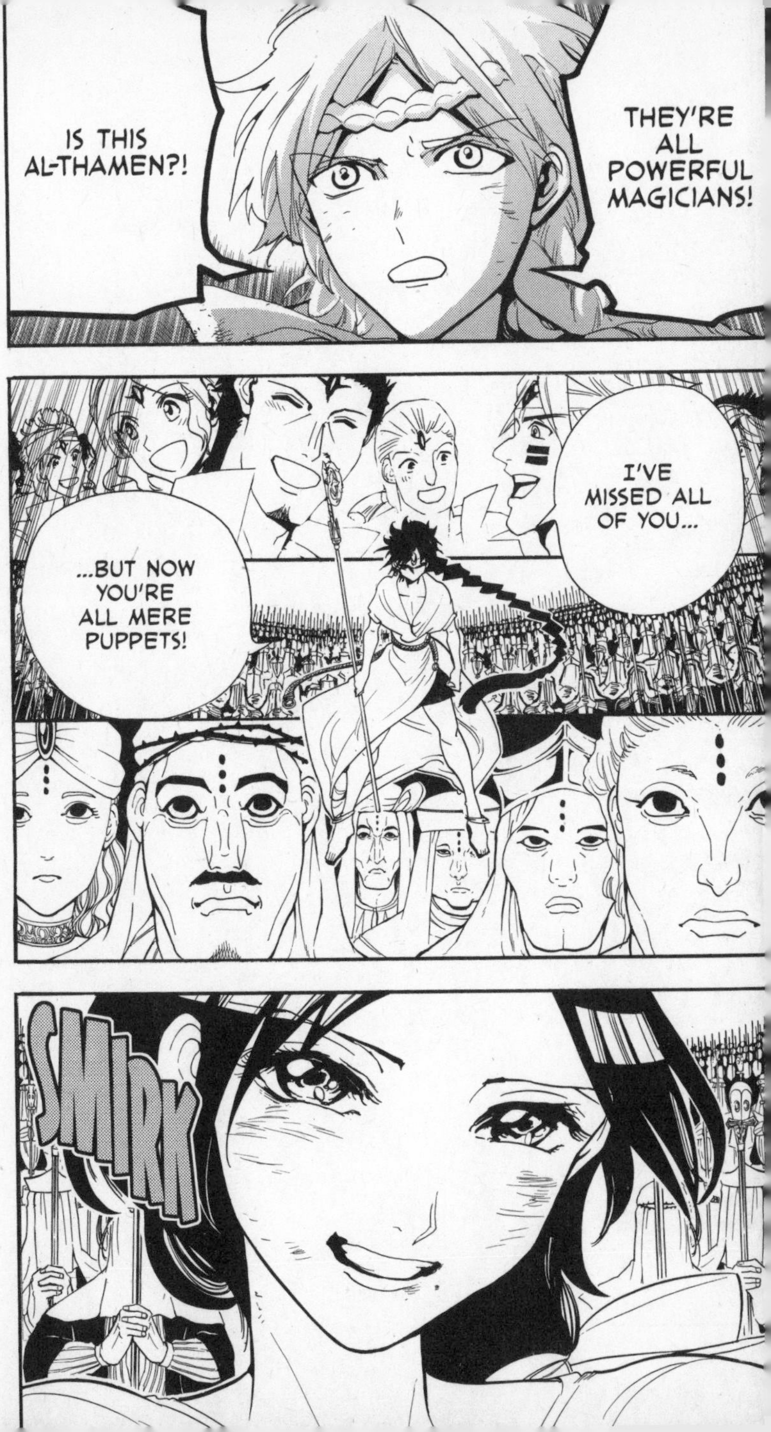
THEY'RE ALL POWERFUL MAGICIANS!
IS THIS AL-THAMEN?!
I'VE MISSED ALL OF YOU...
...BUT NOW YOU'RE ALL MERE PUPPETS!
SMIRK

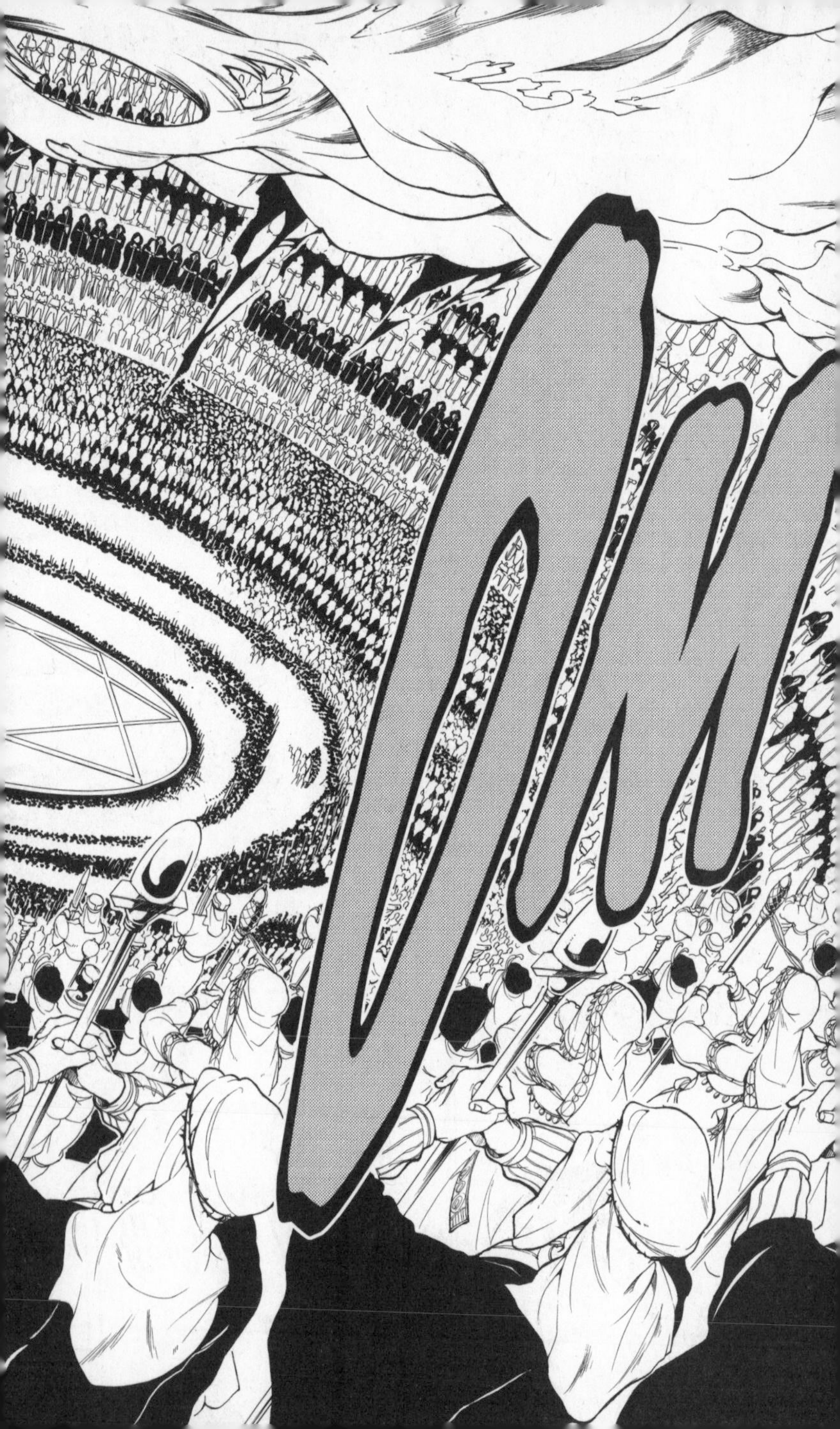

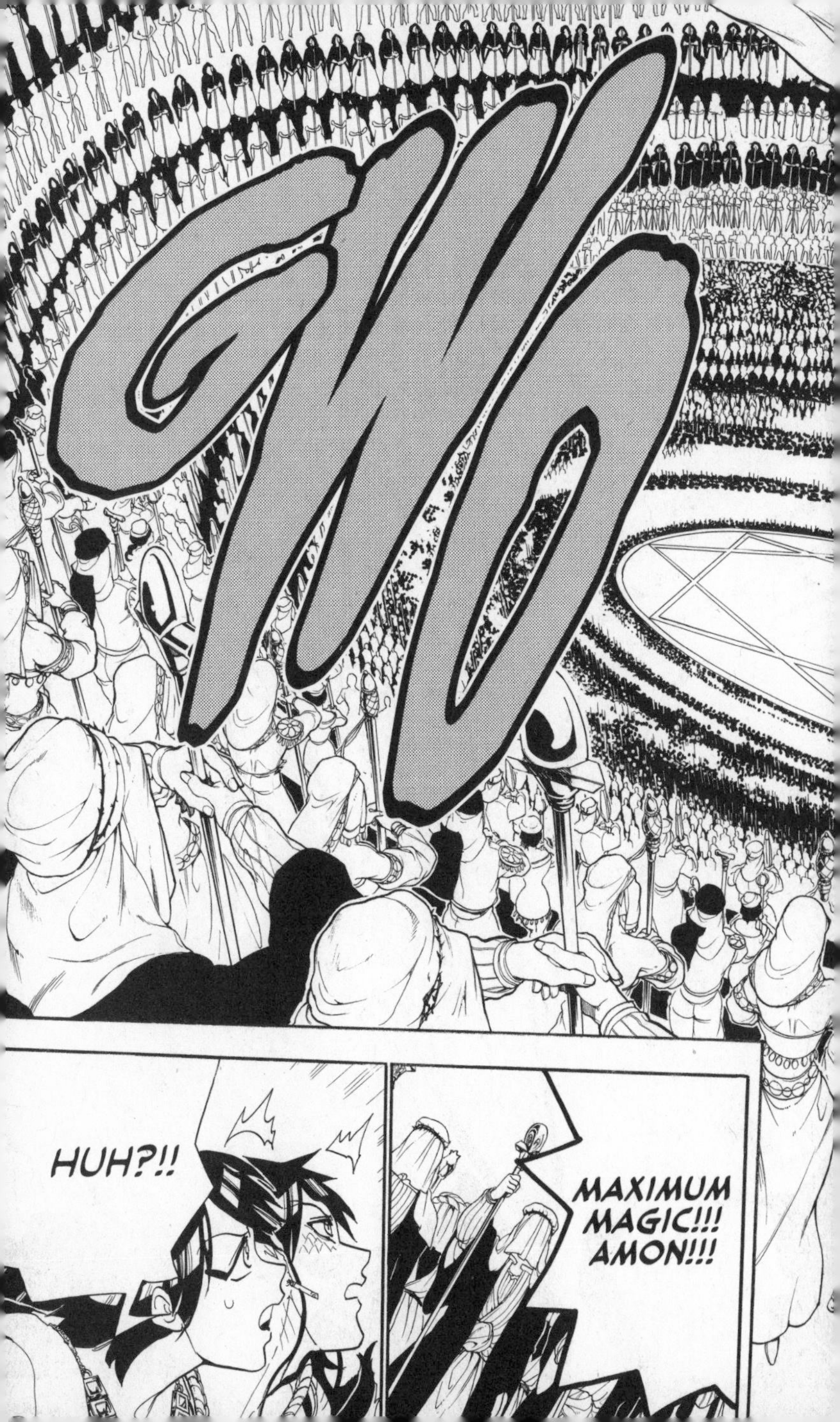
MAXIMUM MAGIC!!! AMON!!!
HUH?!!

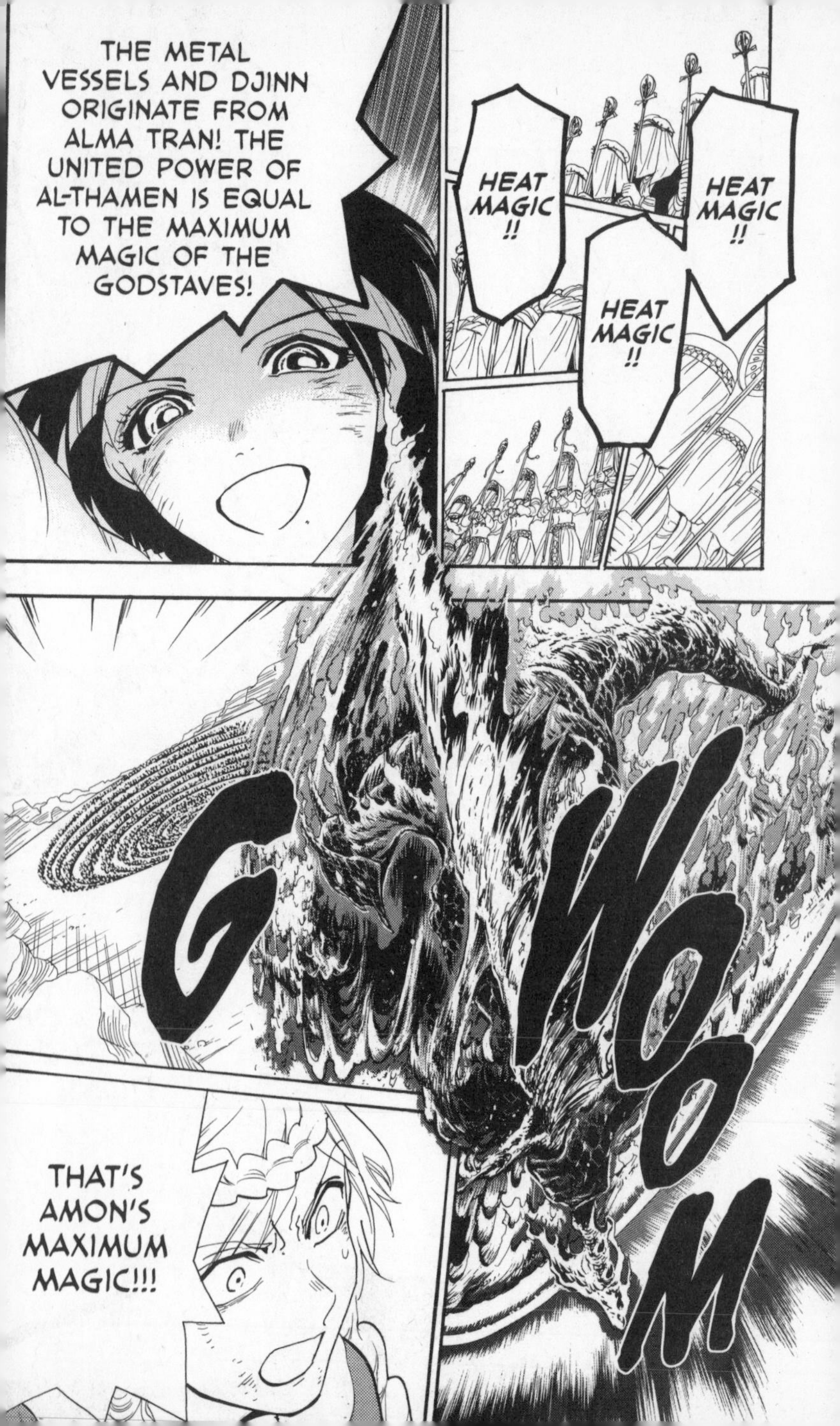
HEAT MAGIC!!
HEAT MAGIC!!
HEAT MAGIC!!
THE METAL VESSELS AND DJINN ORIGINATE FROM ALMA TRAN! THE UNITED POWER OF AL-THAMEN IS EQUAL TO THE MAXIMUM MAGIC OF THE GODSTAVES!
GWOOM
THAT'S AMON'S MAXIMUM MAGIC!!!

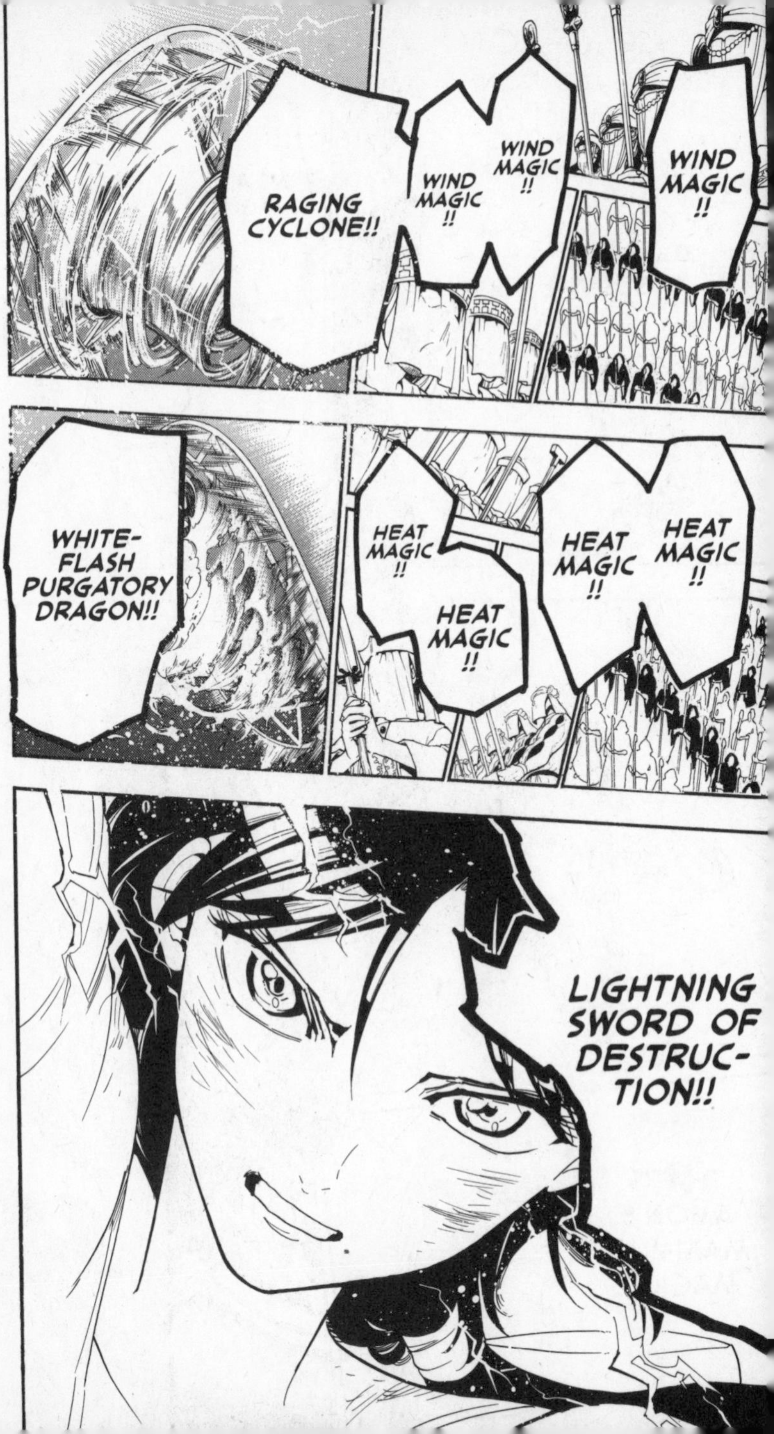
WIND MAGIC!!
WIND MAGIC!!
WIND MAGIC!!
RAGING CYCLONE!!
HEAT MAGIC!!
HEAT MAGIC!!
HEAT MAGIC!!
HEAT MAGIC!!
WHITE-FLASH PURGATORY DRAGON!!
LIGHTNING SWORD OF DESTRUCTION!!

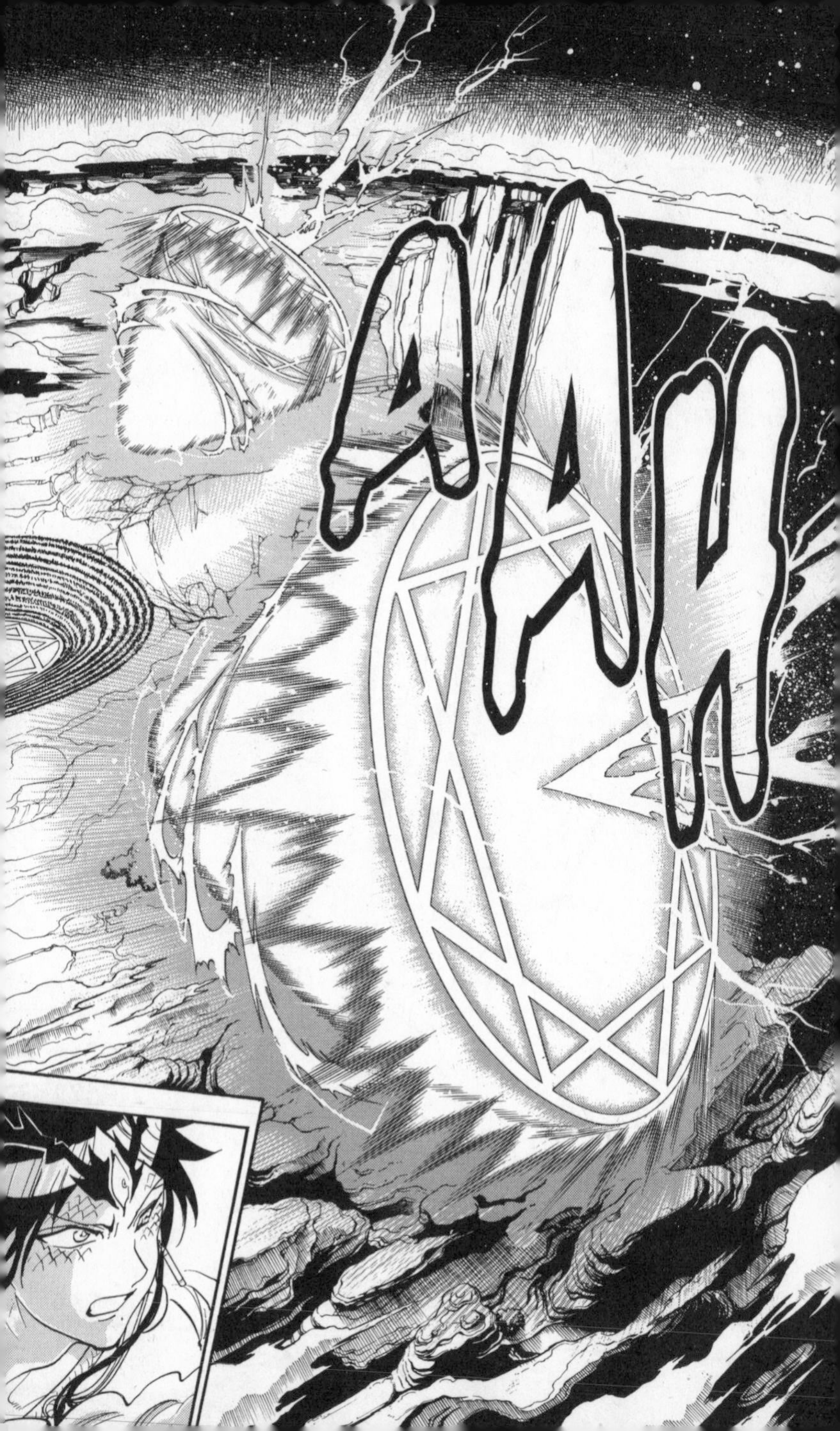
AAH

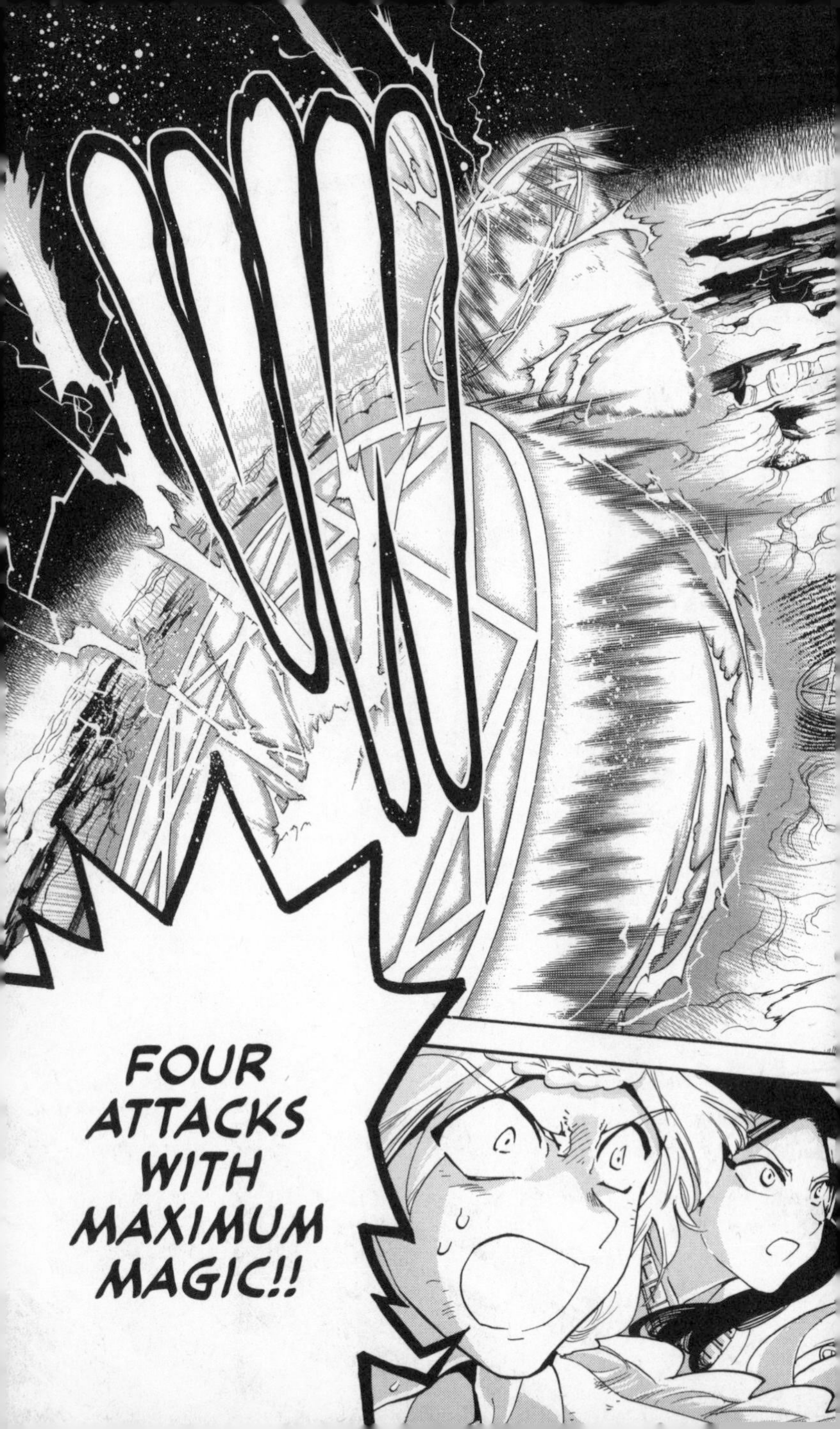
FOUR ATTACKS WITH MAXIMUM MAGIC!!

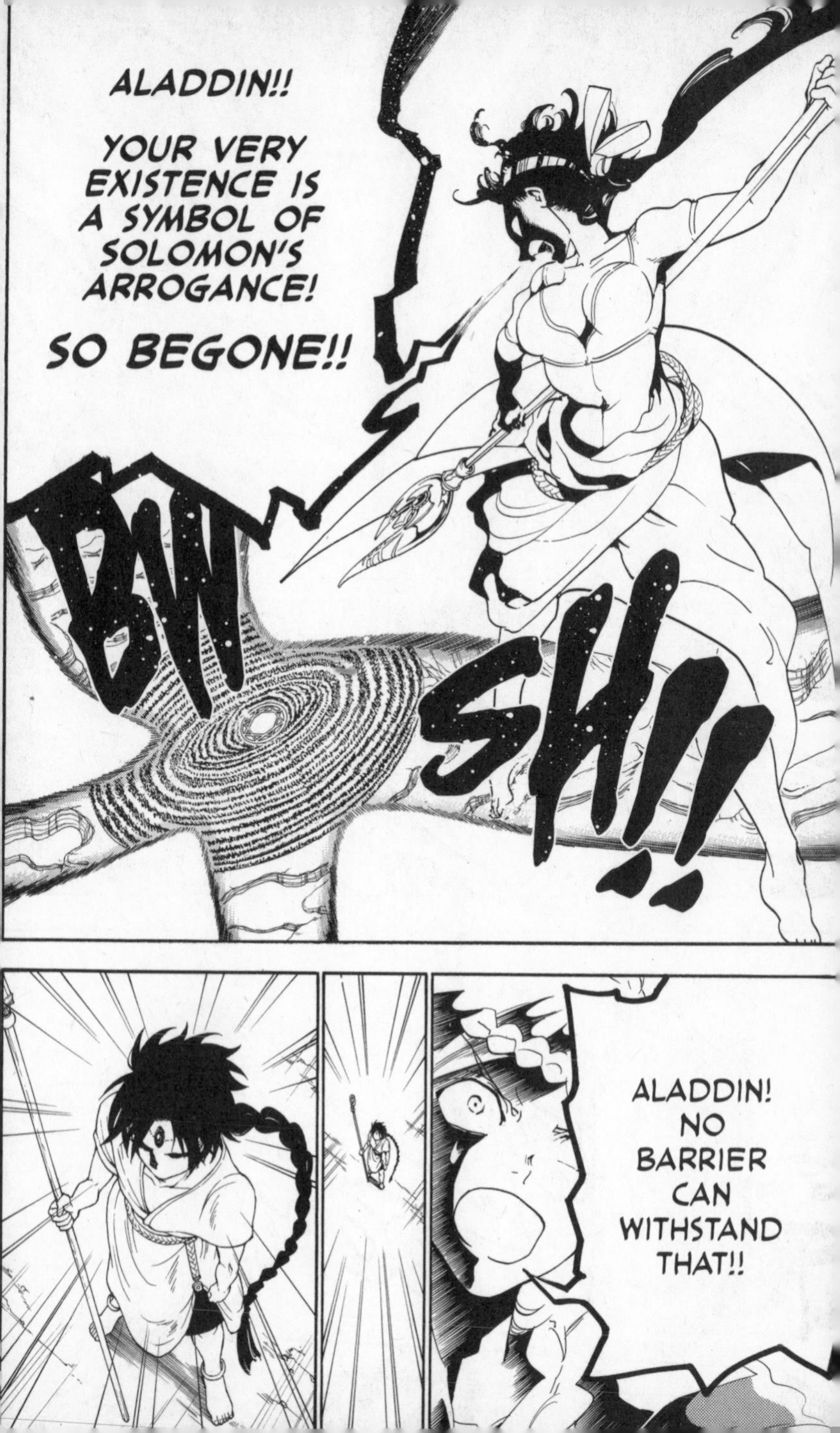
ALADDIN!!
YOUR VERY EXISTENCE IS A SYMBOL OF SOLOMON'S ARROGANCE!
SO BEGONE!!
BWSH!!
ALADDIN! NO BARRIER CAN WITHSTAND THAT!!

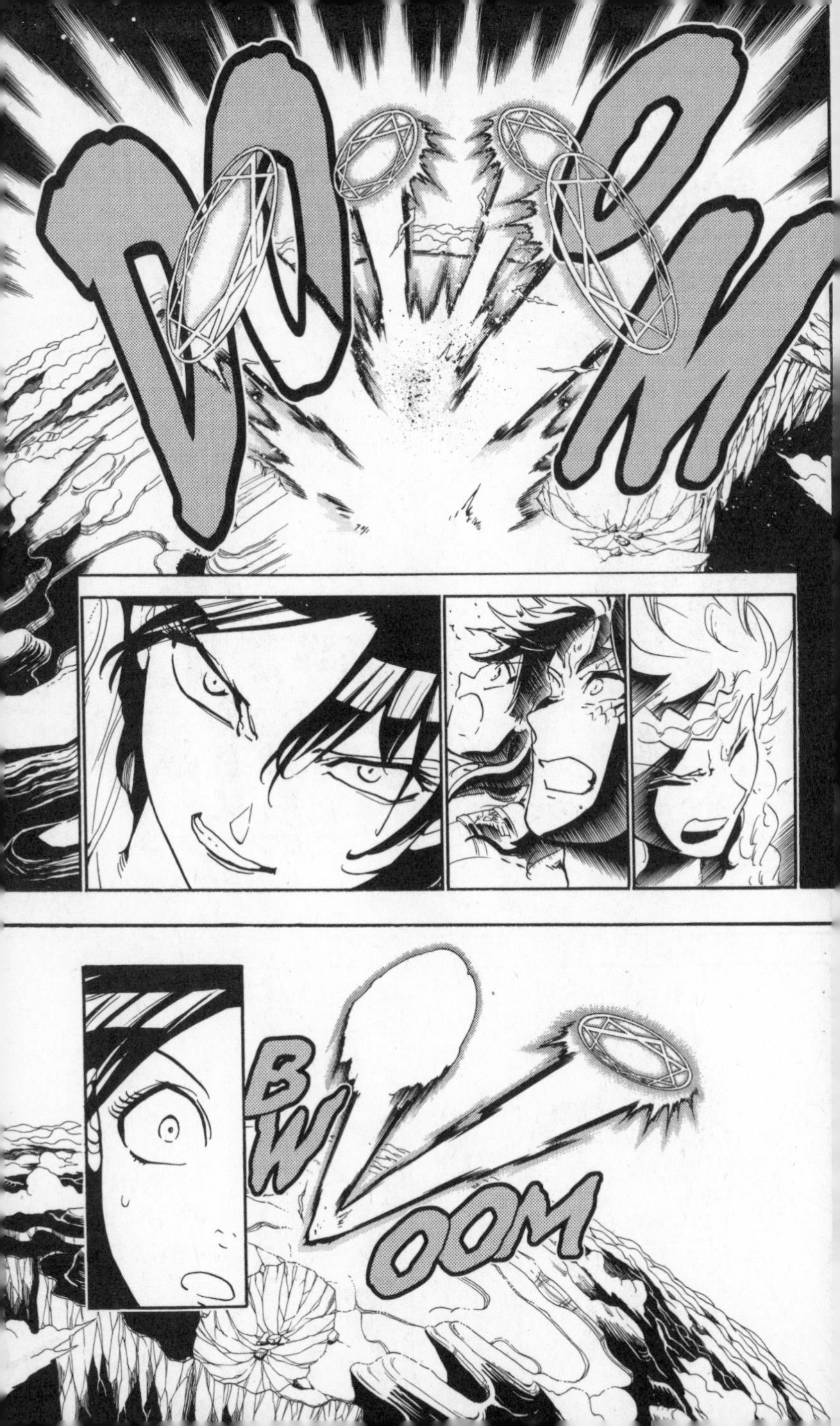
DOOM
BWOOM

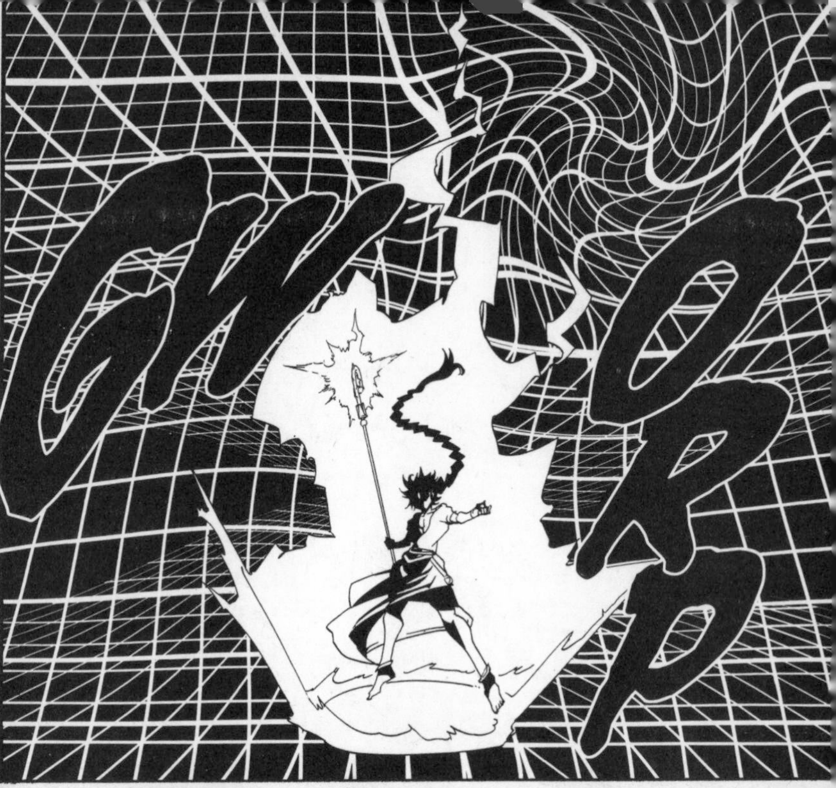
GWORP
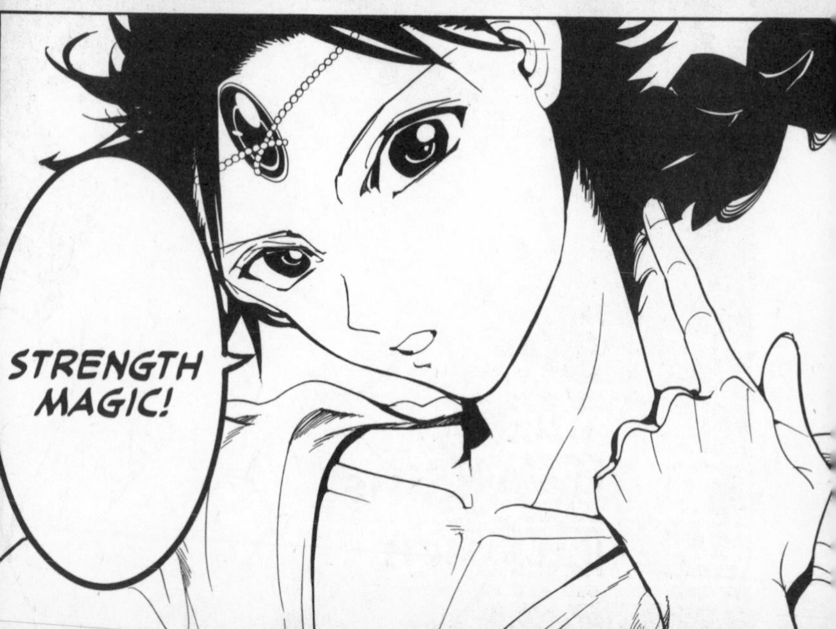
STRENGTH MAGIC!

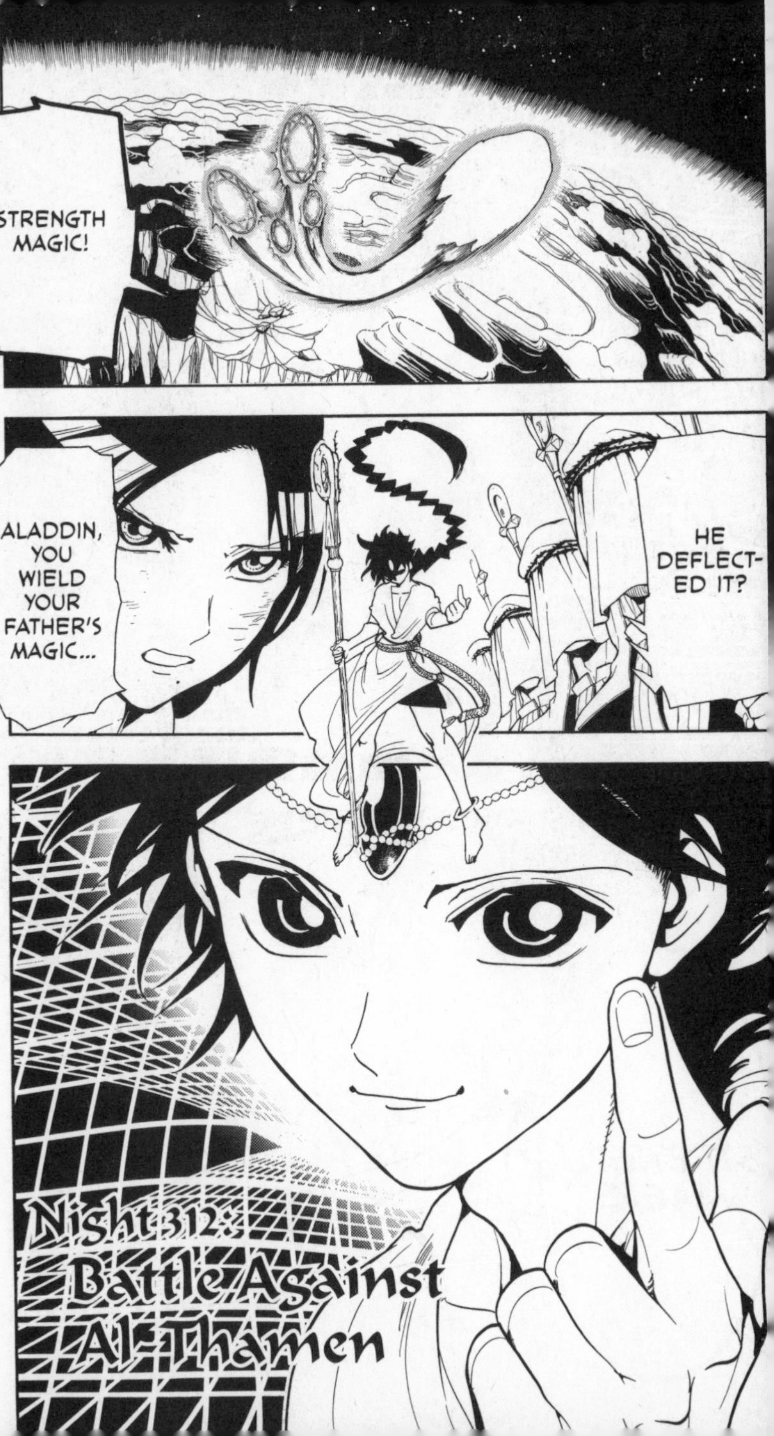
STRENGTH MAGIC!
HE DEFLECT-ED IT?
ALADDIN, YOU WIELD YOUR FATHER'S MAGIC...
Night 312: Battle Against Al-Thamen

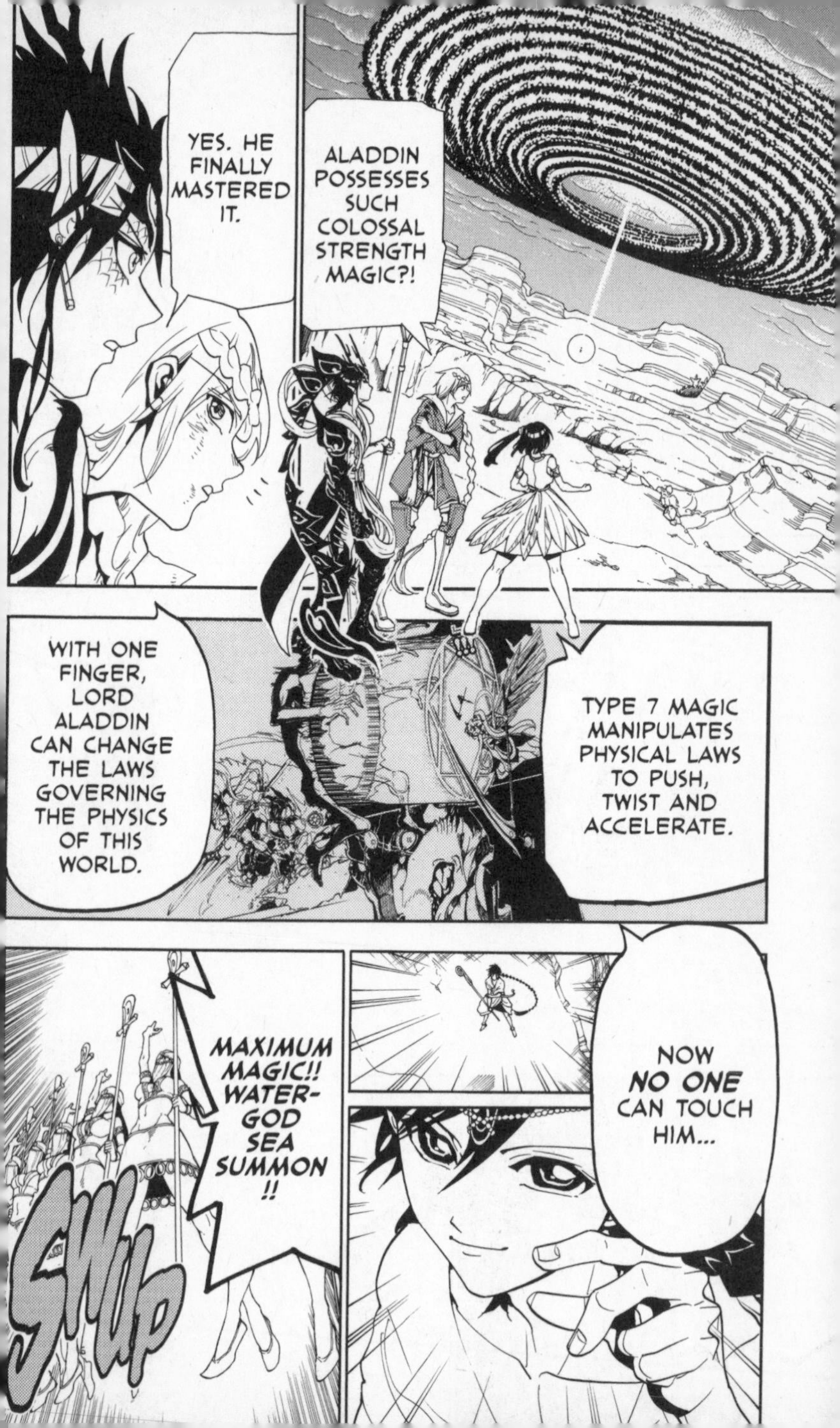
ALADDIN POSSESSES SUCH COLOSSAL STRENGTH MAGIC?!
YES. HE FINALLY MASTERED IT.
TYPE 7 MAGIC MANIPULATES PHYSICAL LAWS TO PUSH, TWIST AND ACCELERATE.
WITH ONE FINGER, LORD ALADDIN CAN CHANGE THE LAWS GOVERNING THE PHYSICS OF THIS WORLD.
NOW *NO ONE* CAN TOUCH HIM...
MAXIMUM MAGIC!! WATER-GOD SEA SUMMON !!
SWUP

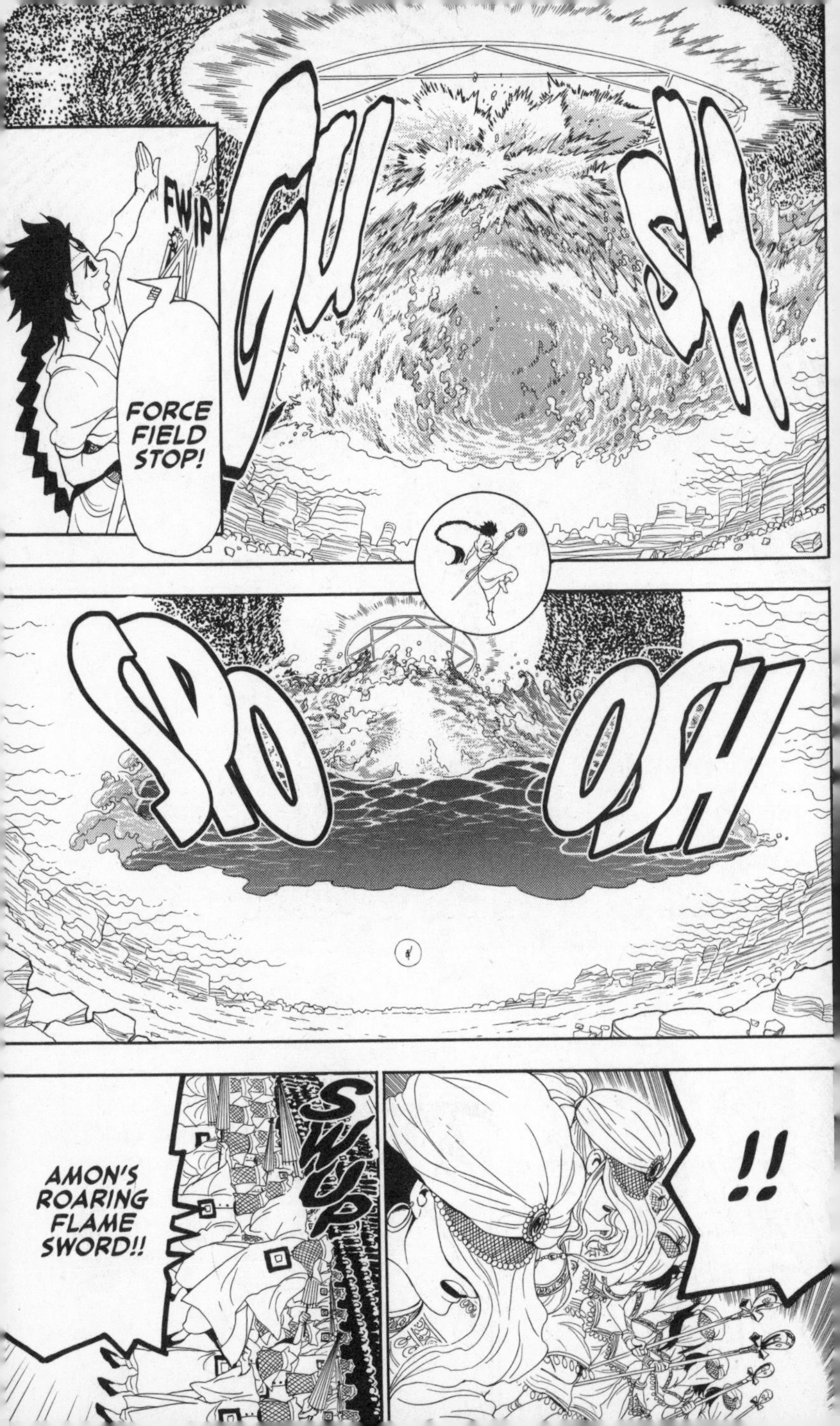
GUSH
FWIP
FORCE FIELD STOP!
SPOOSH
!!
SWOP
AMON'S ROARING FLAME SWORD!!

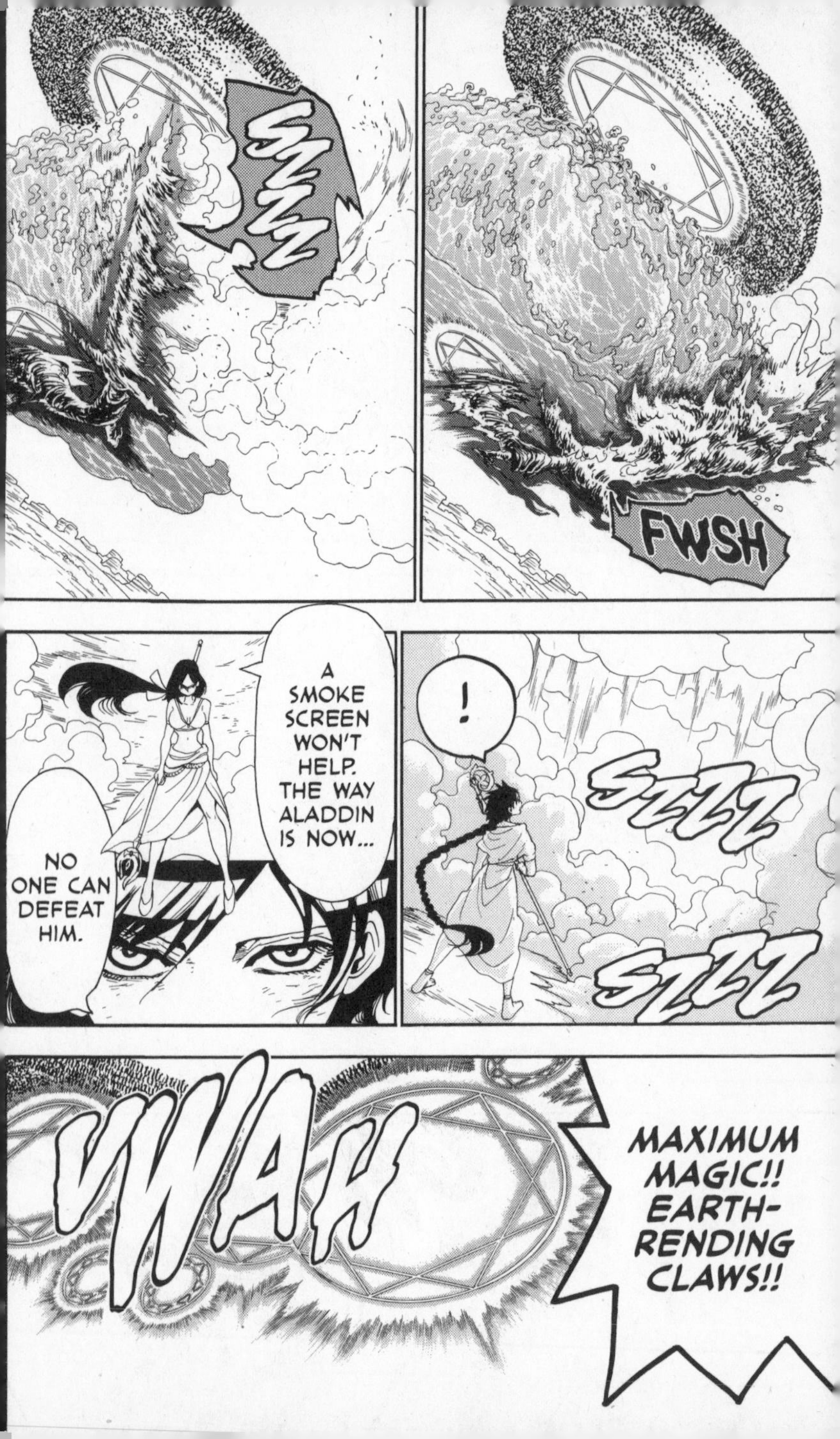
FWSH
!
SZZZ
SZZZ
A SMOKE SCREEN WON'T HELP. THE WAY ALADDIN IS NOW...
NO ONE CAN DEFEAT HIM.
MAXIMUM MAGIC!! EARTH-RENDING CLAWS!!
VWAH

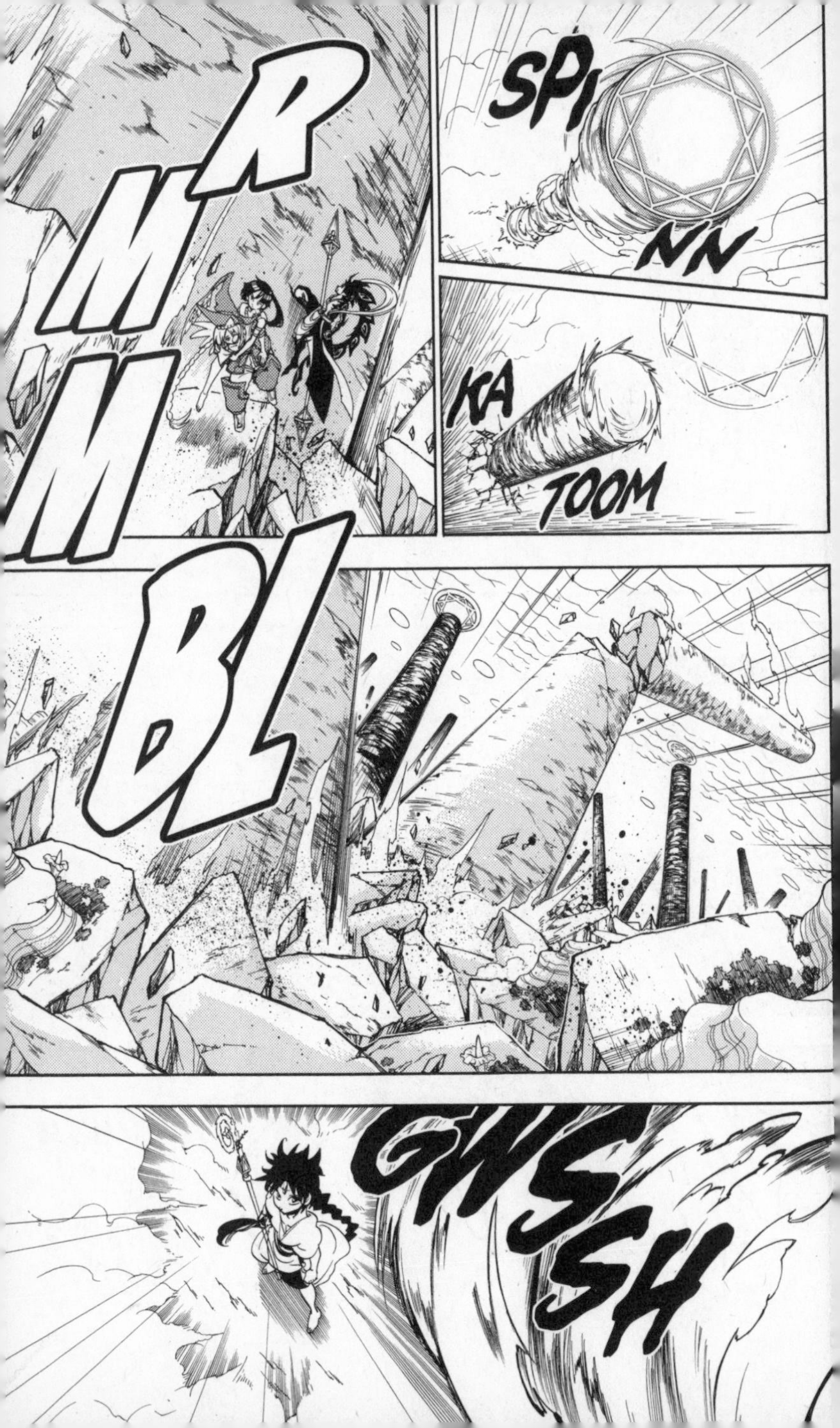
SPI
NN
KA
TOOM
RMMM
BL
GWSSH

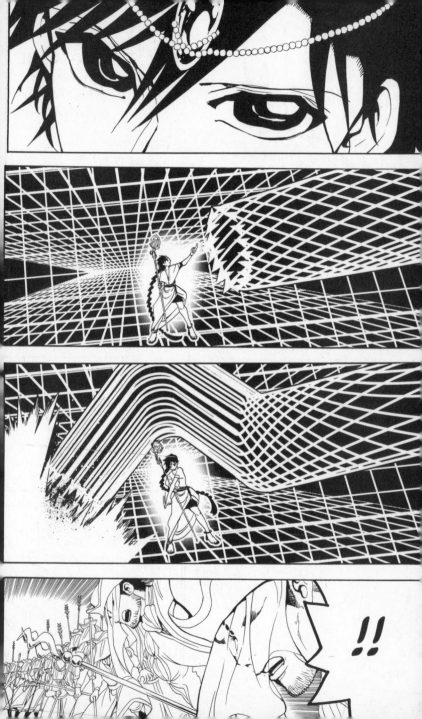

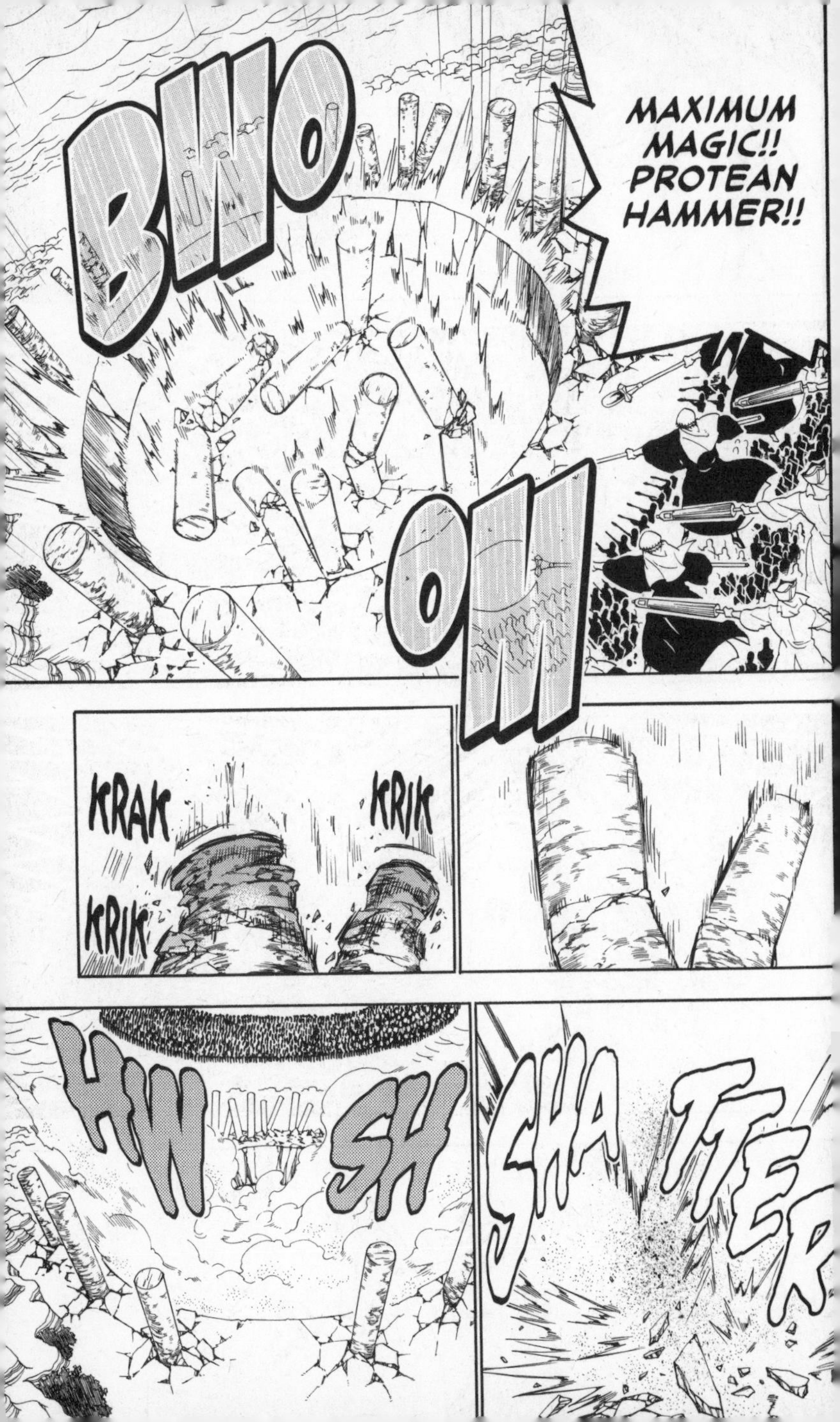
MAXIMUM MAGIC!! PROTEAN HAMMER!!
BWOOM
KRIK
KRAK
KRIK
SHATTER
HWSH

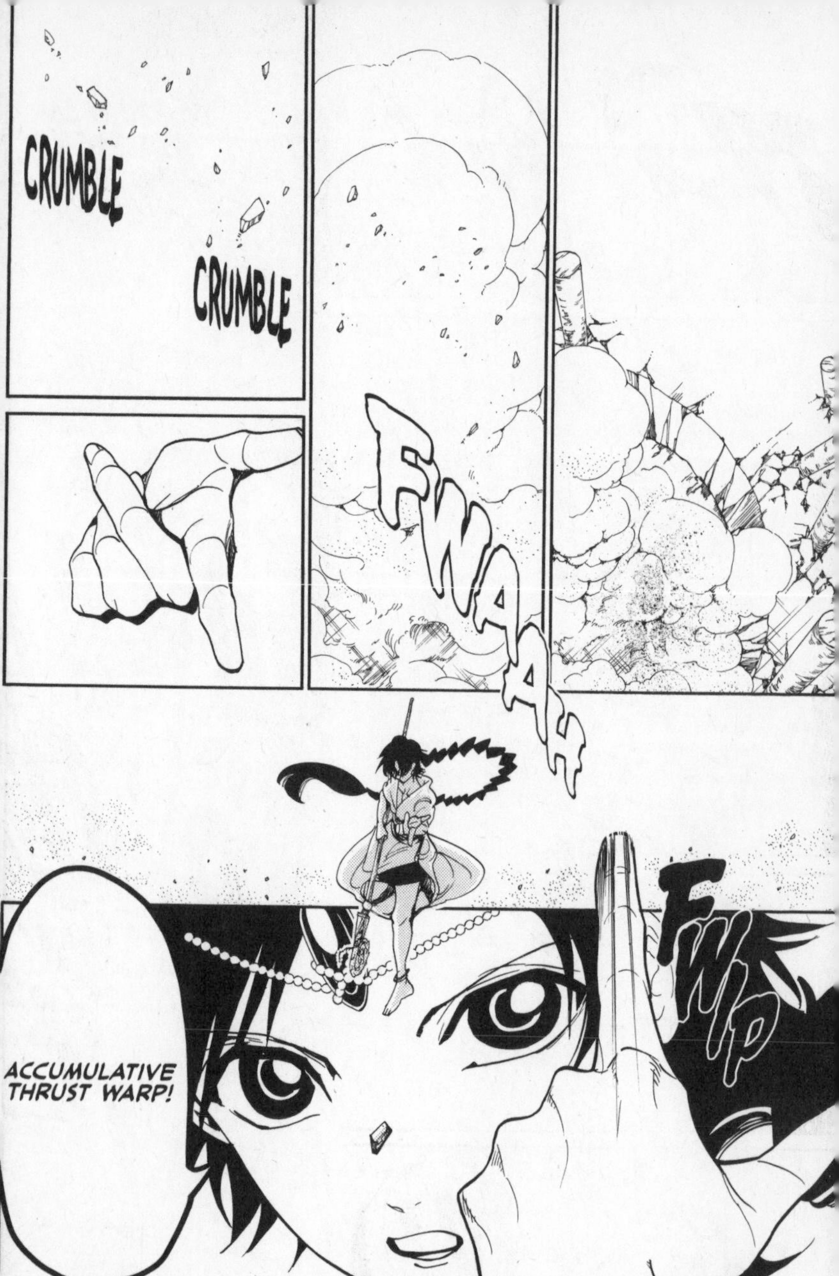
FWAAH
CRUMBLE
CRUMBLE
FWIP
ACCUMULATIVE THRUST WARP!

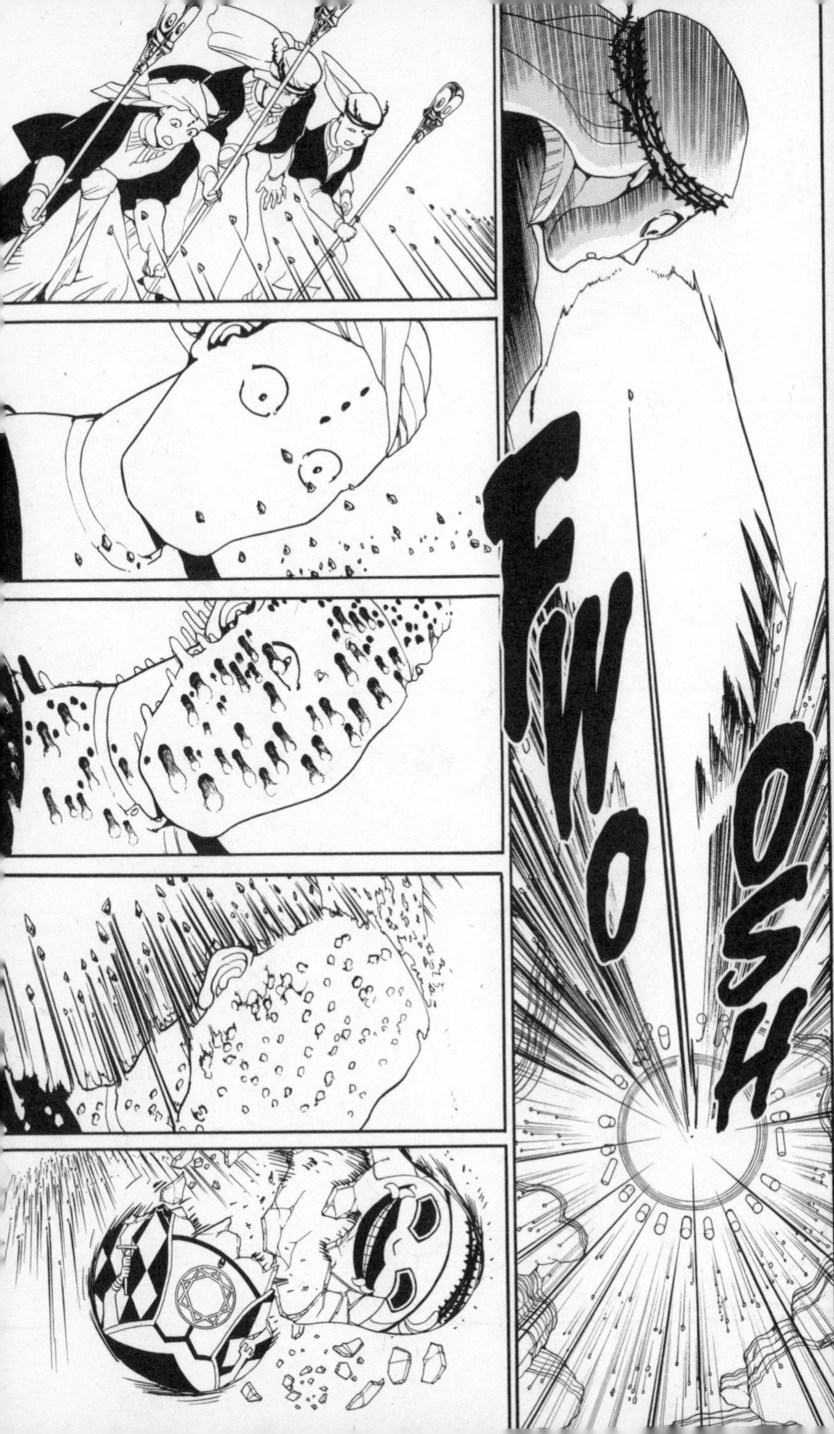
FWOOSH

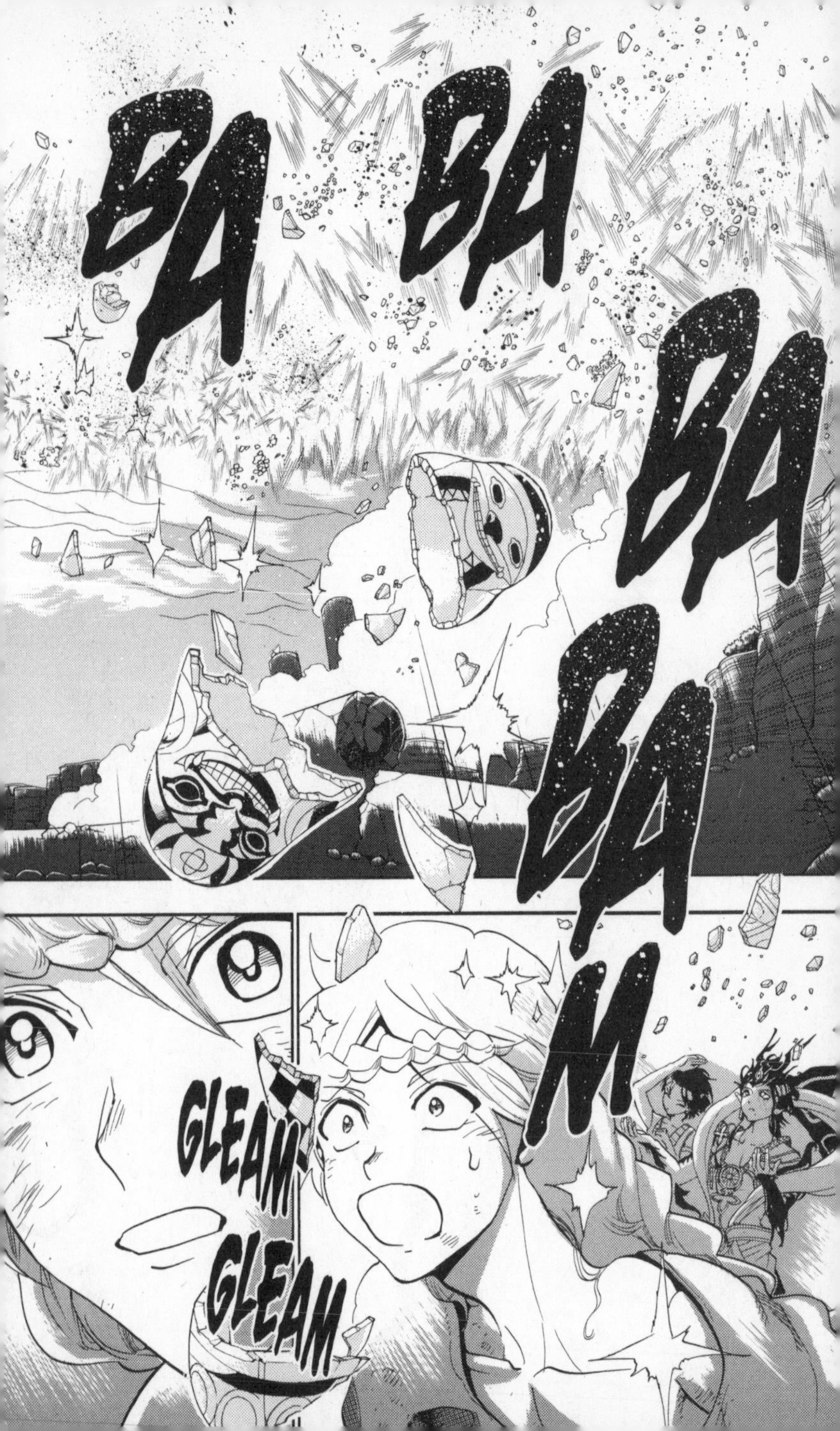
BA BA BA BA BAM
GLEAM GLEAM

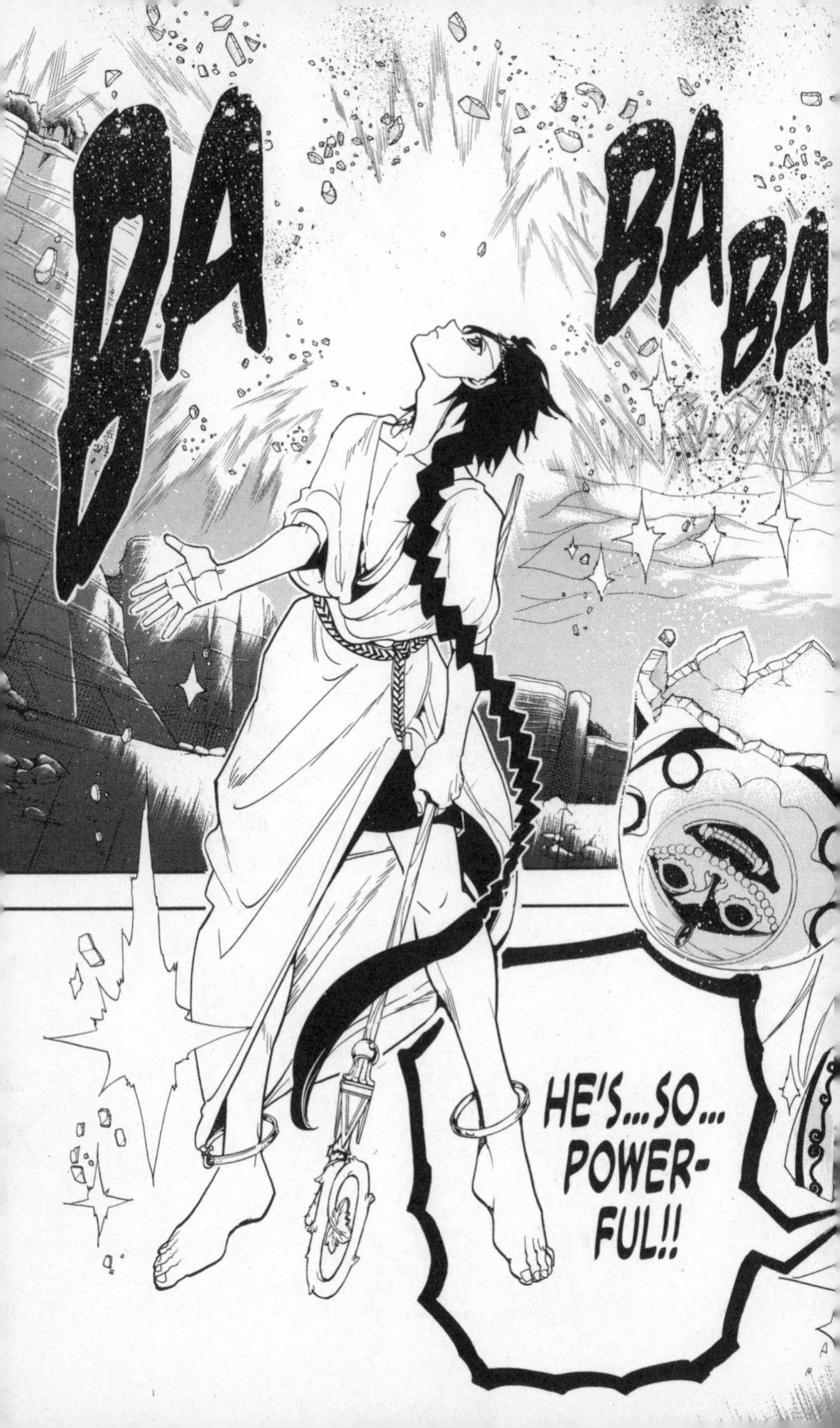
BA BA BA
HE'S... SO... POWER-FUL!!

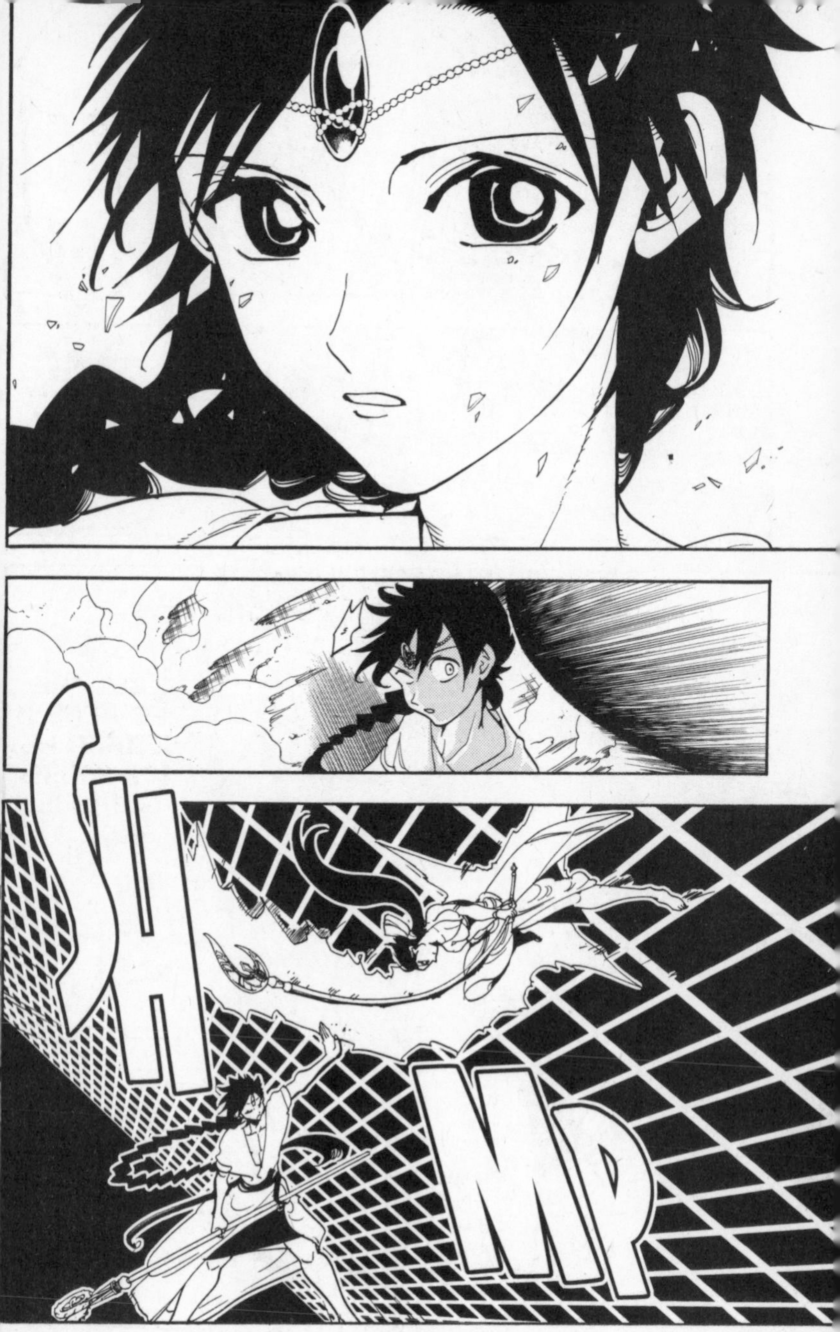
SHMP

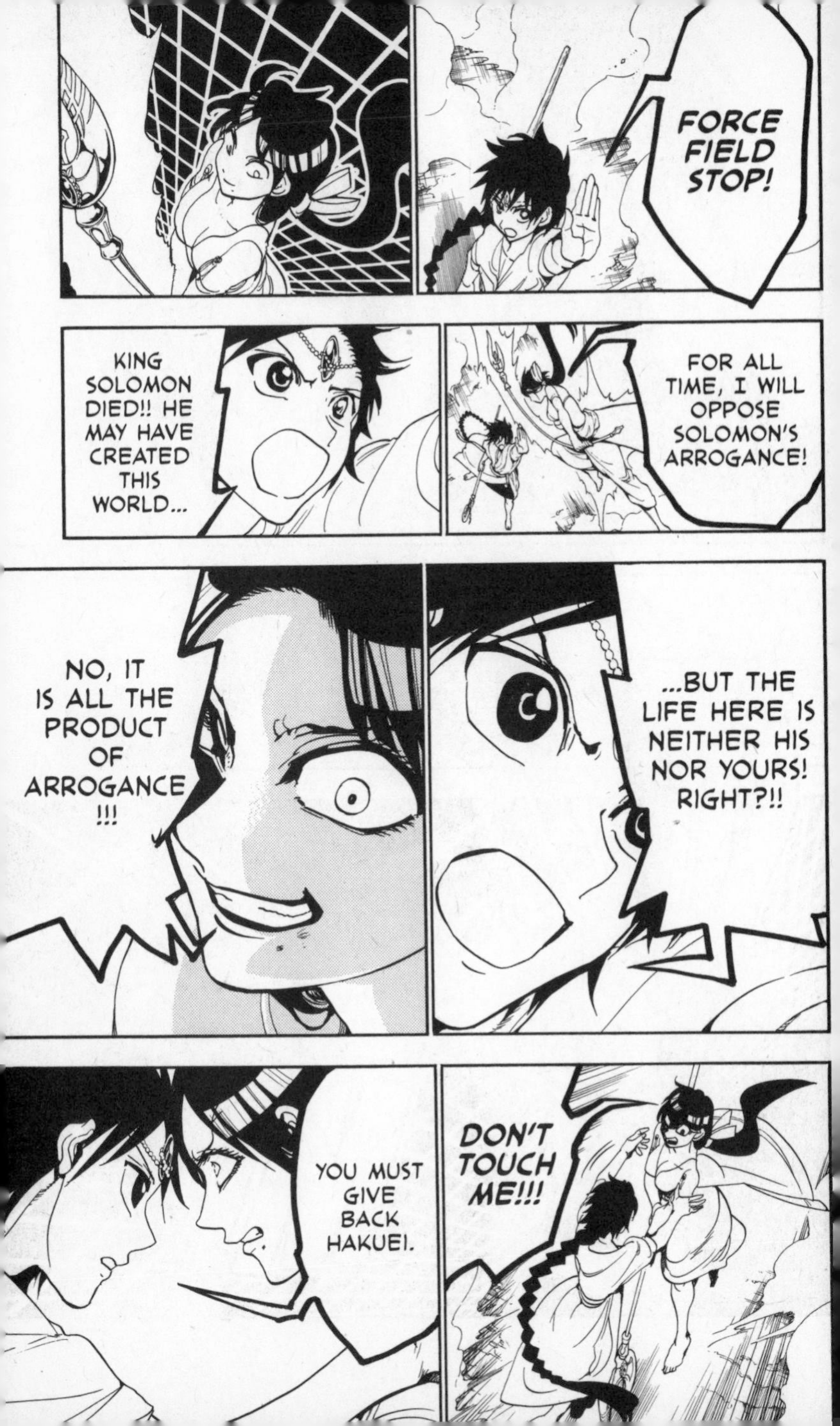
FORCE FIELD STOP!
FOR ALL TIME, I WILL OPPOSE SOLOMON'S ARROGANCE!
KING SOLOMON DIED!! HE MAY HAVE CREATED THIS WORLD...
...BUT THE LIFE HERE IS NEITHER HIS NOR YOURS! RIGHT?!!
NO, IT IS ALL THE PRODUCT OF ARROGANCE!!!
DON'T TOUCH ME!!!
YOU MUST GIVE BACK HAKUEI.

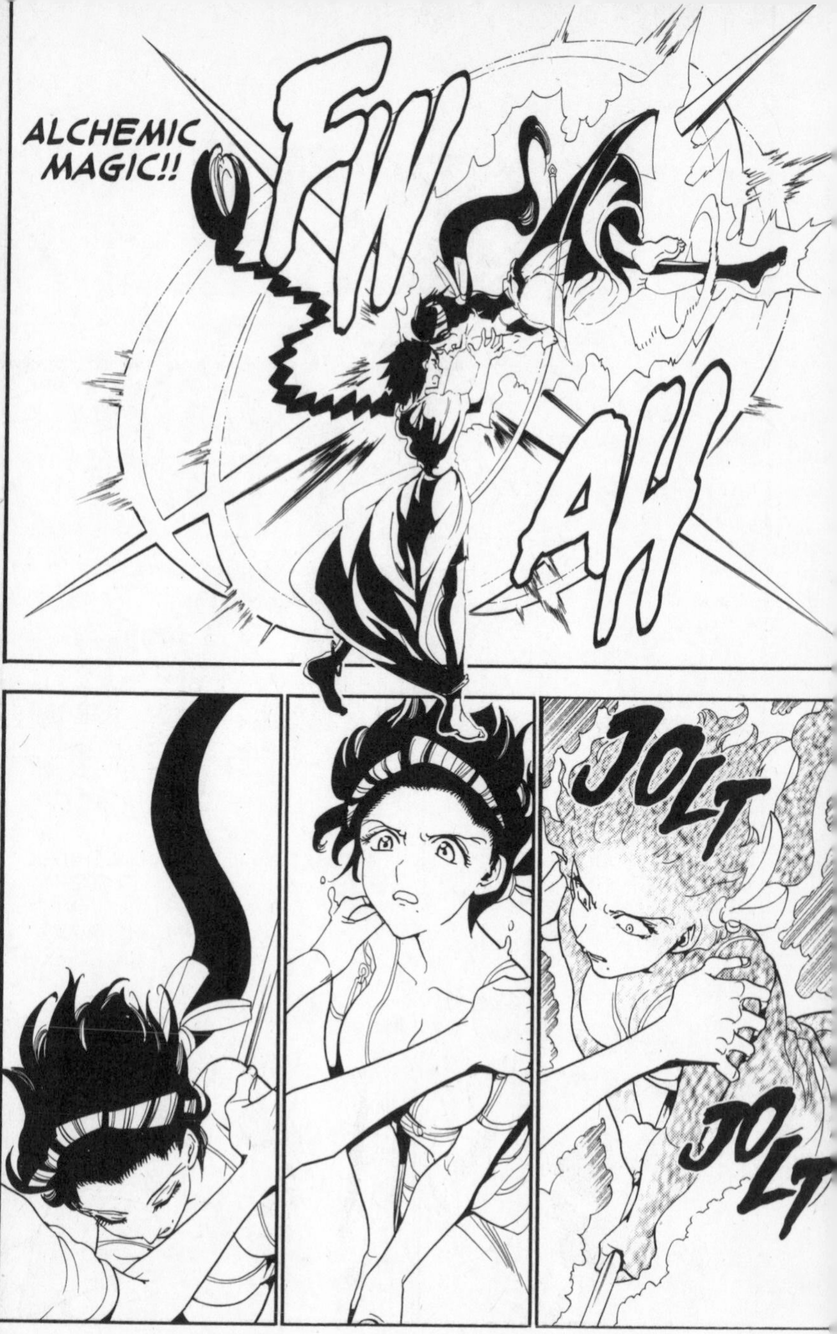
ALCHEMIC MAGIC!!
FWAAH
JOLT
JOLT

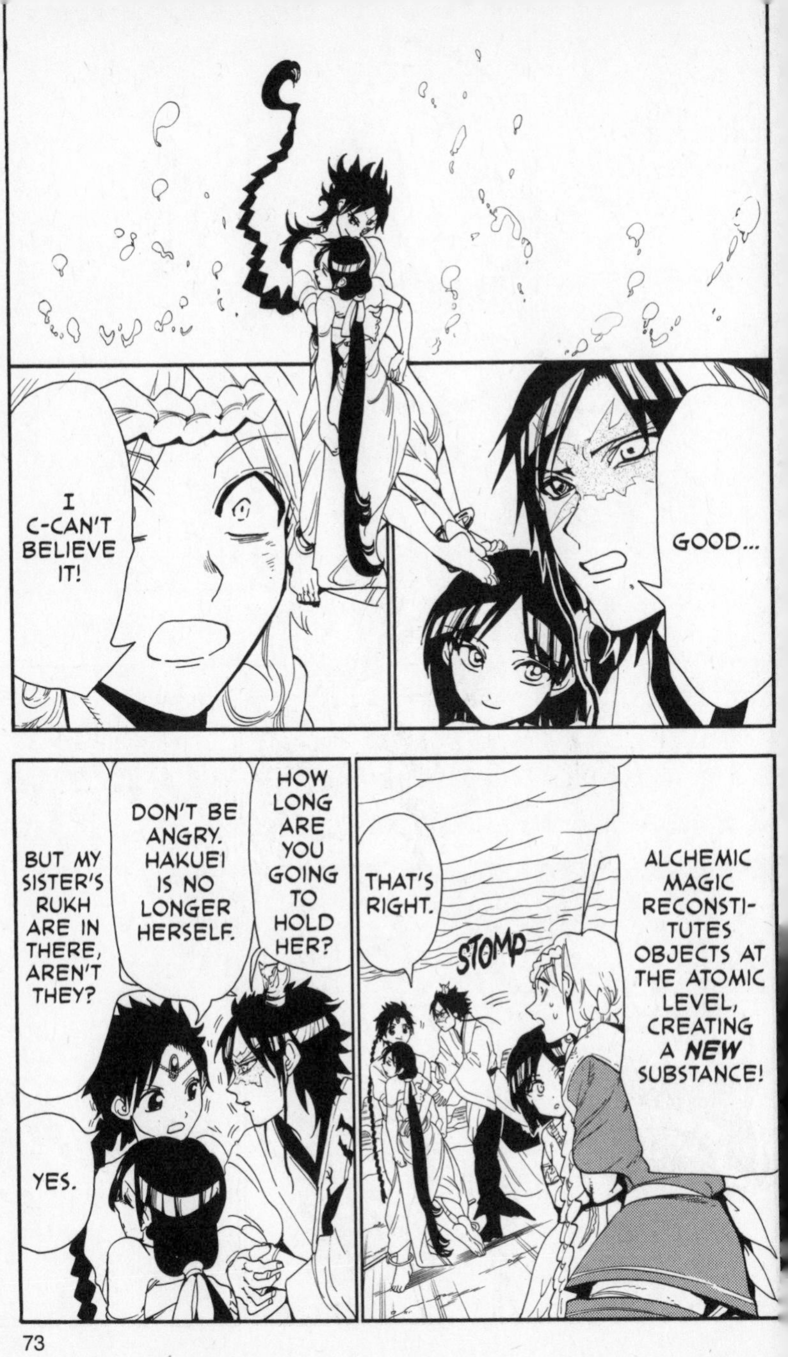
GOOD...
I C-CAN'T BELIEVE IT!
ALCHEMIC MAGIC RECONSTITUTES OBJECTS AT THE ATOMIC LEVEL, CREATING A *NEW* SUBSTANCE!
THAT'S RIGHT.
STOMP
HOW LONG ARE YOU GOING TO HOLD HER?
DON'T BE ANGRY. HAKUEI IS NO LONGER HERSELF.
BUT MY SISTER'S RUKH ARE IN THERE, AREN'T THEY?
YES.

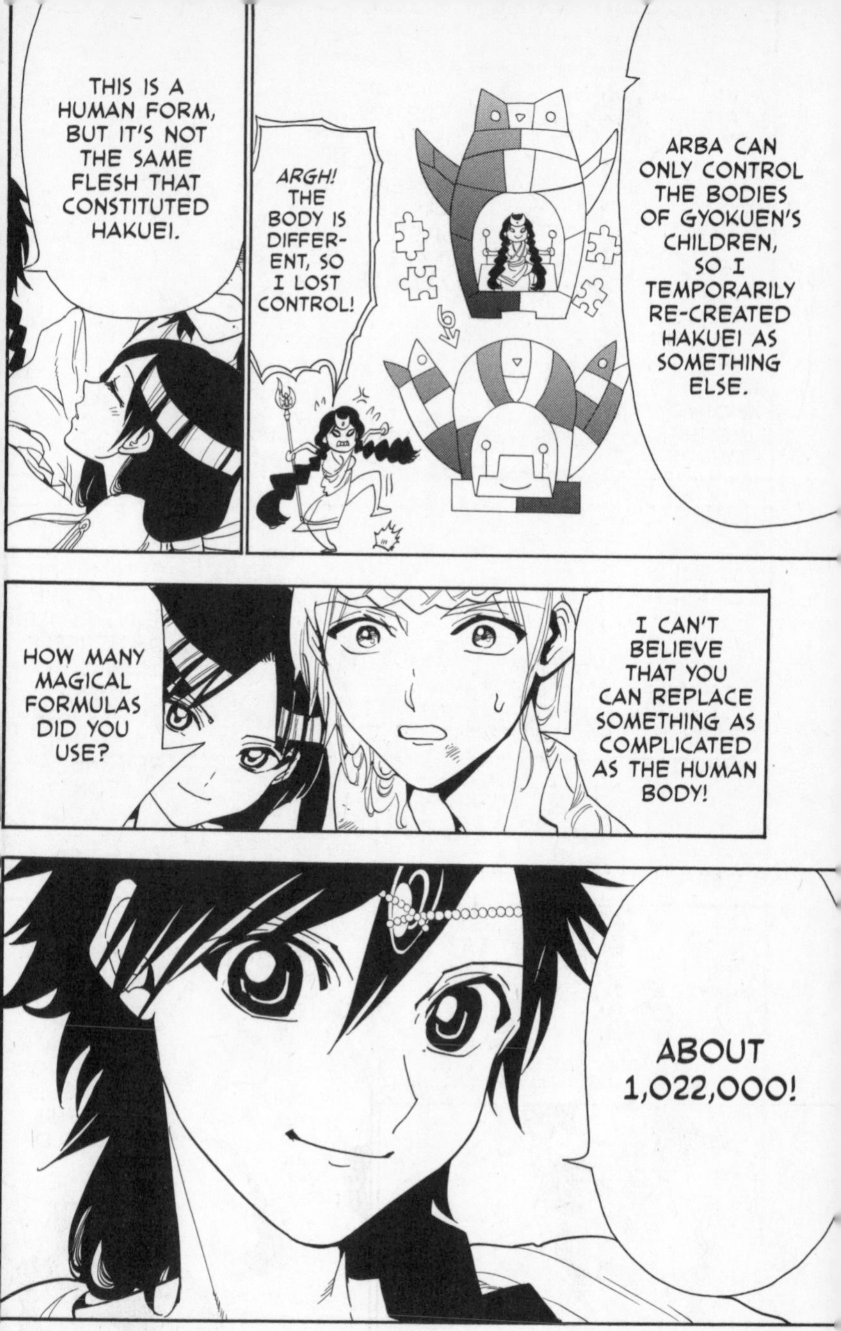
ARBA CAN ONLY CONTROL THE BODIES OF GYOKUEN'S CHILDREN, SO I TEMPORARILY RE-CREATED HAKUEI AS SOMETHING ELSE.
ARGH! THE BODY IS DIFFER-ENT, SO I LOST CONTROL!
THIS IS A HUMAN FORM, BUT IT'S NOT THE SAME FLESH THAT CONSTITUTED HAKUEI.
I CAN'T BELIEVE THAT YOU CAN REPLACE SOMETHING AS COMPLICATED AS THE HUMAN BODY!
HOW MANY MAGICAL FORMULAS DID YOU USE?
ABOUT 1,022,000!

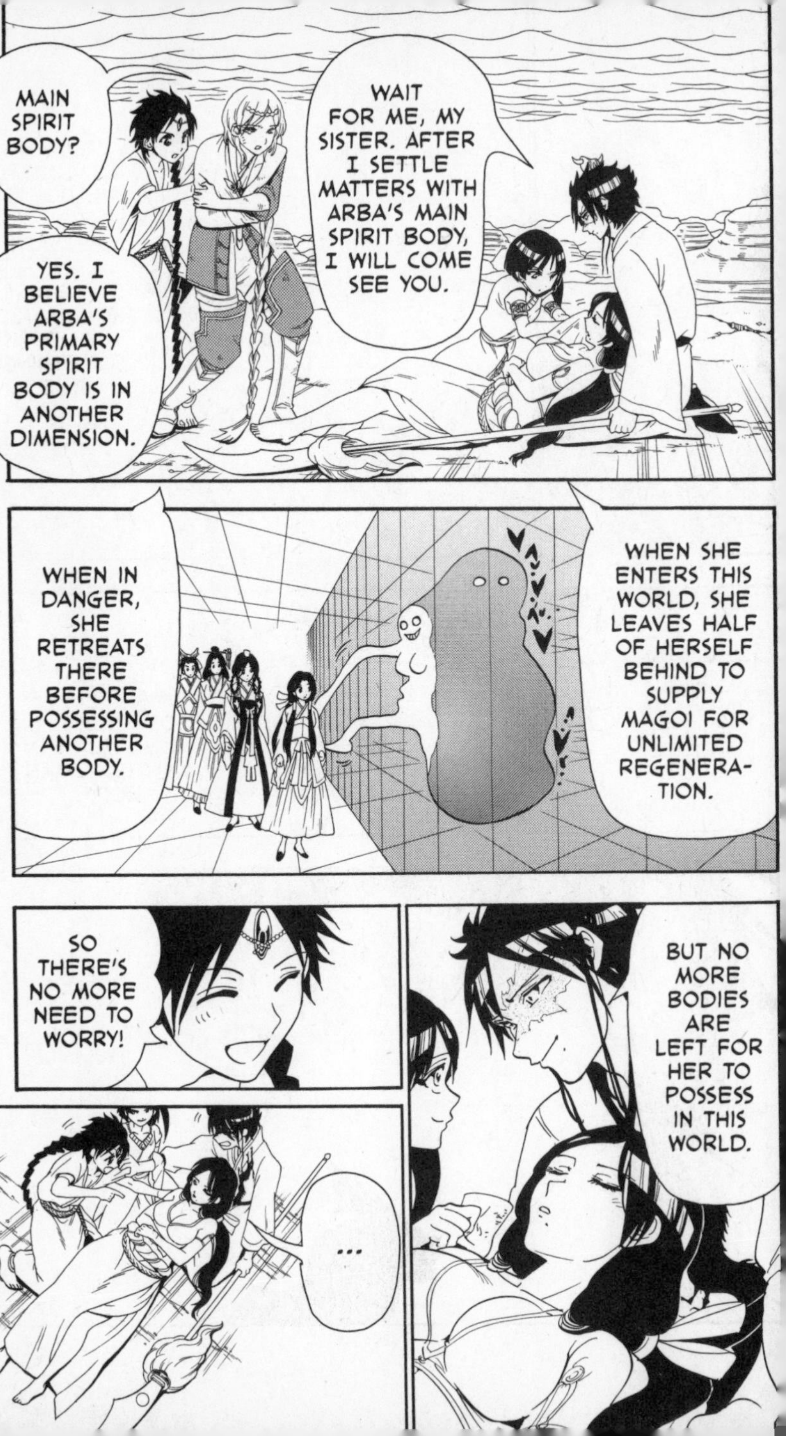
WAIT FOR ME, MY SISTER. AFTER I SETTLE MATTERS WITH ARBA'S MAIN SPIRIT BODY, I WILL COME SEE YOU.
MAIN SPIRIT BODY?
YES. I BELIEVE ARBA'S PRIMARY SPIRIT BODY IS IN ANOTHER DIMENSION.
WHEN SHE ENTERS THIS WORLD, SHE LEAVES HALF OF HERSELF BEHIND TO SUPPLY MAGOI FOR UNLIMITED REGENERA-TION.
WHEN IN DANGER, SHE RETREATS THERE BEFORE POSSESSING ANOTHER BODY.
BUT NO MORE BODIES ARE LEFT FOR HER TO POSSESS IN THIS WORLD.
SO THERE'S NO MORE NEED TO WORRY!
...

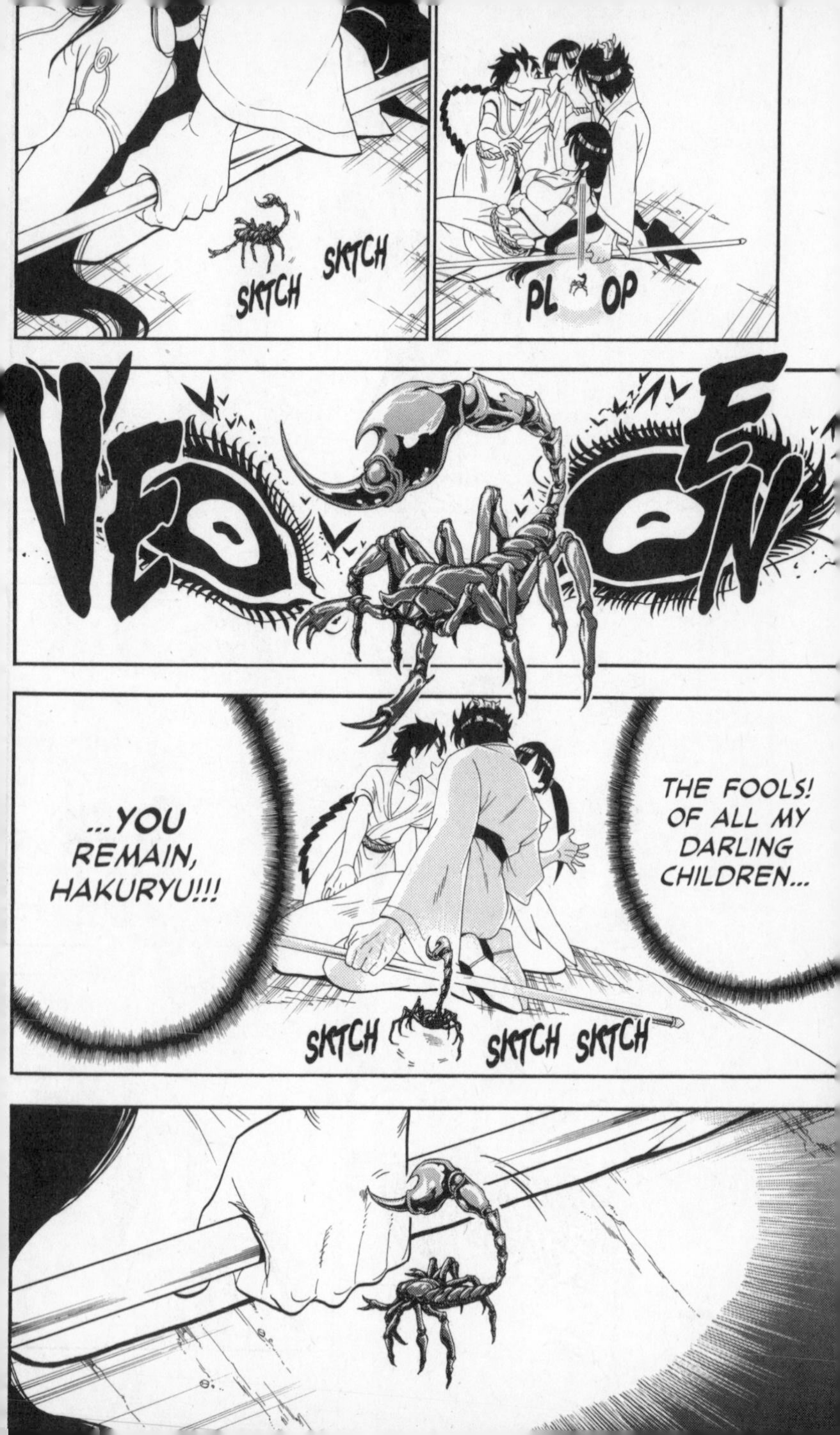
PL OP
SKTCH
SKTCH
VENOM
THE FOOLS! OF ALL MY DARLING CHILDREN...
...YOU REMAIN, HAKURYU!!!
SKTCH
SKTCH SKTCH

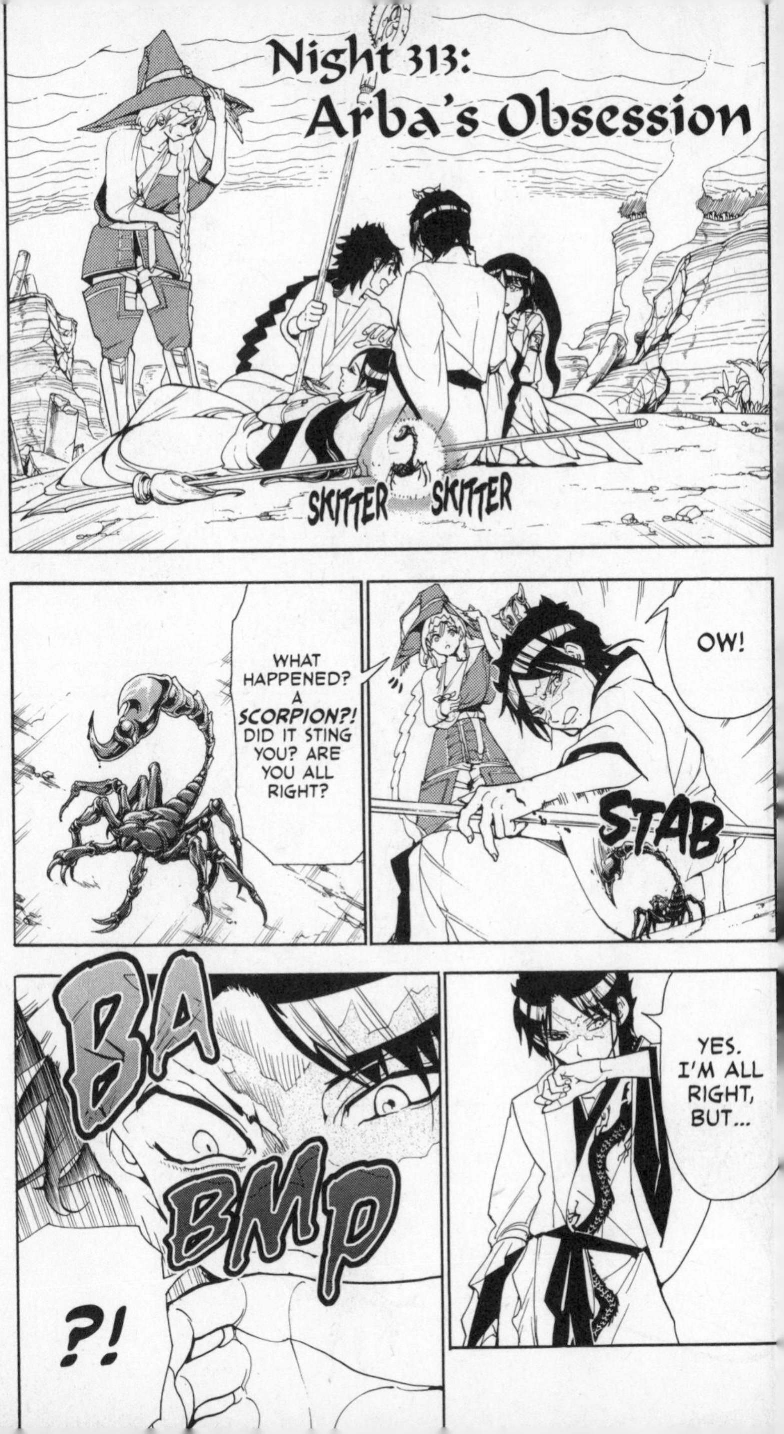
Night 313:
Arba's Obsession
SKITTER SKITTER
OW!
STAB
WHAT HAPPENED? A SCORPION?! DID IT STING YOU? ARE YOU ALL RIGHT?
YES. I'M ALL RIGHT, BUT...
BA
BMP
?!

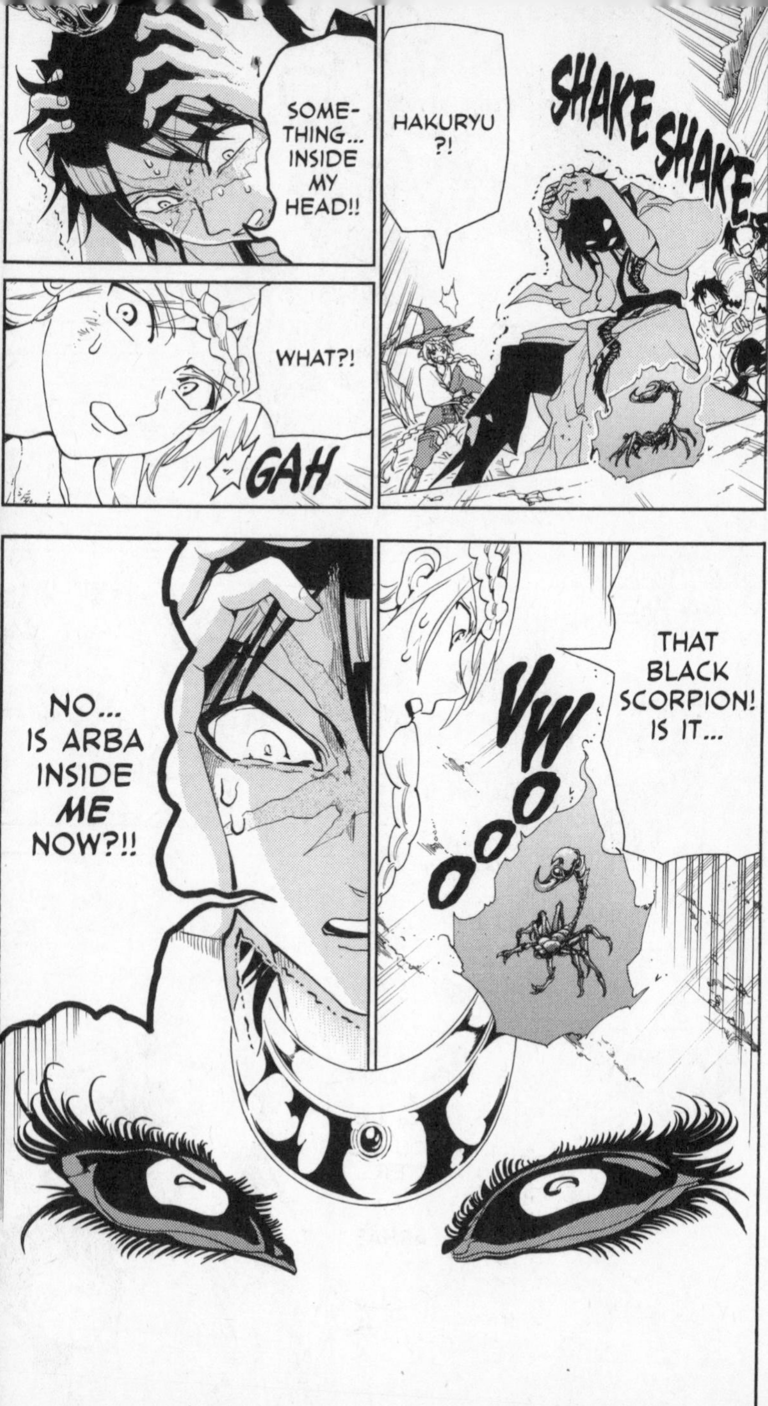
HAKURYU ?!
SHAKE SHAKE
SOME-THING... INSIDE MY HEAD!!
WHAT?!
GAH
THAT BLACK SCORPION! IS IT...
VWOOOO
NO... IS ARBA INSIDE *ME* NOW?!!

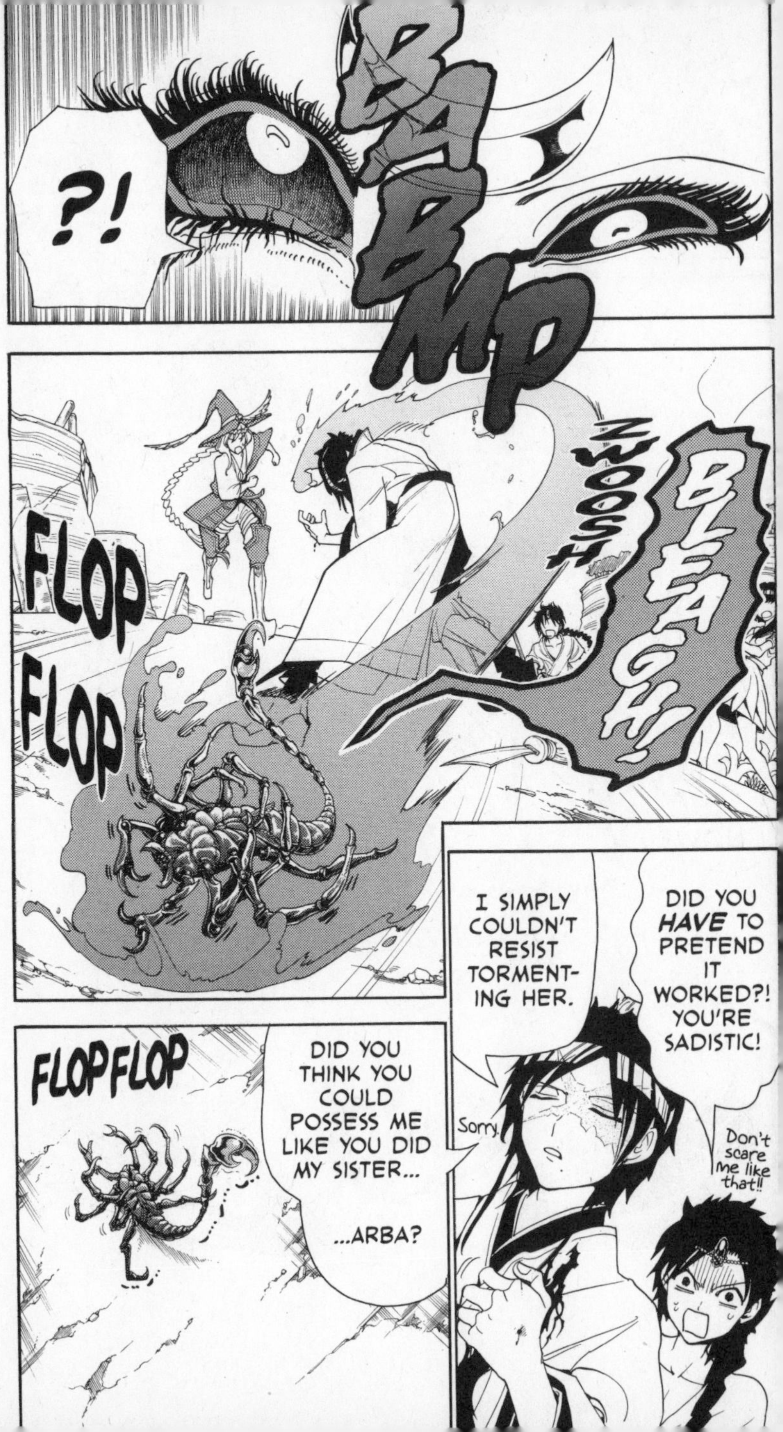

?!
BA-BUMP
BLEAGH!
WHOOSH
FLOP FLOP
DID YOU HAVE TO PRETEND IT WORKED?! YOU'RE SADISTIC!
I SIMPLY COULDN'T RESIST TORMENT-ING HER.
Don't scare me like that!!
Sorry.
DID YOU THINK YOU COULD POSSESS ME LIKE YOU DID MY SISTER...
...ARBA?
FLOPFLOP

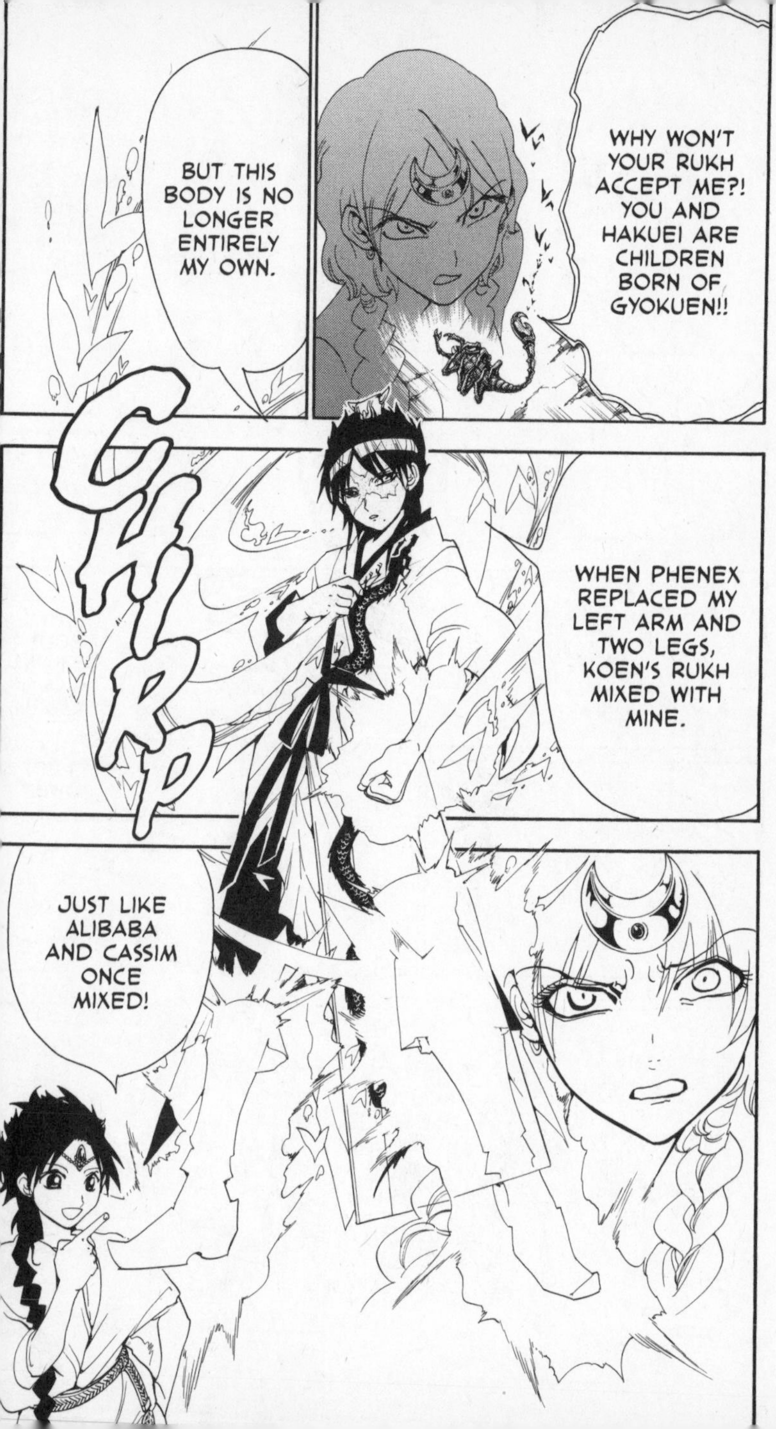
WHY WON'T YOUR RUKH ACCEPT ME?! YOU AND HAKUEI ARE CHILDREN BORN OF GYOKUEN!!
BUT THIS BODY IS NO LONGER ENTIRELY MY OWN.
WHEN PHENEX REPLACED MY LEFT ARM AND TWO LEGS, KOEN'S RUKH MIXED WITH MINE.
CHIRP
JUST LIKE ALIBABA AND CASSIM ONCE MIXED!

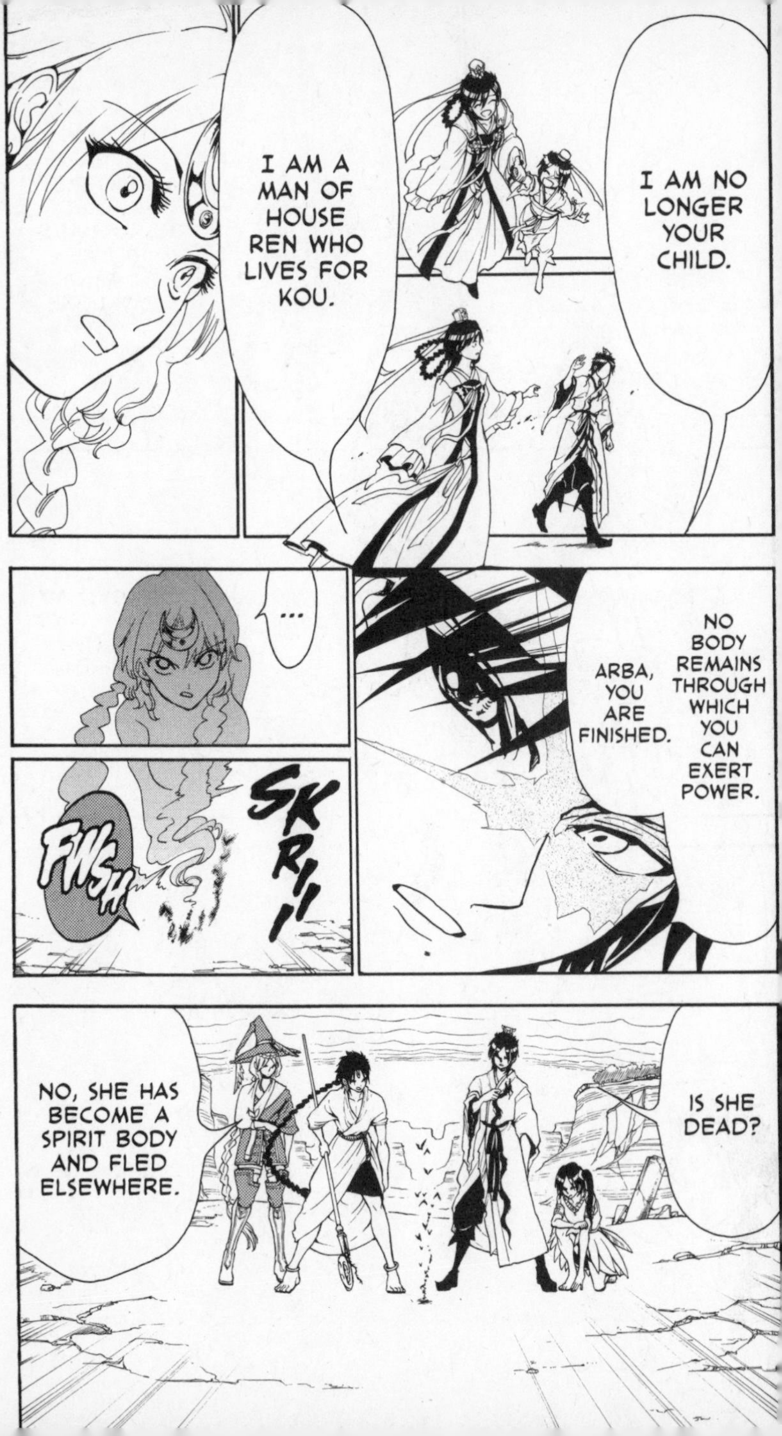
I AM NO LONGER YOUR CHILD.
I AM A MAN OF HOUSE REN WHO LIVES FOR KOU.
NO BODY REMAINS THROUGH WHICH YOU CAN EXERT POWER.
ARBA, YOU ARE FINISHED.
...
FWSH
SKRIII
IS SHE DEAD?
NO, SHE HAS BECOME A SPIRIT BODY AND FLED ELSEWHERE.

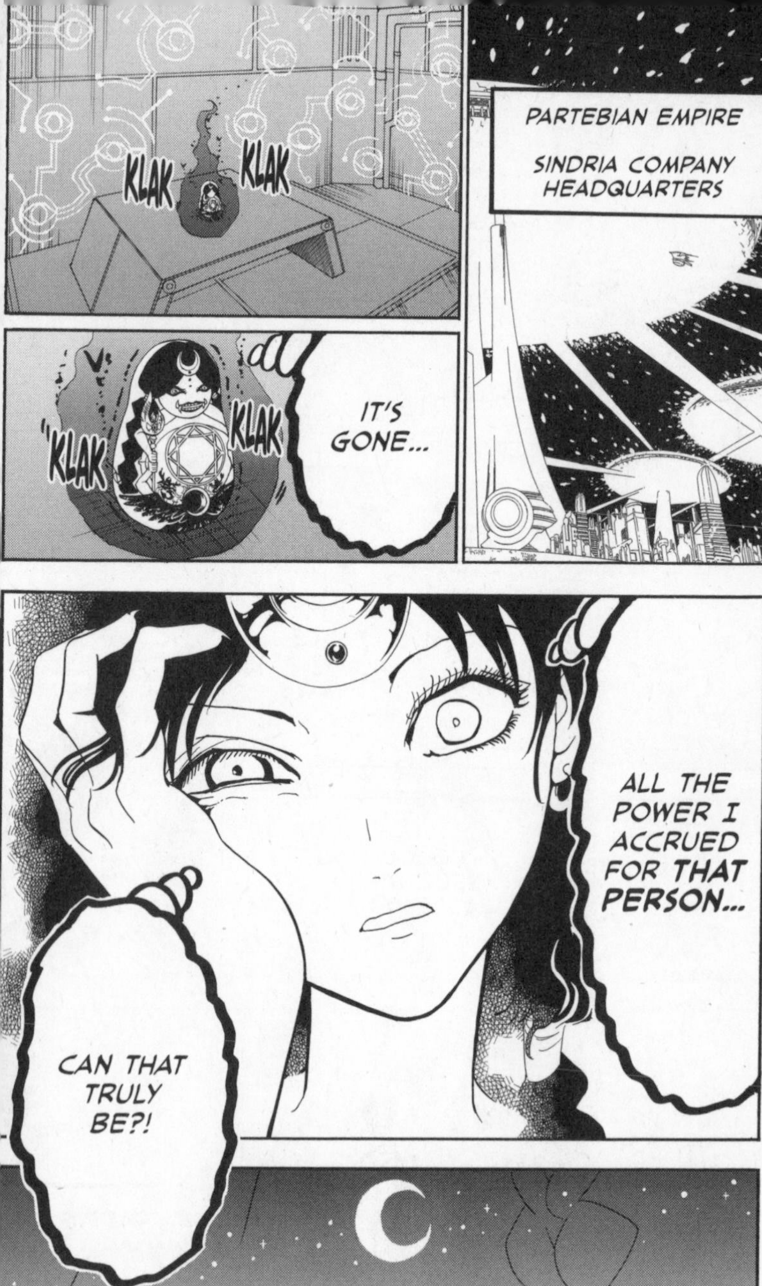
PARTEBIAN EMPIRE
SINDRIA COMPANY HEADQUARTERS
KLAK
KLAK
IT'S GONE...
KLAK
KLAK
ALL THE POWER I ACCRUED FOR THAT PERSON...
CAN THAT TRULY BE?!

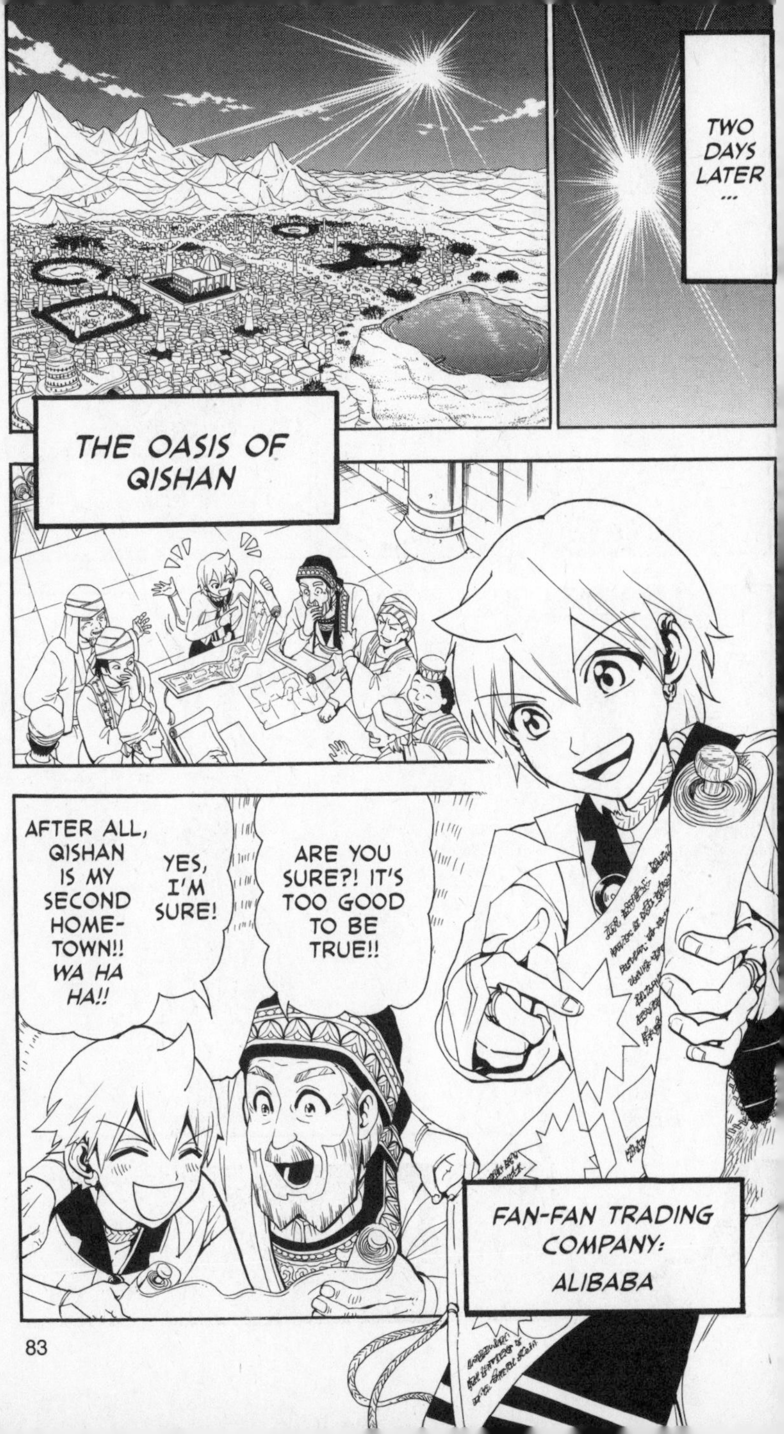
TWO DAYS LATER...
THE OASIS OF QISHAN
ARE YOU SURE?! IT'S TOO GOOD TO BE TRUE!!
YES, I'M SURE!
AFTER ALL, QISHAN IS MY SECOND HOME-TOWN!! WA HA HA!!
FAN-FAN TRADING COMPANY: ALIBABA

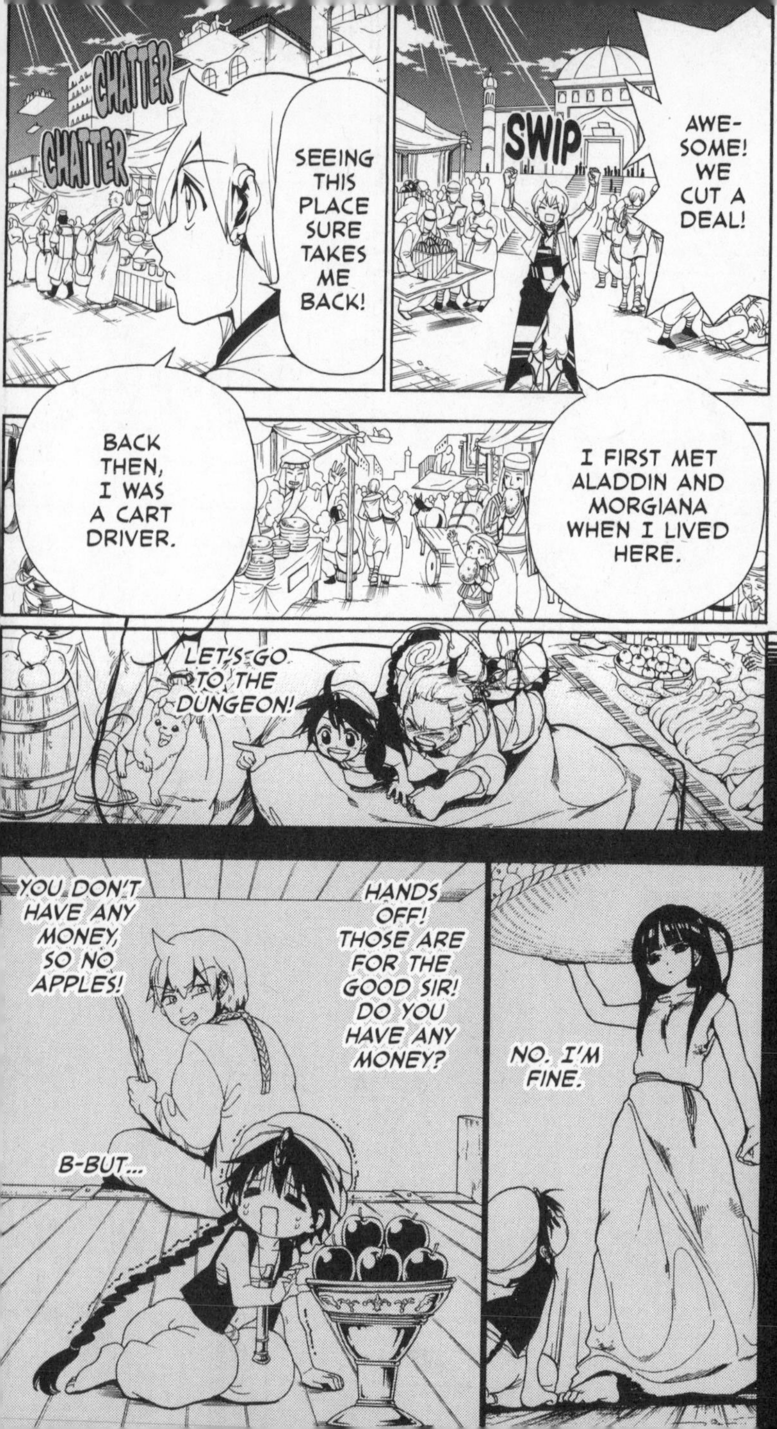
SWIP
AWE-SOME! WE CUT A DEAL!
CHATTER
CHATTER
SEEING THIS PLACE SURE TAKES ME BACK!
I FIRST MET ALADDIN AND MORGIANA WHEN I LIVED HERE.
BACK THEN, I WAS A CART DRIVER.
LET'S GO TO THE DUNGEON!
NO. I'M FINE.
HANDS OFF! THOSE ARE FOR THE GOOD SIR! DO YOU HAVE ANY MONEY?
YOU DON'T HAVE ANY MONEY, SO NO APPLES!
B-BUT...

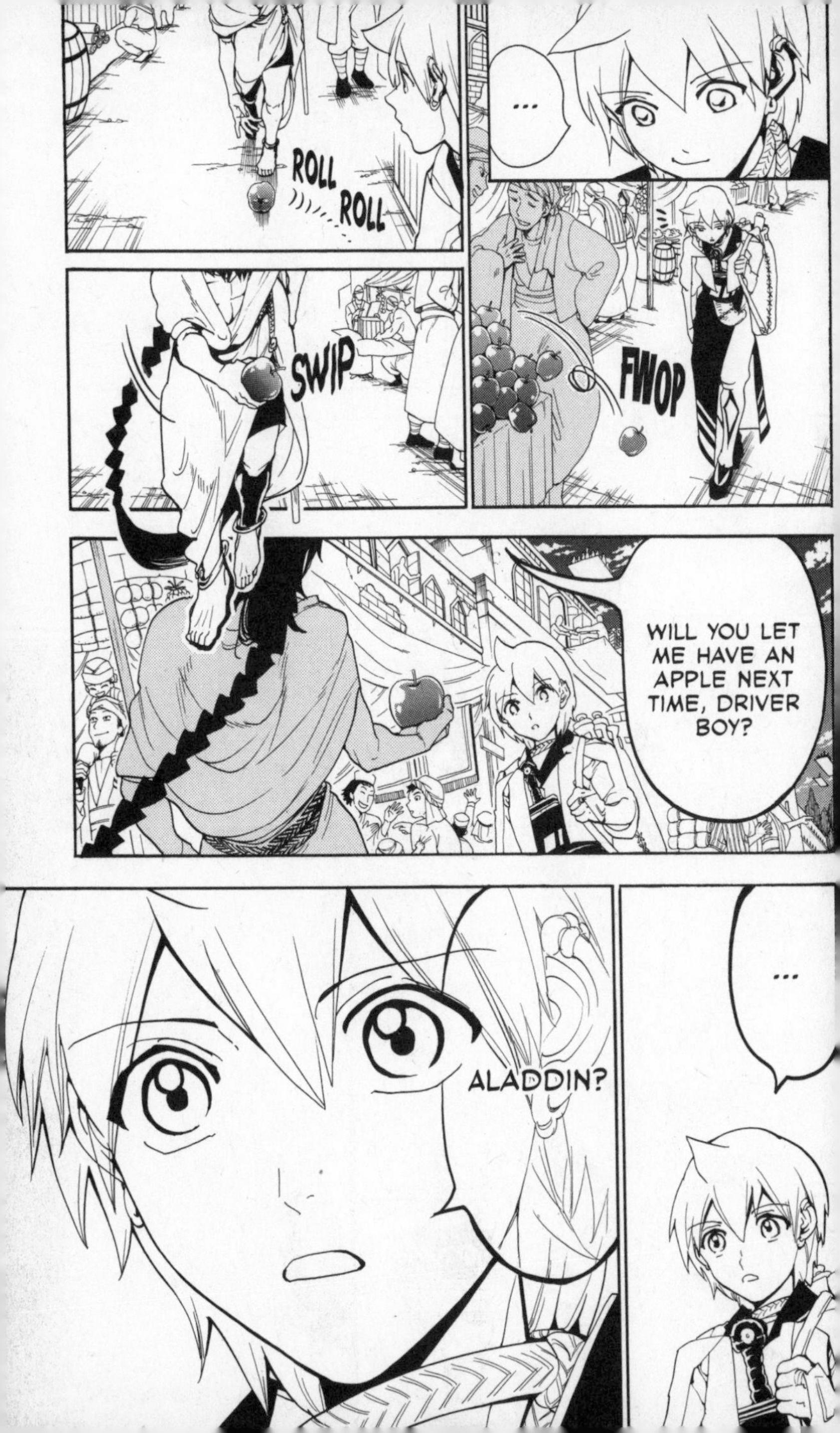
...
FWOP
ROLL ROLL
SWIP
WILL YOU LET ME HAVE AN APPLE NEXT TIME, DRIVER BOY?
...
ALADDIN?

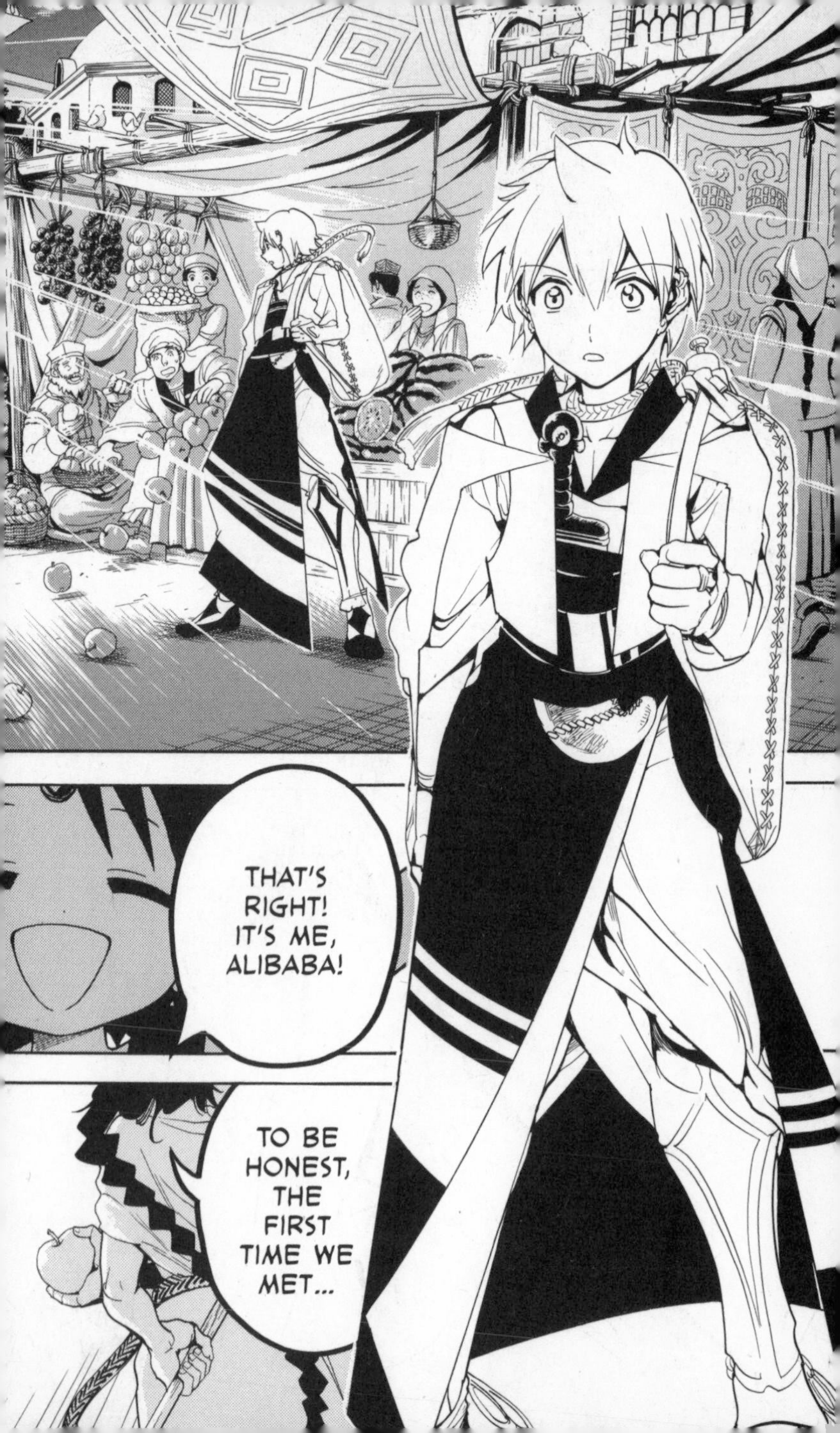
THAT'S RIGHT! IT'S ME, ALIBABA!
TO BE HONEST, THE FIRST TIME WE MET...

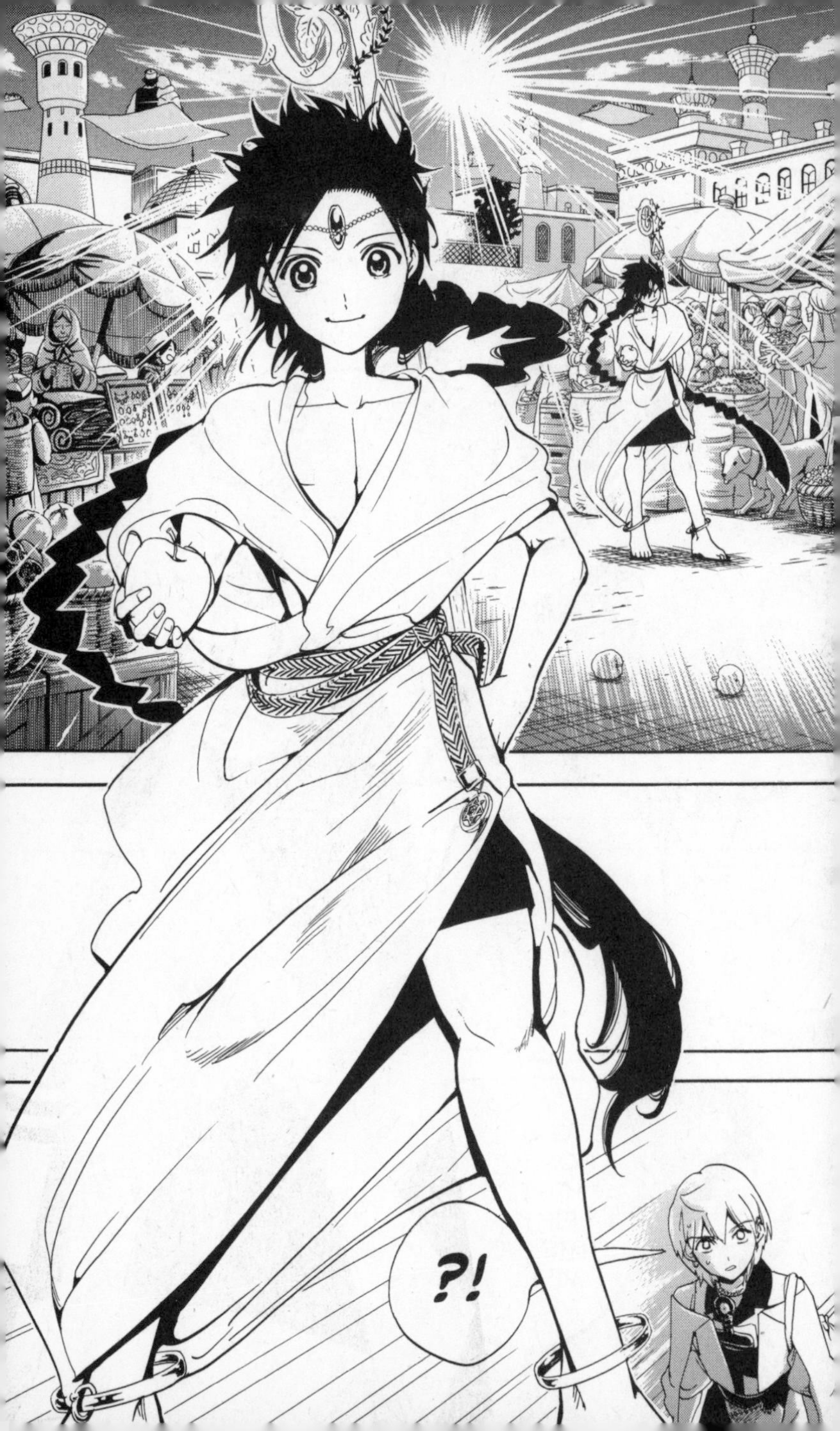
?!

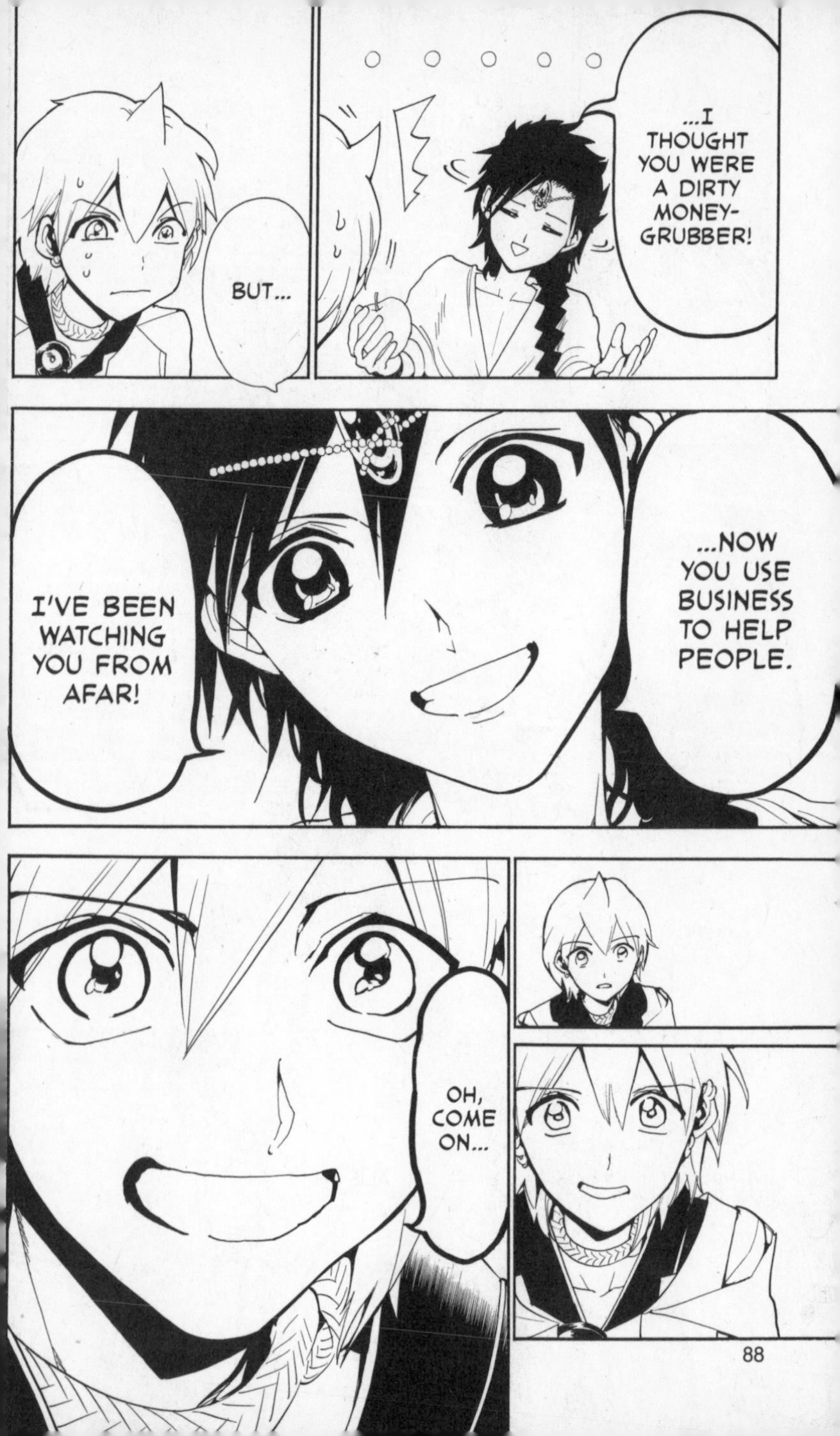
...I THOUGHT YOU WERE A DIRTY MONEY-GRUBBER!
BUT...
...NOW YOU USE BUSINESS TO HELP PEOPLE.
I'VE BEEN WATCHING YOU FROM AFAR!
OH, COME ON...

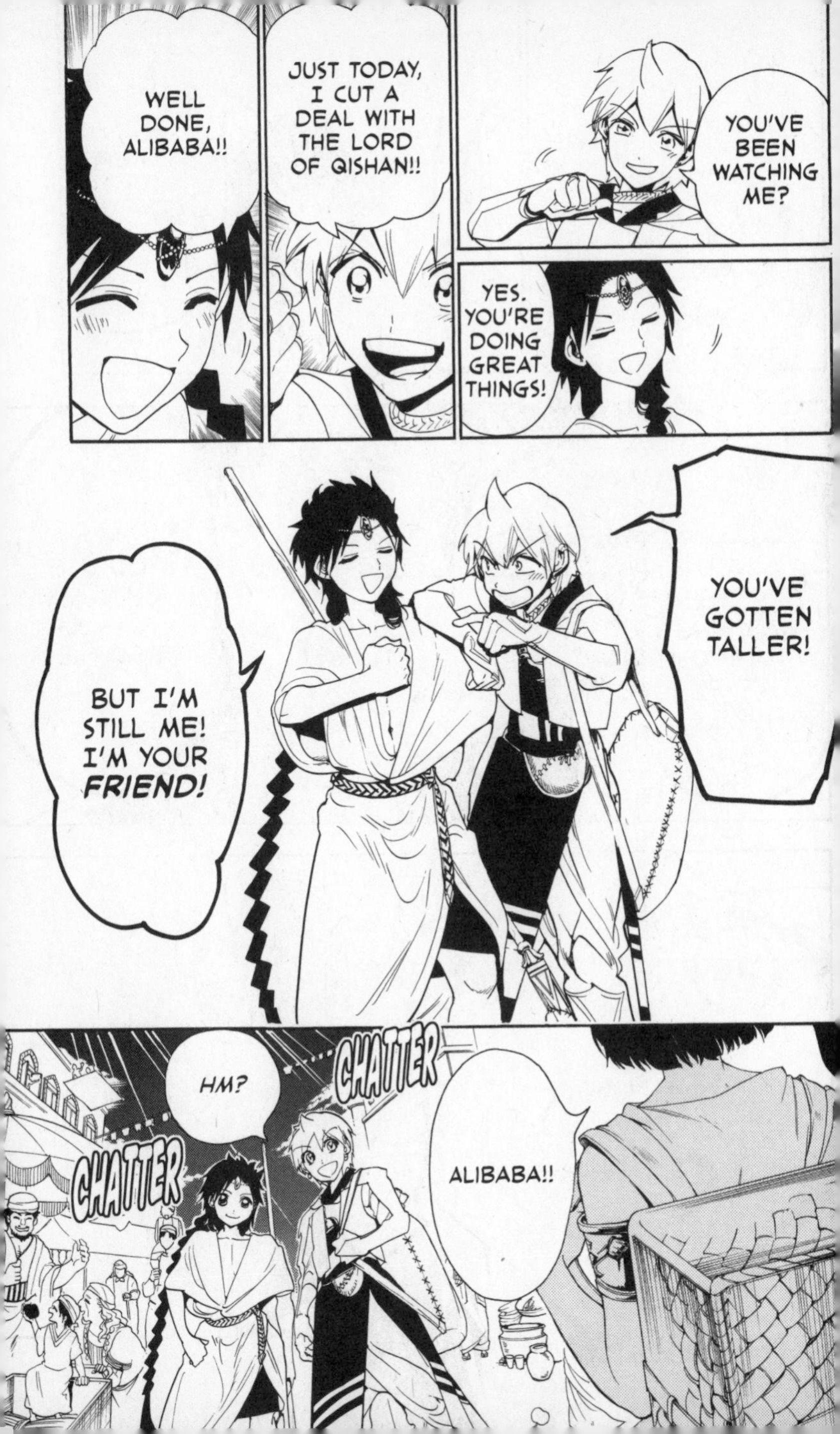

YOU'VE BEEN WATCHING ME?
YES. YOU'RE DOING GREAT THINGS!
JUST TODAY, I CUT A DEAL WITH THE LORD OF QISHAN!!
WELL DONE, ALIBABA!!
YOU'VE GOTTEN TALLER!
BUT I'M STILL ME! I'M YOUR *FRIEND!*
ALIBABA!!
CHATTER
HM?
CHATTER

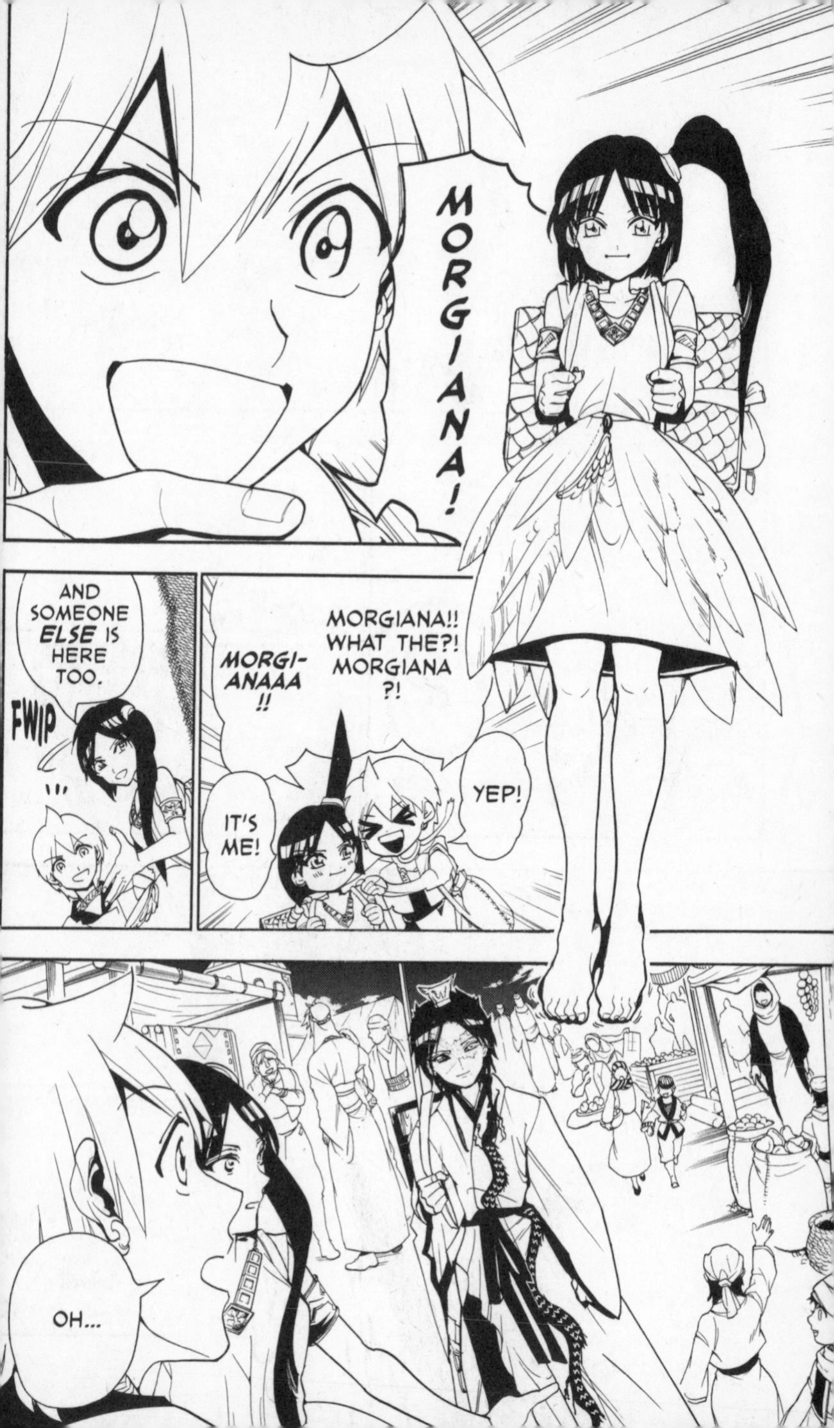
MORGIANA!
MORGIANA!! WHAT THE?! MORGIANA ?!
MORGI-ANAAA !!
YEP!
IT'S ME!
AND SOMEONE ELSE IS HERE TOO.
FWIP
OH...

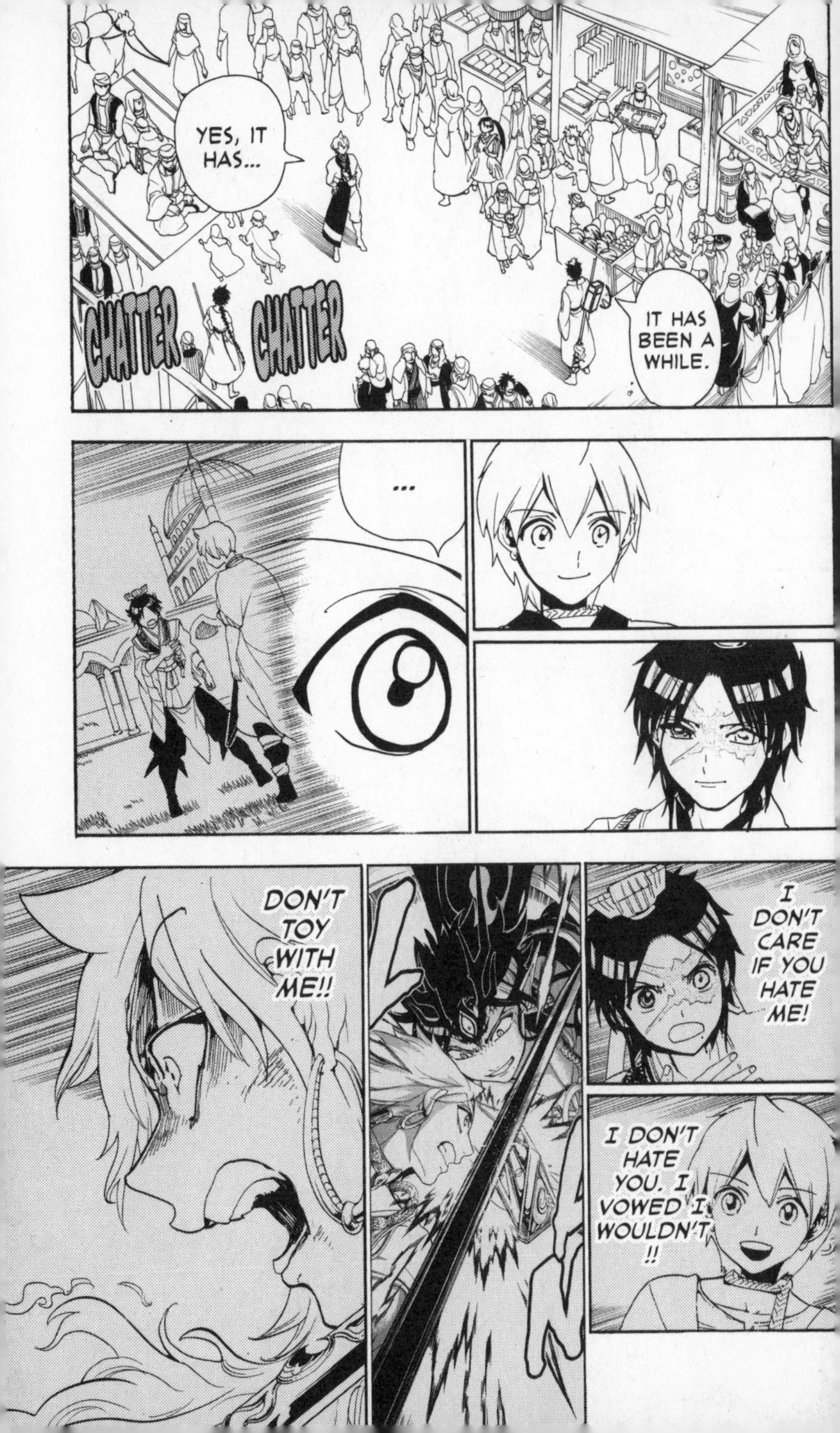
IT HAS BEEN A WHILE.
YES, IT HAS...
CHATTER
CHATTER
...
I DON'T CARE IF YOU HATE ME!
I DON'T HATE YOU. I VOWED I WOULDN'T!!
DON'T TOY WITH ME!!

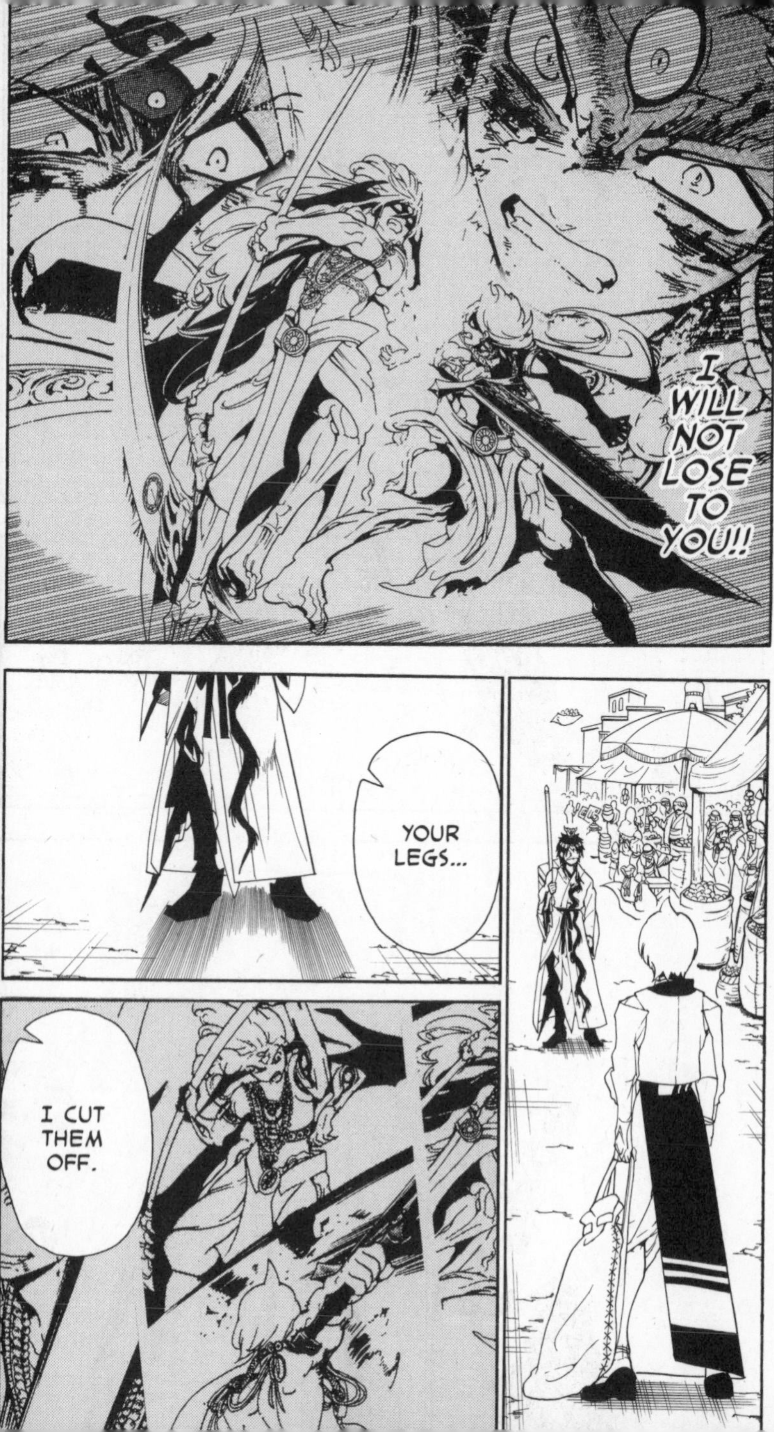
I WILL NOT LOSE TO YOU!!
YOUR LEGS...
I CUT THEM OFF.

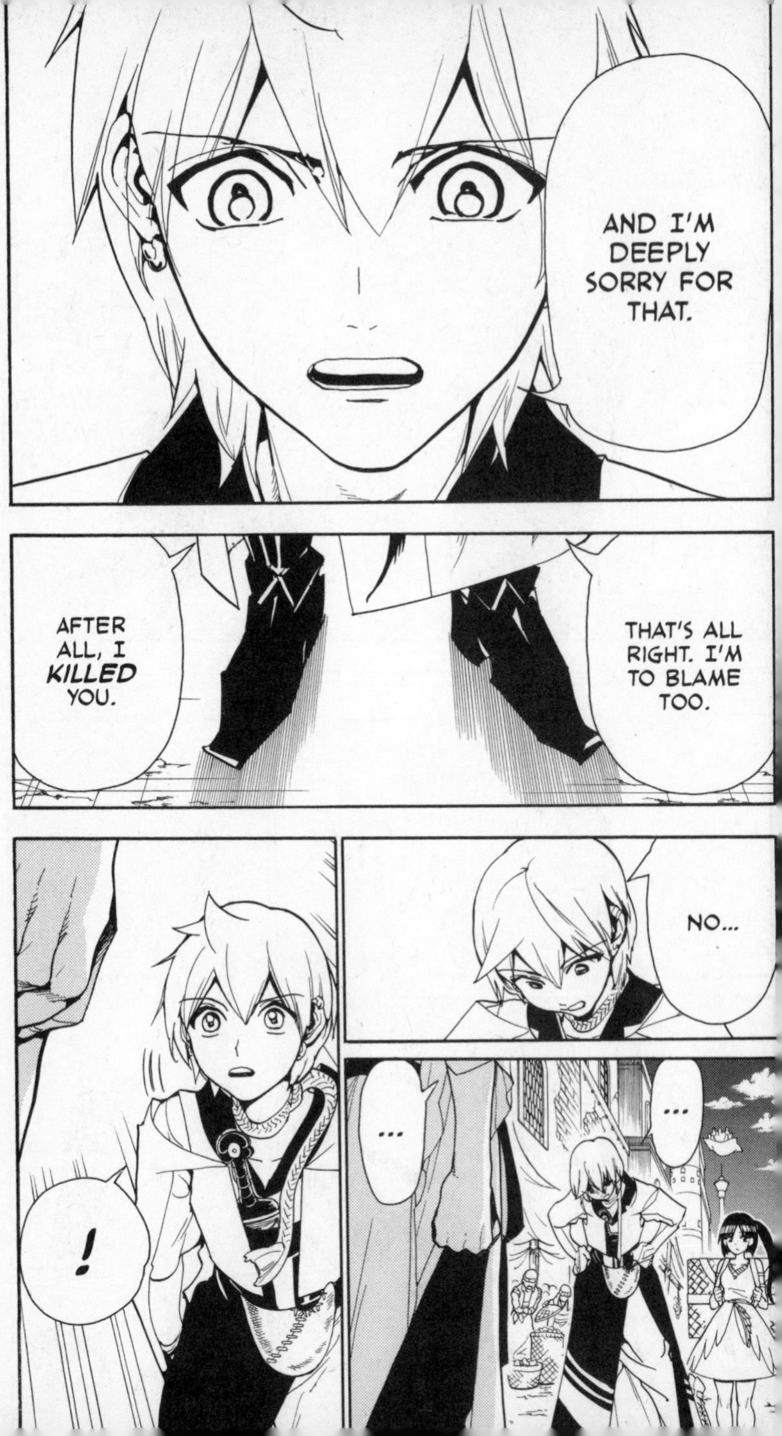
AND I'M DEEPLY SORRY FOR THAT.
THAT'S ALL RIGHT. I'M TO BLAME TOO.
AFTER ALL, I *KILLED* YOU.
NO...
...
...
!

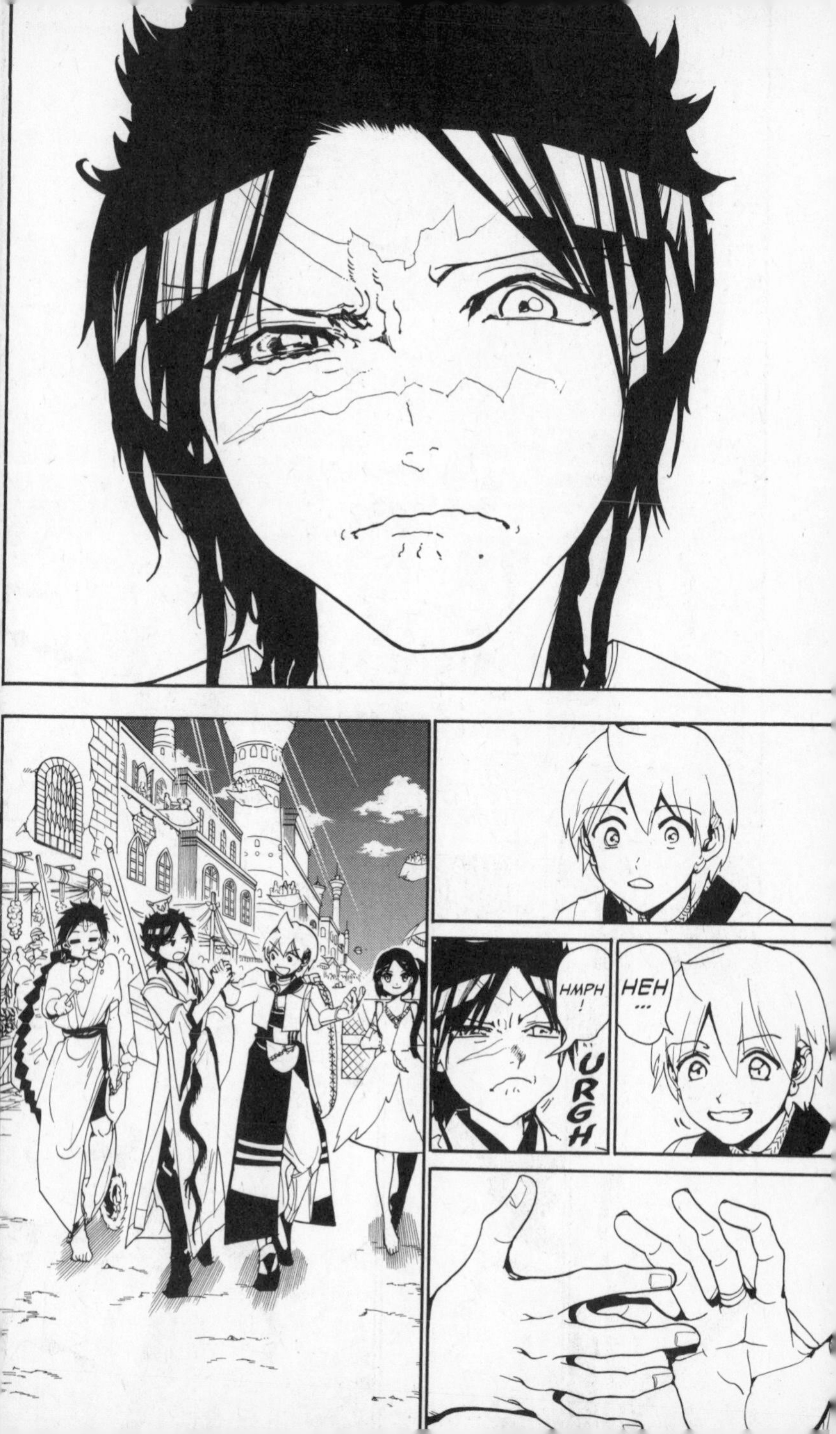
HEH ...
HMPH!
URGH

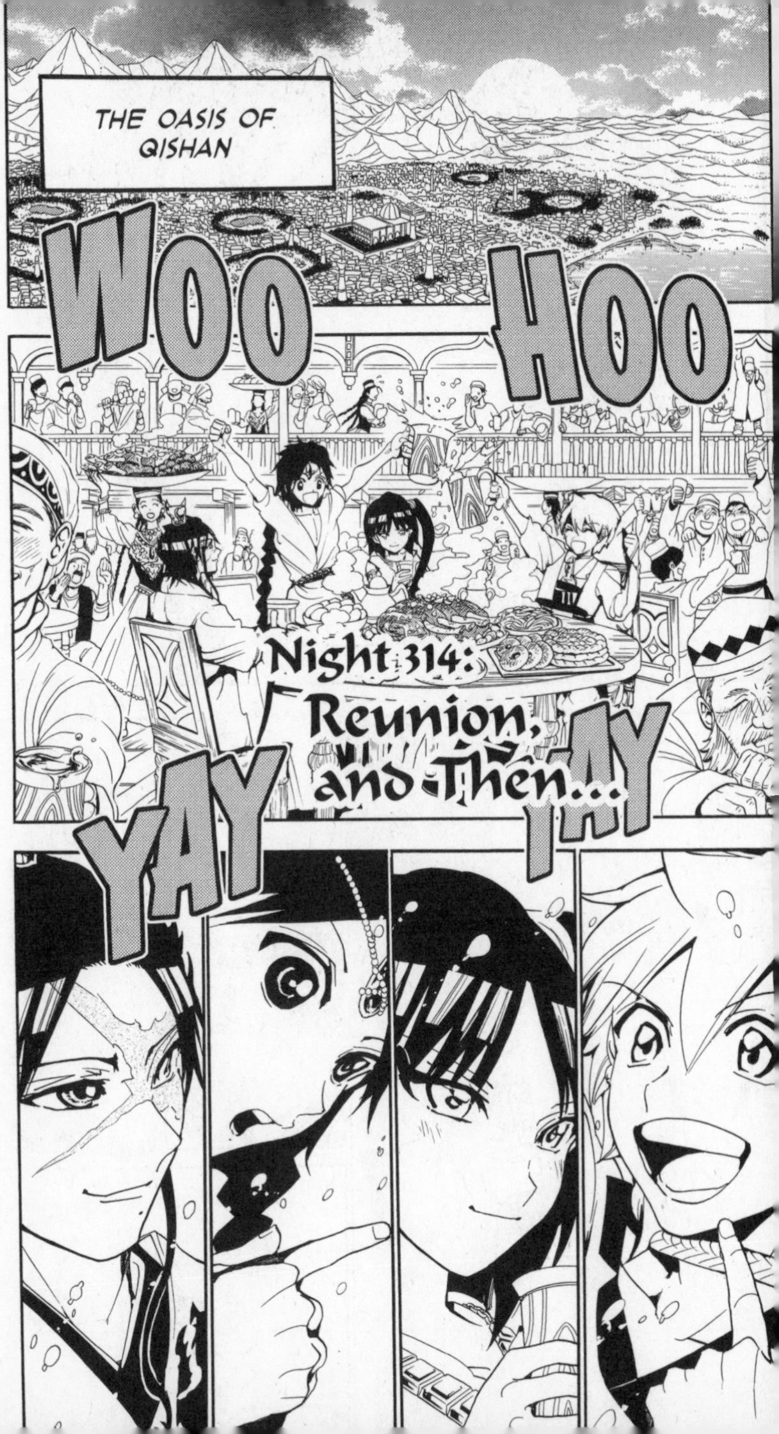
THE OASIS OF QISHAN
WOO HOO
Night 314: Reunion, and Then...
YAY YAY

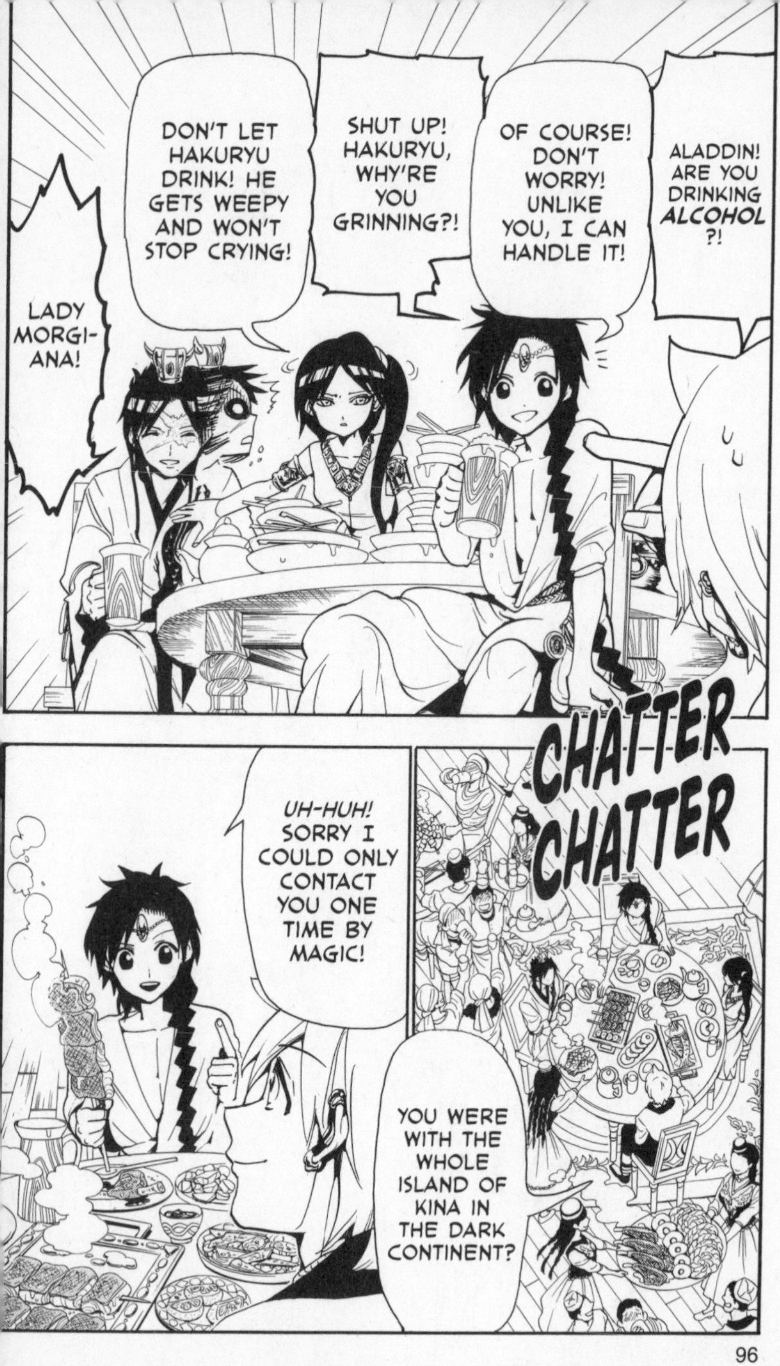
ALADDIN! ARE YOU DRINKING ALCOHOL?!
OF COURSE! DON'T WORRY! UNLIKE YOU, I CAN HANDLE IT!
SHUT UP! HAKURYU, WHY'RE YOU GRINNING?!
DON'T LET HAKURYU DRINK! HE GETS WEEPY AND WON'T STOP CRYING!
LADY MORGIANA!
CHATTER CHATTER
YOU WERE WITH THE WHOLE ISLAND OF KINA IN THE DARK CONTINENT?
UH-HUH! SORRY I COULD ONLY CONTACT YOU ONE TIME BY MAGIC!

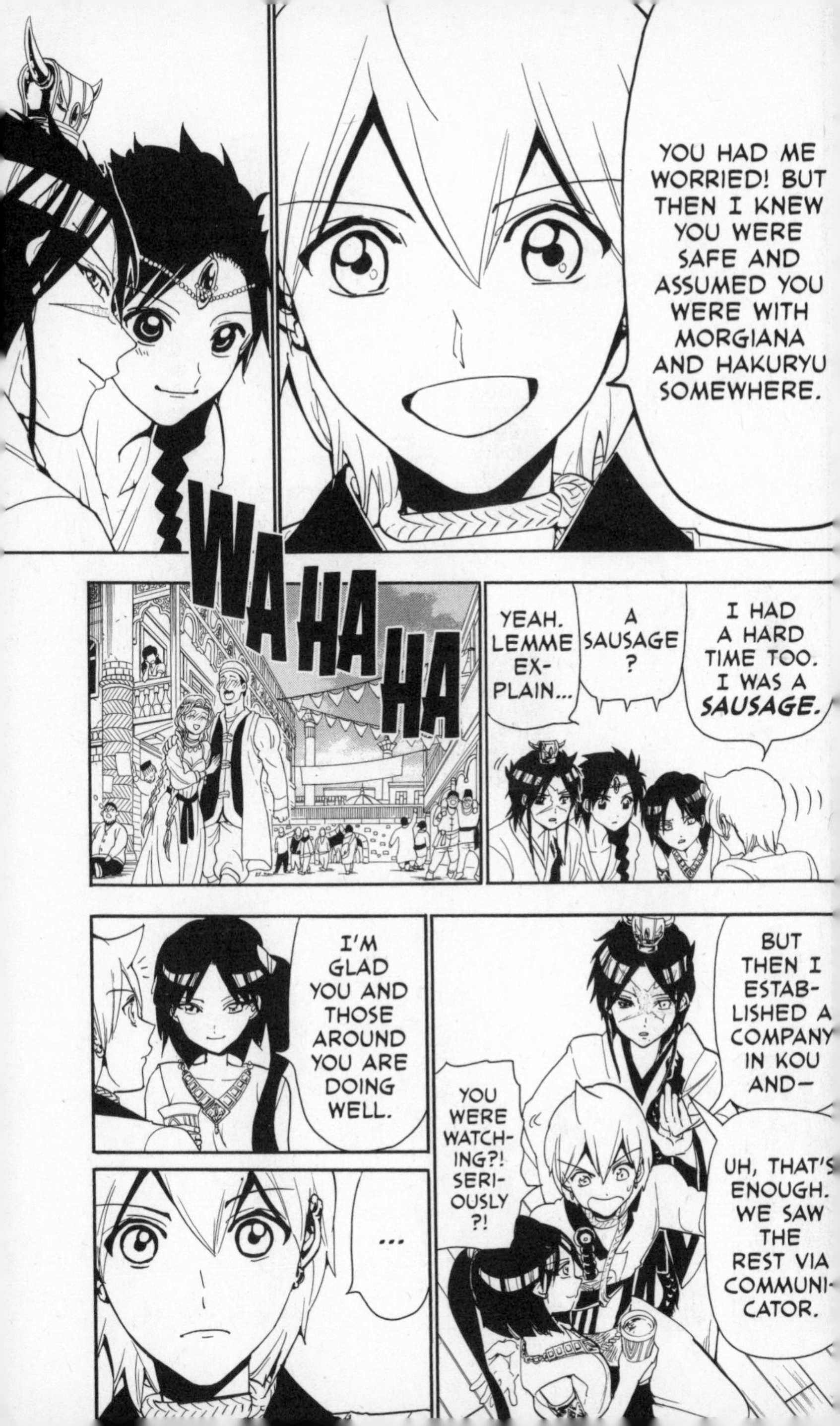
YOU HAD ME WORRIED! BUT THEN I KNEW YOU WERE SAFE AND ASSUMED YOU WERE WITH MORGIANA AND HAKURYU SOMEWHERE.
I HAD A HARD TIME TOO. I WAS A SAUSAGE.
A SAUSAGE?
YEAH. LEMME EXPLAIN...
WAHAHAHA
BUT THEN I ESTABLISHED A COMPANY IN KOU AND—
UH, THAT'S ENOUGH. WE SAW THE REST VIA COMMUNICATOR.
YOU WERE WATCHING?! SERIOUSLY?!
I'M GLAD YOU AND THOSE AROUND YOU ARE DOING WELL.
...

YOU'RE STILL WEARING THAT NECKLACE?
YES.
GLINT
ALIBABA! WHAT'S WRONG? YOU'RE HARDLY DRINKING!!
WELL... I DON'T NEED MUCH!
BECAUSE I WANT TO SAY SOMETHING WHILE I'M SOBER!
OH, WHAT IS IT?
MORGIANA!
WHAT I HAVE TO SAY IS FOR *YOU.*
HA HA HA
CHATTER
CHATTER
OH-HO! LOOK OVER THERE!

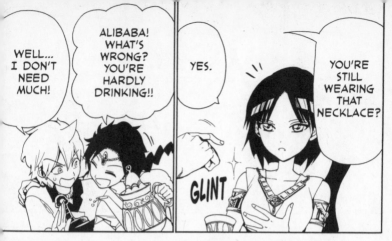

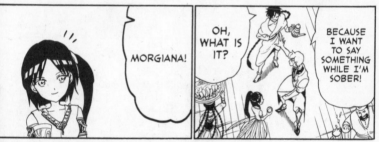

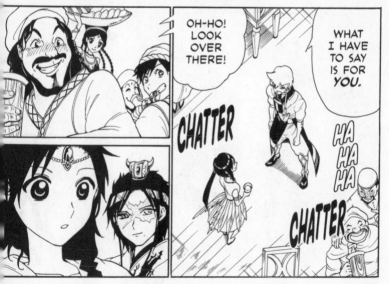

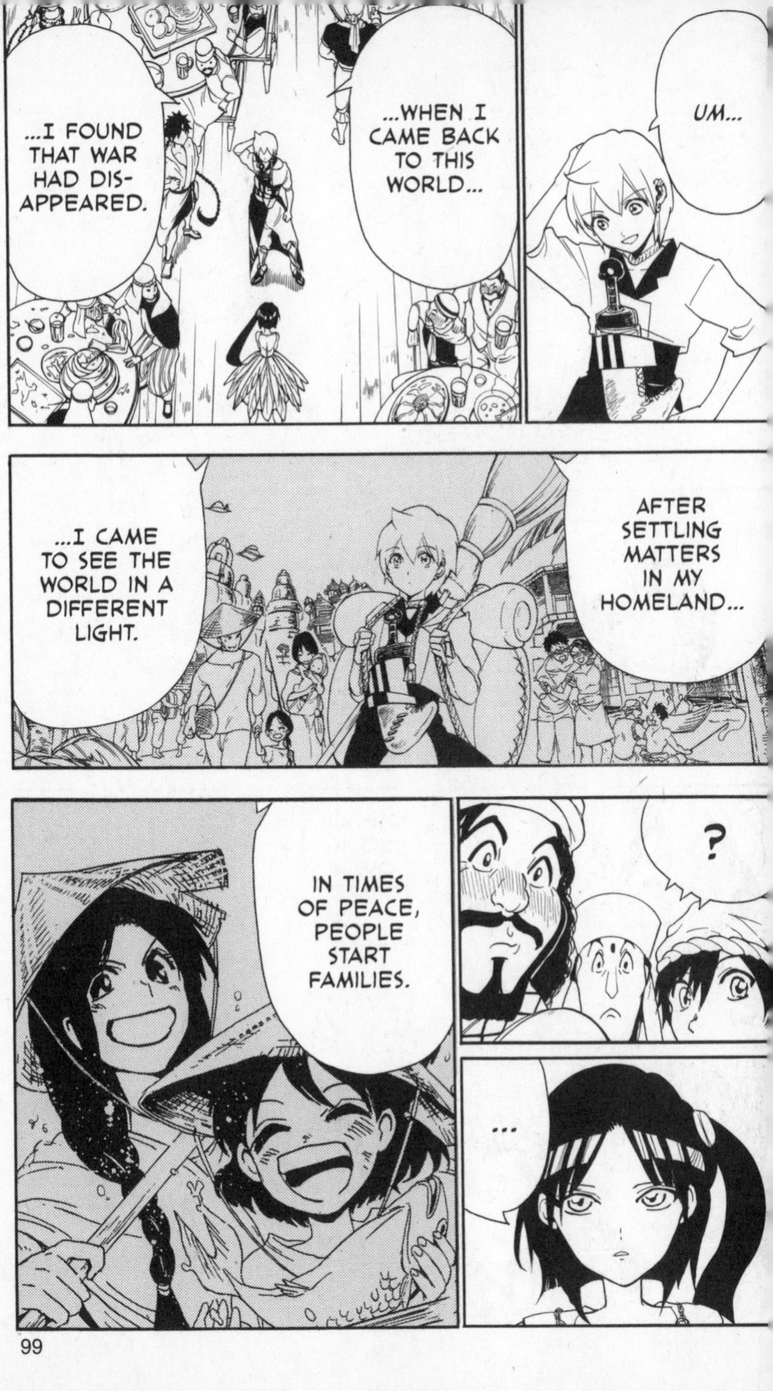
UM...
...WHEN I CAME BACK TO THIS WORLD...
...I FOUND THAT WAR HAD DIS-APPEARED.
AFTER SETTLING MATTERS IN MY HOMELAND...
...I CAME TO SEE THE WORLD IN A DIFFERENT LIGHT.
?
...
IN TIMES OF PEACE, PEOPLE START FAMILIES.

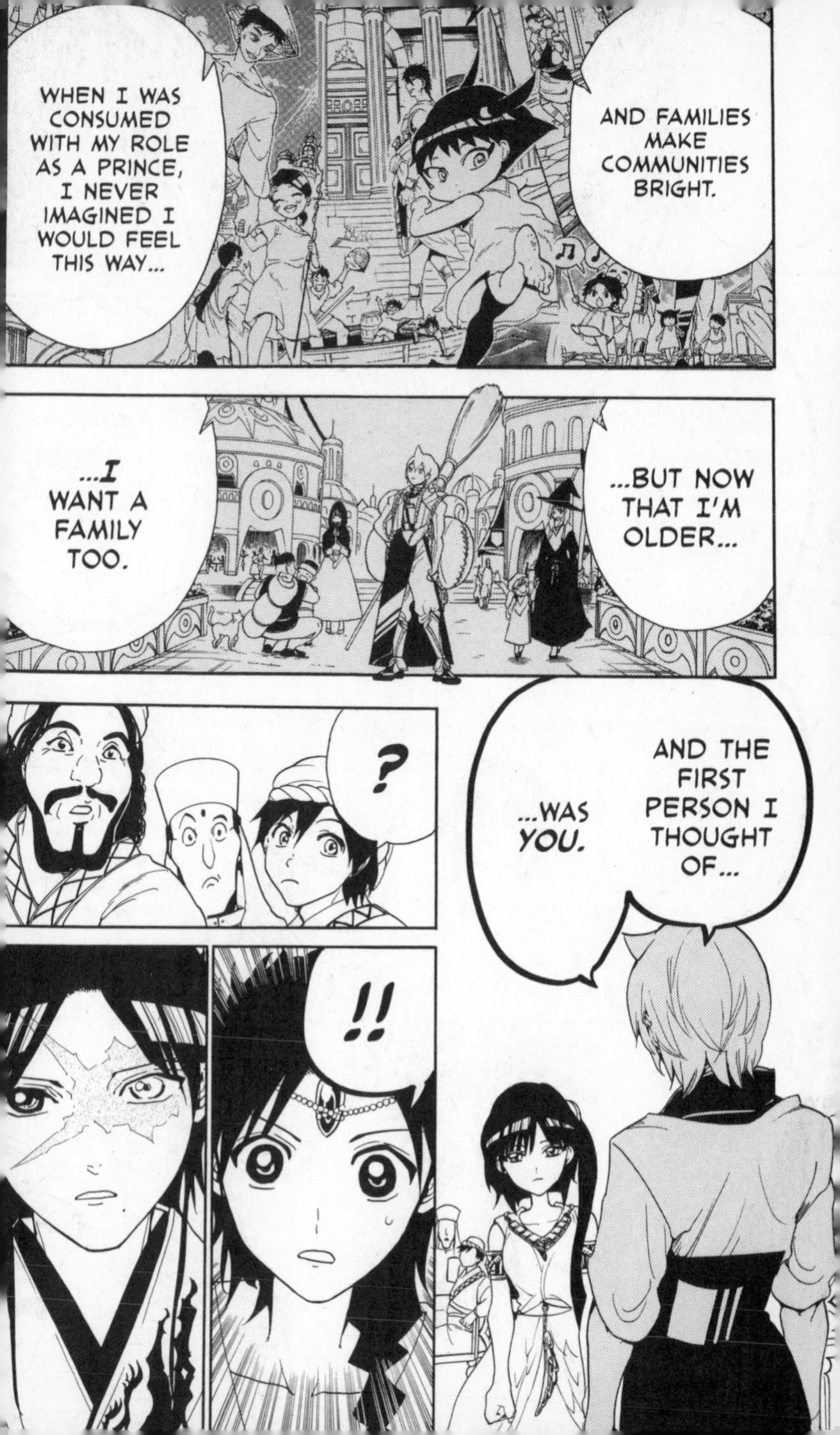
AND FAMILIES MAKE COMMUNITIES BRIGHT.
WHEN I WAS CONSUMED WITH MY ROLE AS A PRINCE, I NEVER IMAGINED I WOULD FEEL THIS WAY...
...BUT NOW THAT I'M OLDER...
...I WANT A FAMILY TOO.
AND THE FIRST PERSON I THOUGHT OF...
...WAS *YOU.*
?
!!

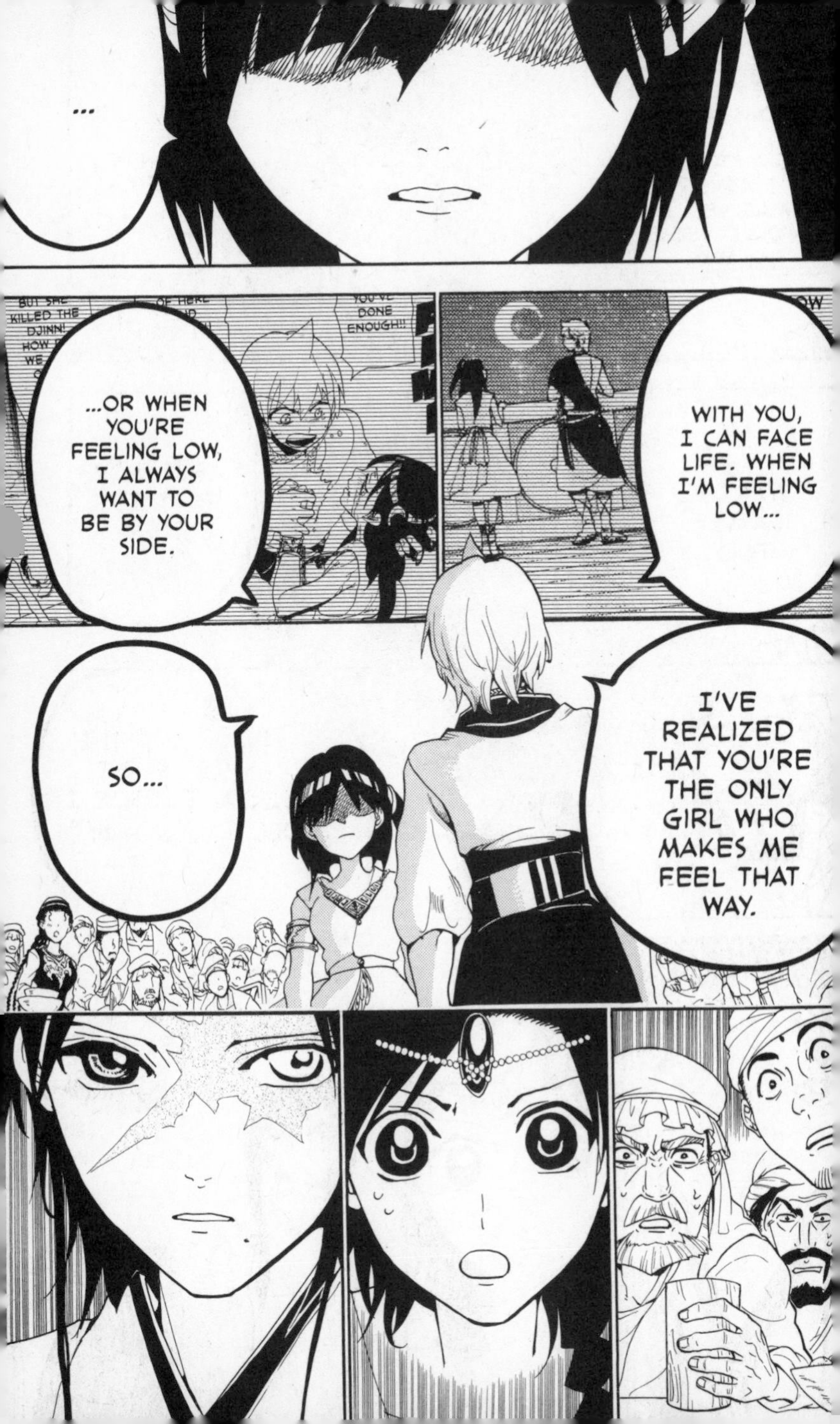
...
WITH YOU, I CAN FACE LIFE. WHEN I'M FEELING LOW...
...OR WHEN YOU'RE FEELING LOW, I ALWAYS WANT TO BE BY YOUR SIDE.
I'VE REALIZED THAT YOU'RE THE ONLY GIRL WHO MAKES ME FEEL THAT WAY.
SO...

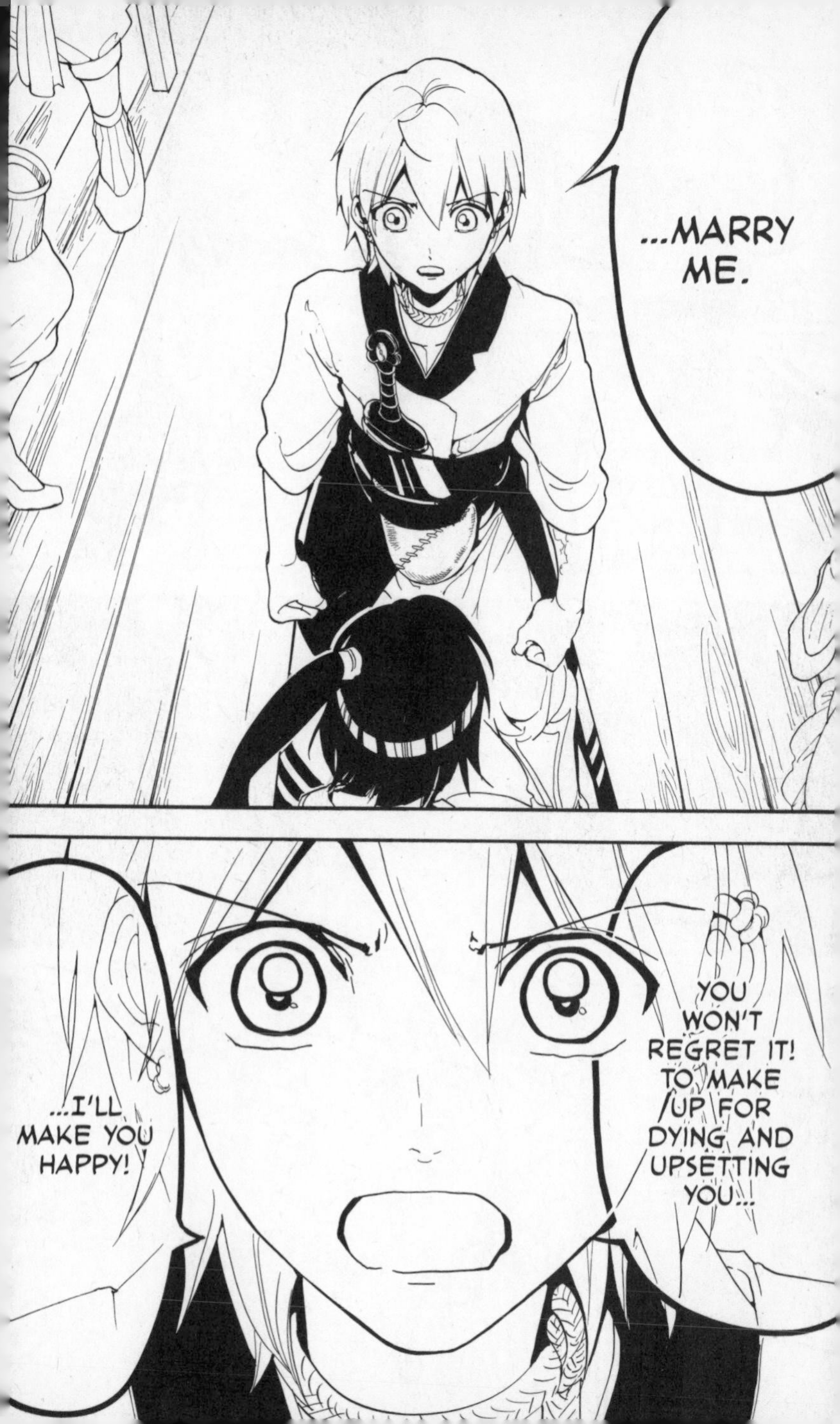
...MARRY ME.
YOU WON'T REGRET IT! TO MAKE UP FOR DYING AND UPSETTING YOU...
...I'LL MAKE YOU HAPPY!

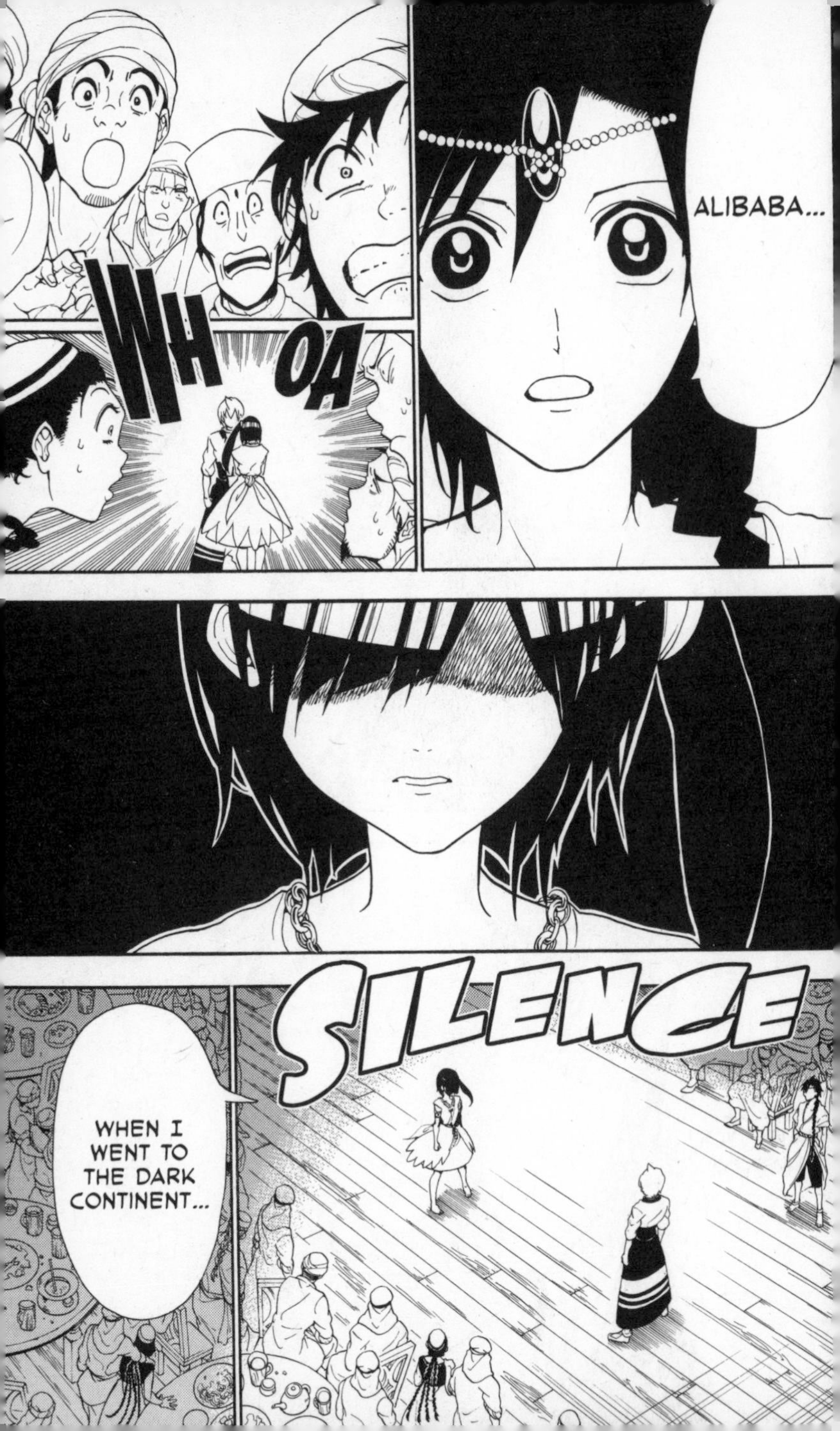
ALIBABA...
WHOA
SILENCE
WHEN I WENT TO THE DARK CONTINENT...

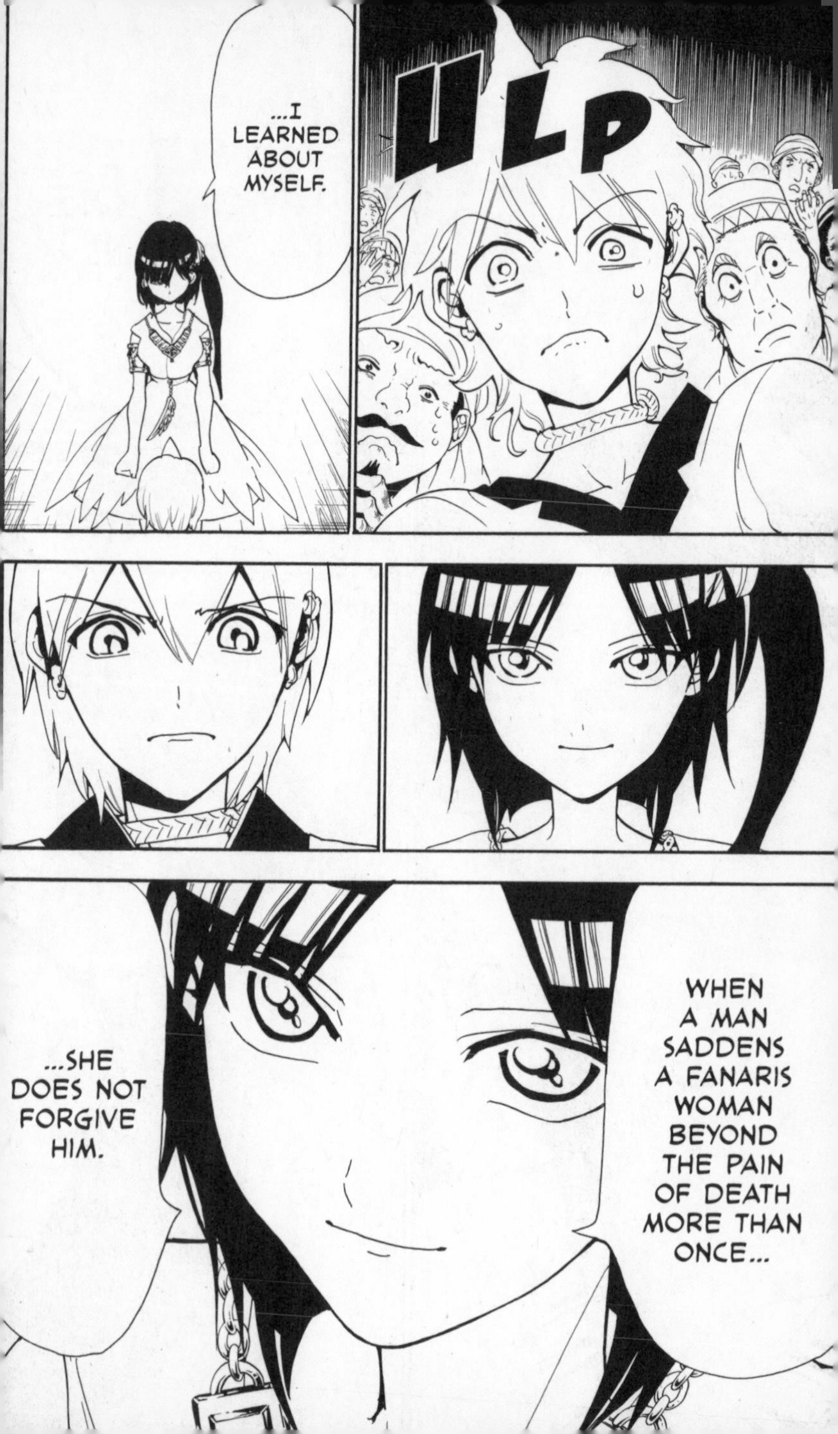
ULP
...I LEARNED ABOUT MYSELF.
WHEN A MAN SADDENS A FANARIS WOMAN BEYOND THE PAIN OF DEATH MORE THAN ONCE...
...SHE DOES NOT FORGIVE HIM.

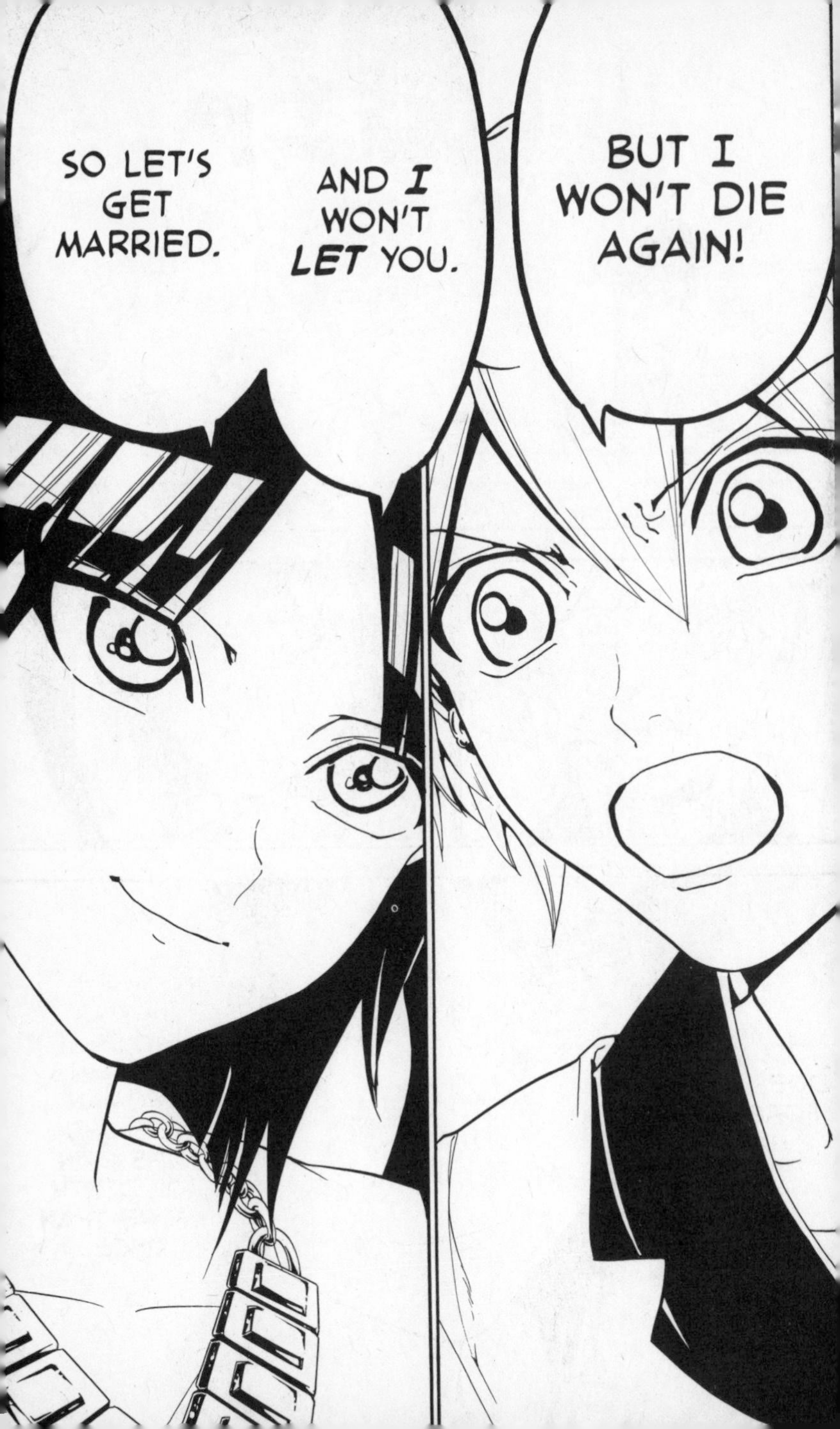
BUT I WON'T DIE AGAIN!
AND I WON'T LET YOU.
SO LET'S GET MARRIED.

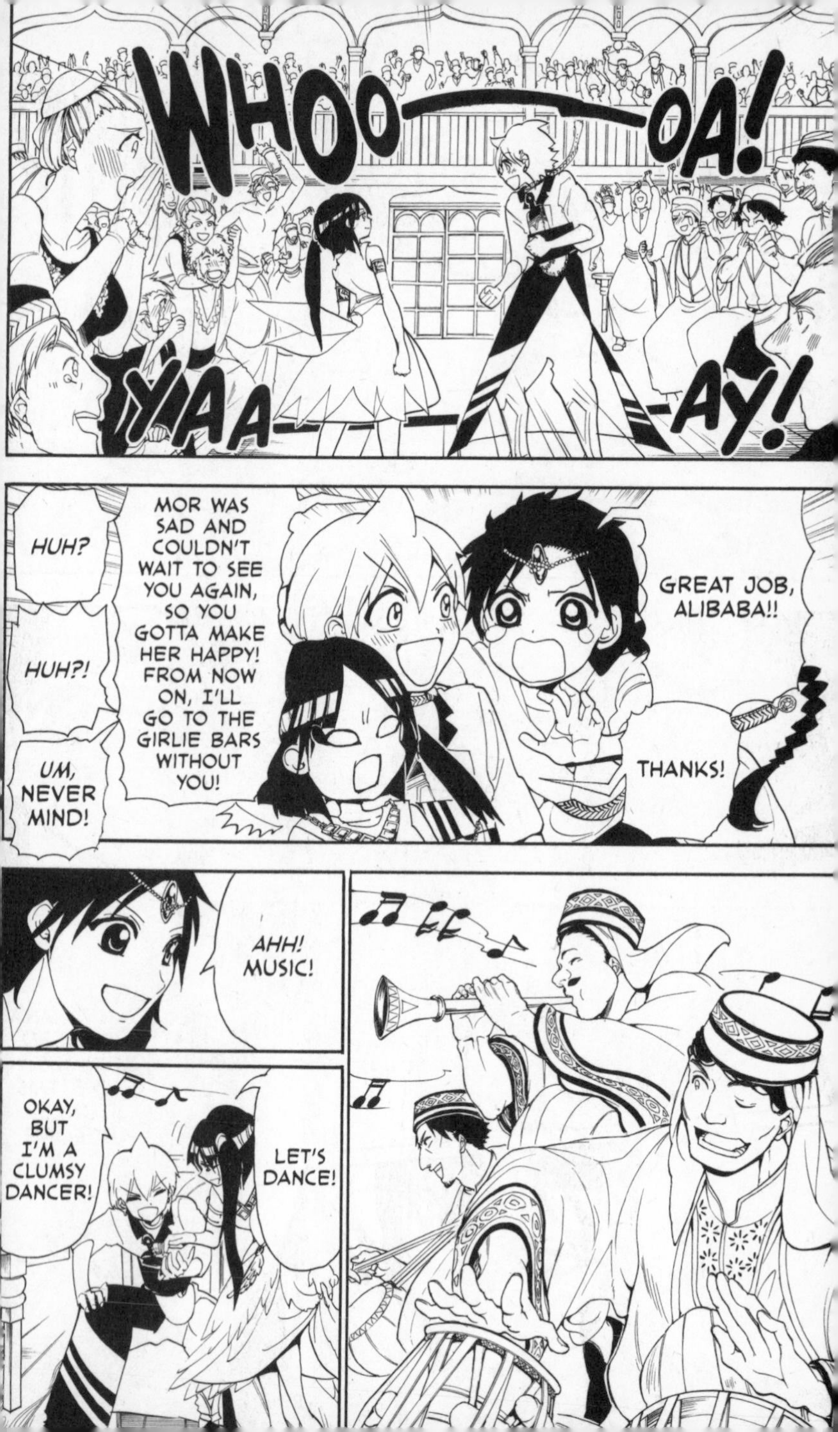
WHOO——OA!
YAA——AY!
GREAT JOB, ALIBABA!!
THANKS!
MOR WAS SAD AND COULDN'T WAIT TO SEE YOU AGAIN, SO YOU GOTTA MAKE HER HAPPY! FROM NOW ON, I'LL GO TO THE GIRLIE BARS WITHOUT YOU!
HUH?
HUH?!
UM, NEVER MIND!
AHH! MUSIC!
LET'S DANCE!
OKAY, BUT I'M A CLUMSY DANCER!

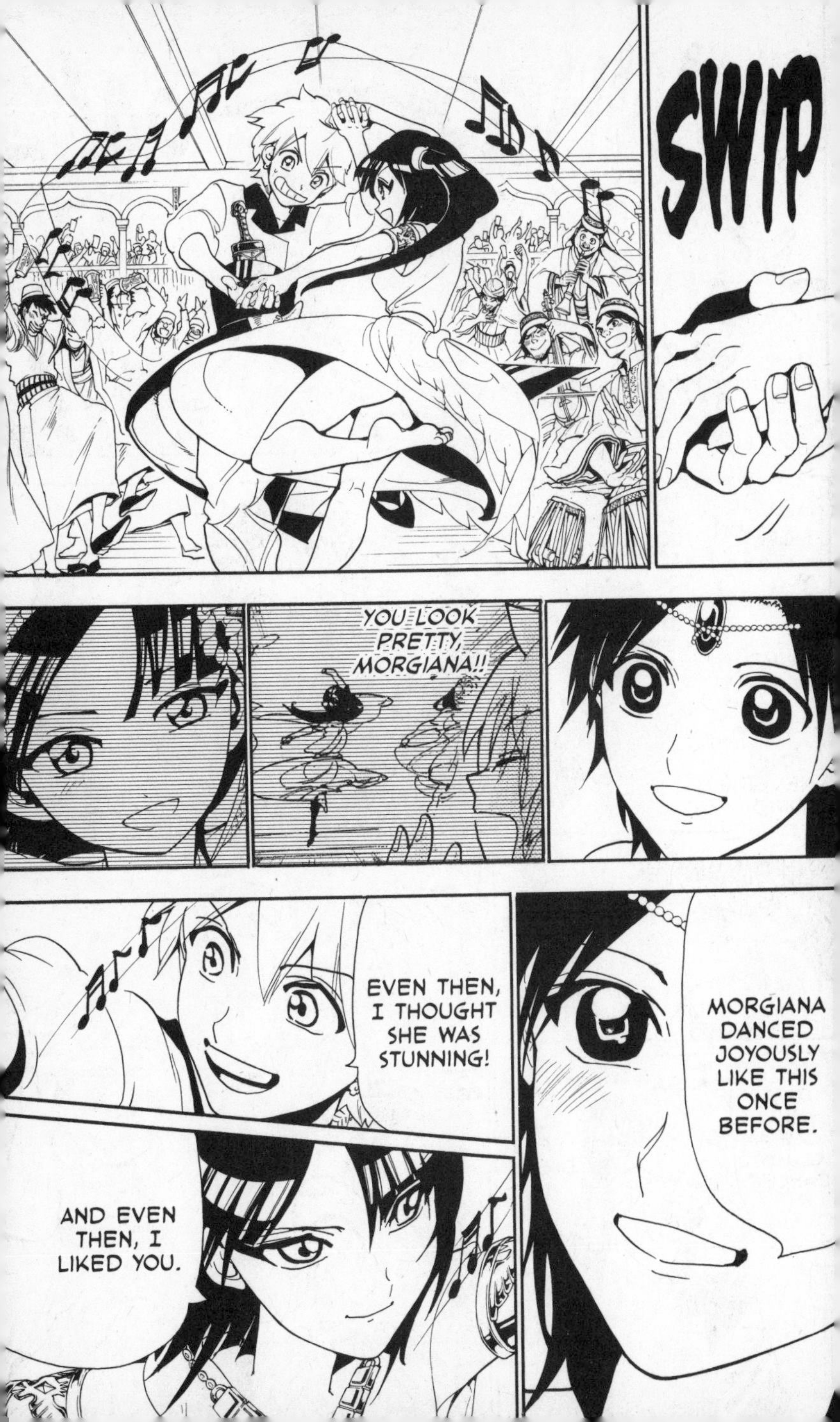
SWIP
YOU LOOK PRETTY, MORGIANA!!
MORGIANA DANCED JOYOUSLY LIKE THIS ONCE BEFORE.
EVEN THEN, I THOUGHT SHE WAS STUNNING!
AND EVEN THEN, I LIKED YOU.

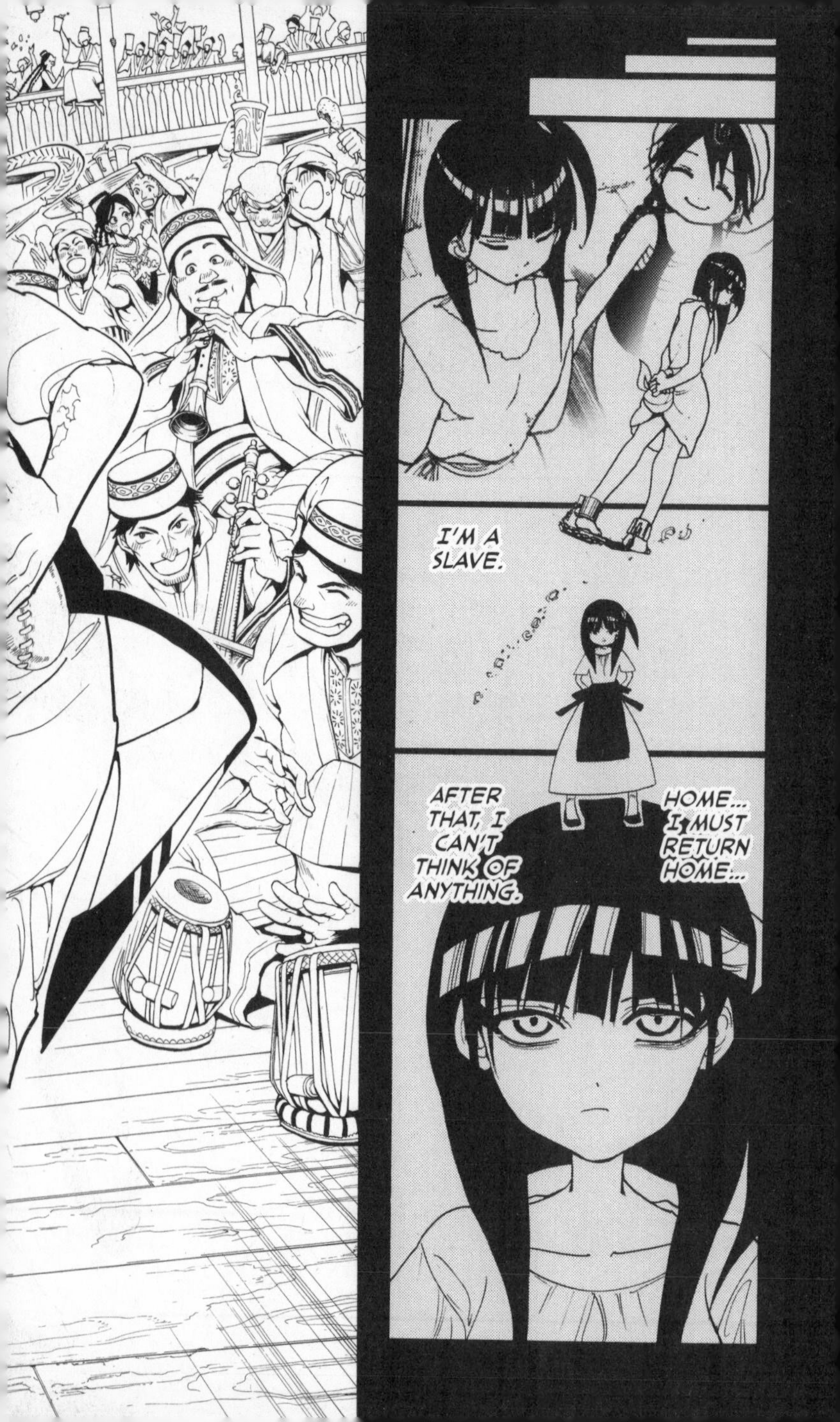
I'M A SLAVE.
HOME... I MUST RETURN HOME...
AFTER THAT, I CAN'T THINK OF ANYTHING.

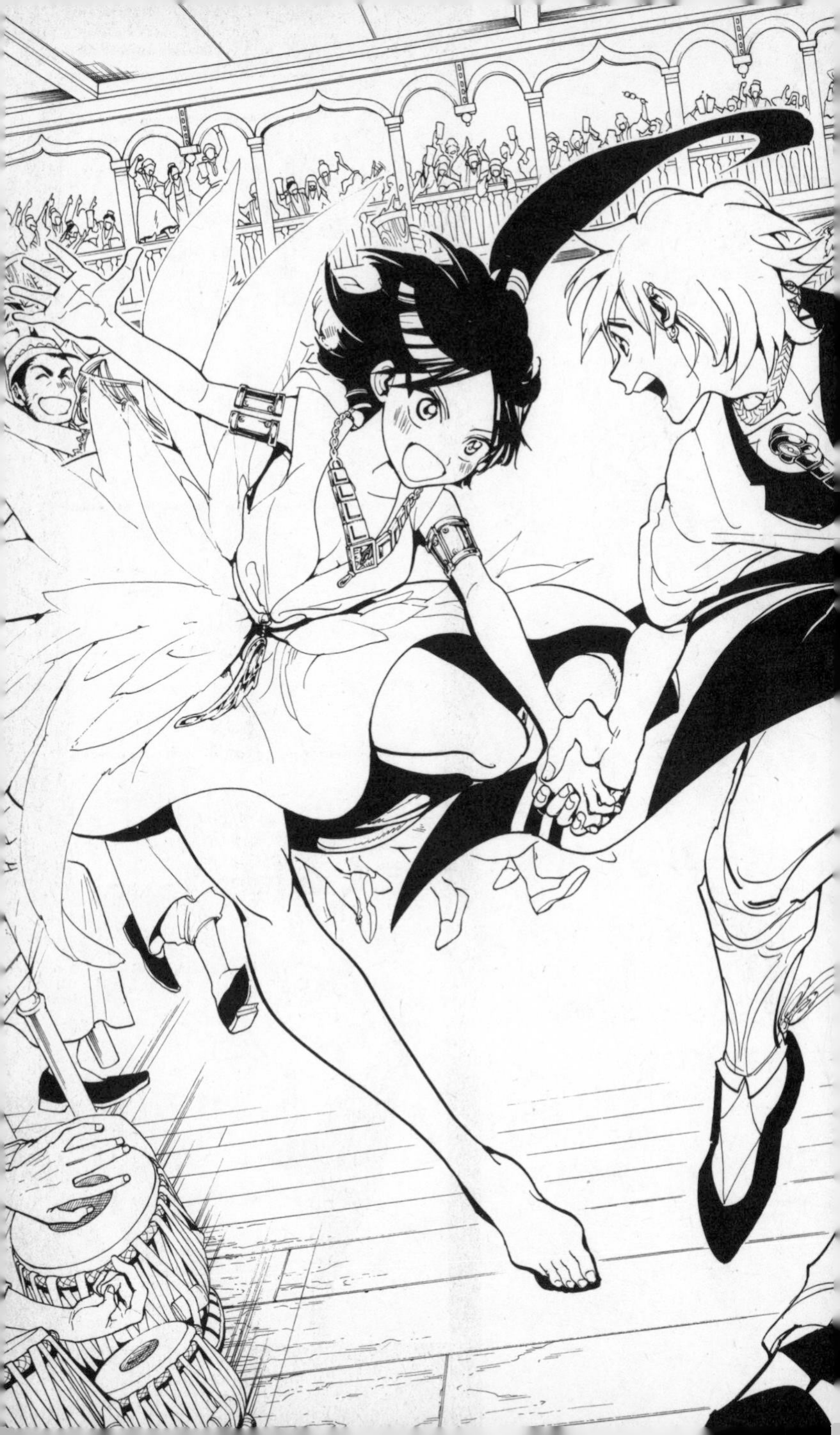

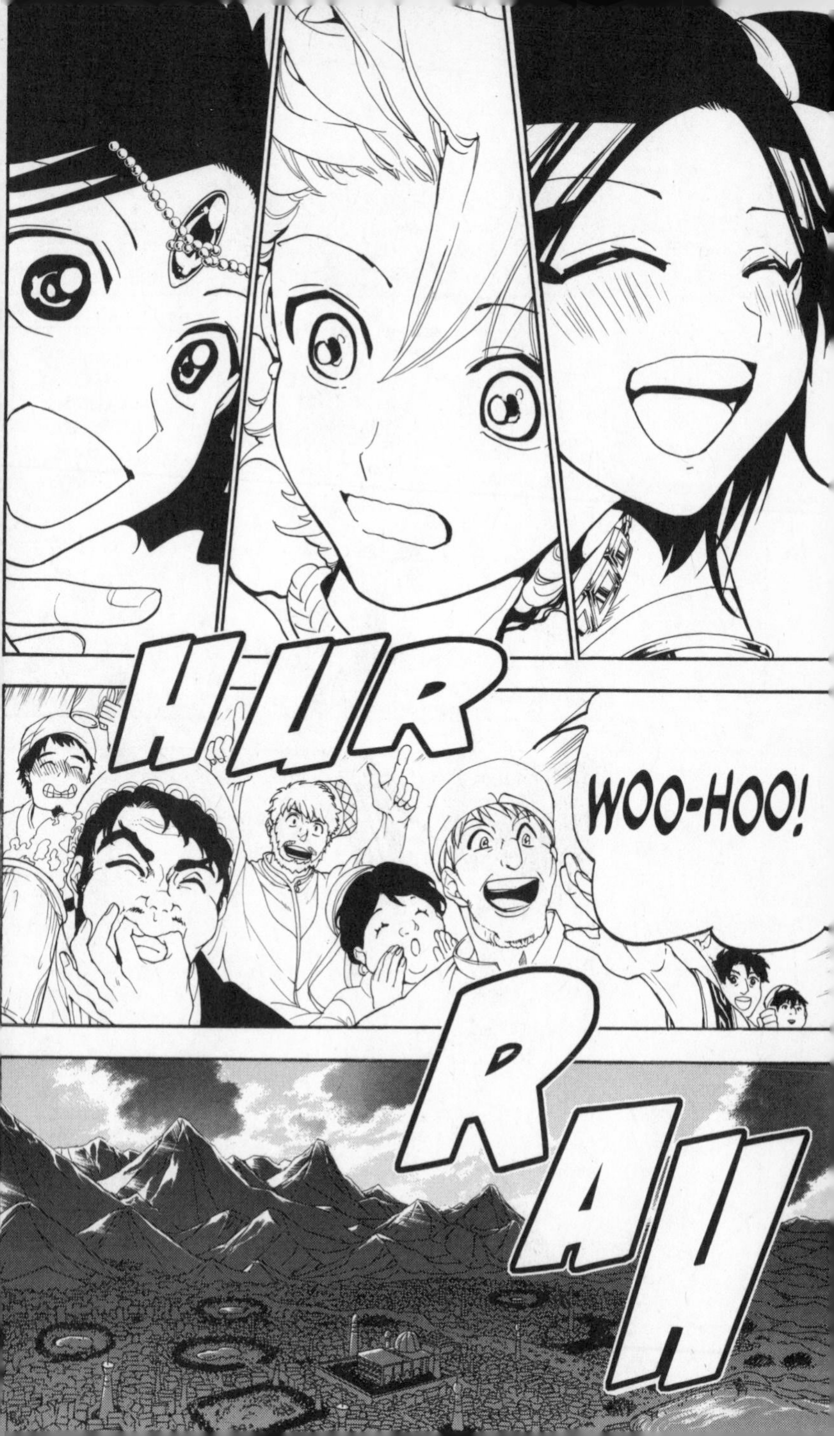

WOO-HOO!
HURRAH

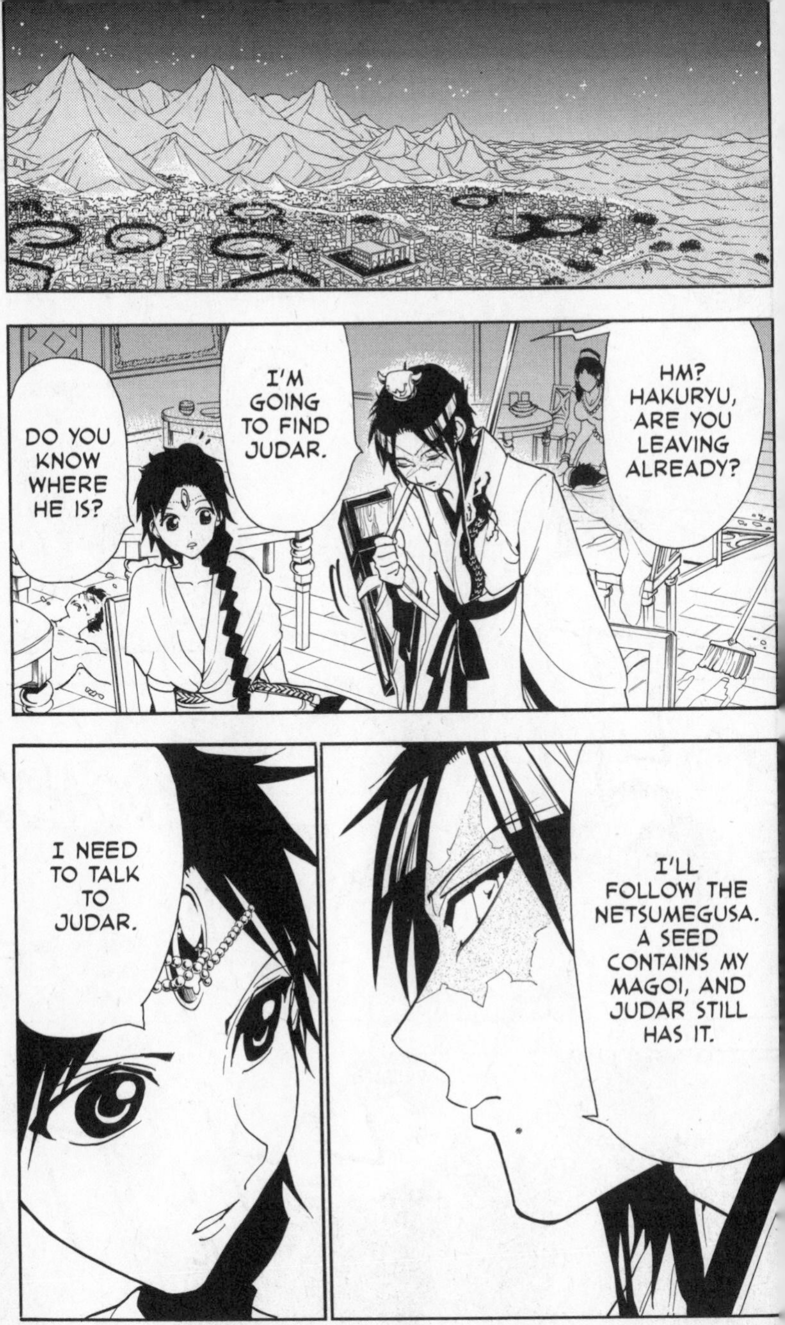
HM? HAKURYU, ARE YOU LEAVING ALREADY?
I'M GOING TO FIND JUDAR.
DO YOU KNOW WHERE HE IS?
I'LL FOLLOW THE NETSUMEGUSA. A SEED CONTAINS MY MAGOI, AND JUDAR STILL HAS IT.
I NEED TO TALK TO JUDAR.

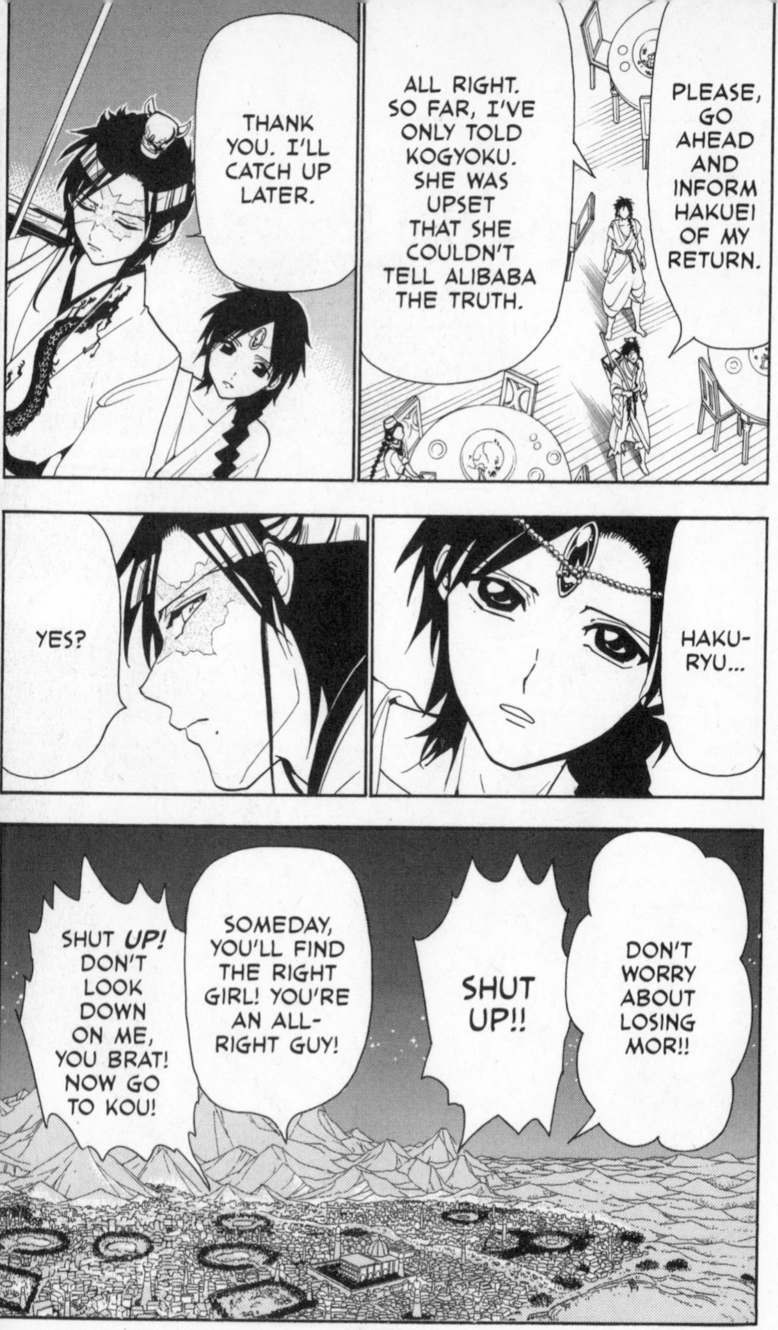
PLEASE, GO AHEAD AND INFORM HAKUEI OF MY RETURN.
ALL RIGHT. SO FAR, I'VE ONLY TOLD KOGYOKU. SHE WAS UPSET THAT SHE COULDN'T TELL ALIBABA THE TRUTH.
THANK YOU. I'LL CATCH UP LATER.
HAKU-RYU...
YES?
DON'T WORRY ABOUT LOSING MOR!!
SHUT UP!!
SOMEDAY, YOU'LL FIND THE RIGHT GIRL! YOU'RE AN ALL-RIGHT GUY!
SHUT *UP!* DON'T LOOK DOWN ON ME, YOU BRAT! NOW GO TO KOU!

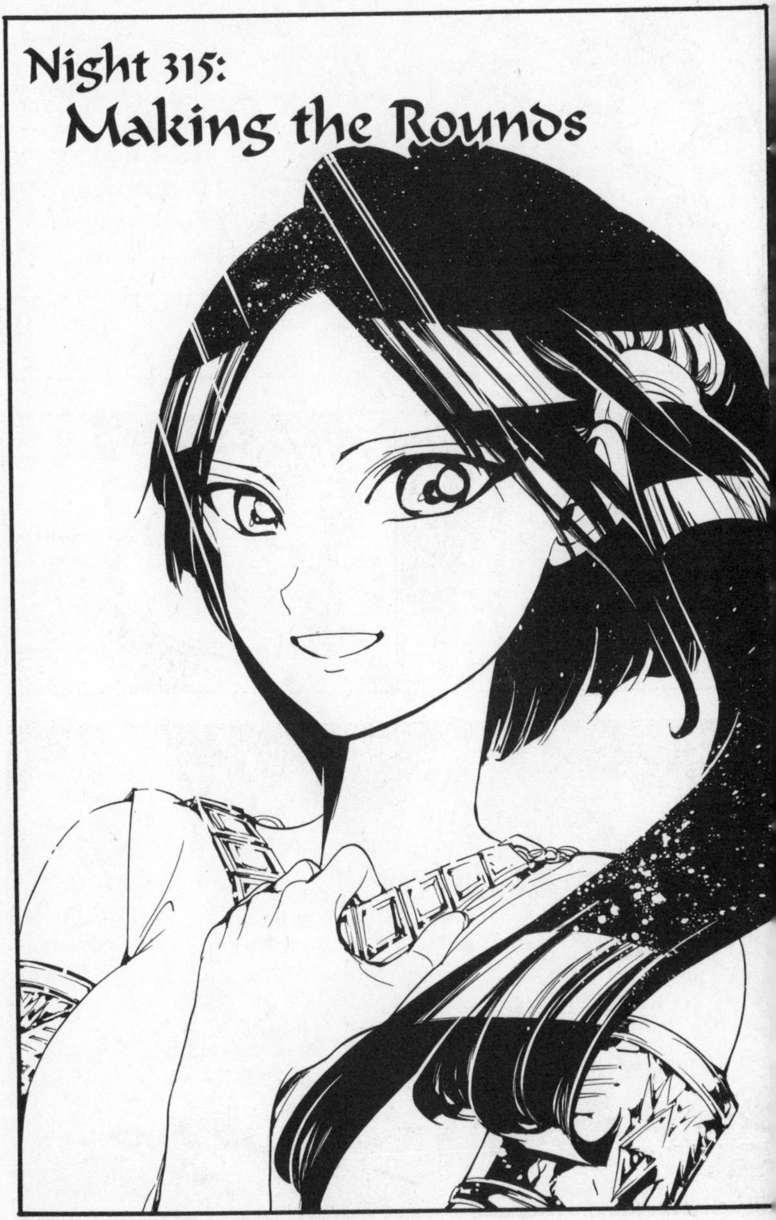
Night 315:
Making the Rounds

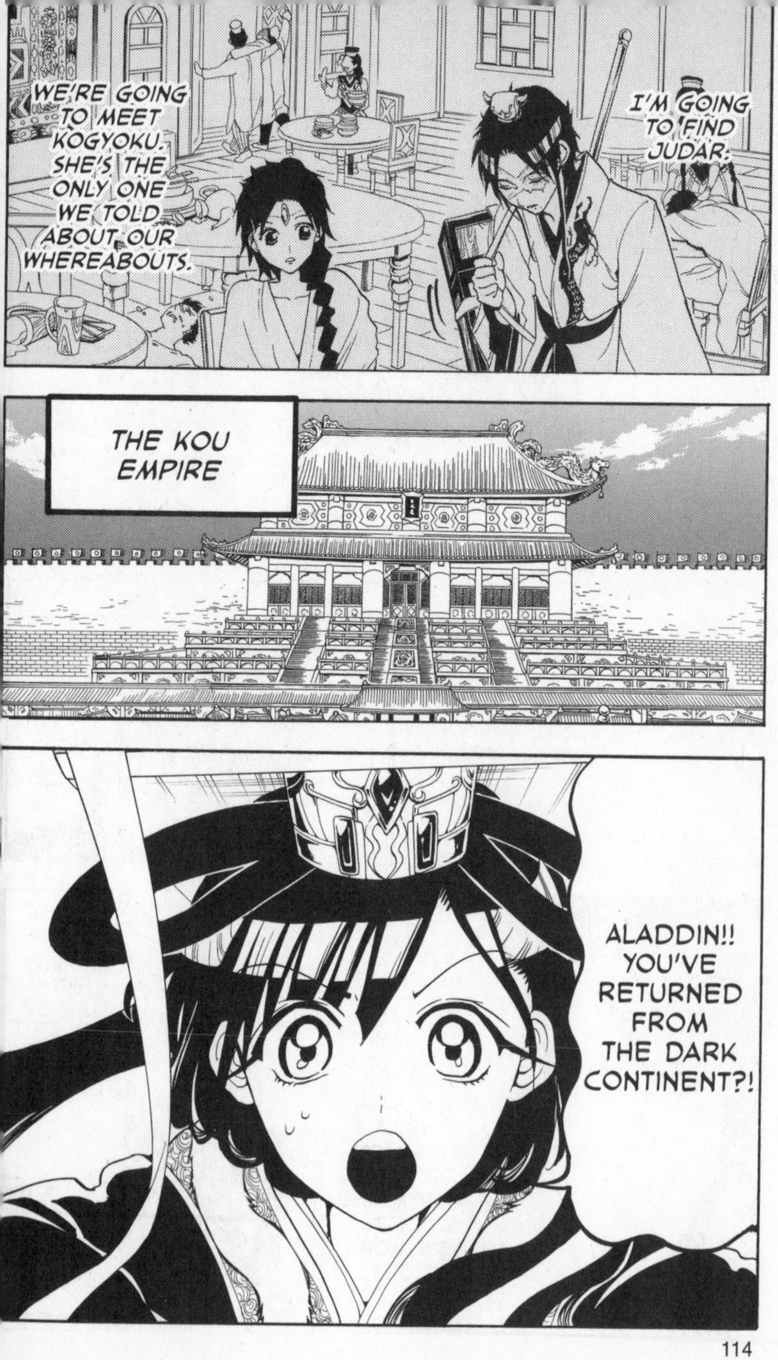
I'M GOING TO FIND JUDAR.
WE'RE GOING TO MEET KOGYOKU. SHE'S THE ONLY ONE WE TOLD ABOUT OUR WHEREABOUTS.
THE KOU EMPIRE
ALADDIN!! YOU'VE RETURNED FROM THE DARK CONTINENT?!

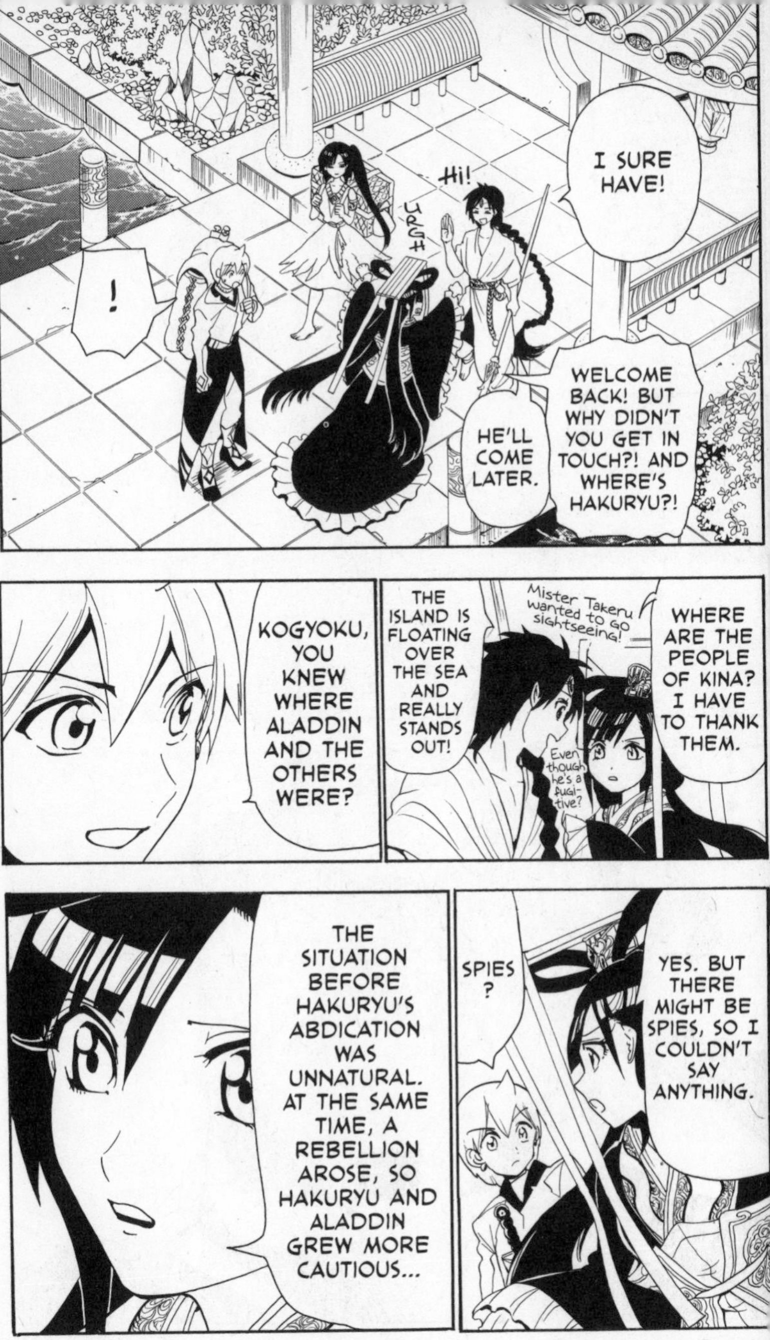
I SURE HAVE!
Hi!
URGH
WELCOME BACK! BUT WHY DIDN'T YOU GET IN TOUCH?! AND WHERE'S HAKURYU?!
HE'LL COME LATER.
!
WHERE ARE THE PEOPLE OF KINA? I HAVE TO THANK THEM.
Mister Takeru wanted to go sightseeing!
Even though he's a fugitive?
THE ISLAND IS FLOATING OVER THE SEA AND REALLY STANDS OUT!
KOGYOKU, YOU KNEW WHERE ALADDIN AND THE OTHERS WERE?
YES. BUT THERE MIGHT BE SPIES, SO I COULDN'T SAY ANYTHING.
SPIES?
THE SITUATION BEFORE HAKURYU'S ABDICATION WAS UNNATURAL. AT THE SAME TIME, A REBELLION AROSE, SO HAKURYU AND ALADDIN GREW MORE CAUTIOUS...

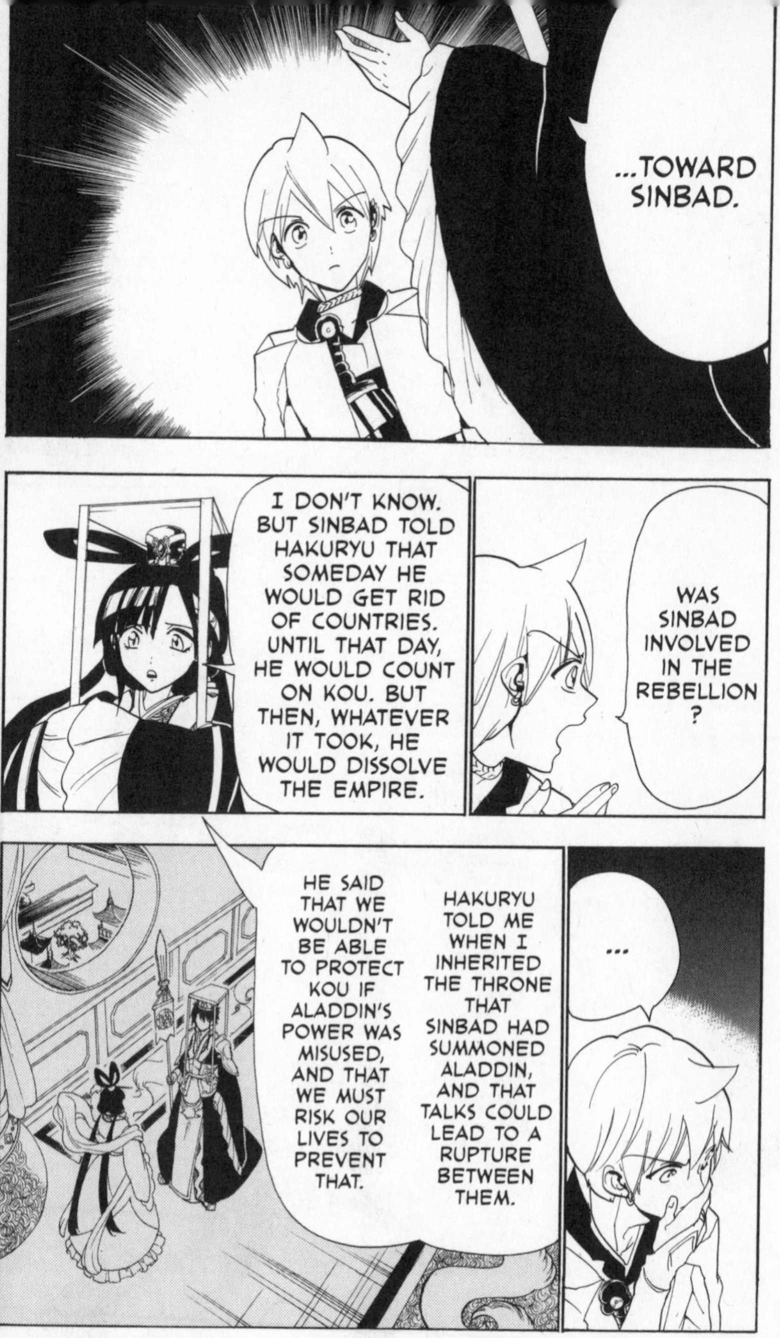
...TOWARD SINBAD.
WAS SINBAD INVOLVED IN THE REBELLION?
I DON'T KNOW. BUT SINBAD TOLD HAKURYU THAT SOMEDAY HE WOULD GET RID OF COUNTRIES. UNTIL THAT DAY, HE WOULD COUNT ON KOU. BUT THEN, WHATEVER IT TOOK, HE WOULD DISSOLVE THE EMPIRE.
...
HAKURYU TOLD ME WHEN I INHERITED THE THRONE THAT SINBAD HAD SUMMONED ALADDIN, AND THAT TALKS COULD LEAD TO A RUPTURE BETWEEN THEM.
HE SAID THAT WE WOULDN'T BE ABLE TO PROTECT KOU IF ALADDIN'S POWER WAS MISUSED, AND THAT WE MUST RISK OUR LIVES TO PREVENT THAT.

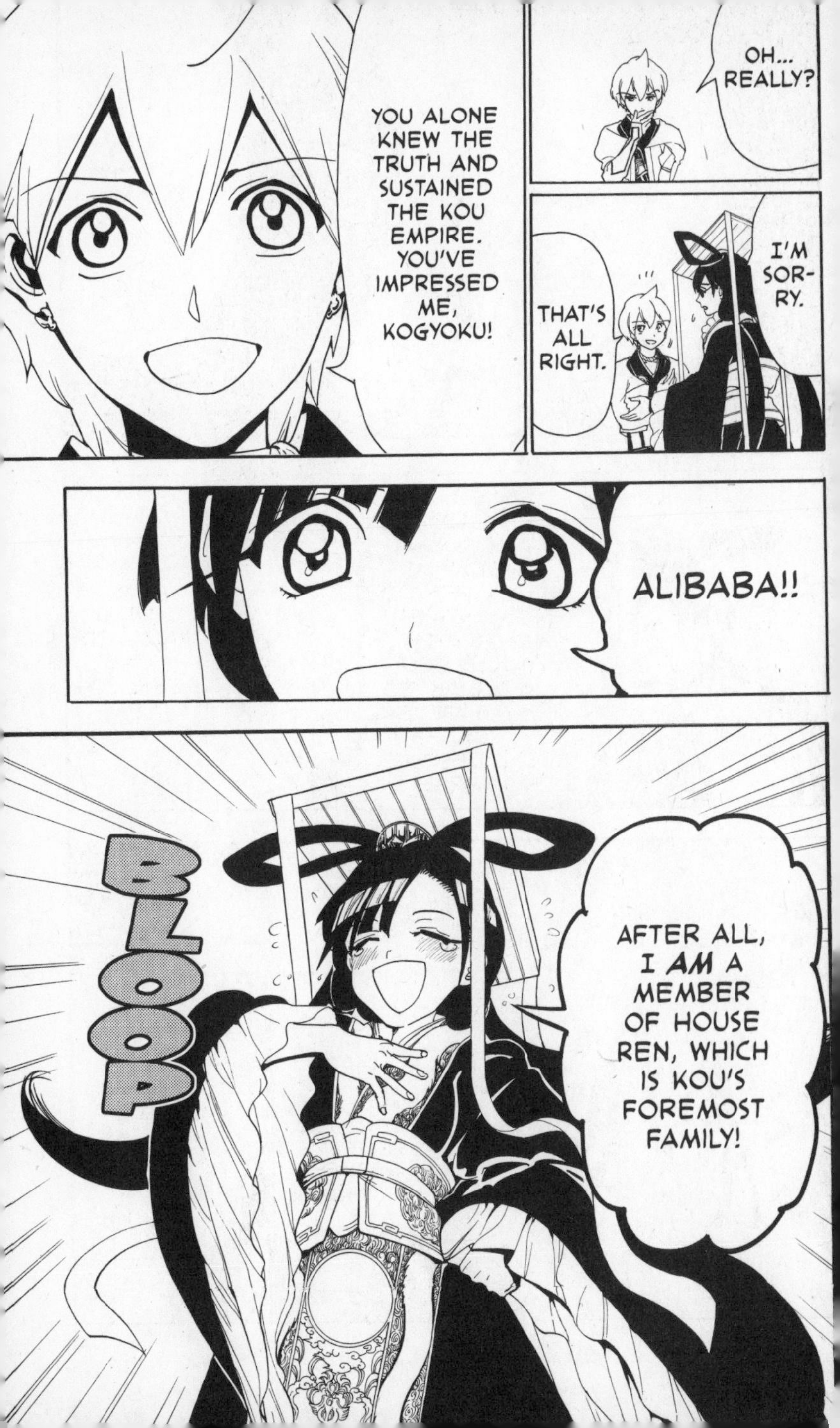
OH... REALLY?
I'M SORRY.
THAT'S ALL RIGHT.
YOU ALONE KNEW THE TRUTH AND SUSTAINED THE KOU EMPIRE. YOU'VE IMPRESSED ME, KOGYOKU!
ALIBABA!!
AFTER ALL, I *AM* A MEMBER OF HOUSE REN, WHICH IS KOU'S FOREMOST FAMILY!
BLOOP

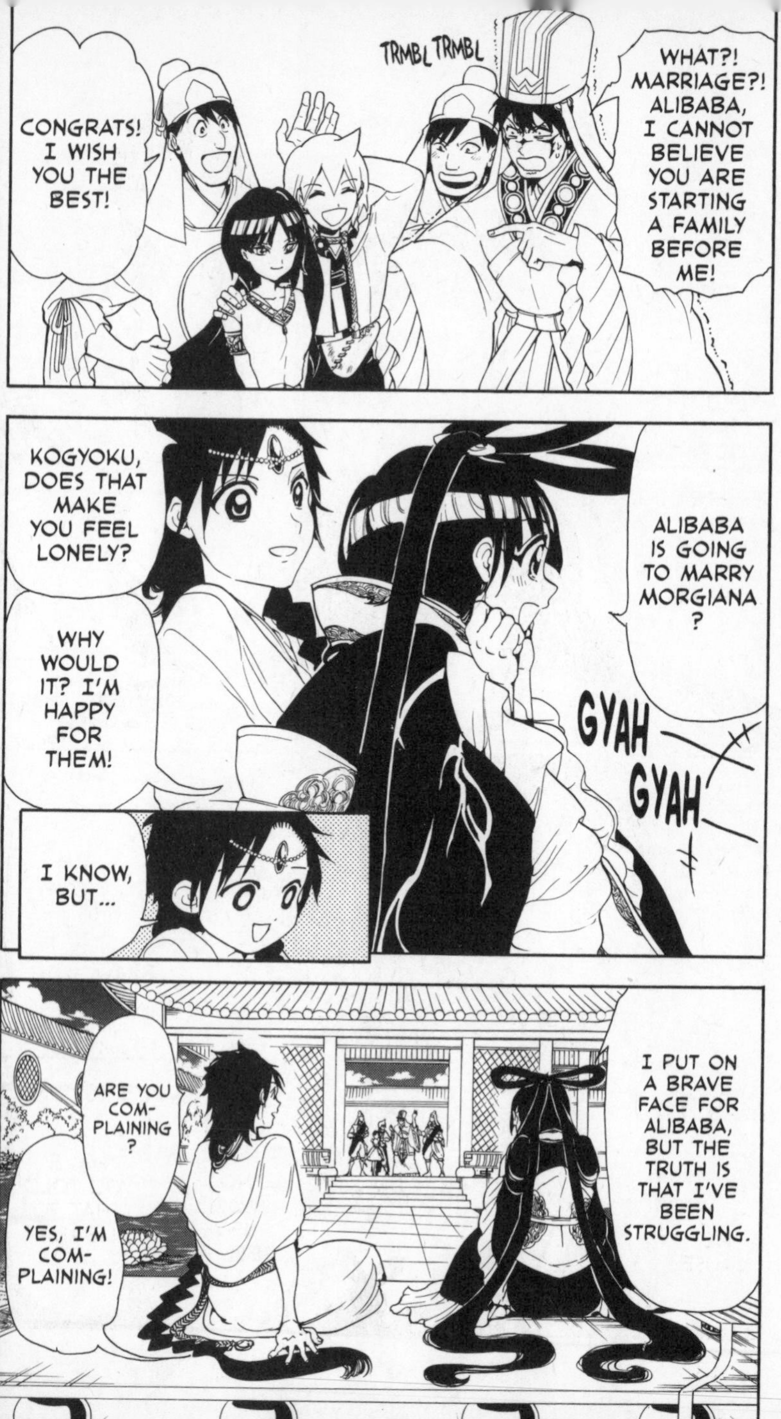
TRMBL TRMBL
WHAT?! MARRIAGE?! ALIBABA, I CANNOT BELIEVE YOU ARE STARTING A FAMILY BEFORE ME!
CONGRATS! I WISH YOU THE BEST!
ALIBABA IS GOING TO MARRY MORGIANA?
GYAH GYAH
KOGYOKU, DOES THAT MAKE YOU FEEL LONELY?
WHY WOULD IT? I'M HAPPY FOR THEM!
I KNOW, BUT...
I PUT ON A BRAVE FACE FOR ALIBABA, BUT THE TRUTH IS THAT I'VE BEEN STRUGGLING.
ARE YOU COM- PLAINING?
YES, I'M COM- PLAINING!

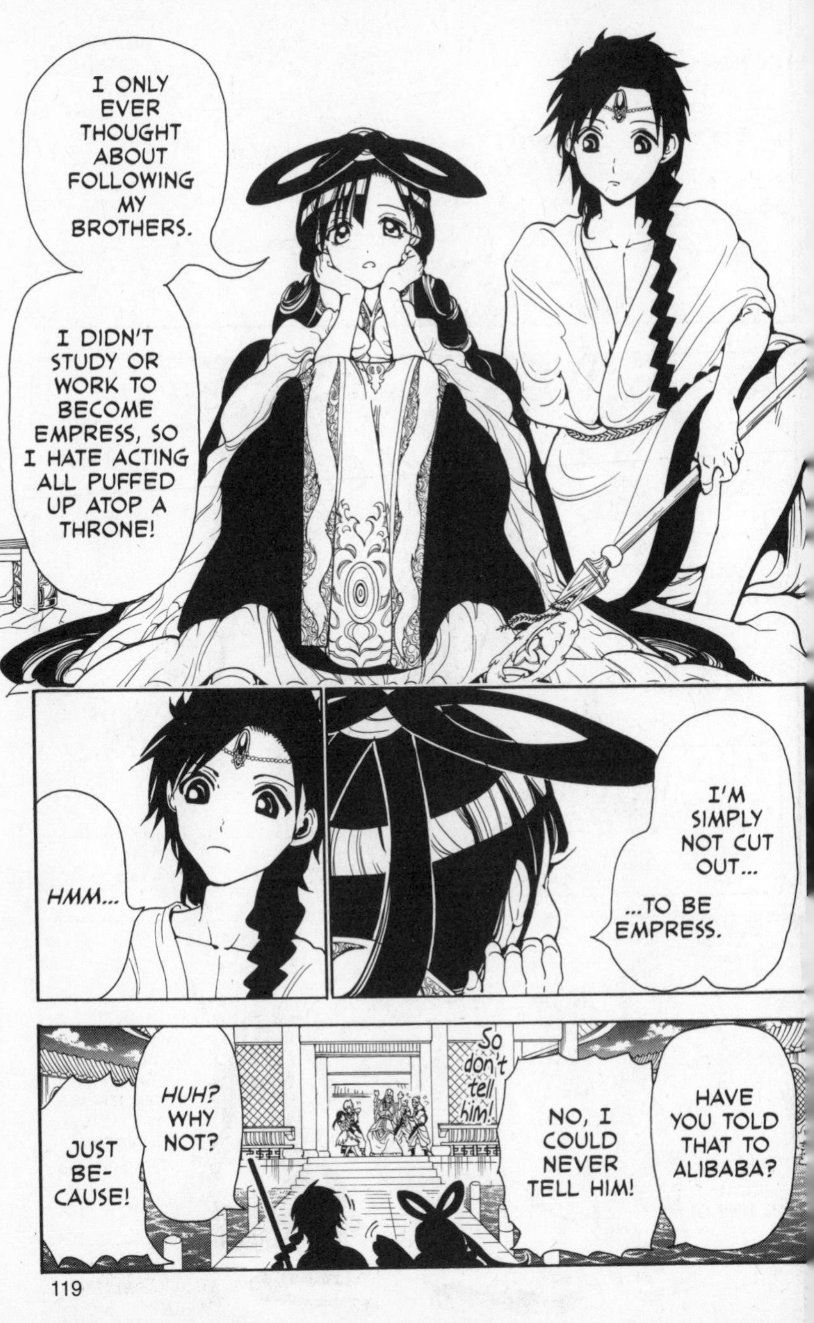
I ONLY EVER THOUGHT ABOUT FOLLOWING MY BROTHERS.
I DIDN'T STUDY OR WORK TO BECOME EMPRESS, SO I HATE ACTING ALL PUFFED UP ATOP A THRONE!
I'M SIMPLY NOT CUT OUT...
...TO BE EMPRESS.
HMM...
HAVE YOU TOLD THAT TO ALIBABA?
NO, I COULD NEVER TELL HIM!
So don't tell him!
HUH? WHY NOT?
JUST BE-CAUSE!

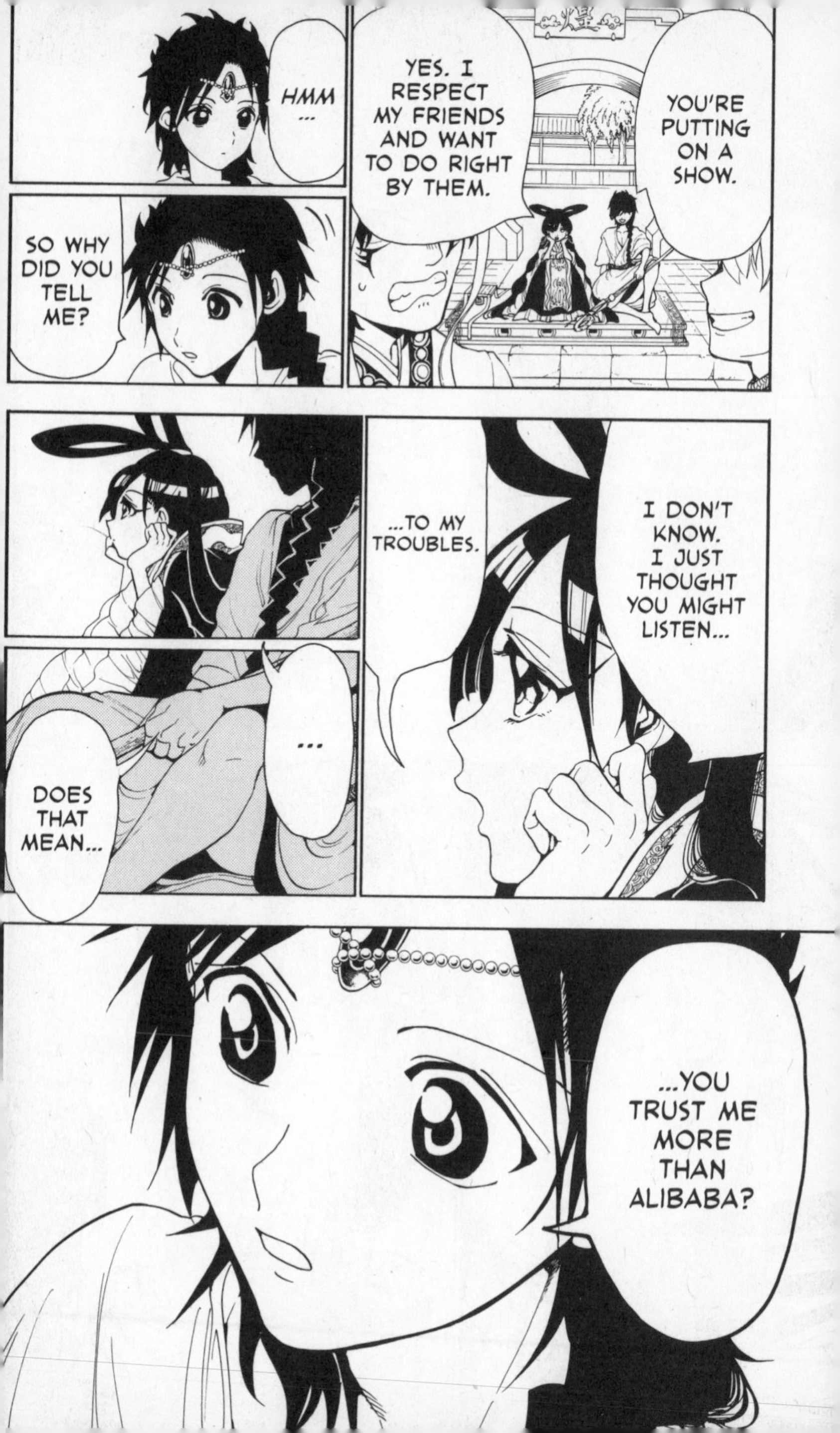

YOU'RE PUTTING ON A SHOW.
YES. I RESPECT MY FRIENDS AND WANT TO DO RIGHT BY THEM.
HMM ...
SO WHY DID YOU TELL ME?
I DON'T KNOW. I JUST THOUGHT YOU MIGHT LISTEN...
...TO MY TROUBLES.
...
DOES THAT MEAN...
...YOU TRUST ME MORE THAN ALIBABA?

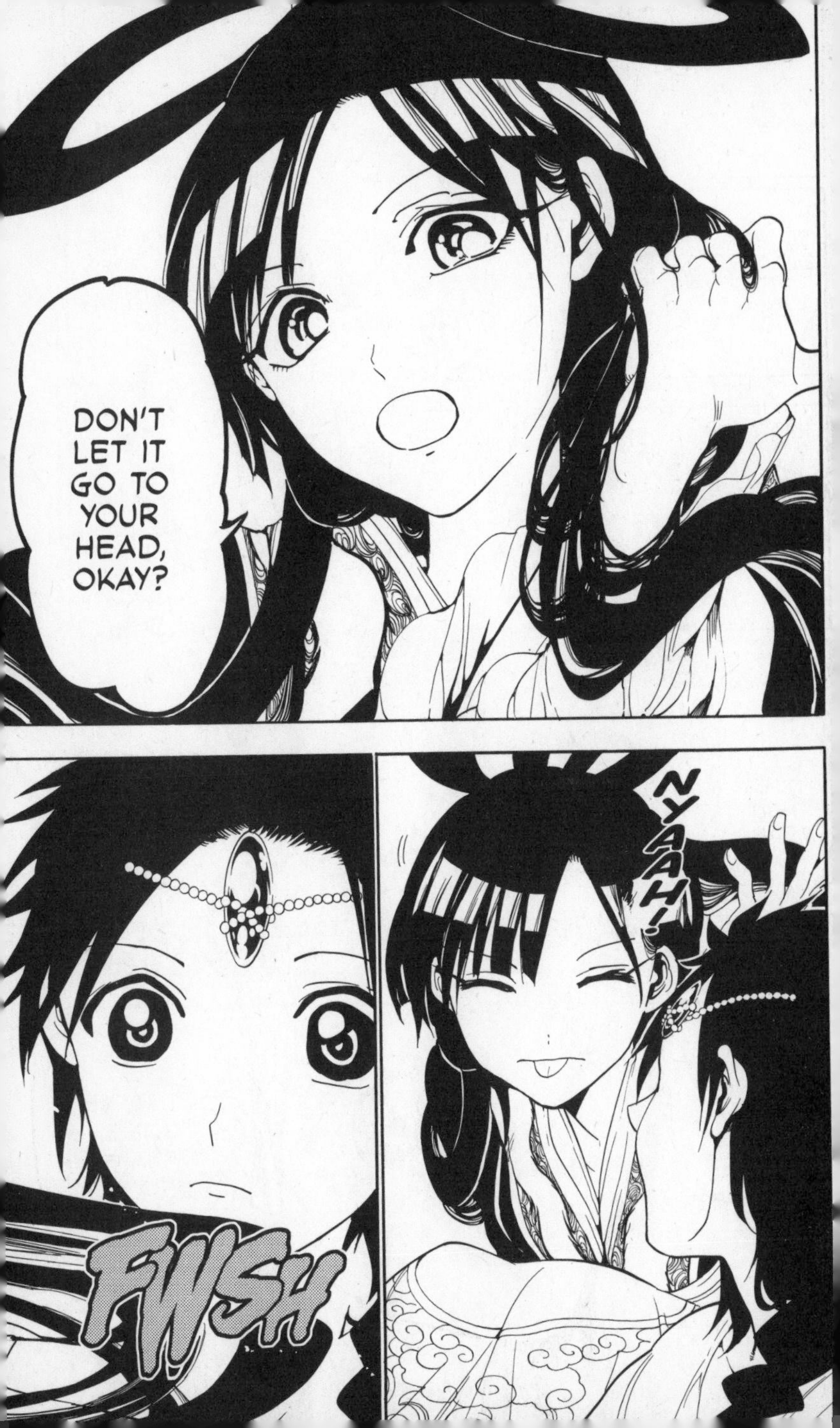
DON'T LET IT GO TO YOUR HEAD, OKAY?
NYAAH!
FWSH

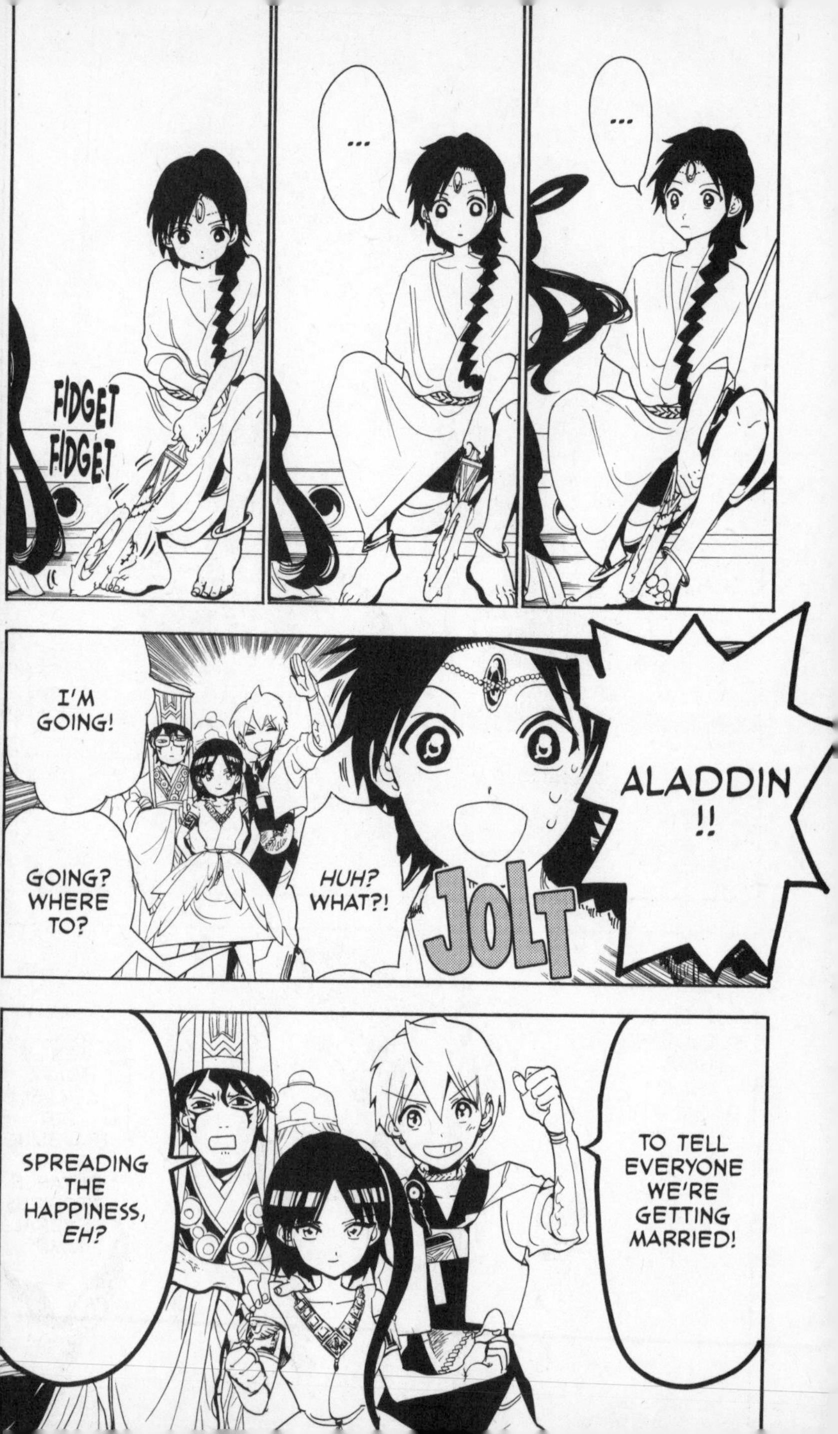
...
...
FIDGET FIDGET
ALADDIN !!
I'M GOING!
HUH? WHAT?!
JOLT
GOING? WHERE TO?
TO TELL EVERYONE WE'RE GETTING MARRIED!
SPREADING THE HAPPINESS, *EH?*

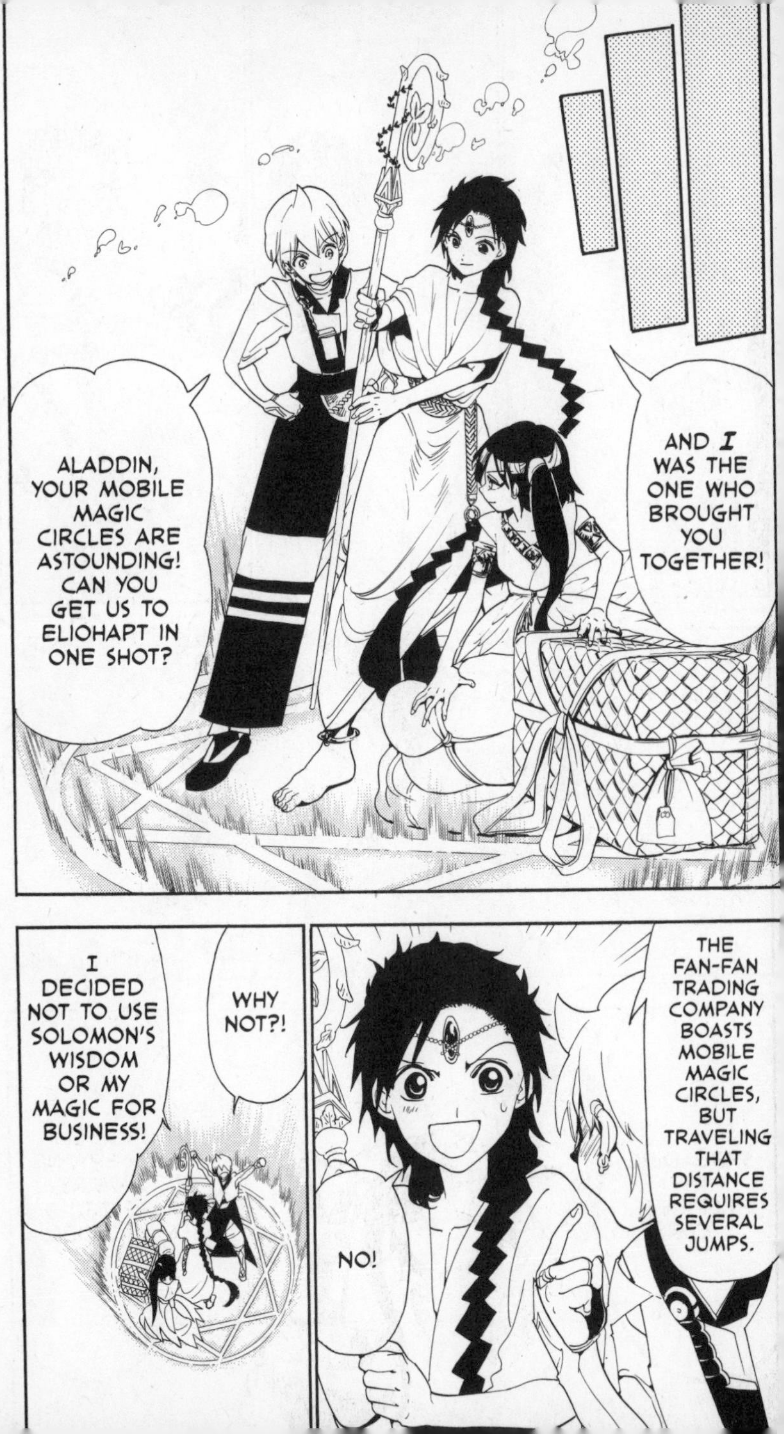
AND I WAS THE ONE WHO BROUGHT YOU TOGETHER!
ALADDIN, YOUR MOBILE MAGIC CIRCLES ARE ASTOUNDING! CAN YOU GET US TO ELIOHAPT IN ONE SHOT?
THE FAN-FAN TRADING COMPANY BOASTS MOBILE MAGIC CIRCLES, BUT TRAVELING THAT DISTANCE REQUIRES SEVERAL JUMPS.
NO!
WHY NOT?!
I DECIDED NOT TO USE SOLOMON'S WISDOM OR MY MAGIC FOR BUSINESS!

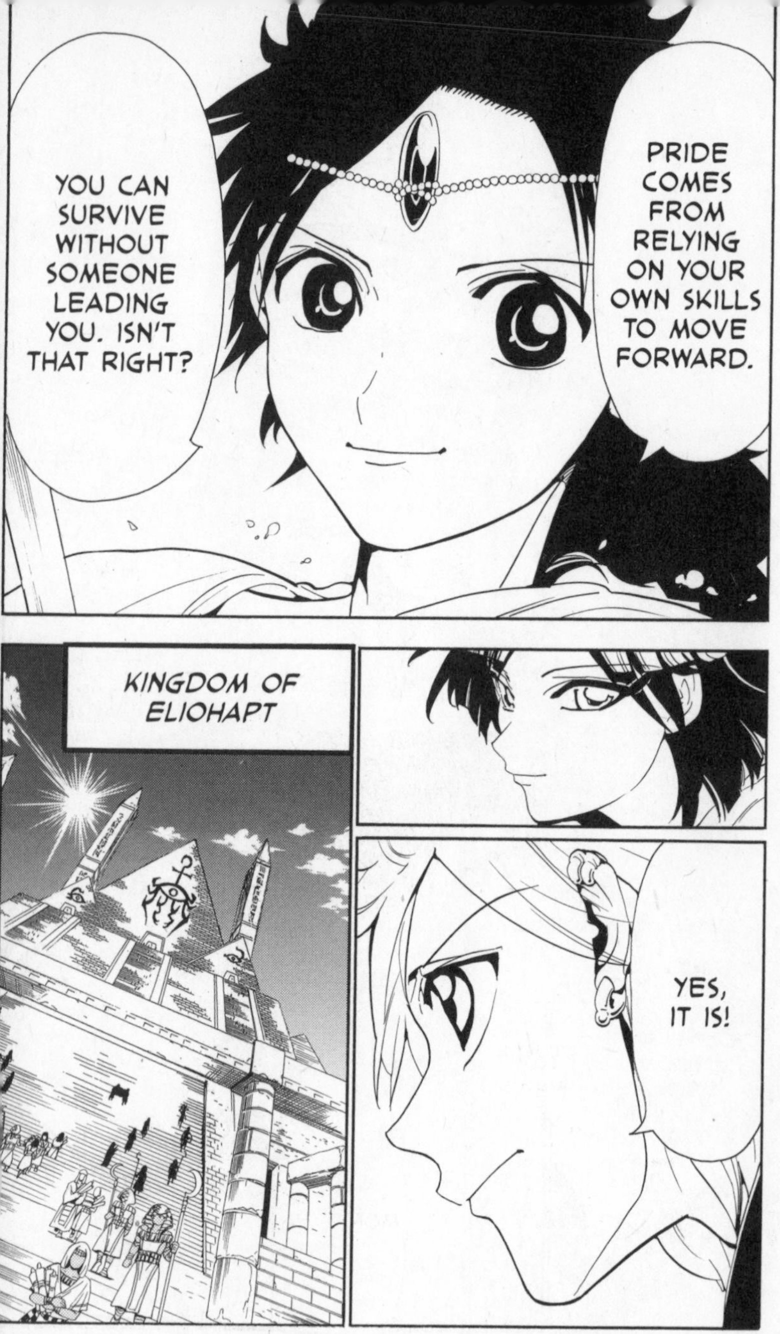
PRIDE COMES FROM RELYING ON YOUR OWN SKILLS TO MOVE FORWARD.
YOU CAN SURVIVE WITHOUT SOMEONE LEADING YOU. ISN'T THAT RIGHT?
YES, IT IS!
KINGDOM OF ELIOHAPT

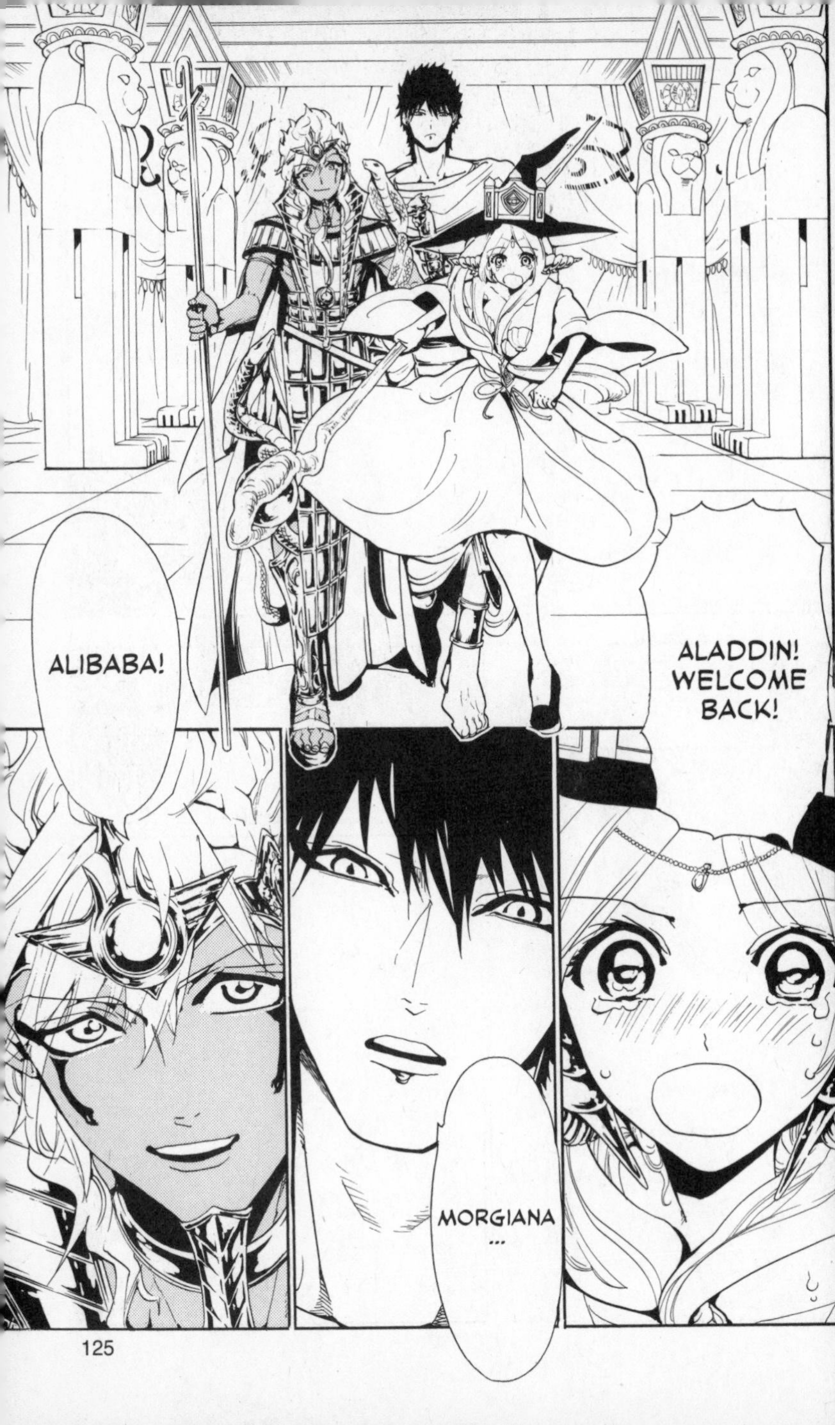
ALADDIN! WELCOME BACK!
ALIBABA!
MORGIANA ...

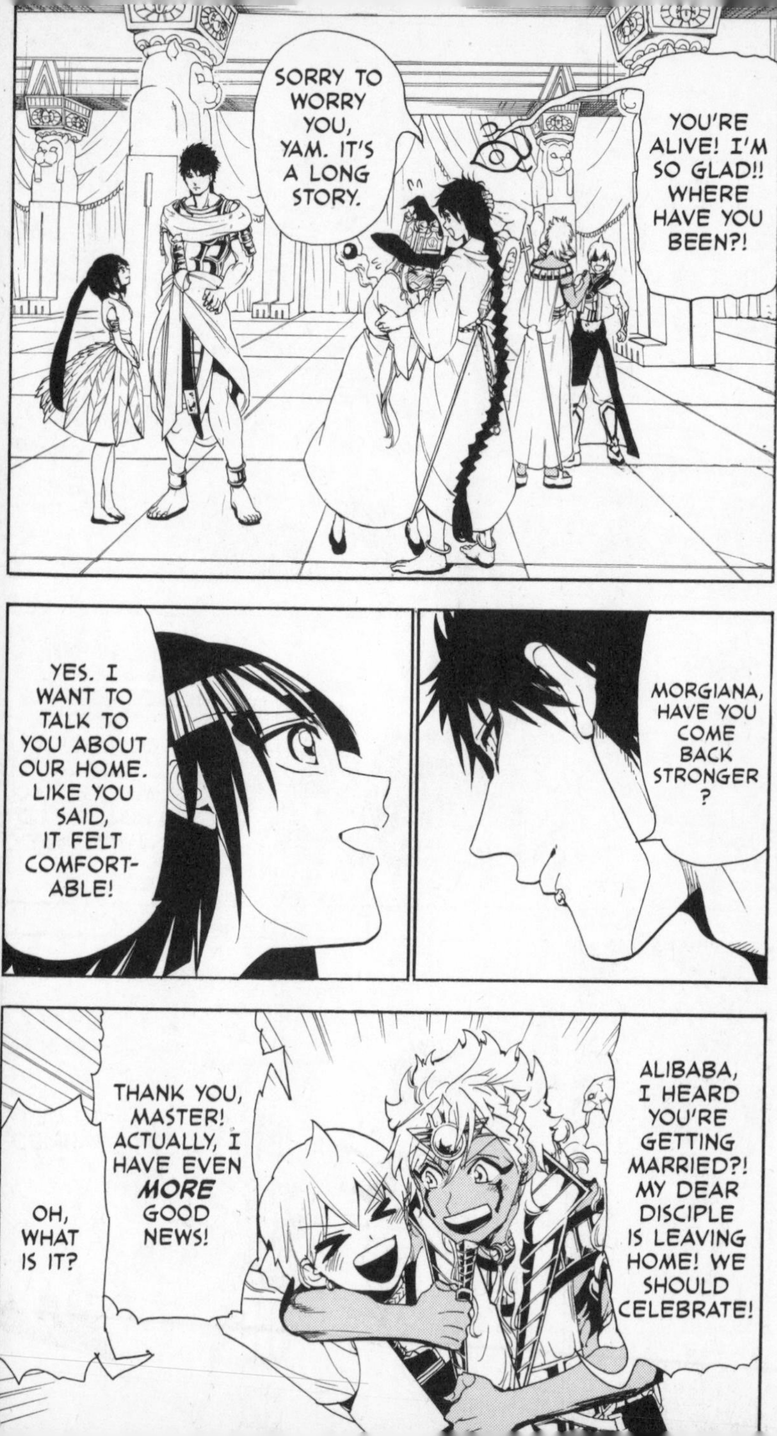
YOU'RE ALIVE! I'M SO GLAD!! WHERE HAVE YOU BEEN?!
SORRY TO WORRY YOU, YAM. IT'S A LONG STORY.
MORGIANA, HAVE YOU COME BACK STRONGER?
YES. I WANT TO TALK TO YOU ABOUT OUR HOME. LIKE YOU SAID, IT FELT COMFORT-ABLE!
ALIBABA, I HEARD YOU'RE GETTING MARRIED?! MY DEAR DISCIPLE IS LEAVING HOME! WE SHOULD CELEBRATE!
THANK YOU, MASTER! ACTUALLY, I HAVE EVEN *MORE* GOOD NEWS!
OH, WHAT IS IT?

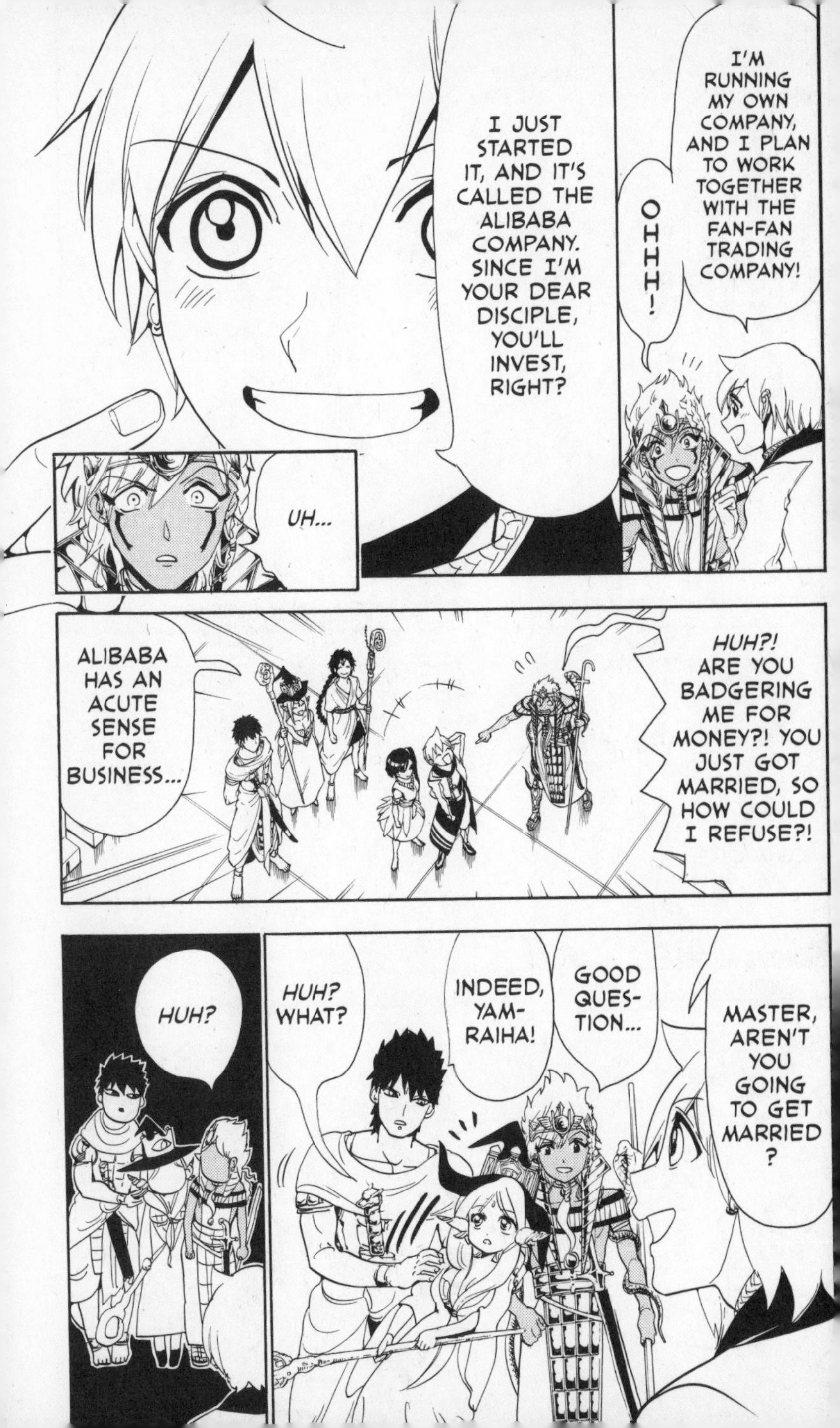
I'M RUNNING MY OWN COMPANY, AND I PLAN TO WORK TOGETHER WITH THE FAN-FAN TRADING COMPANY!
OHHH!
I JUST STARTED IT, AND IT'S CALLED THE ALIBABA COMPANY. SINCE I'M YOUR DEAR DISCIPLE, YOU'LL INVEST, RIGHT?
UH...
HUH?! ARE YOU BADGERING ME FOR MONEY?! YOU JUST GOT MARRIED, SO HOW COULD I REFUSE?!
ALIBABA HAS AN ACUTE SENSE FOR BUSINESS...
MASTER, AREN'T YOU GOING TO GET MARRIED?
GOOD QUES-TION...
INDEED, YAM-RAIHA!
HUH? WHAT?
HUH?

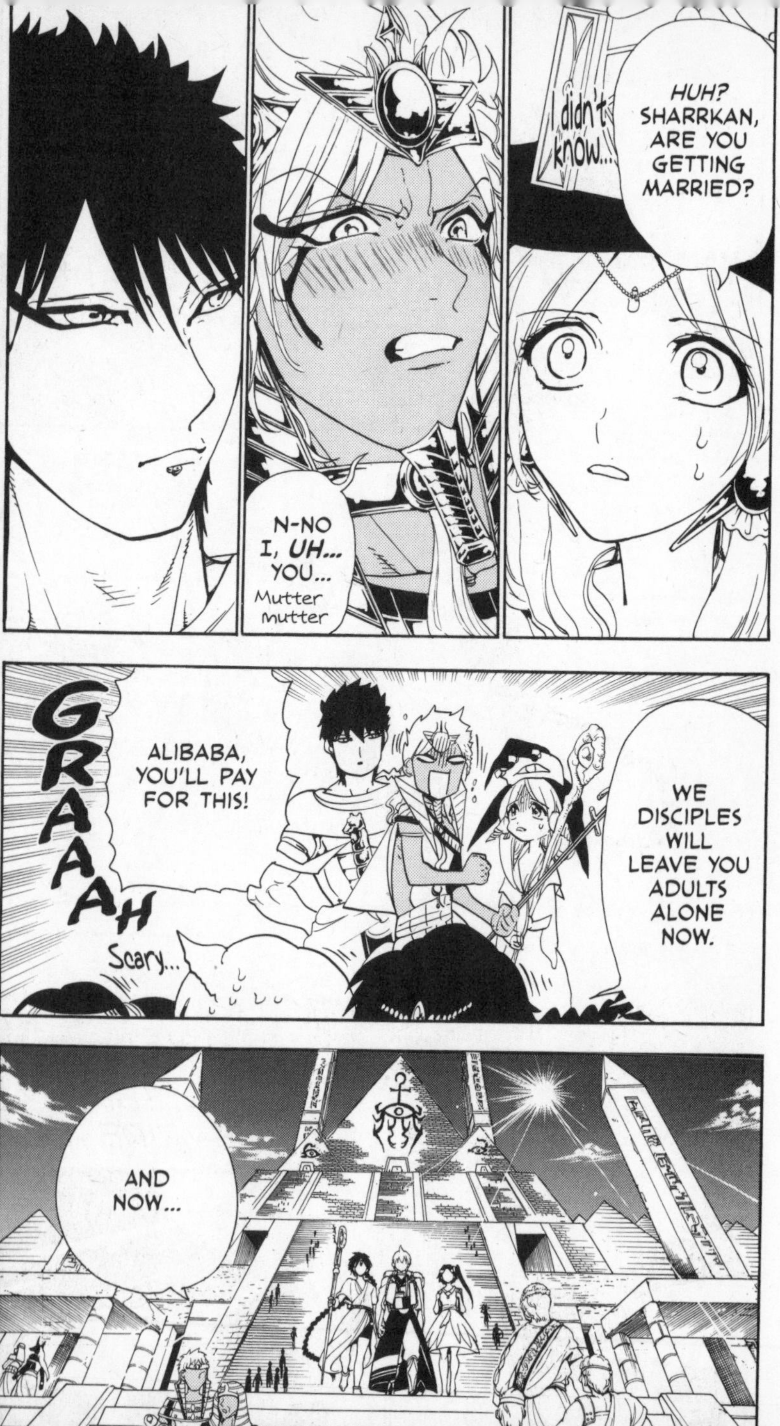
HUH? SHARRKAN, ARE YOU GETTING MARRIED?
I didn't know...!
N-NO I, UH... YOU...
Mutter mutter
WE DISCIPLES WILL LEAVE YOU ADULTS ALONE NOW.
ALIBABA, YOU'LL PAY FOR THIS!
GRAAAH
Scary...
AND NOW...

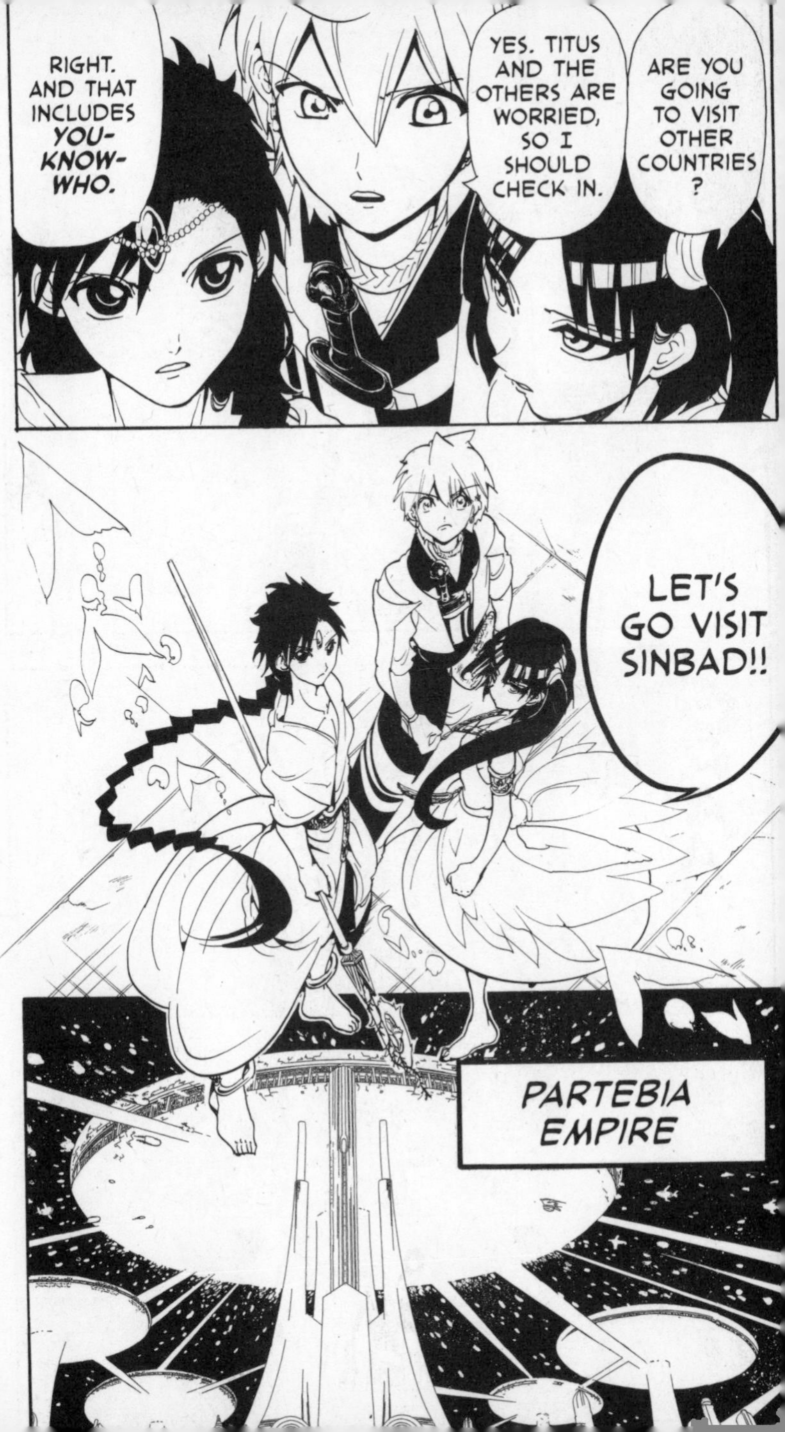
ARE YOU GOING TO VISIT OTHER COUNTRIES?
YES. TITUS AND THE OTHERS ARE WORRIED, SO I SHOULD CHECK IN.
RIGHT. AND THAT INCLUDES *YOU-KNOW-WHO.*
LET'S GO VISIT SINBAD!!
PARTEBIA EMPIRE

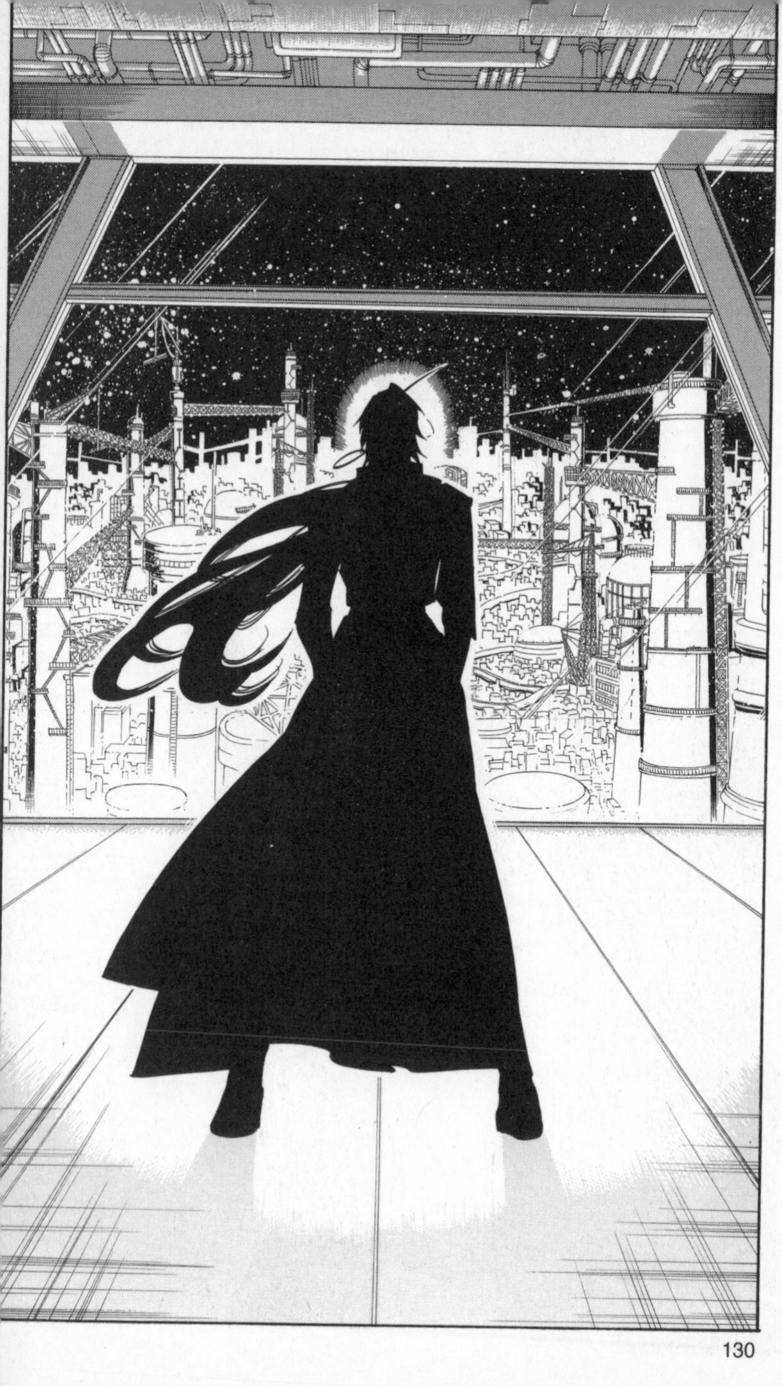

Night 316: David's Whispers

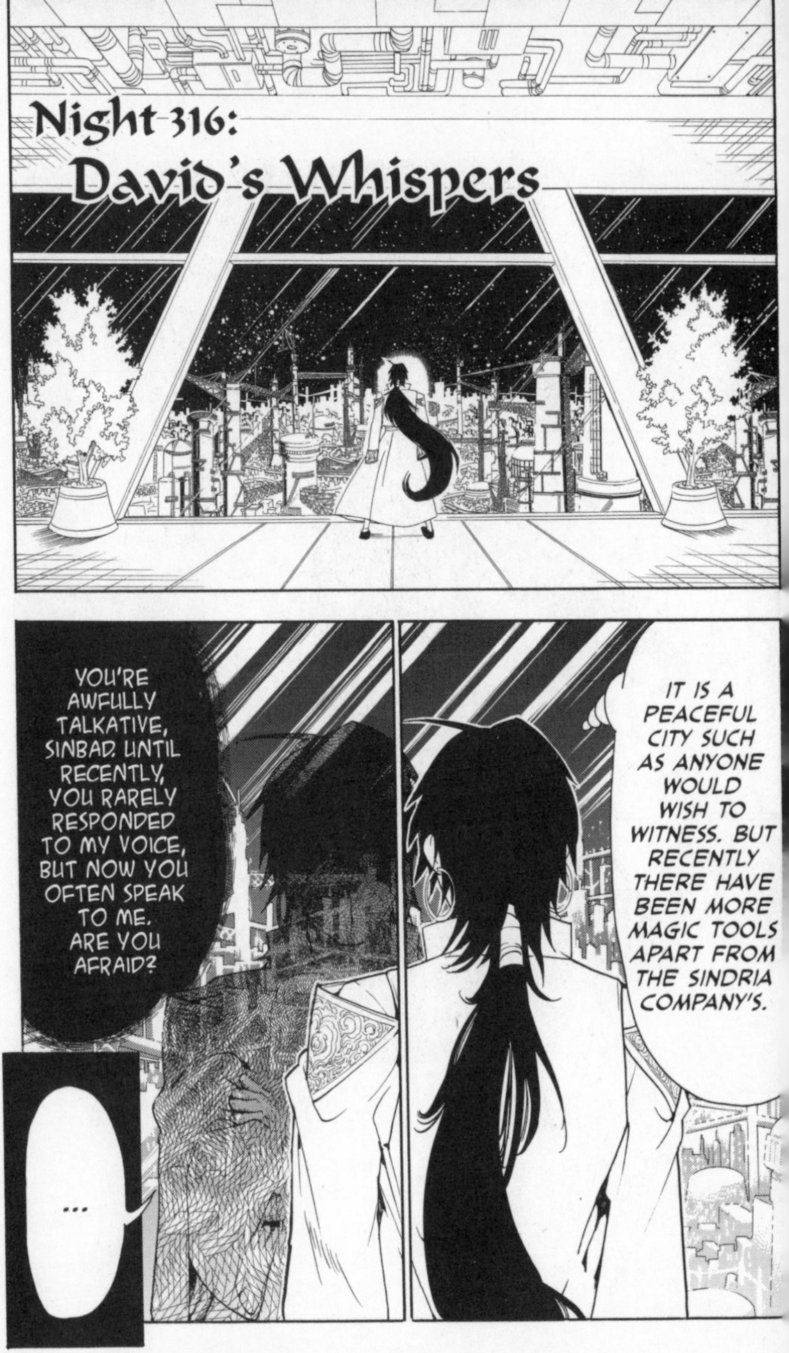
IT IS A PEACEFUL CITY SUCH AS ANYONE WOULD WISH TO WITNESS. BUT RECENTLY THERE HAVE BEEN MORE MAGIC TOOLS APART FROM THE SINDRIA COMPANY'S.
YOU'RE AWFULLY TALKATIVE, SINBAD. UNTIL RECENTLY, YOU RARELY RESPONDED TO MY VOICE, BUT NOW YOU OFTEN SPEAK TO ME. ARE YOU AFRAID?
...

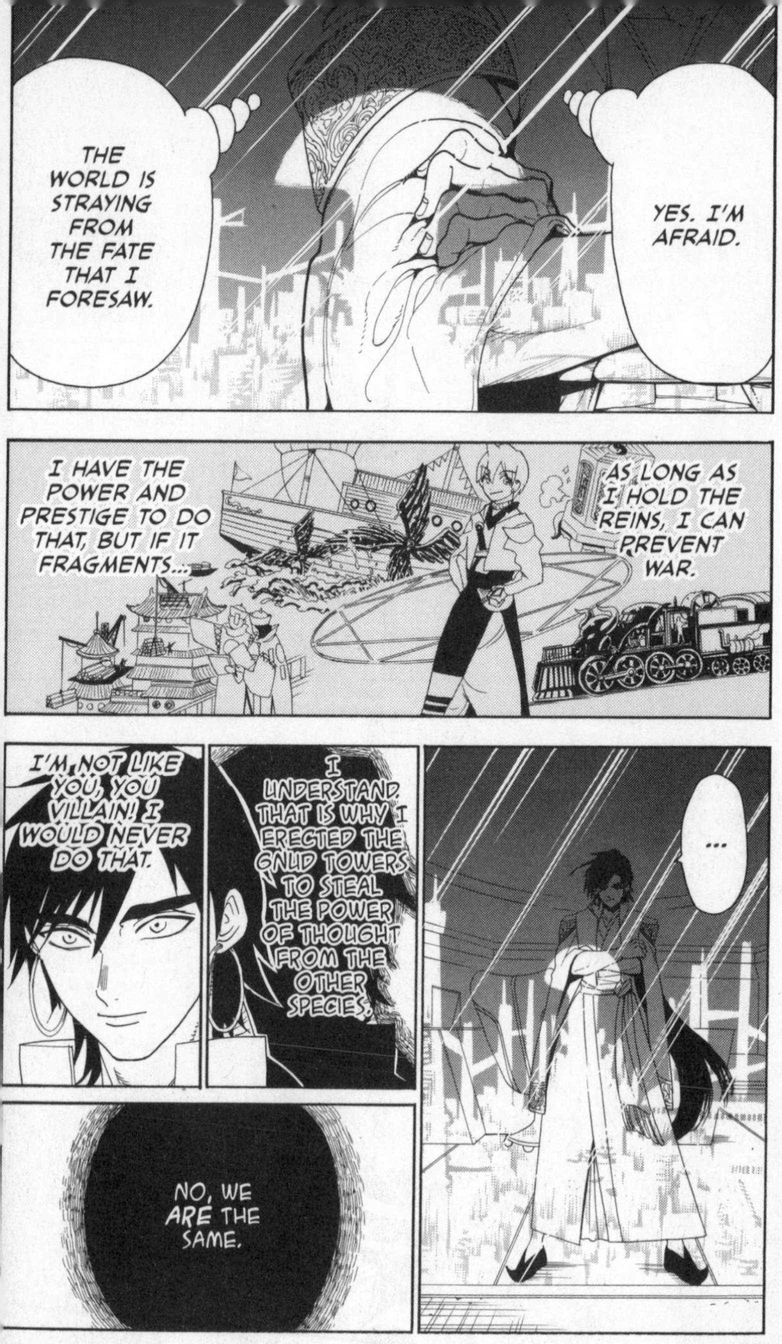
YES. I'M AFRAID.
THE WORLD IS STRAYING FROM THE FATE THAT I FORESAW.
AS LONG AS I HOLD THE REINS, I CAN PREVENT WAR.
I HAVE THE POWER AND PRESTIGE TO DO THAT, BUT IF IT FRAGMENTS...
...
I UNDERSTAND. THAT IS WHY I ERECTED THE GNUD TOWERS TO STEAL THE POWER OF THOUGHT FROM THE OTHER SPECIES.
I'M NOT LIKE YOU, YOU VILLAIN! I WOULD NEVER DO THAT.
NO, WE ARE THE SAME.

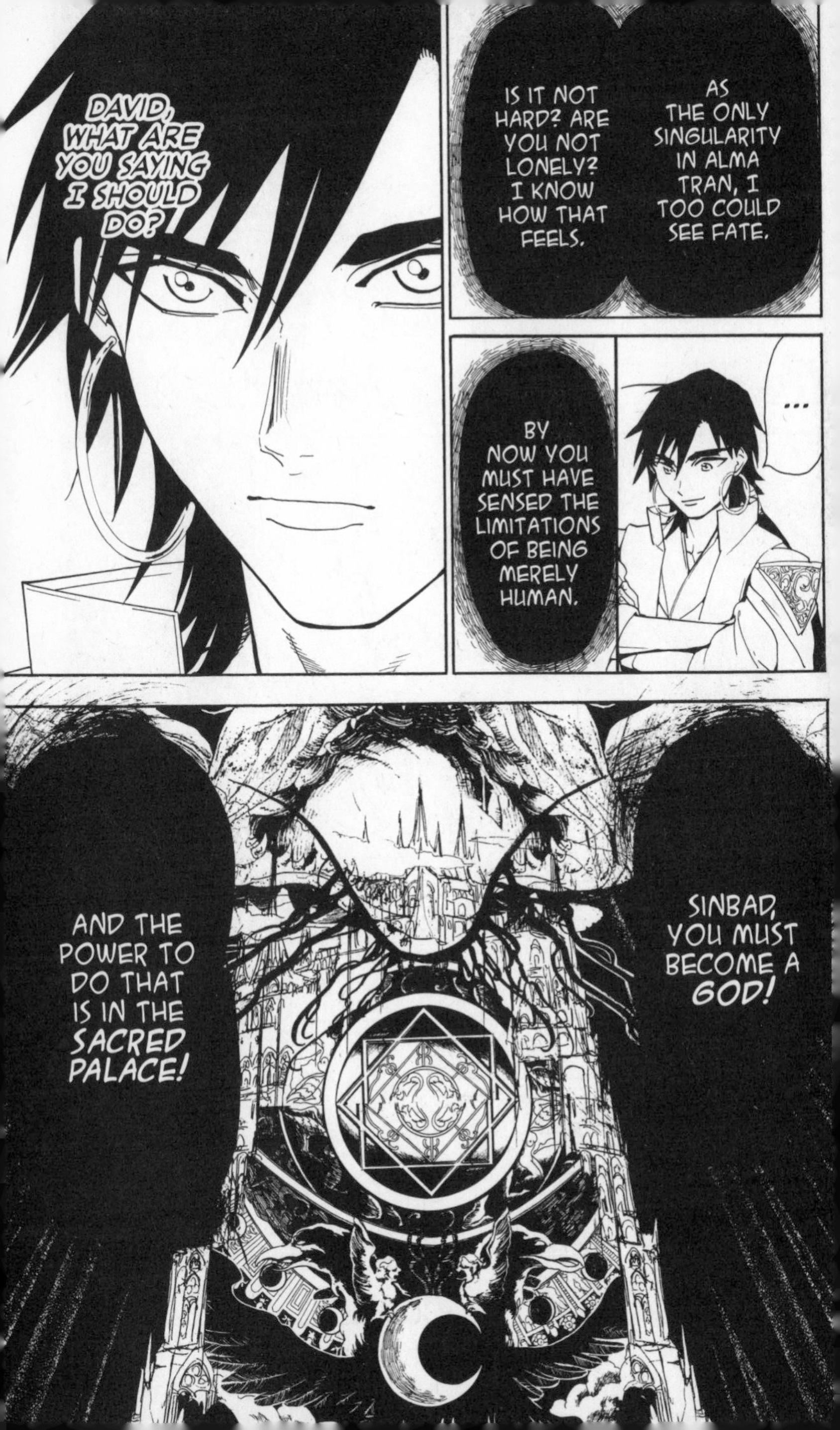
AS THE ONLY SINGULARITY IN ALMA TRAN, I TOO COULD SEE FATE.
IS IT NOT HARD? ARE YOU NOT LONELY? I KNOW HOW THAT FEELS.
...
BY NOW YOU MUST HAVE SENSED THE LIMITATIONS OF BEING MERELY HUMAN.
DAVID, WHAT ARE YOU SAYING I SHOULD DO?
SINBAD, YOU MUST BECOME A GOD!
AND THE POWER TO DO THAT IS IN THE SACRED PALACE!

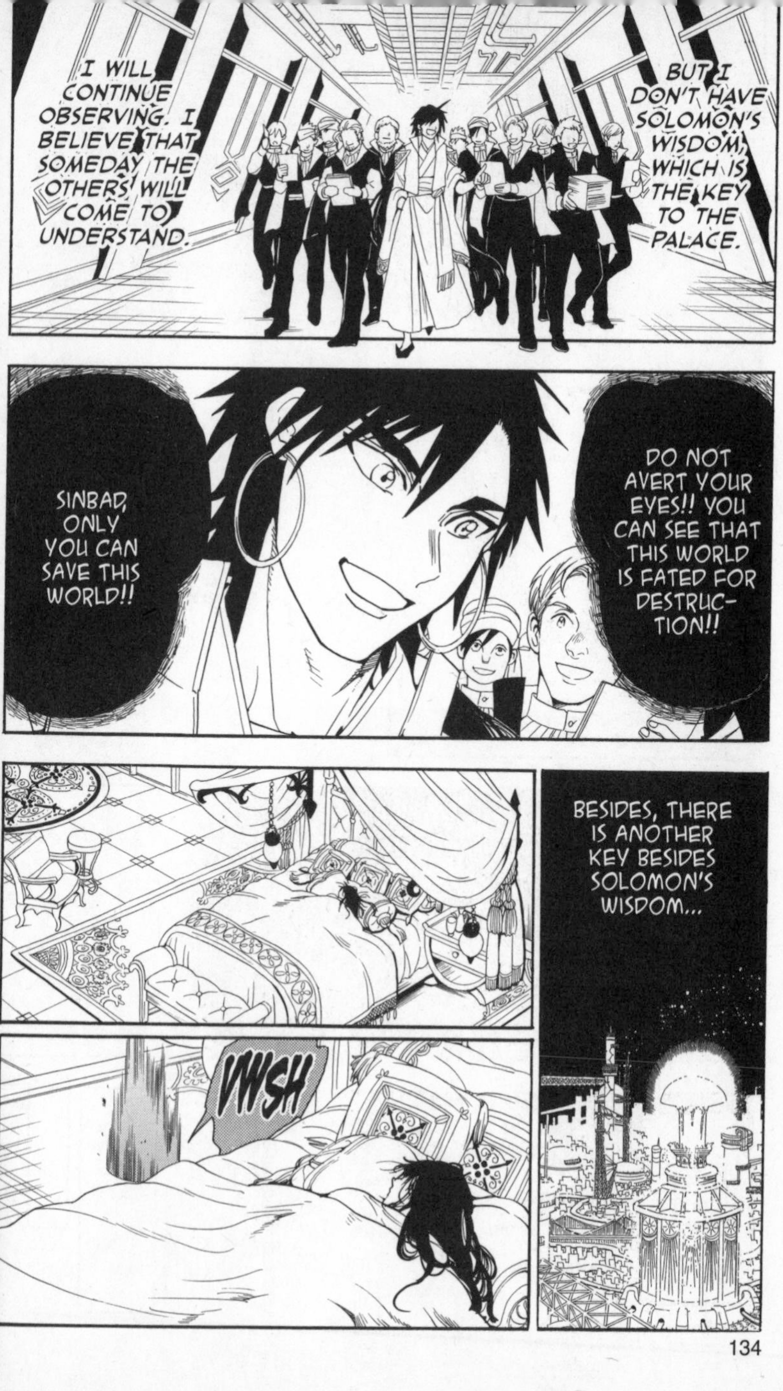
BUT I DON'T HAVE SOLOMON'S WISDOM, WHICH IS THE KEY TO THE PALACE.
I WILL CONTINUE OBSERVING. I BELIEVE THAT SOMEDAY THE OTHERS WILL COME TO UNDERSTAND.
DO NOT AVERT YOUR EYES!! YOU CAN SEE THAT THIS WORLD IS FATED FOR DESTRUC-TION!!
SINBAD, ONLY YOU CAN SAVE THIS WORLD!!
BESIDES, THERE IS ANOTHER KEY BESIDES SOLOMON'S WISDOM...
VWSH

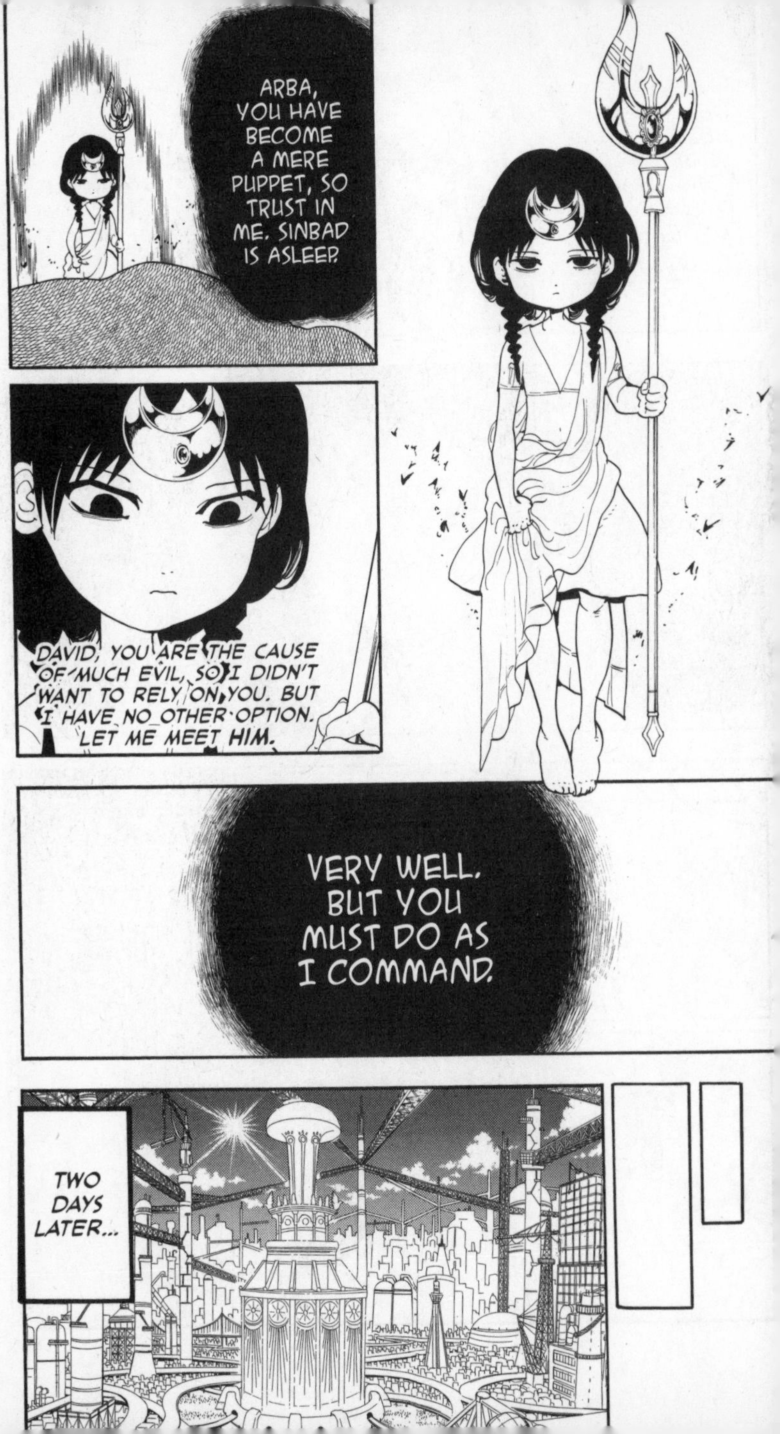
ARBA, YOU HAVE BECOME A MERE PUPPET, SO TRUST IN ME. SINBAD IS ASLEEP.
DAVID, YOU ARE THE CAUSE OF MUCH EVIL, SO I DIDN'T WANT TO RELY ON YOU. BUT I HAVE NO OTHER OPTION. LET ME MEET HIM.
VERY WELL. BUT YOU MUST DO AS I COMMAND.
TWO DAYS LATER...

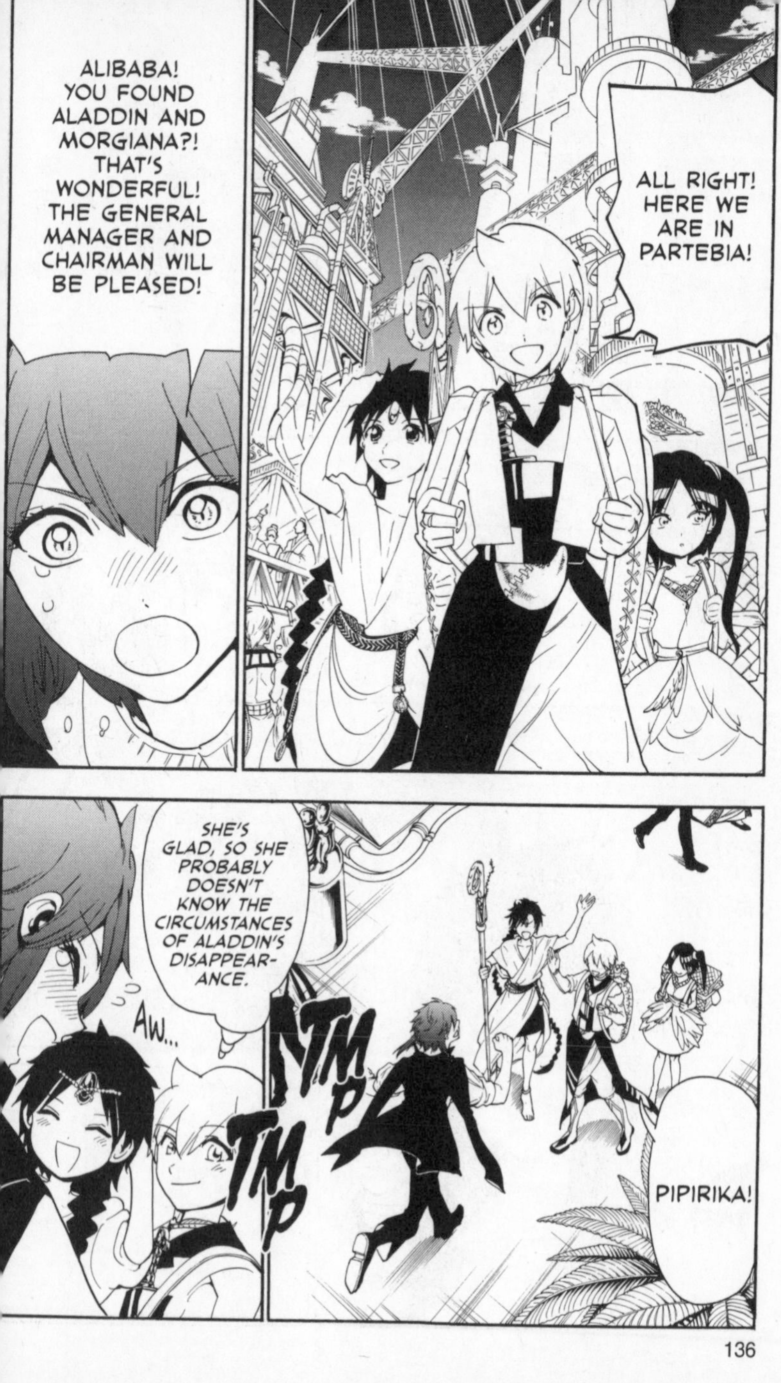
ALL RIGHT! HERE WE ARE IN PARTEBIA!
ALIBABA! YOU FOUND ALADDIN AND MORGIANA?! THAT'S WONDERFUL! THE GENERAL MANAGER AND CHAIRMAN WILL BE PLEASED!
PIPIRIKA!
TMP TMP
SHE'S GLAD, SO SHE PROBABLY DOESN'T KNOW THE CIRCUMSTANCES OF ALADDIN'S DISAPPEARANCE.
AW...

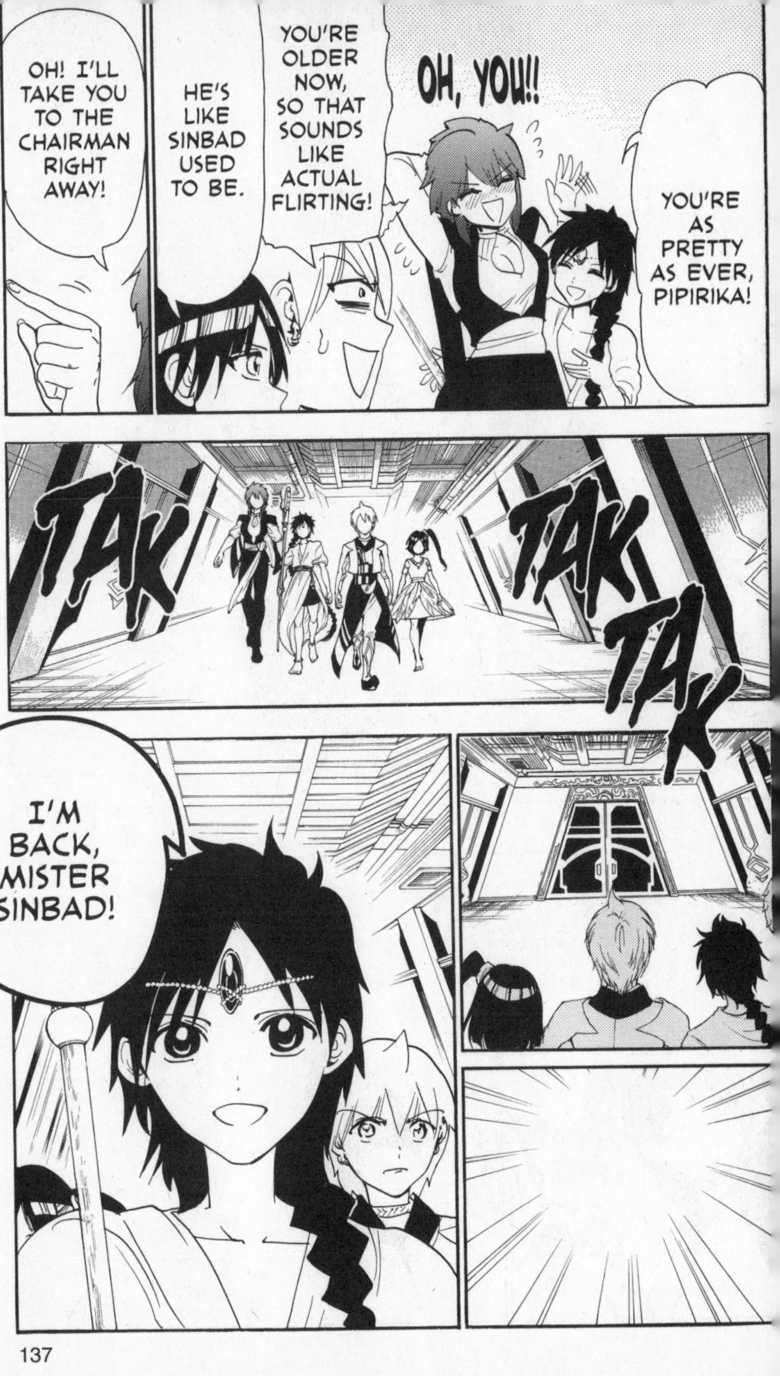
YOU'RE AS PRETTY AS EVER, PIPIRIKA!
OH, YOU!!
YOU'RE OLDER NOW, SO THAT SOUNDS LIKE ACTUAL FLIRTING!
HE'S LIKE SINBAD USED TO BE.
OH! I'LL TAKE YOU TO THE CHAIRMAN RIGHT AWAY!
TAK
TAK
TAK
TAK
I'M BACK, MISTER SINBAD!

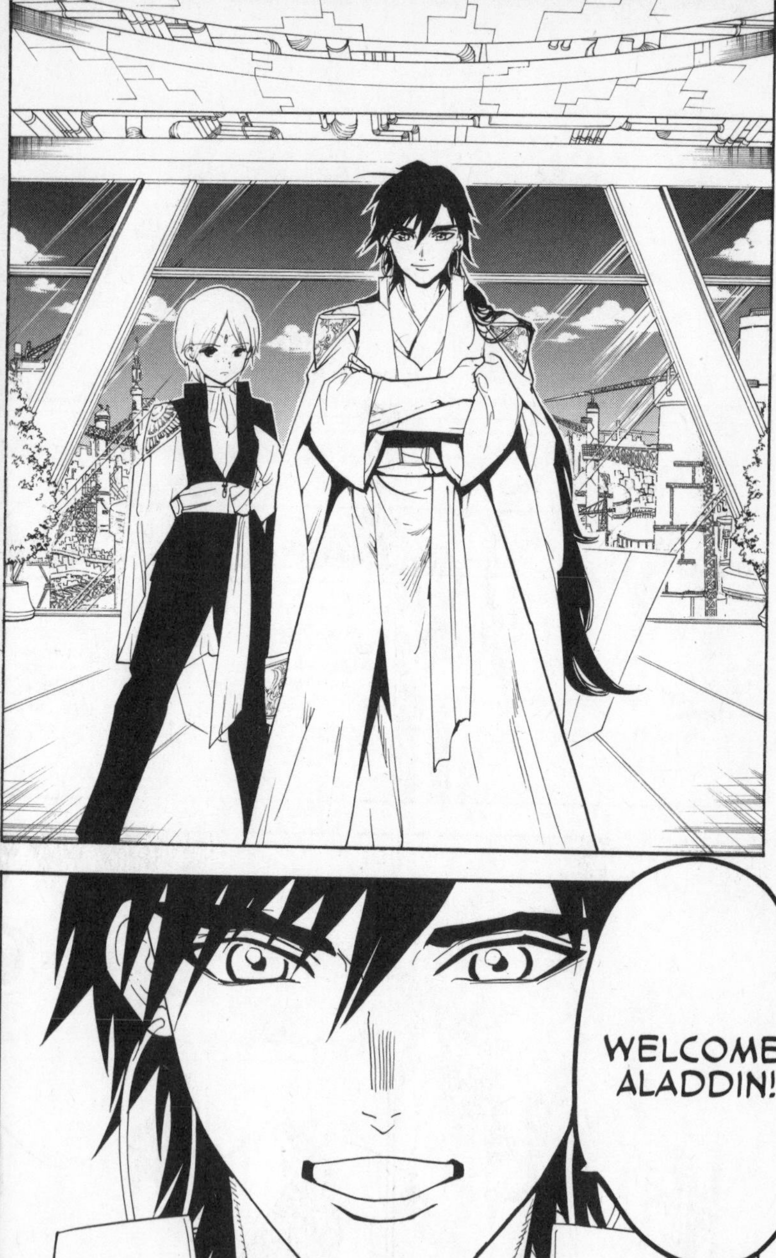
WELCOME, ALADDIN!

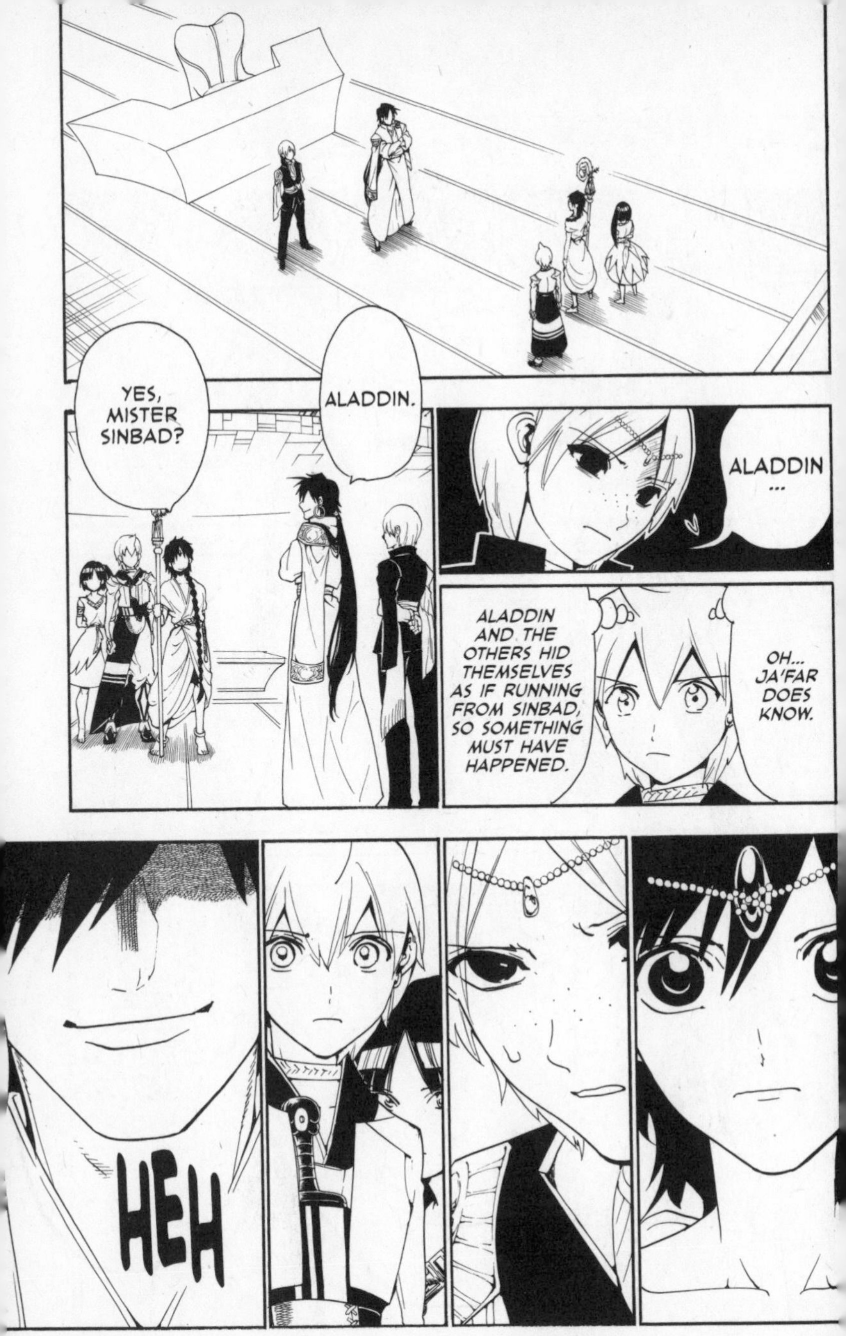
ALADDIN ...
OH... JA'FAR DOES KNOW.
ALADDIN AND THE OTHERS HID THEMSELVES AS IF RUNNING FROM SINBAD, SO SOMETHING MUST HAVE HAPPENED.
ALADDIN.
YES, MISTER SINBAD?
HEH

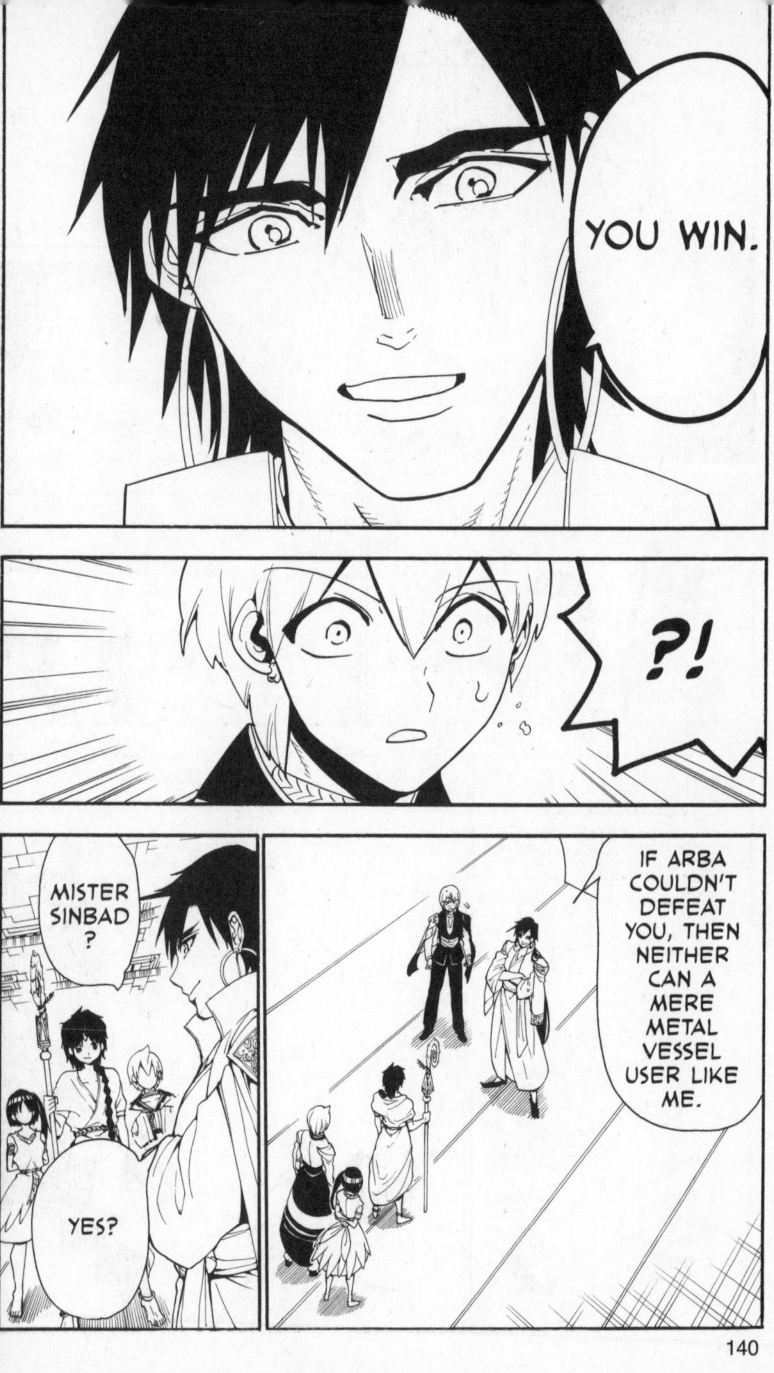
YOU WIN.
?!
IF ARBA COULDN'T DEFEAT YOU, THEN NEITHER CAN A MERE METAL VESSEL USER LIKE ME.
MISTER SINBAD?
YES?

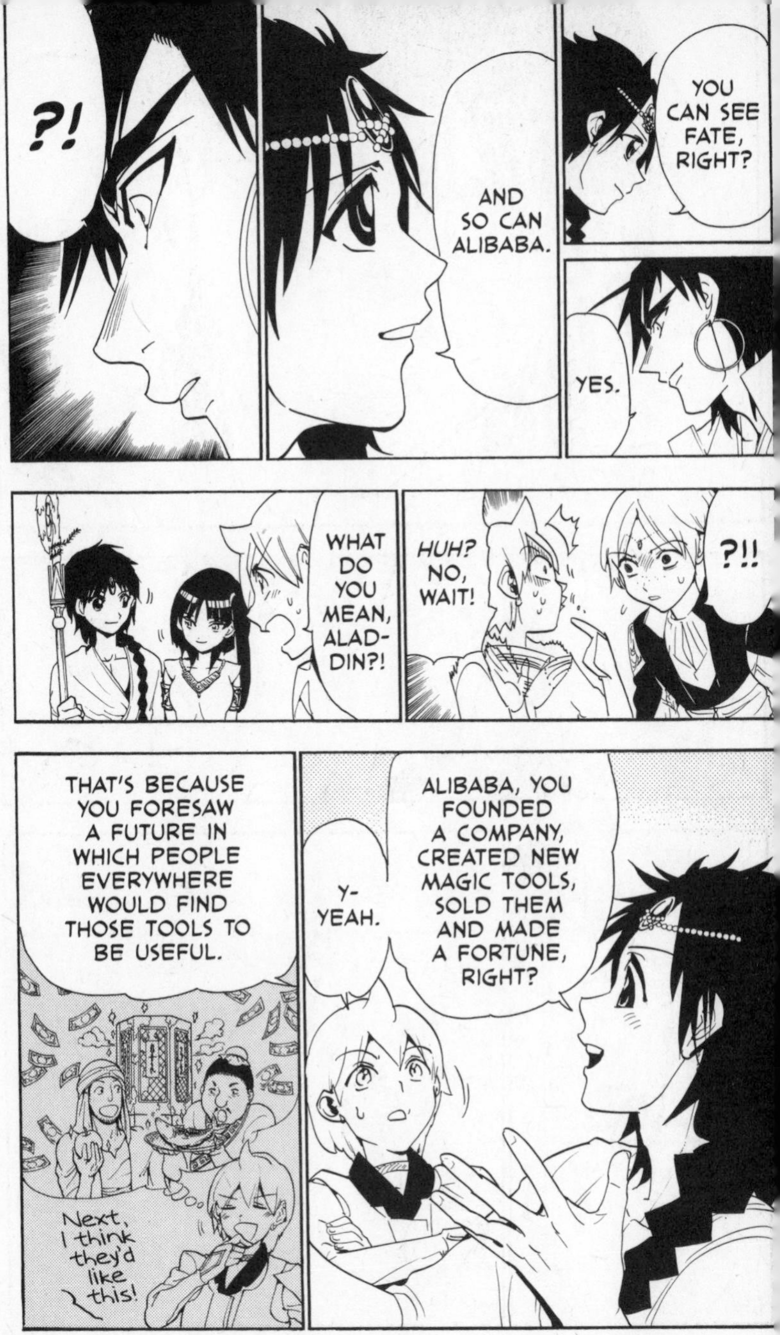
YOU CAN SEE FATE, RIGHT?
YES.
AND SO CAN ALIBABA.
?!
?!!
HUH? NO, WAIT!
WHAT DO YOU MEAN, ALAD-DIN?!
ALIBABA, YOU FOUNDED A COMPANY, CREATED NEW MAGIC TOOLS, SOLD THEM AND MADE A FORTUNE, RIGHT?
Y-YEAH.
THAT'S BECAUSE YOU FORESAW A FUTURE IN WHICH PEOPLE EVERYWHERE WOULD FIND THOSE TOOLS TO BE USEFUL.
Next, I think they'd like this!

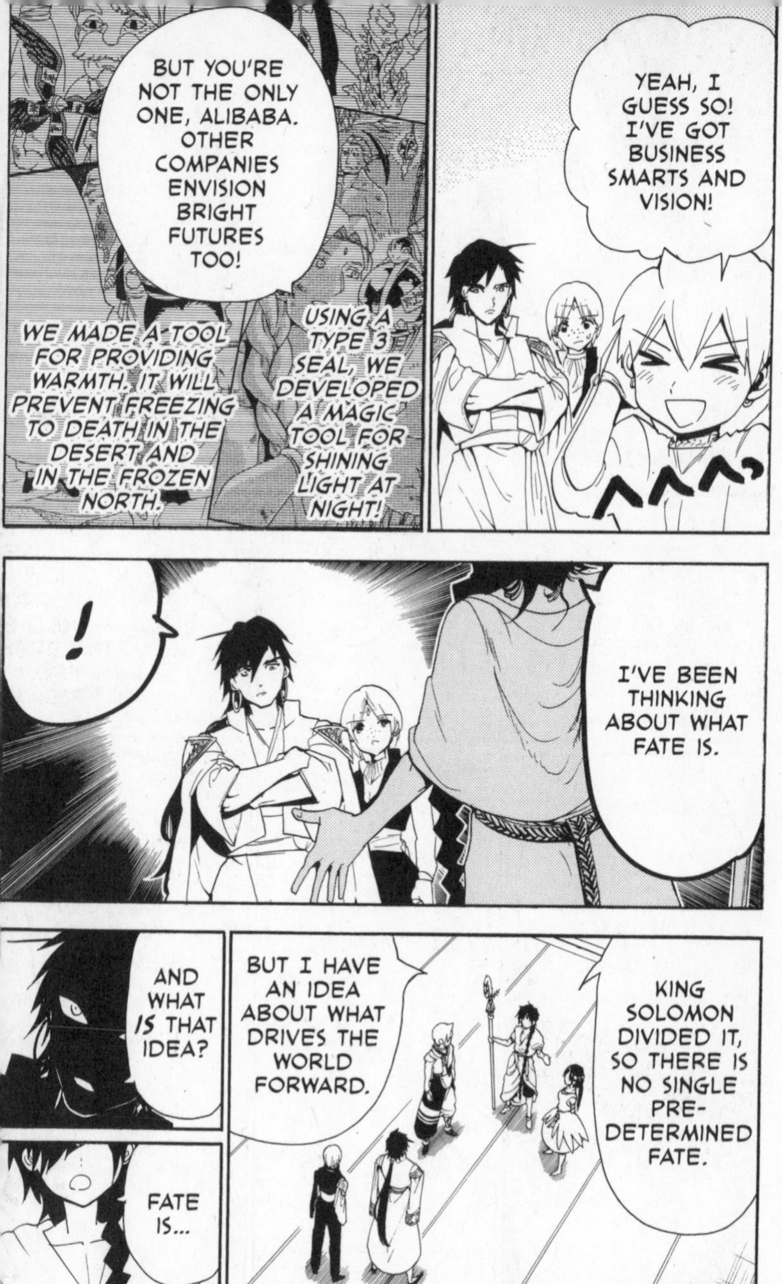
YEAH, I GUESS SO! I'VE GOT BUSINESS SMARTS AND VISION!
BUT YOU'RE NOT THE ONLY ONE, ALIBABA. OTHER COMPANIES ENVISION BRIGHT FUTURES TOO!
USING A TYPE 3 SEAL, WE DEVELOPED A MAGIC TOOL FOR SHINING LIGHT AT NIGHT!
WE MADE A TOOL FOR PROVIDING WARMTH. IT WILL PREVENT FREEZING TO DEATH IN THE DESERT AND IN THE FROZEN NORTH.
I'VE BEEN THINKING ABOUT WHAT FATE IS.
!
KING SOLOMON DIVIDED IT, SO THERE IS NO SINGLE PRE-DETERMINED FATE.
BUT I HAVE AN IDEA ABOUT WHAT DRIVES THE WORLD FORWARD.
AND WHAT *IS* THAT IDEA?
FATE IS...

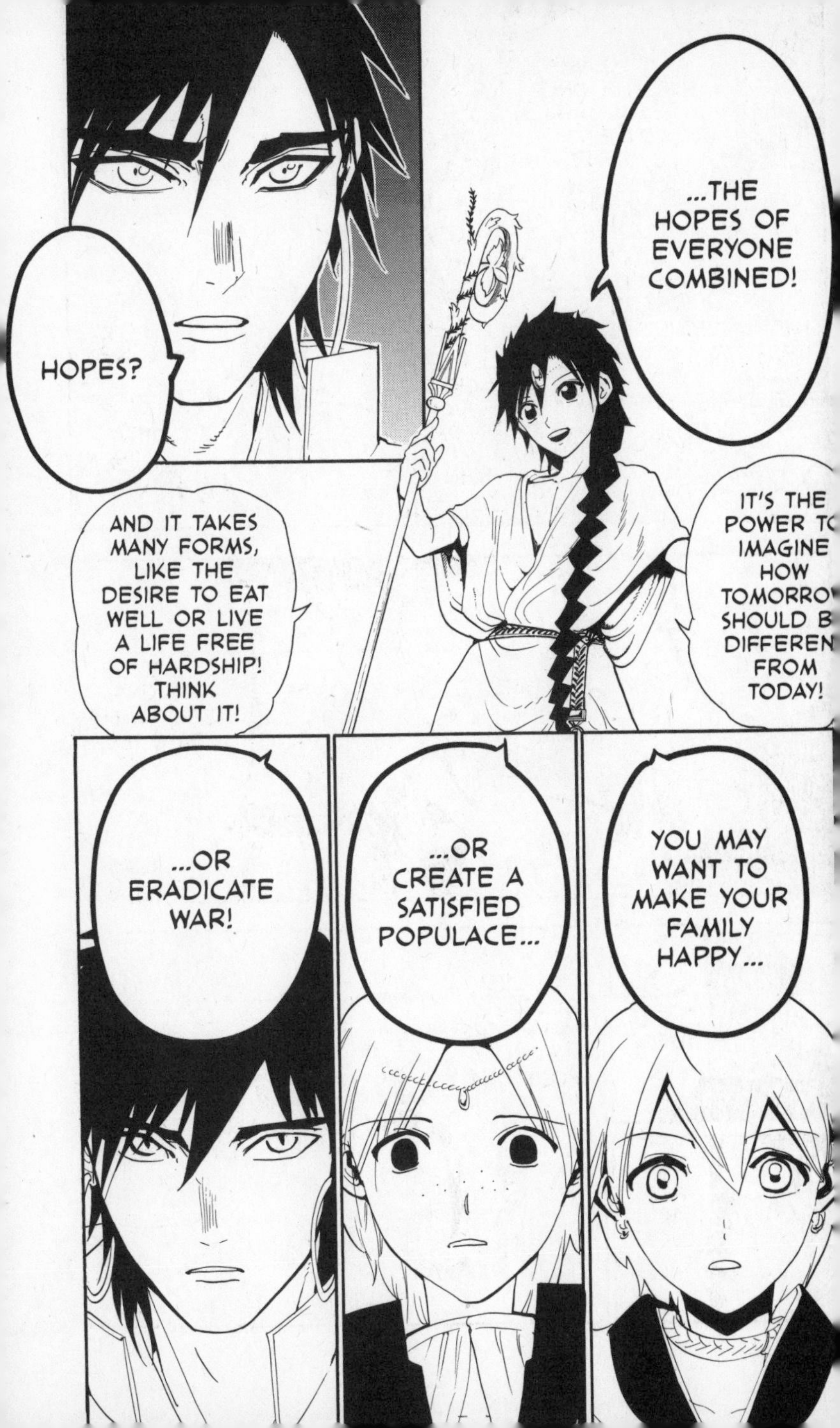
...THE HOPES OF EVERYONE COMBINED!
HOPES?
IT'S THE POWER T IMAGINE HOW TOMORRO SHOULD B DIFFEREN FROM TODAY!
AND IT TAKES MANY FORMS, LIKE THE DESIRE TO EAT WELL OR LIVE A LIFE FREE OF HARDSHIP! THINK ABOUT IT!
YOU MAY WANT TO MAKE YOUR FAMILY HAPPY...
...OR CREATE A SATISFIED POPULACE...
...OR ERADICATE WAR!

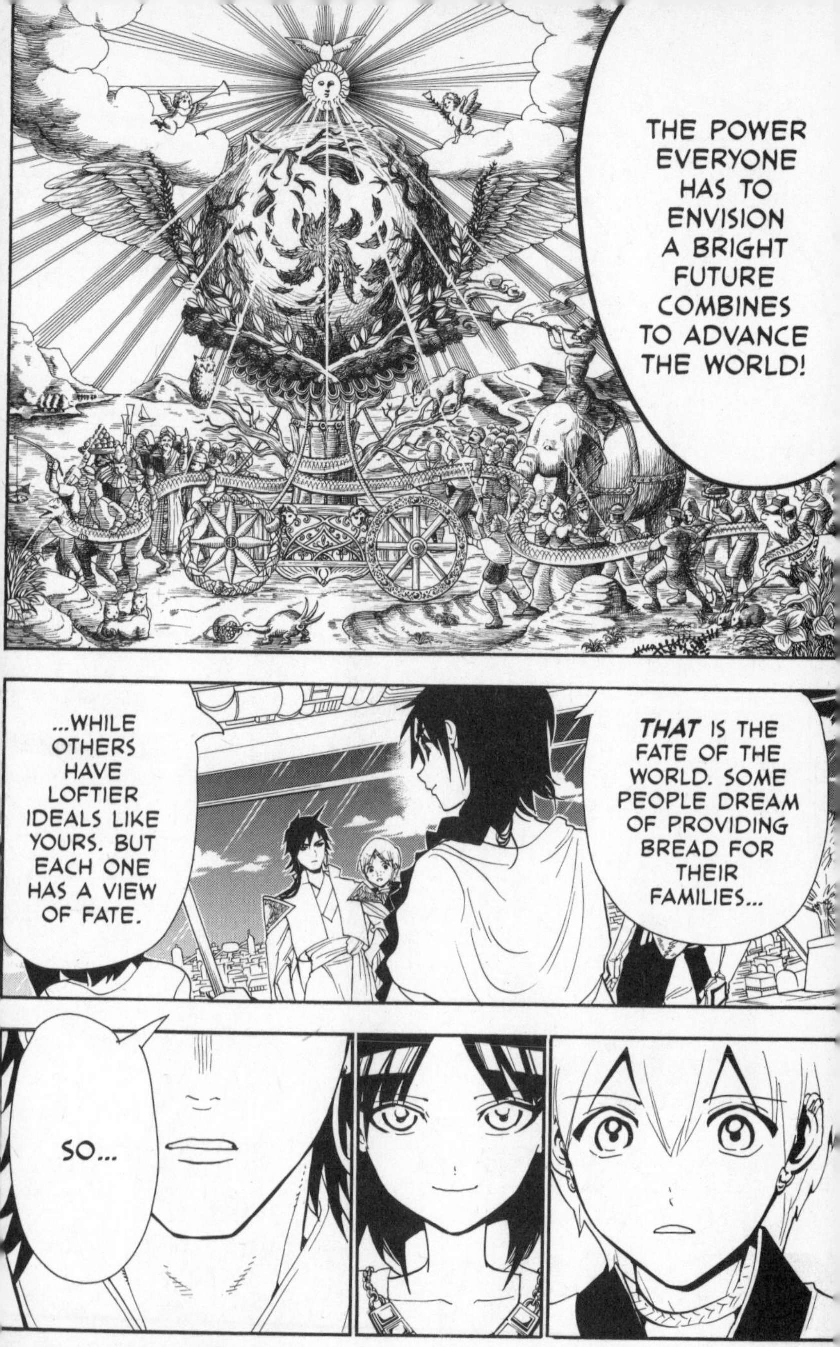
THE POWER EVERYONE HAS TO ENVISION A BRIGHT FUTURE COMBINES TO ADVANCE THE WORLD!
THAT IS THE FATE OF THE WORLD. SOME PEOPLE DREAM OF PROVIDING BREAD FOR THEIR FAMILIES...
...WHILE OTHERS HAVE LOFTIER IDEALS LIKE YOURS. BUT EACH ONE HAS A VIEW OF FATE.
SO...

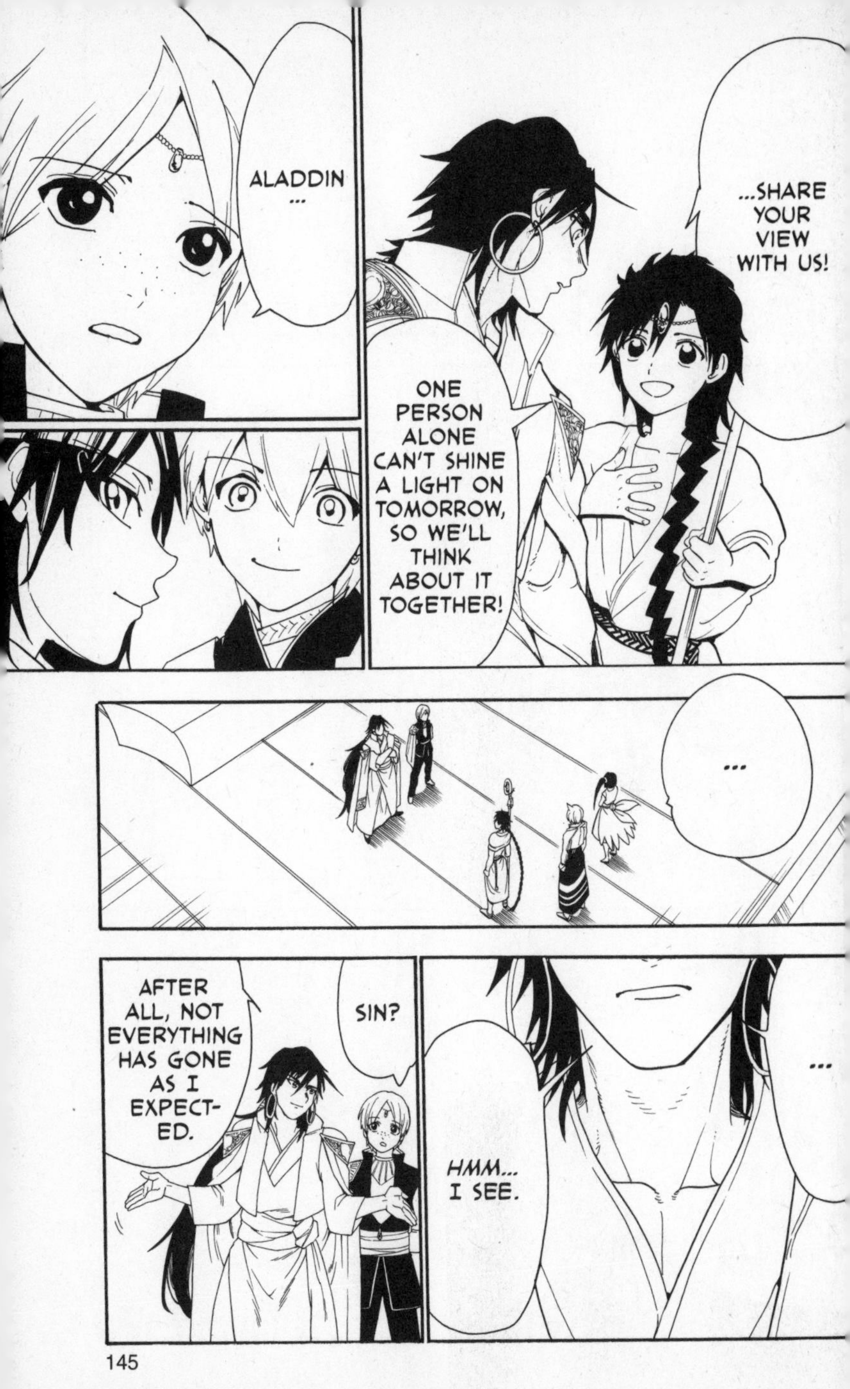
...SHARE YOUR VIEW WITH US!
ONE PERSON ALONE CAN'T SHINE A LIGHT ON TOMORROW, SO WE'LL THINK ABOUT IT TOGETHER!
ALADDIN ...
...
...
HMM... I SEE.
SIN?
AFTER ALL, NOT EVERYTHING HAS GONE AS I EXPECT-ED.

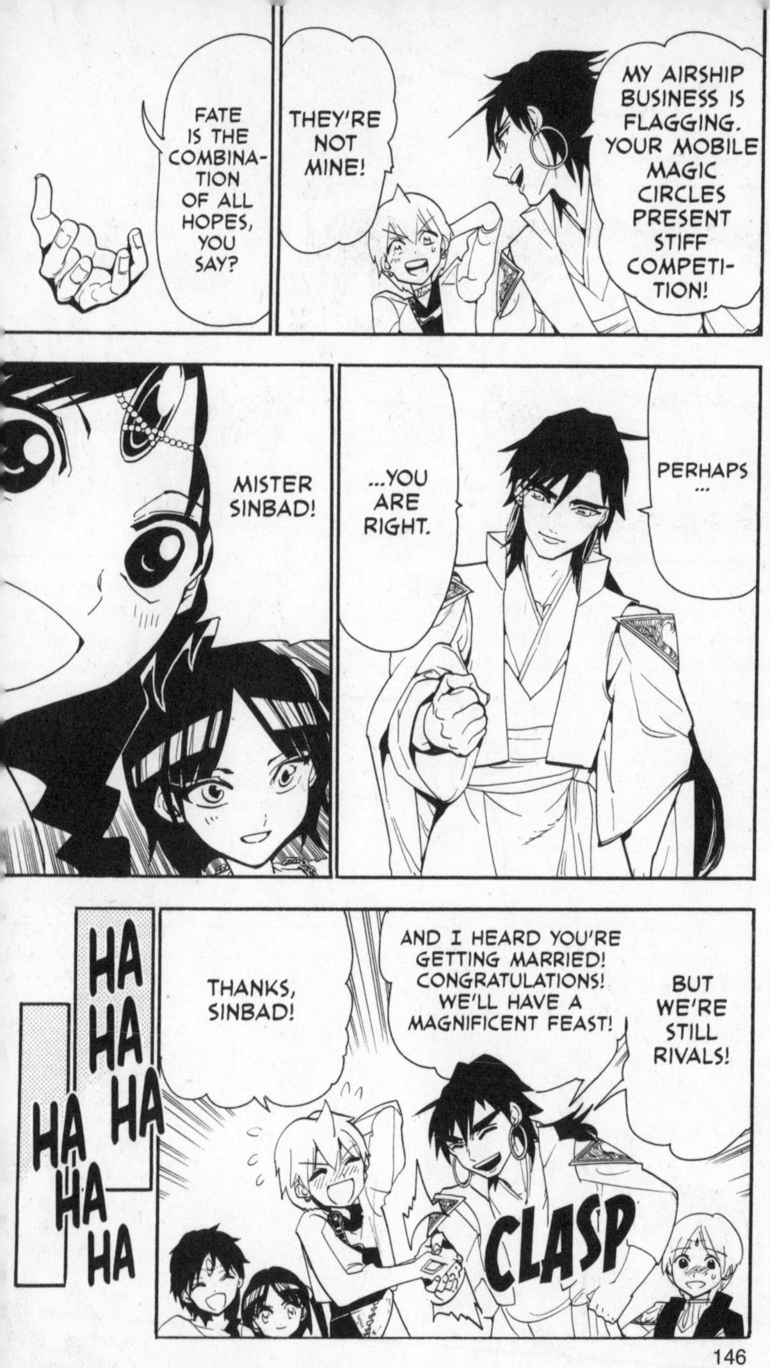
MY AIRSHIP BUSINESS IS FLAGGING. YOUR MOBILE MAGIC CIRCLES PRESENT STIFF COMPETITION!
THEY'RE NOT MINE!
FATE IS THE COMBINATION OF ALL HOPES, YOU SAY?
PERHAPS...
...YOU ARE RIGHT.
MISTER SINBAD!
BUT WE'RE STILL RIVALS!
AND I HEARD YOU'RE GETTING MARRIED! CONGRATULATIONS! WE'LL HAVE A MAGNIFICENT FEAST!
CLASP
THANKS, SINBAD!
HA HA HA
HA HA HA

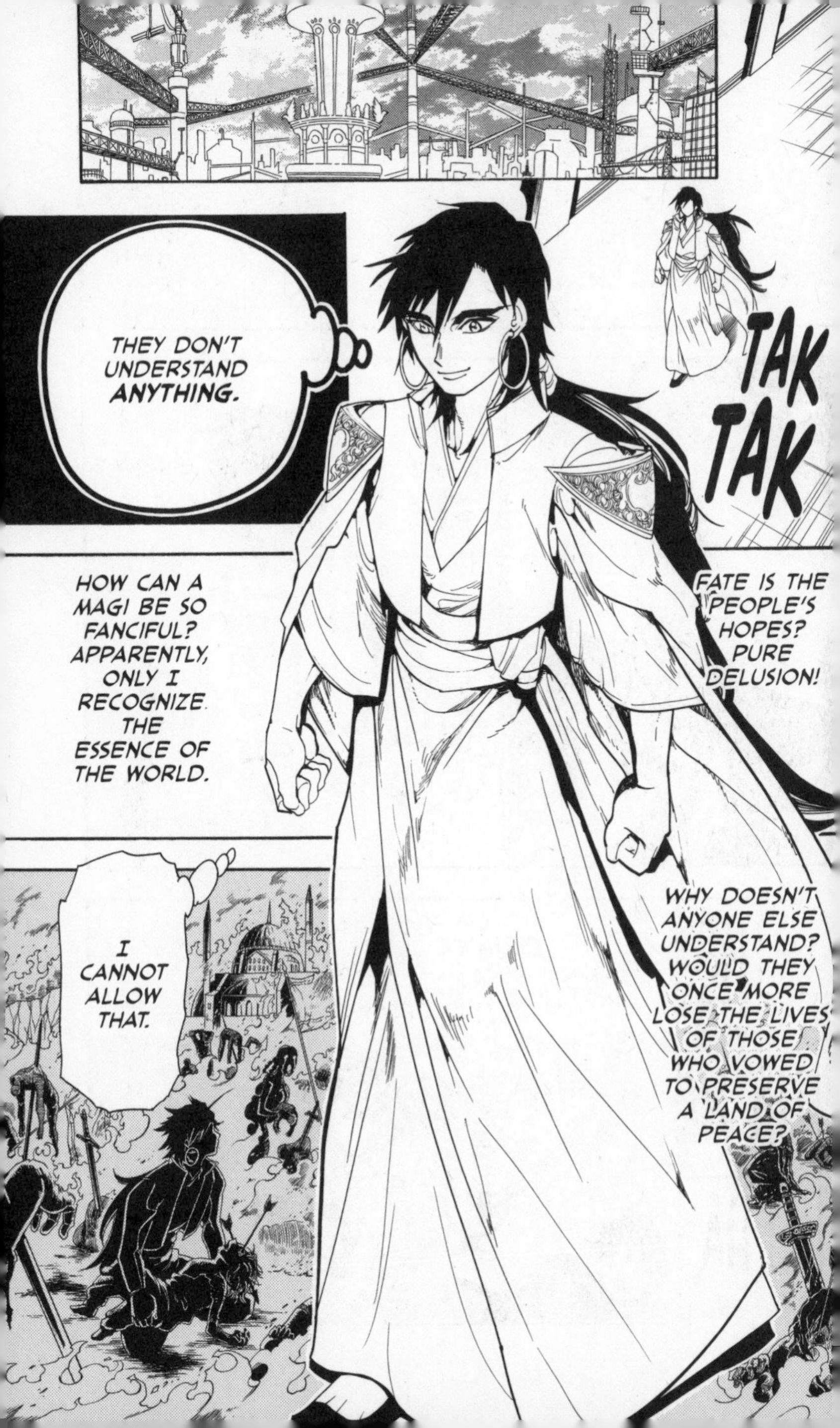

TAK TAK
FATE IS THE PEOPLE'S HOPES? PURE DELUSION!
WHY DOESN'T ANYONE ELSE UNDERSTAND? WOULD THEY ONCE MORE LOSE THE LIVES OF THOSE WHO VOWED TO PRESERVE A LAND OF PEACE?
THEY DON'T UNDERSTAND **ANYTHING.**
HOW CAN A MAGI BE SO FANCIFUL? APPARENTLY, ONLY I RECOGNIZE THE ESSENCE OF THE WORLD.
I CANNOT ALLOW THAT.

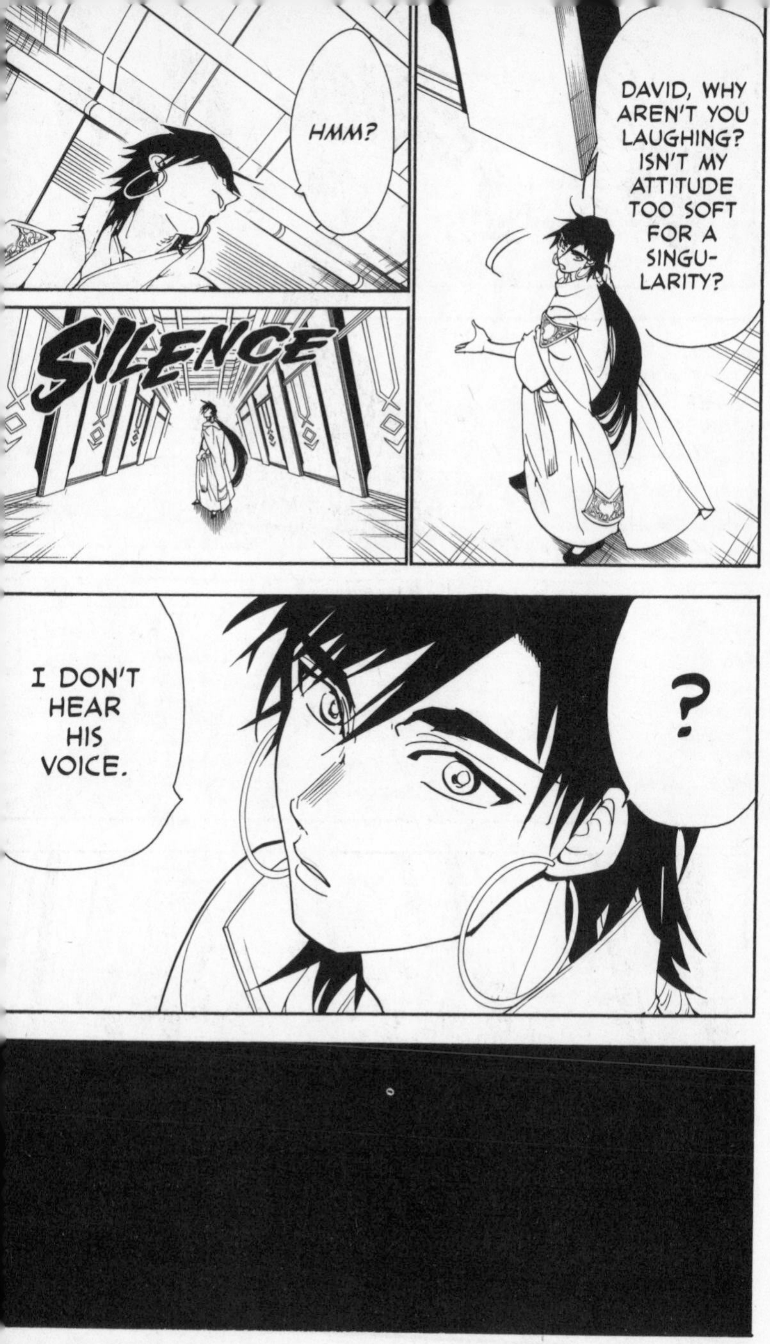
DAVID, WHY AREN'T YOU LAUGHING? ISN'T MY ATTITUDE TOO SOFT FOR A SINGU-LARITY?
HMM?
SILENCE
?
I DON'T HEAR HIS VOICE.

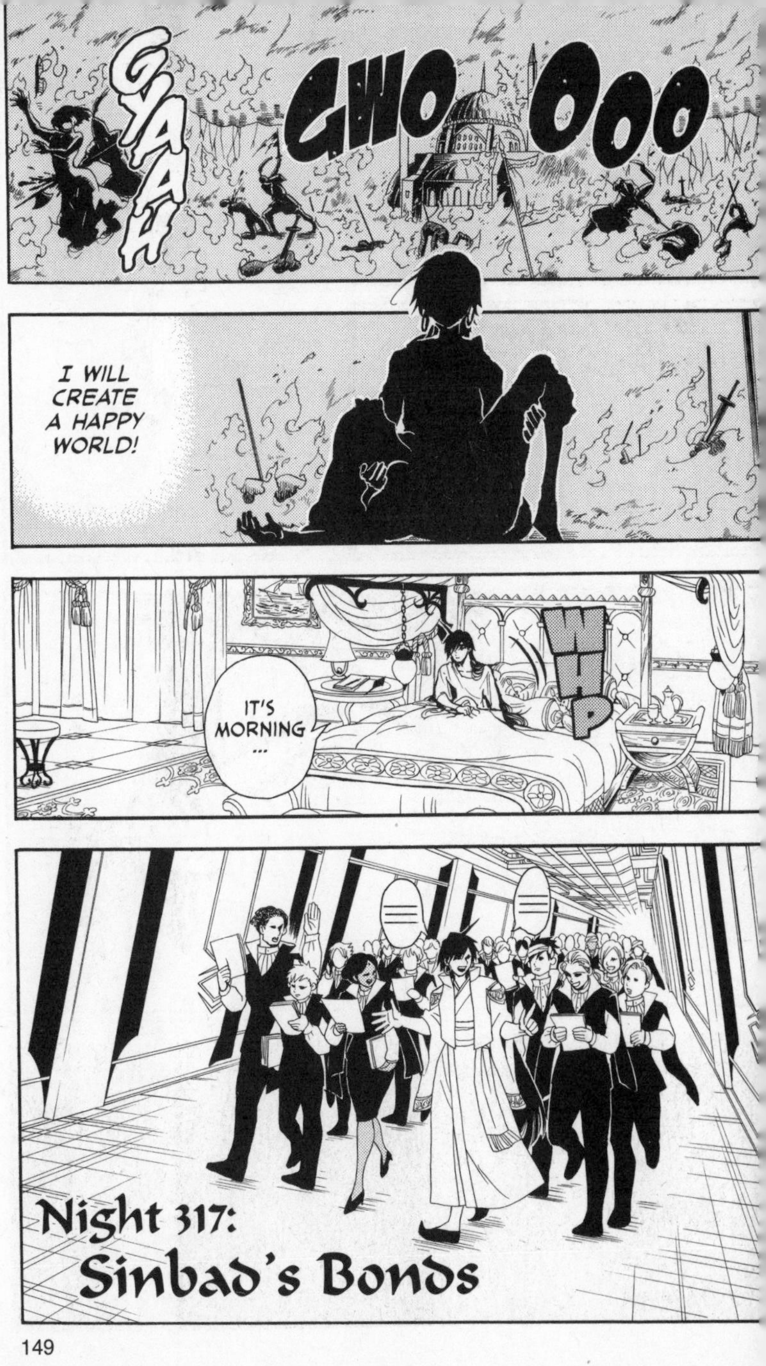
GYAAH
GWO OOO
I WILL CREATE A HAPPY WORLD!
WHP
IT'S MORNING ...
Night 317:
Sinbad's Bonds

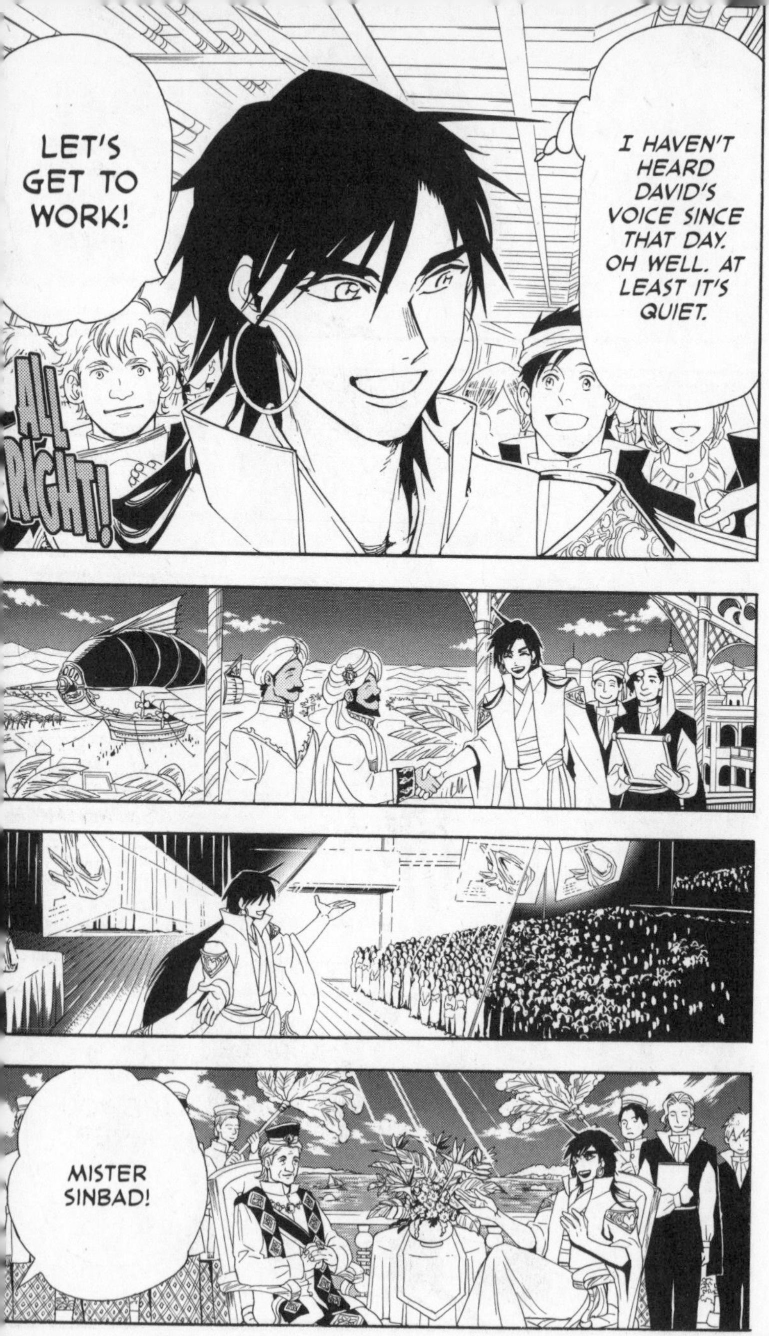
I HAVEN'T HEARD DAVID'S VOICE SINCE THAT DAY. OH WELL. AT LEAST IT'S QUIET.
LET'S GET TO WORK!
ALL RIGHT!!
MISTER SINBAD!

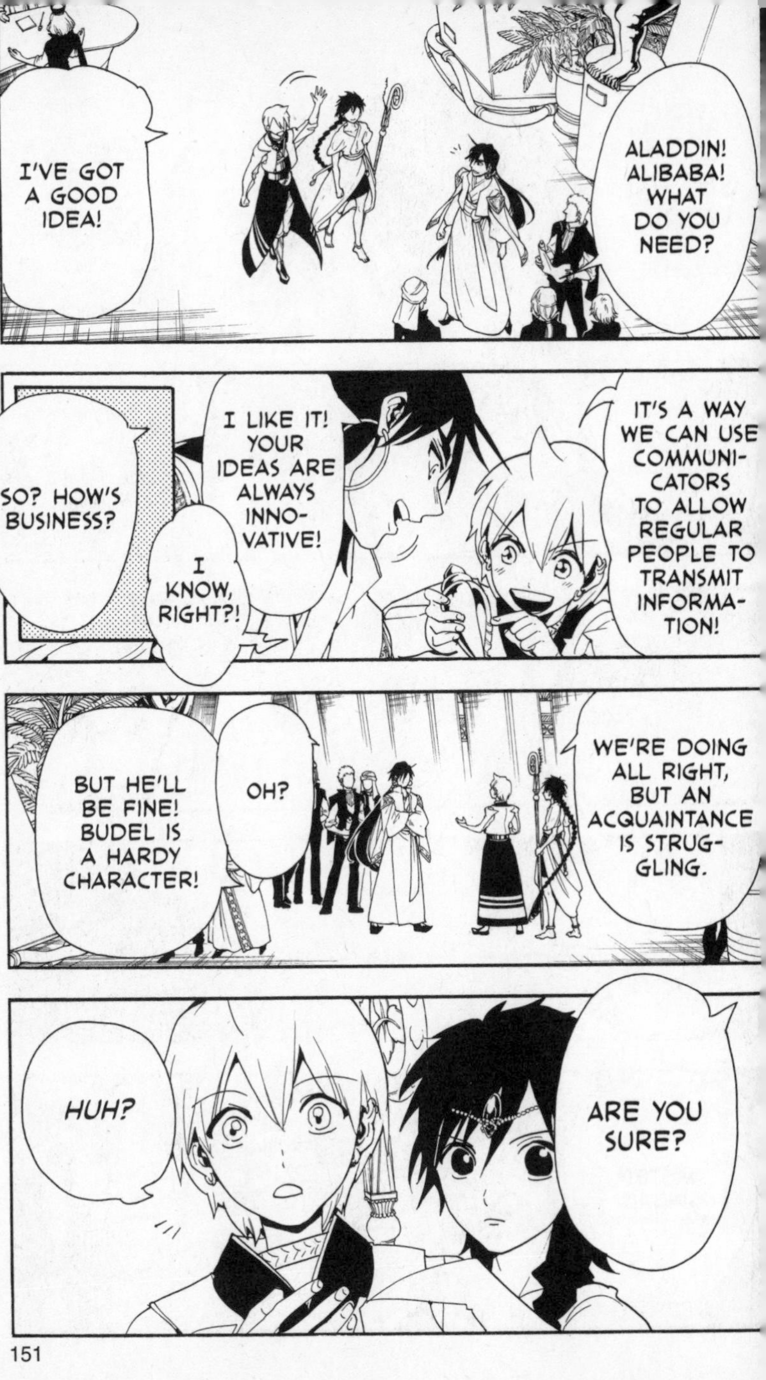
ALADDIN! ALIBABA! WHAT DO YOU NEED?
I'VE GOT A GOOD IDEA!
IT'S A WAY WE CAN USE COMMUNI-CATORS TO ALLOW REGULAR PEOPLE TO TRANSMIT INFORMA-TION!
I LIKE IT! YOUR IDEAS ARE ALWAYS INNO-VATIVE!
I KNOW, RIGHT?!
SO? HOW'S BUSINESS?
WE'RE DOING ALL RIGHT, BUT AN ACQUAINTANCE IS STRUG-GLING.
OH?
BUT HE'LL BE FINE! BUDEL IS A HARDY CHARACTER!
ARE YOU SURE?
HUH?

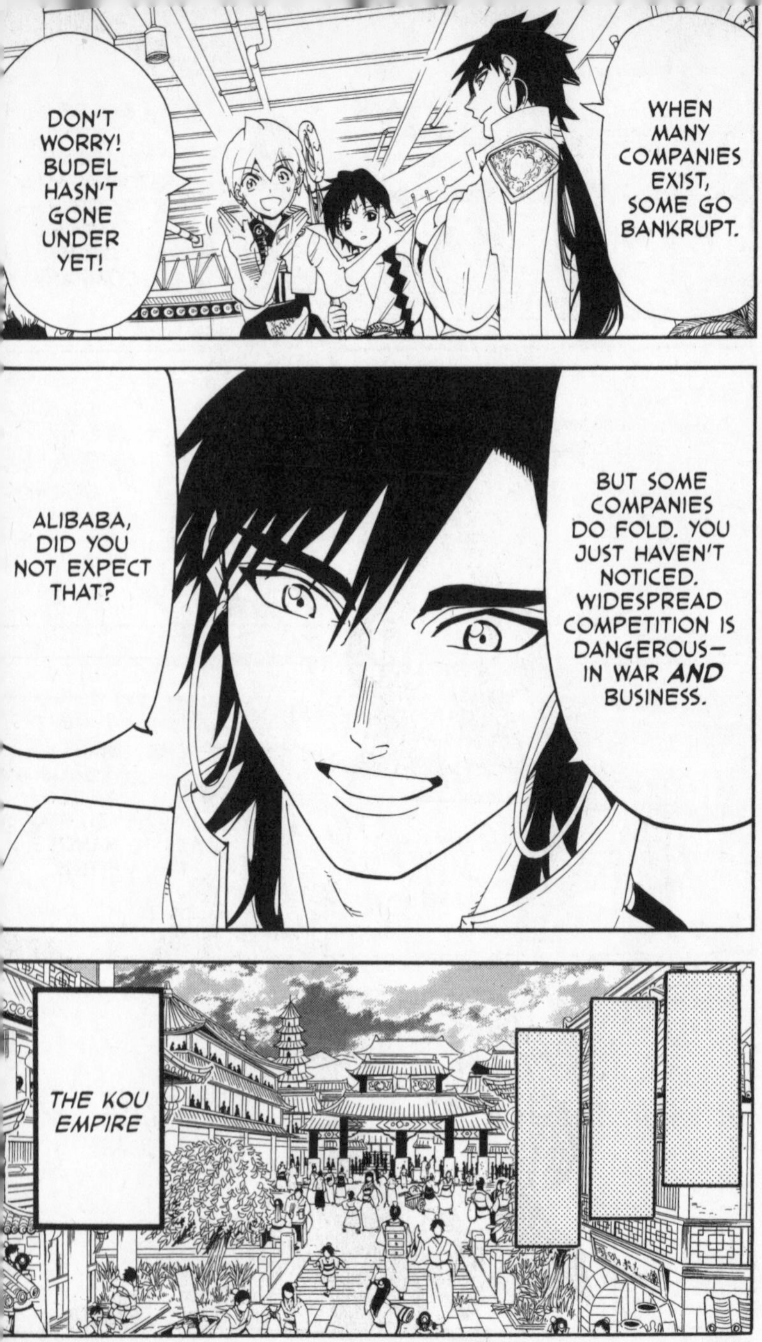
WHEN MANY COMPANIES EXIST, SOME GO BANKRUPT.
DON'T WORRY! BUDEL HASN'T GONE UNDER YET!
BUT SOME COMPANIES DO FOLD. YOU JUST HAVEN'T NOTICED. WIDESPREAD COMPETITION IS DANGEROUS— IN WAR *AND* BUSINESS.
ALIBABA, DID YOU NOT EXPECT THAT?
THE KOU EMPIRE

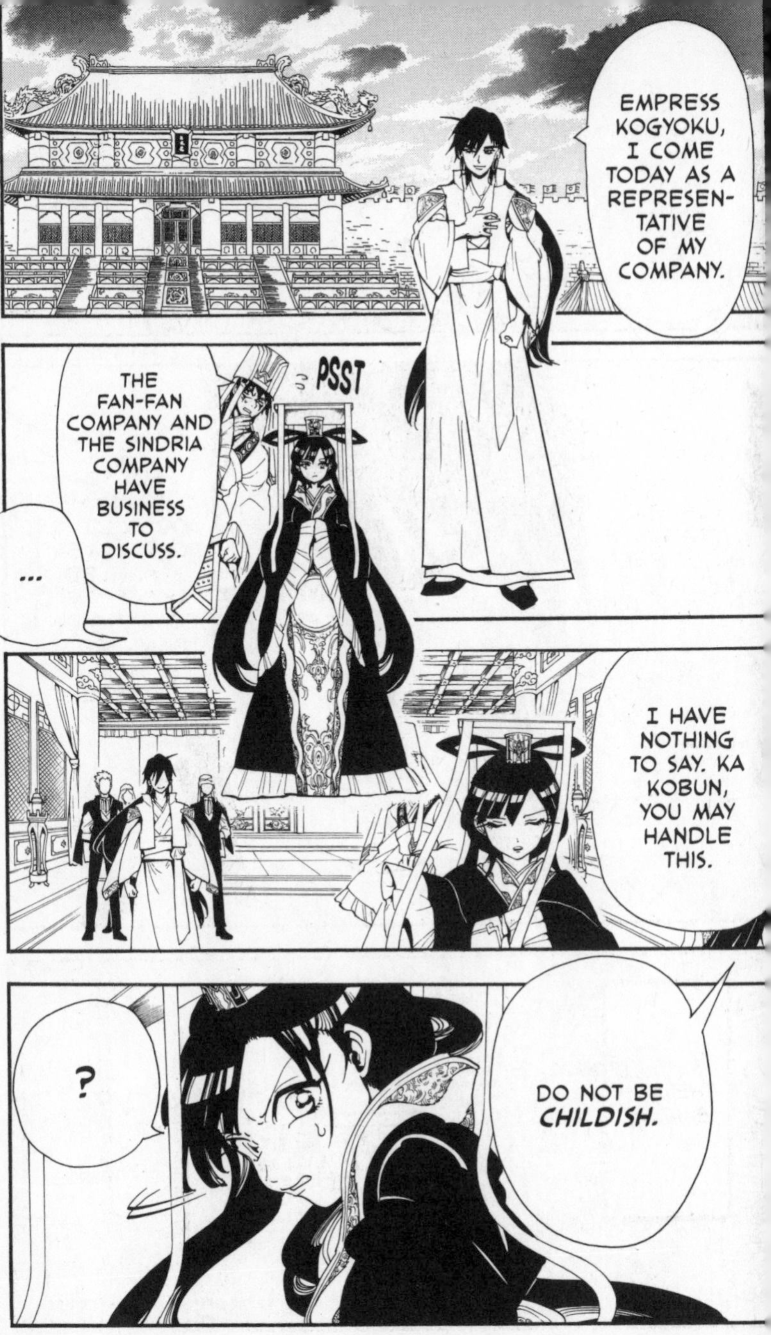
EMPRESS KOGYOKU, I COME TODAY AS A REPRESEN-TATIVE OF MY COMPANY.
PSST
THE FAN-FAN COMPANY AND THE SINDRIA COMPANY HAVE BUSINESS TO DISCUSS.
...
I HAVE NOTHING TO SAY. KA KOBUN, YOU MAY HANDLE THIS.
DO NOT BE *CHILDISH.*
?

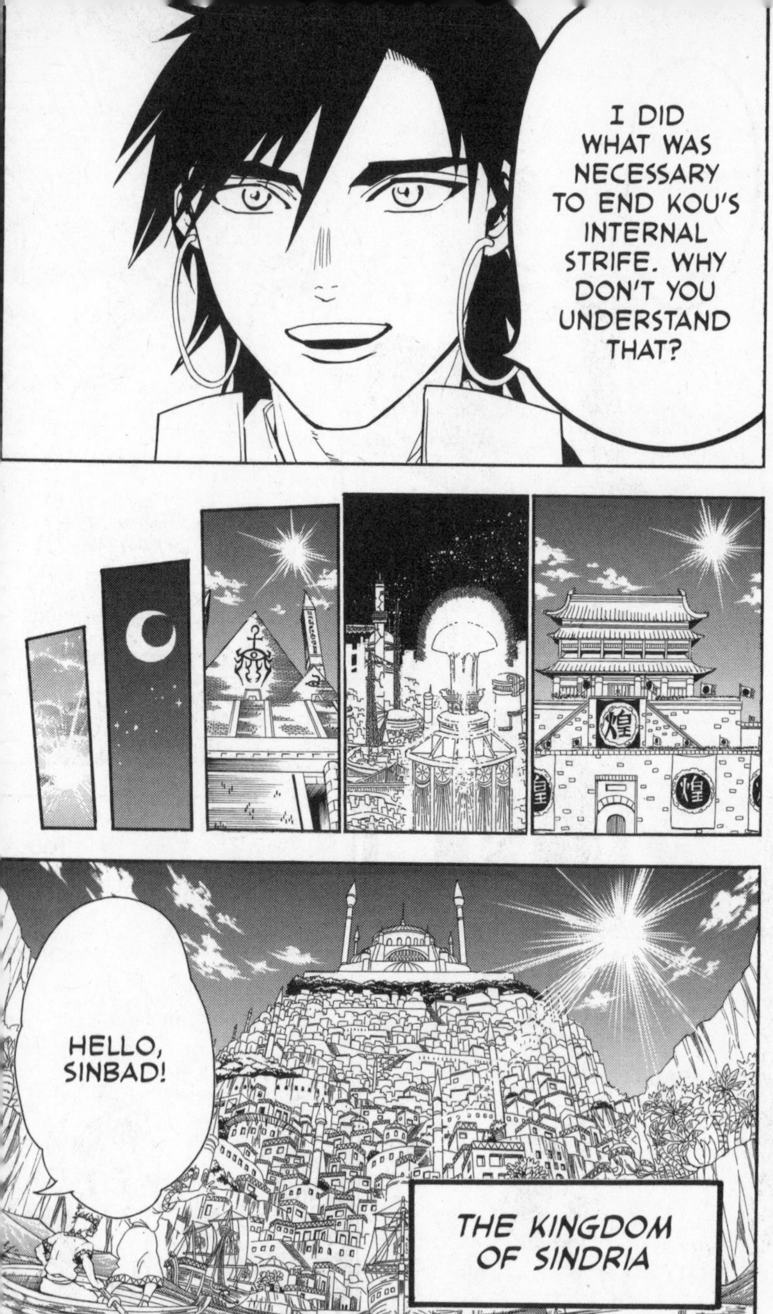
I DID WHAT WAS NECESSARY TO END KOU'S INTERNAL STRIFE. WHY DON'T YOU UNDERSTAND THAT?
煌
煌
HELLO, SINBAD!
THE KINGDOM OF SINDRIA

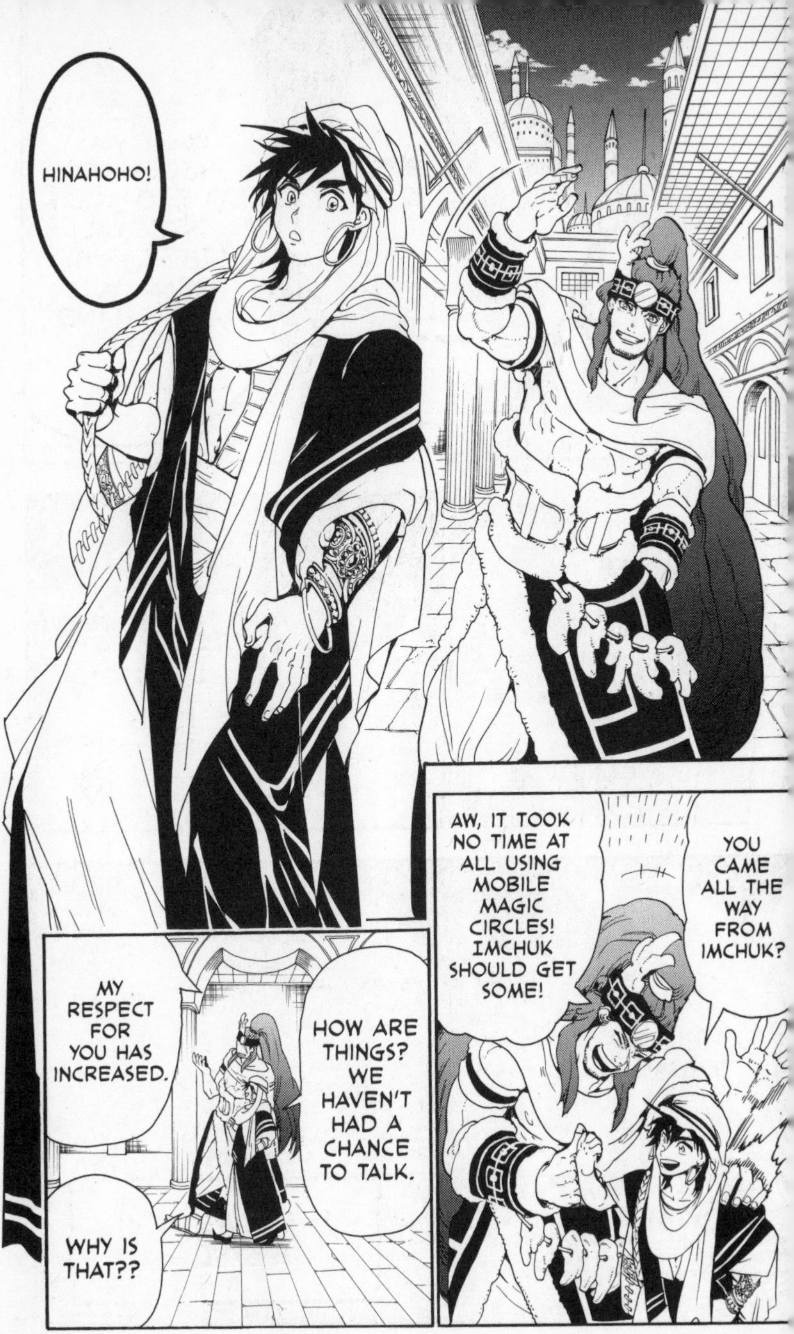
HINAHOHO!
YOU CAME ALL THE WAY FROM IMCHUK?
AW, IT TOOK NO TIME AT ALL USING MOBILE MAGIC CIRCLES! IMCHUK SHOULD GET SOME!
HOW ARE THINGS? WE HAVEN'T HAD A CHANCE TO TALK.
MY RESPECT FOR YOU HAS INCREASED.
WHY IS THAT??

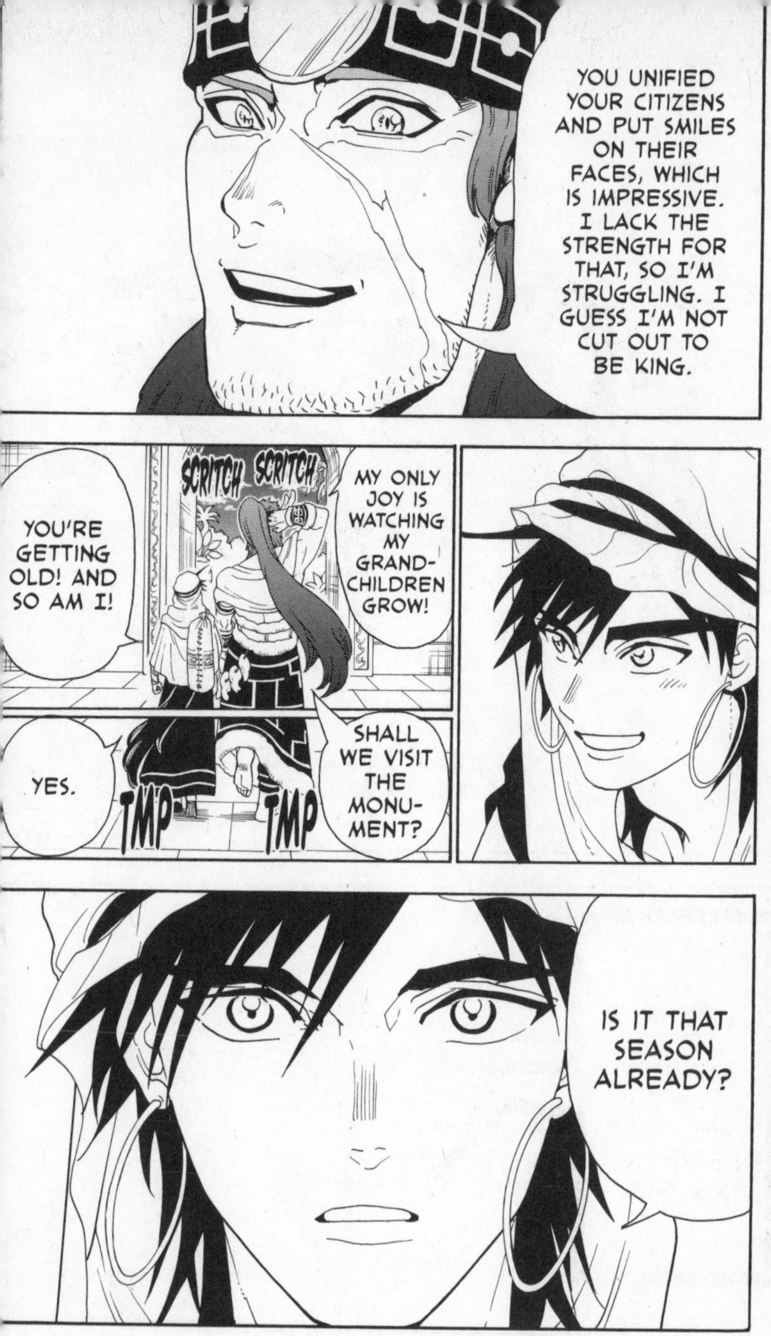
YOU UNIFIED YOUR CITIZENS AND PUT SMILES ON THEIR FACES, WHICH IS IMPRESSIVE. I LACK THE STRENGTH FOR THAT, SO I'M STRUGGLING. I GUESS I'M NOT CUT OUT TO BE KING.
MY ONLY JOY IS WATCHING MY GRAND-CHILDREN GROW!
SCRITCH SCRITCH
YOU'RE GETTING OLD! AND SO AM I!
SHALL WE VISIT THE MONU-MENT?
TMP TMP
YES.
IS IT THAT SEASON ALREADY?

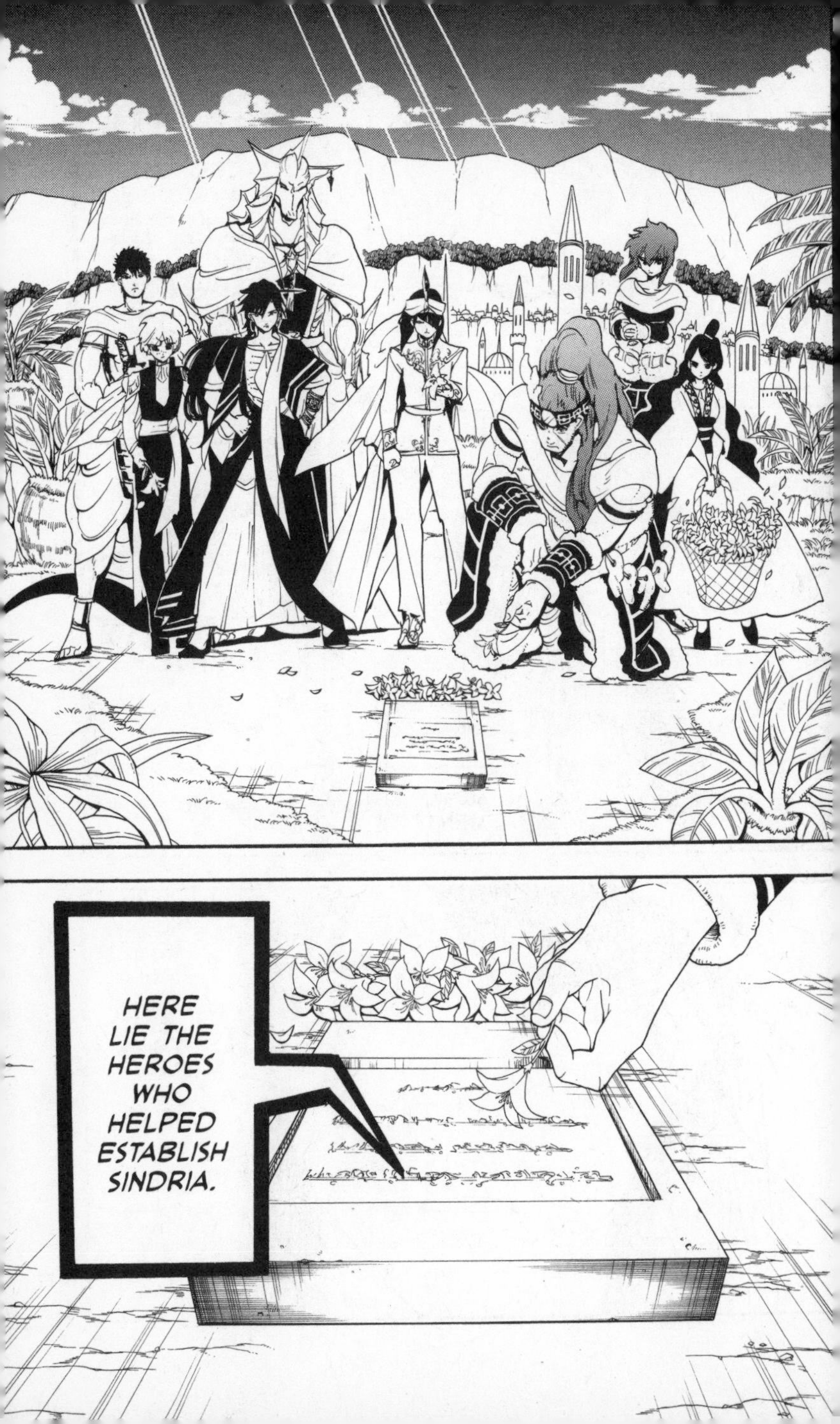
HERE LIE THE HEROES WHO HELPED ESTABLISH SINDRIA.

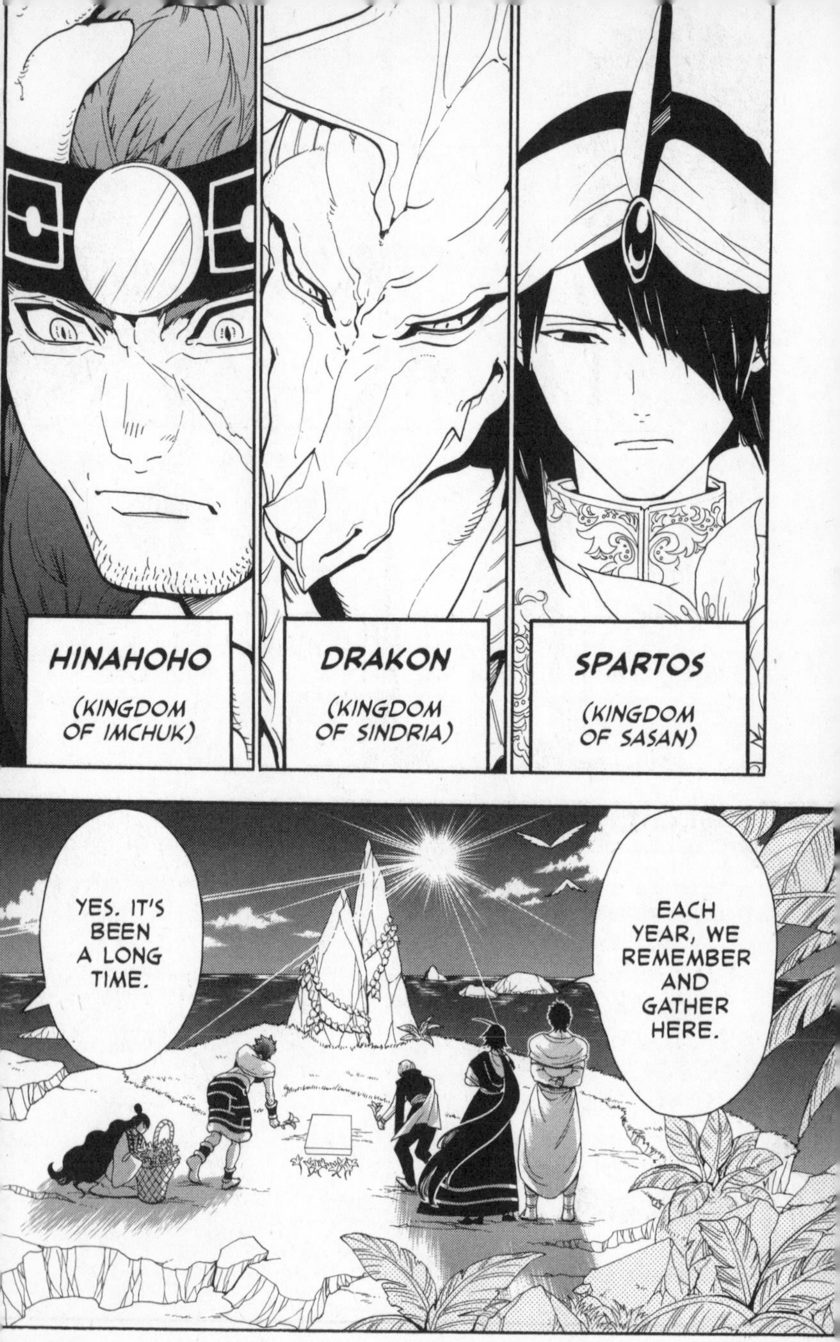
SPARTOS
(KINGDOM OF SASAN)
DRAKON
(KINGDOM OF SINDRIA)
HINAHOHO
(KINGDOM OF IMCHUK)
EACH YEAR, WE REMEMBER AND GATHER HERE.
YES. IT'S BEEN A LONG TIME.

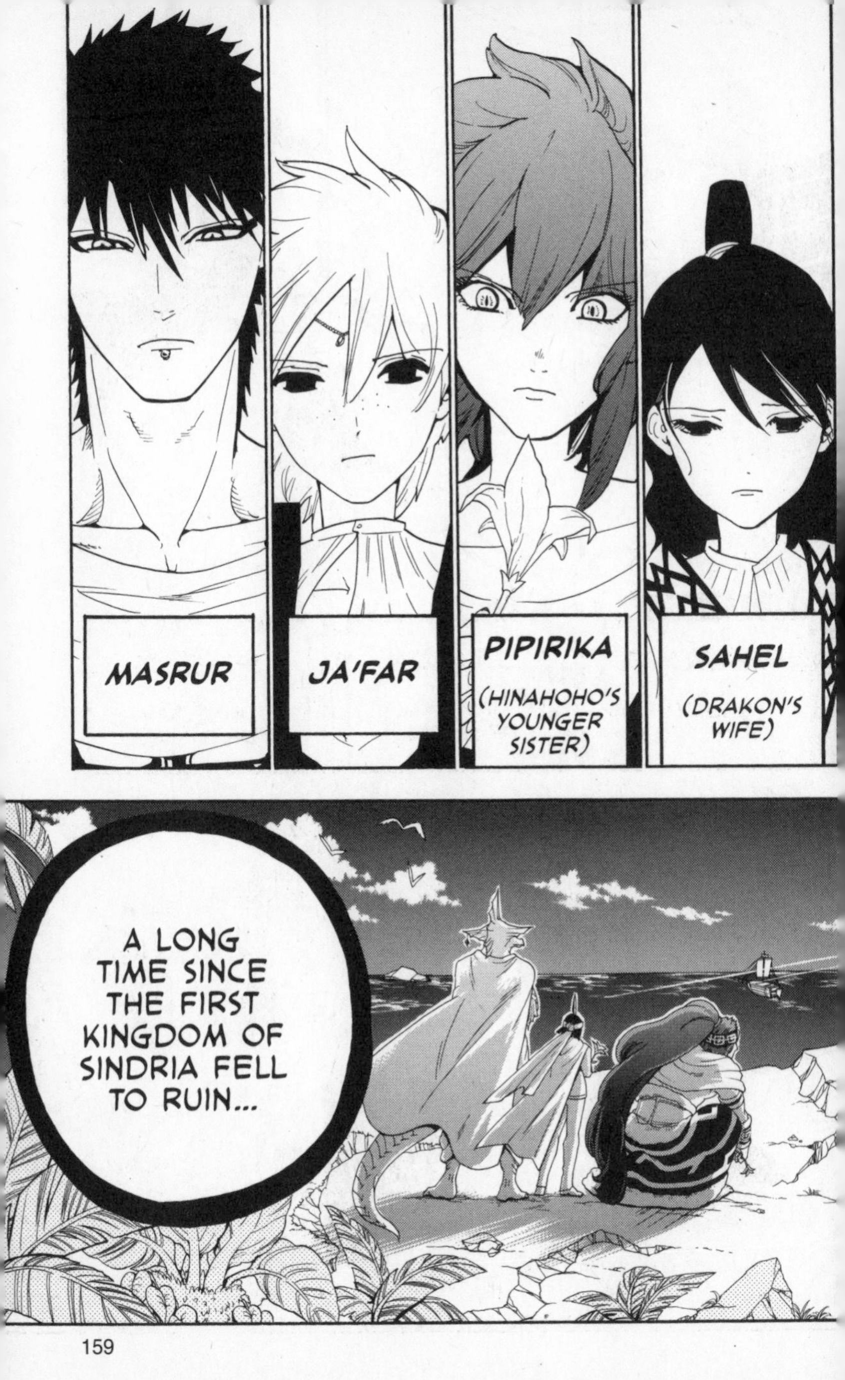
SAHEL
(DRAKON'S WIFE)
PIPIRIKA
(HINAHOHO'S YOUNGER SISTER)
JA'FAR
MASRUR
A LONG TIME SINCE THE FIRST KINGDOM OF SINDRIA FELL TO RUIN...

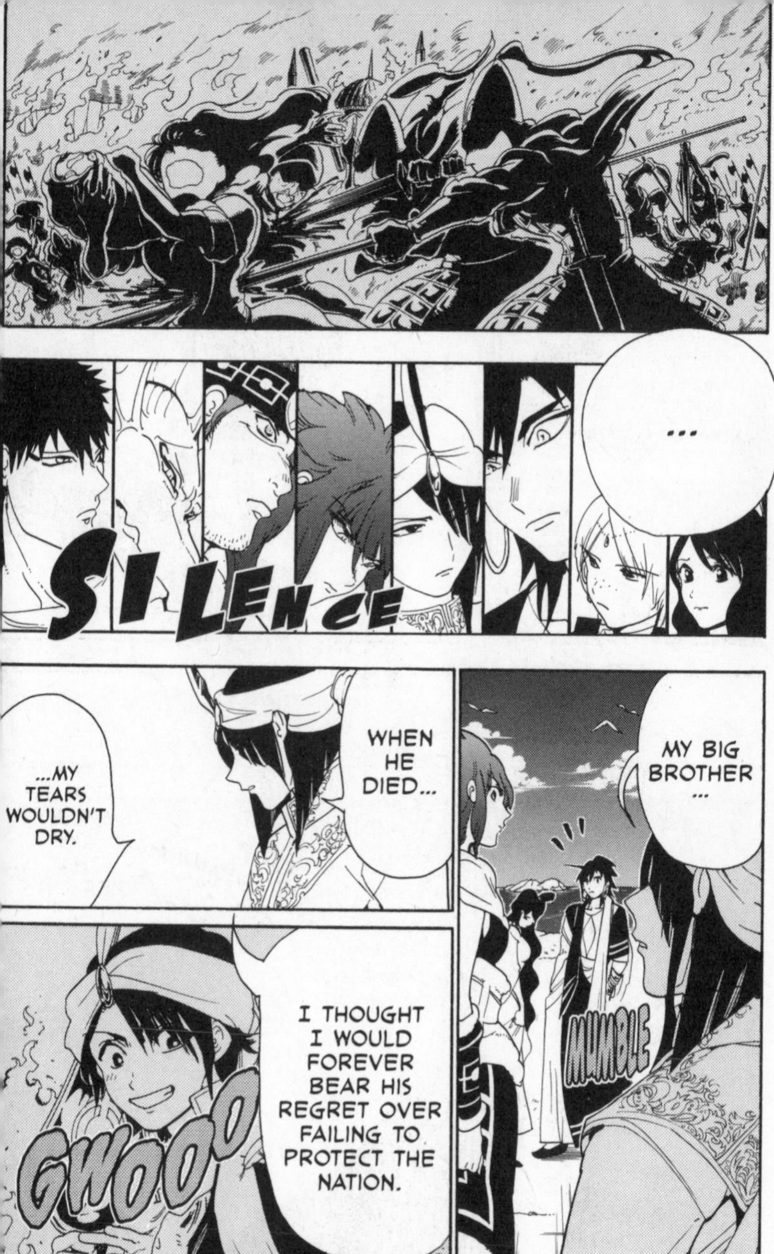

...
SILENCE
MY BIG BROTHER ...
MUMBLE
WHEN HE DIED...
...MY TEARS WOULDN'T DRY.
I THOUGHT I WOULD FOREVER BEAR HIS REGRET OVER FAILING TO PROTECT THE NATION.
GWOOO

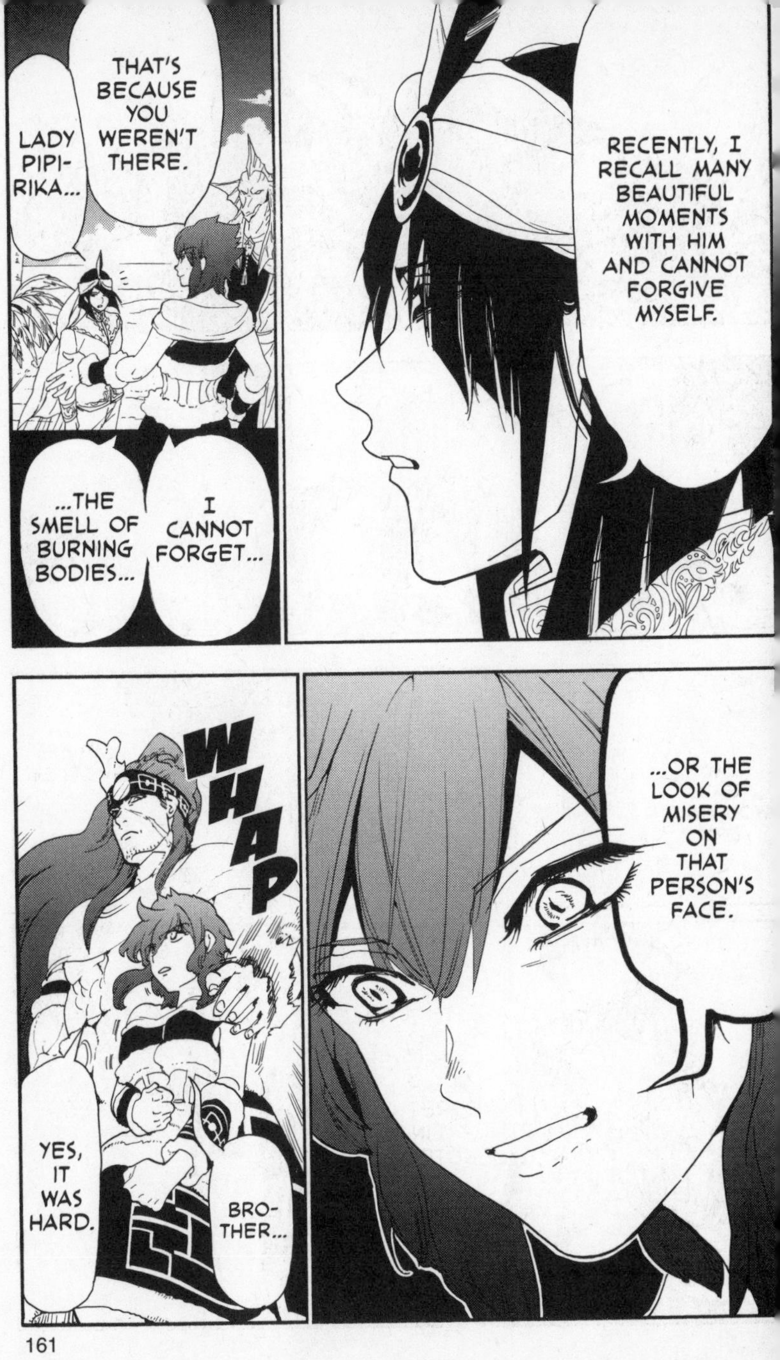
RECENTLY, I RECALL MANY BEAUTIFUL MOMENTS WITH HIM AND CANNOT FORGIVE MYSELF.
THAT'S BECAUSE YOU WEREN'T THERE.
LADY PIPI-RIKA...
I CANNOT FORGET...
...THE SMELL OF BURNING BODIES...
...OR THE LOOK OF MISERY ON THAT PERSON'S FACE.
WHAP
BRO-THER...
YES, IT WAS HARD.

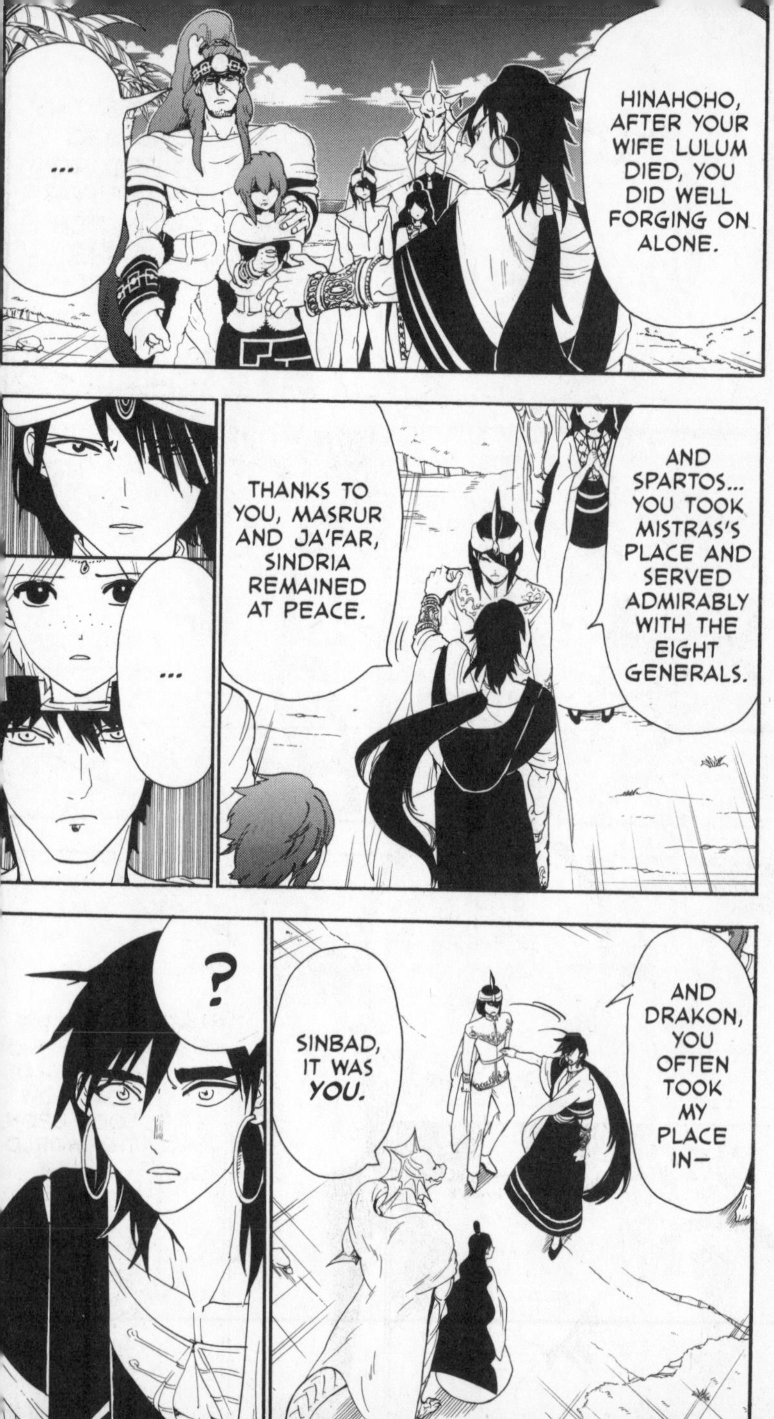
HINAHOHO, AFTER YOUR WIFE LULUM DIED, YOU DID WELL FORGING ON ALONE.
...
AND SPARTOS... YOU TOOK MISTRAS'S PLACE AND SERVED ADMIRABLY WITH THE EIGHT GENERALS.
THANKS TO YOU, MASRUR AND JA'FAR, SINDRIA REMAINED AT PEACE.
...
AND DRAKON, YOU OFTEN TOOK MY PLACE IN—
SINBAD, IT WAS *YOU*.
?

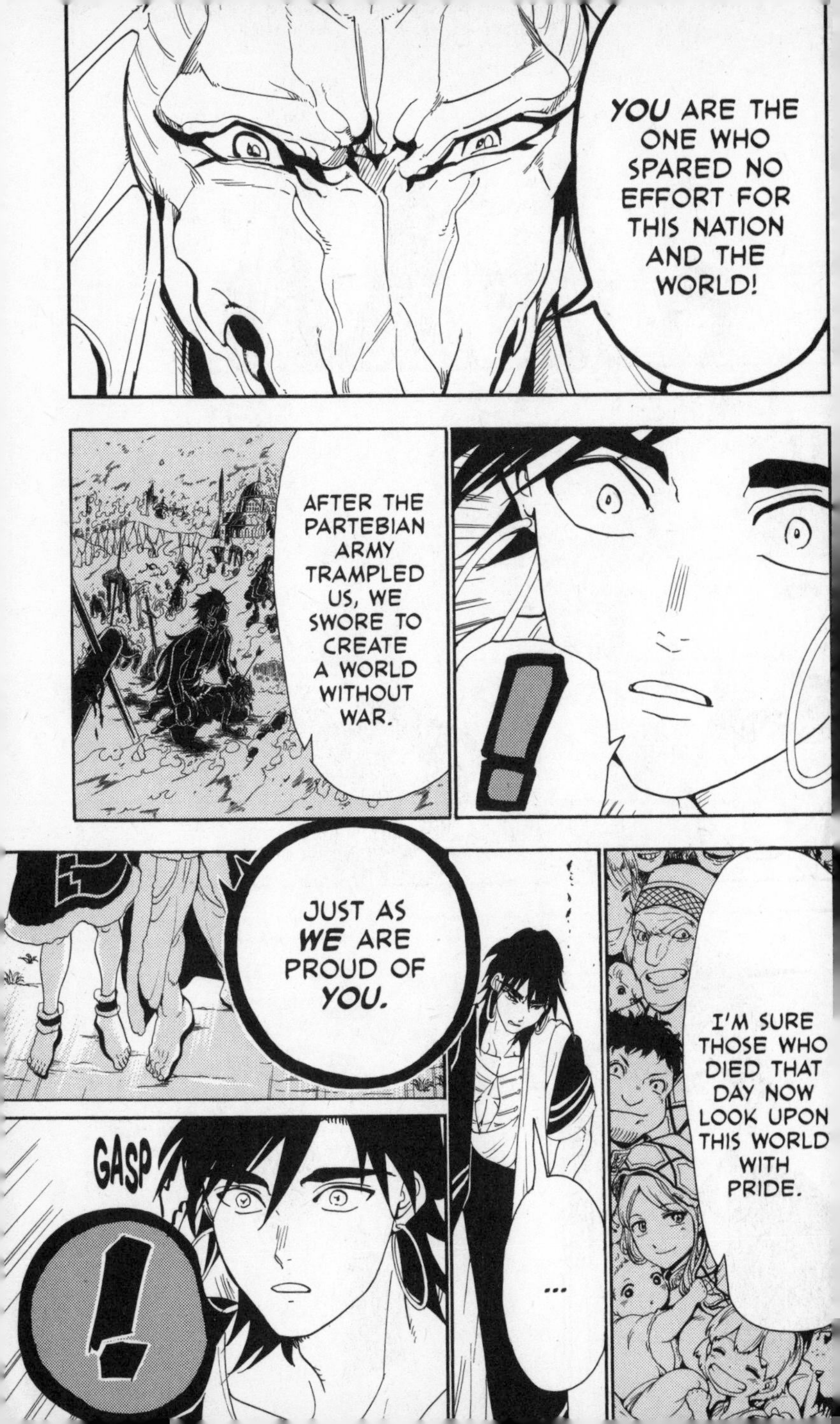
YOU ARE THE ONE WHO SPARED NO EFFORT FOR THIS NATION AND THE WORLD!
!
AFTER THE PARTEBIAN ARMY TRAMPLED US, WE SWORE TO CREATE A WORLD WITHOUT WAR.
I'M SURE THOSE WHO DIED THAT DAY NOW LOOK UPON THIS WORLD WITH PRIDE.
...
JUST AS WE ARE PROUD OF YOU.
GASP
!

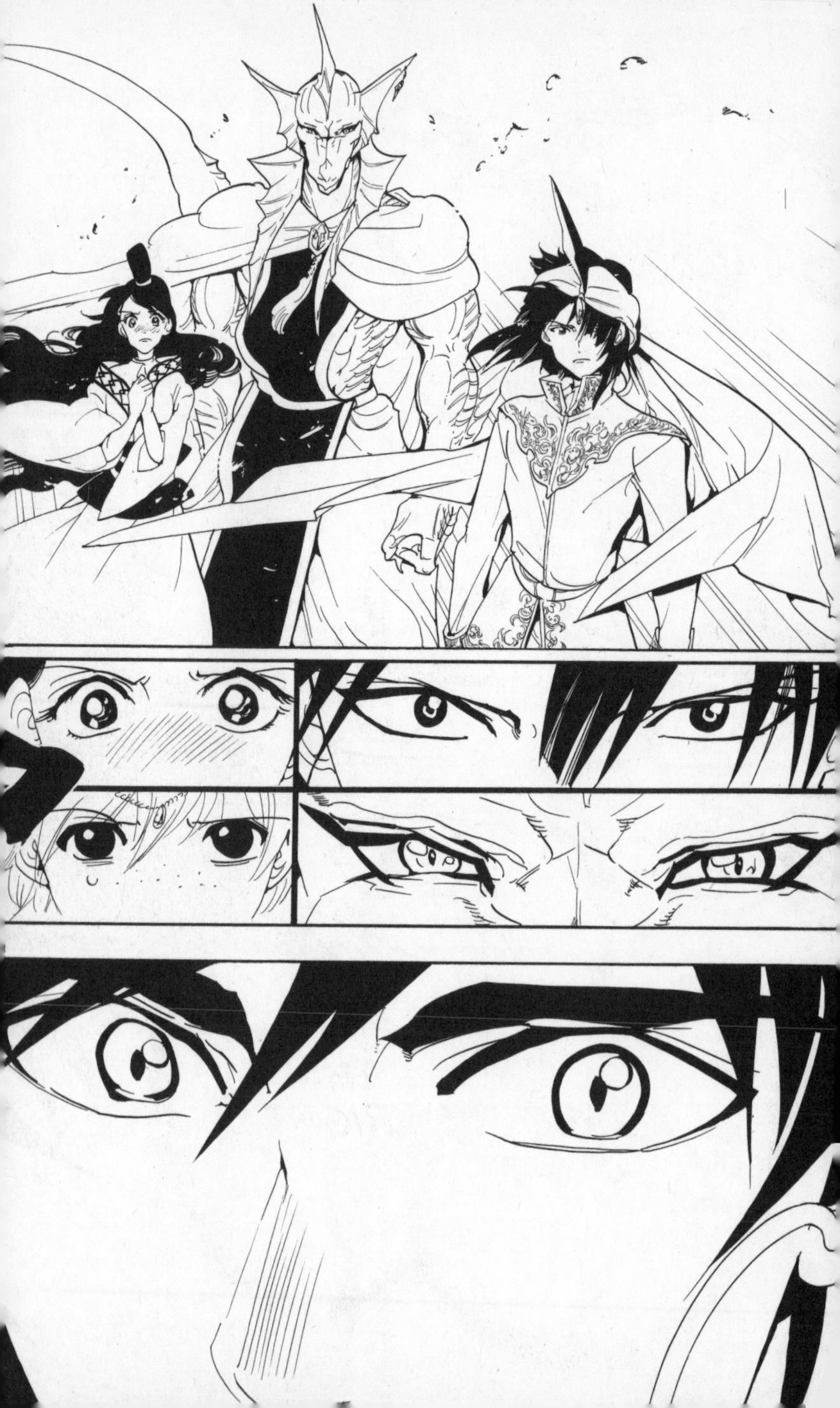

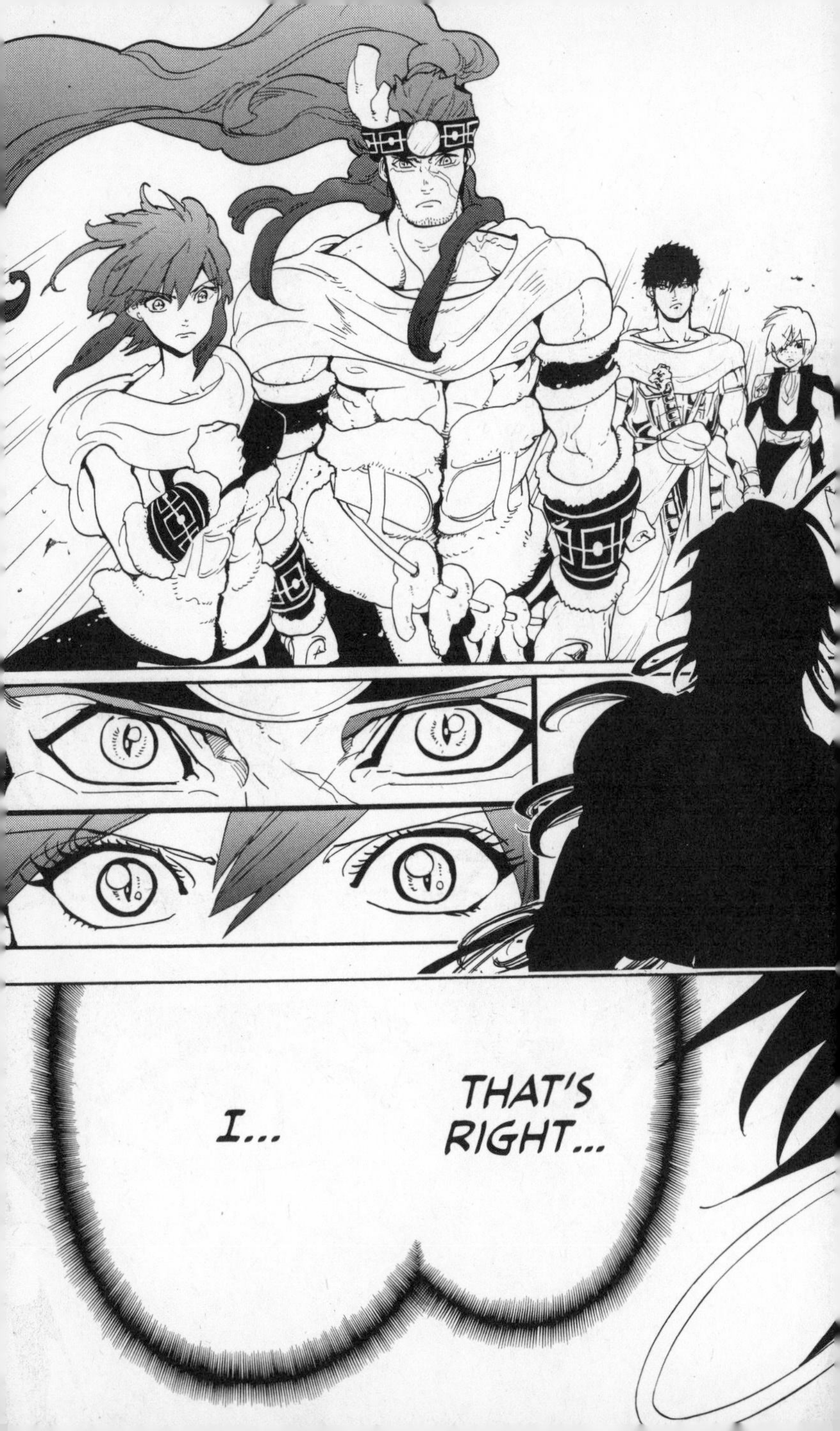
THAT'S RIGHT...
I...

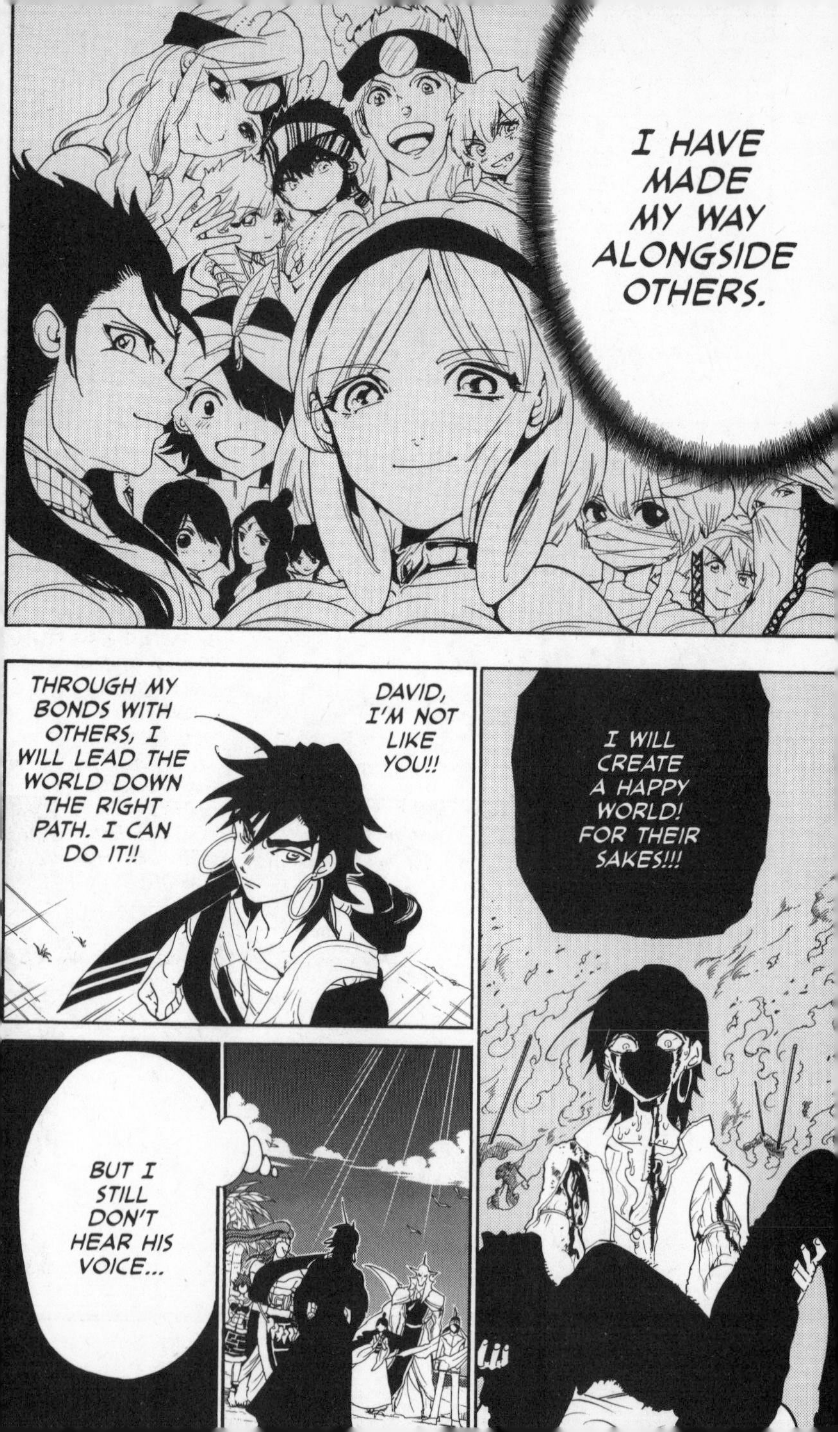
I HAVE MADE MY WAY ALONGSIDE OTHERS.
I WILL CREATE A HAPPY WORLD! FOR THEIR SAKES!!!
DAVID, I'M NOT LIKE YOU!!
THROUGH MY BONDS WITH OTHERS, I WILL LEAD THE WORLD DOWN THE RIGHT PATH. I CAN DO IT!!
BUT I STILL DON'T HEAR HIS VOICE...

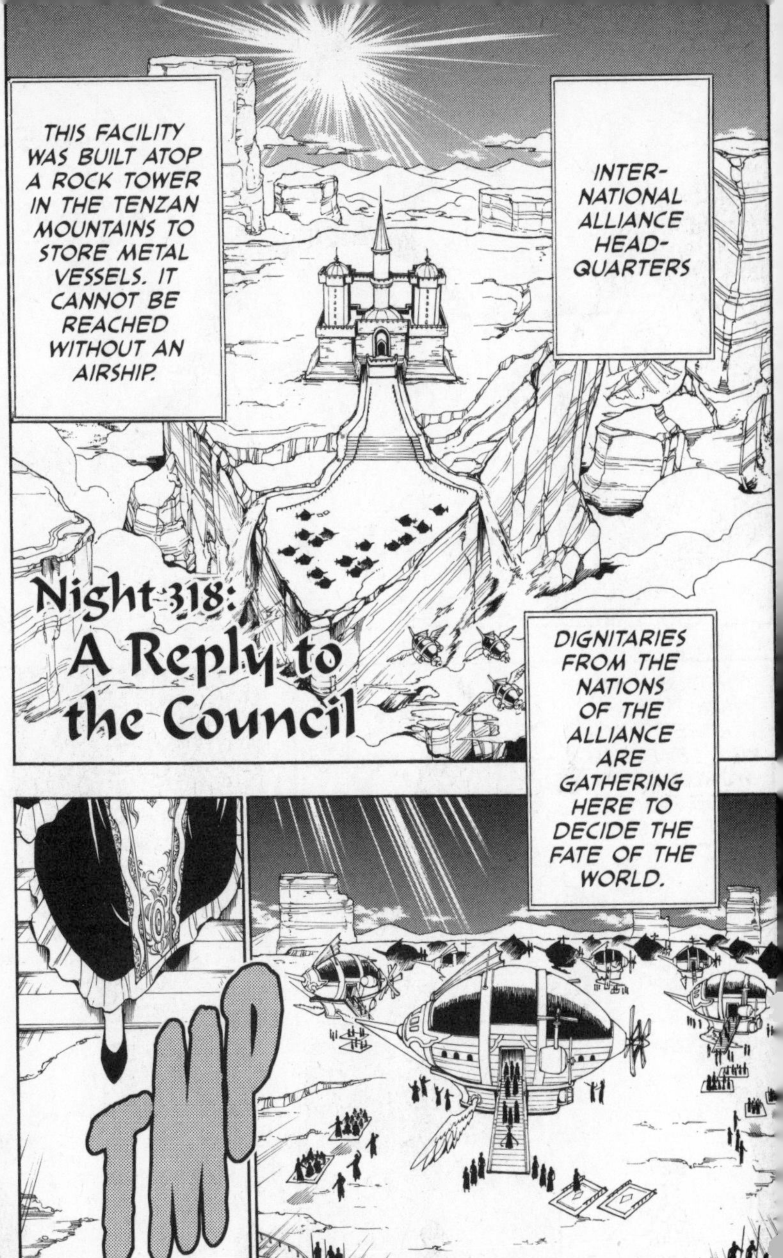
INTER-NATIONAL ALLIANCE HEAD-QUARTERS
THIS FACILITY WAS BUILT ATOP A ROCK TOWER IN THE TENZAN MOUNTAINS TO STORE METAL VESSELS. IT CANNOT BE REACHED WITHOUT AN AIRSHIP.
Night 318: A Reply to the Council
DIGNITARIES FROM THE NATIONS OF THE ALLIANCE ARE GATHERING HERE TO DECIDE THE FATE OF THE WORLD.
THMP

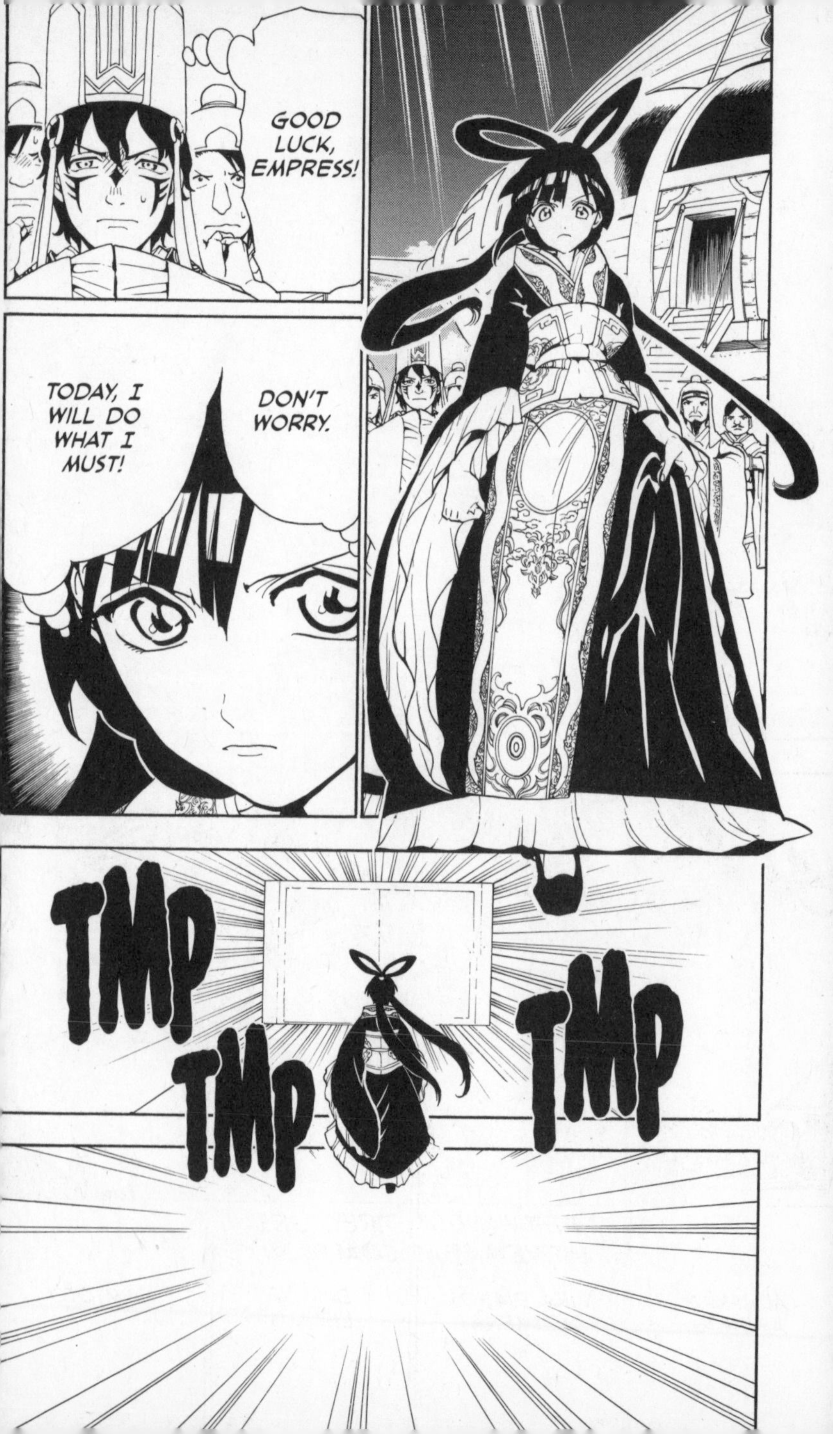
GOOD LUCK, EMPRESS!
DON'T WORRY.
TODAY, I WILL DO WHAT I MUST!
TMP
TMP
TMP

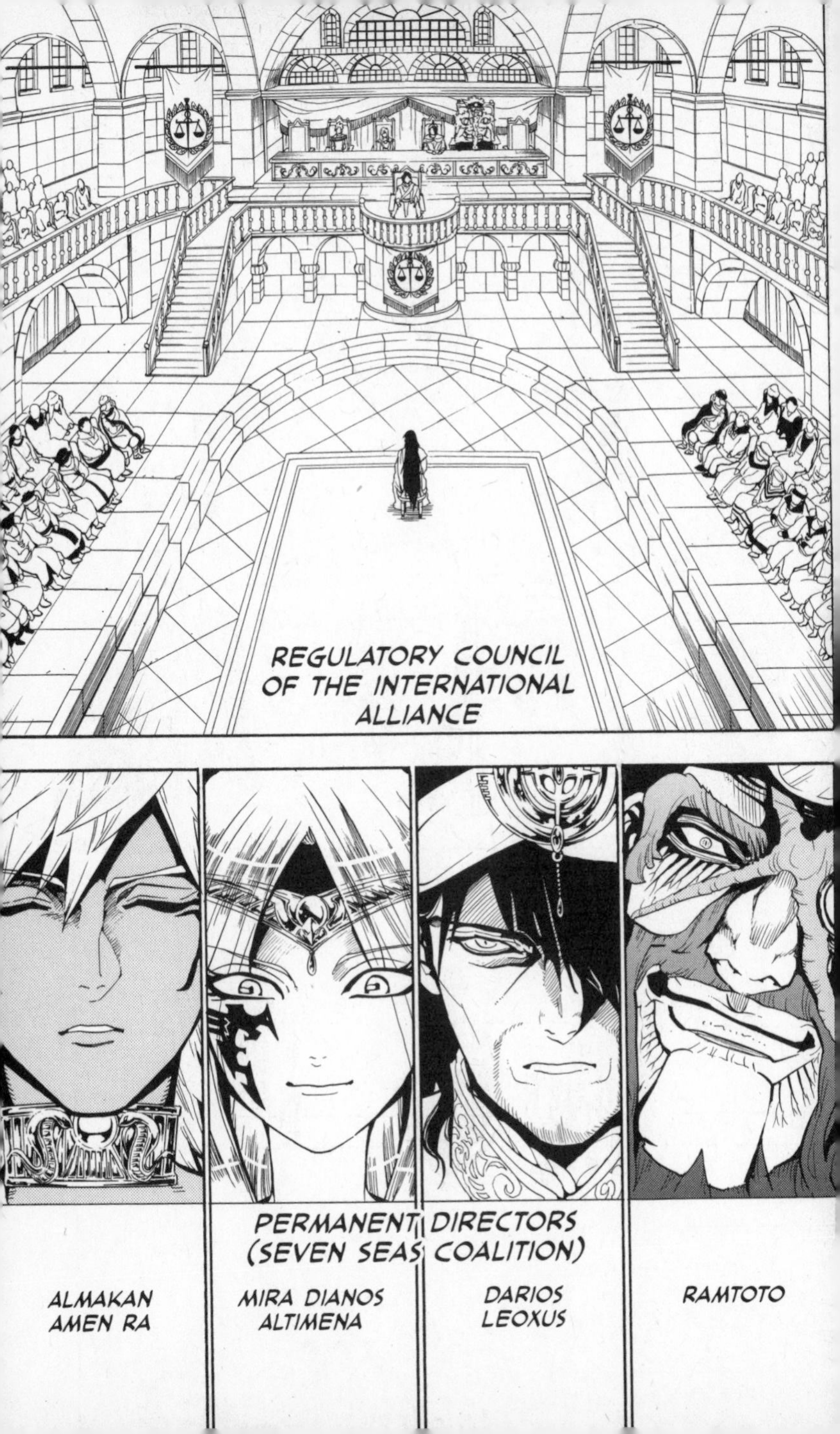
REGULATORY COUNCIL OF THE INTERNATIONAL ALLIANCE
PERMANENT DIRECTORS (SEVEN SEAS COALITION)
RAMTOTO
DARIOS LEOXUS
MIRA DIANOS ALTIMENA
ALMAKAN AMEN RA

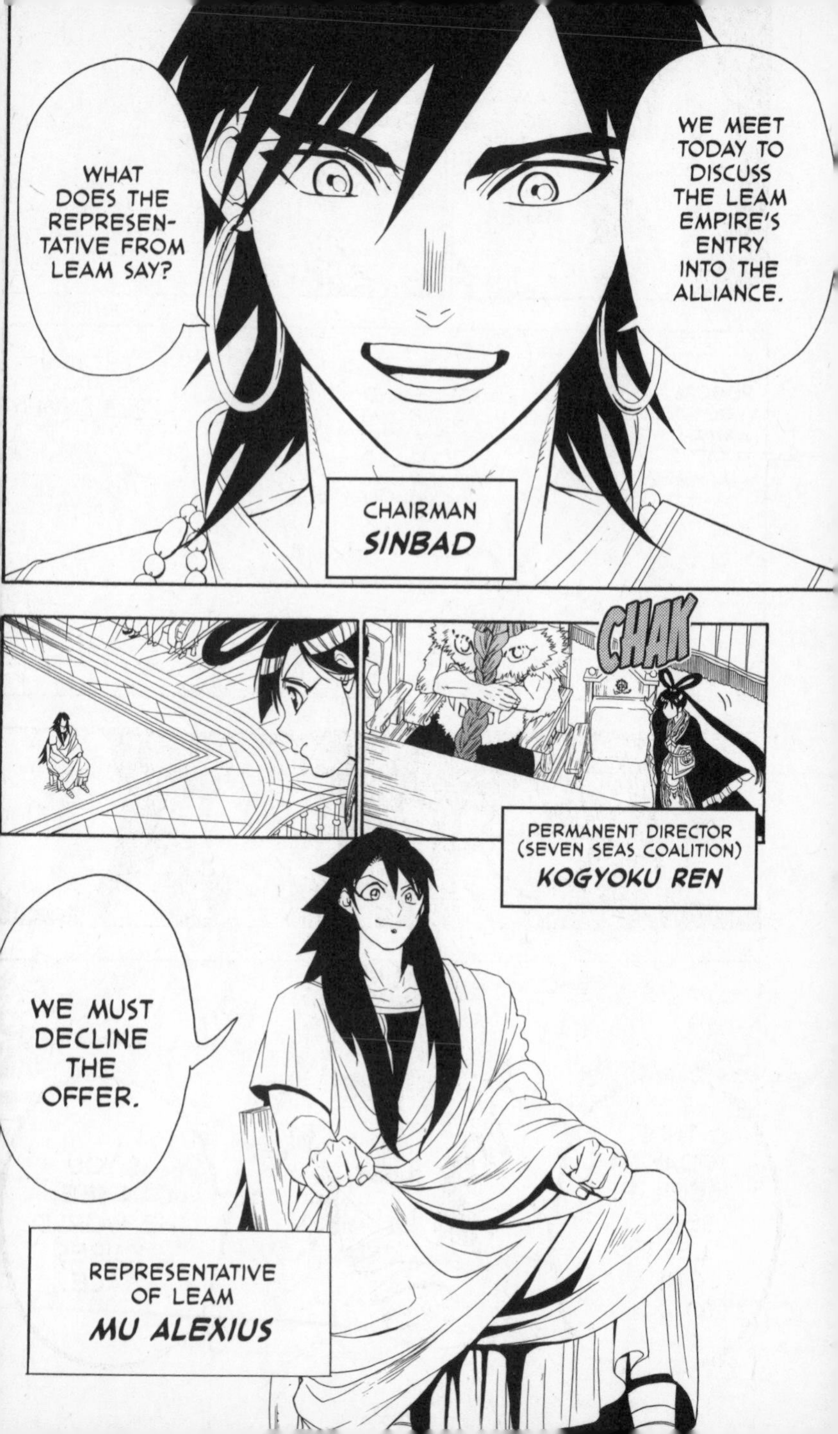
WE MEET TODAY TO DISCUSS THE LEAM EMPIRE'S ENTRY INTO THE ALLIANCE.
WHAT DOES THE REPRESEN-TATIVE FROM LEAM SAY?
CHAIRMAN SINBAD
CHAK
PERMANENT DIRECTOR (SEVEN SEAS COALITION) KOGYOKU REN
WE MUST DECLINE THE OFFER.
REPRESENTATIVE OF LEAM MU ALEXIUS

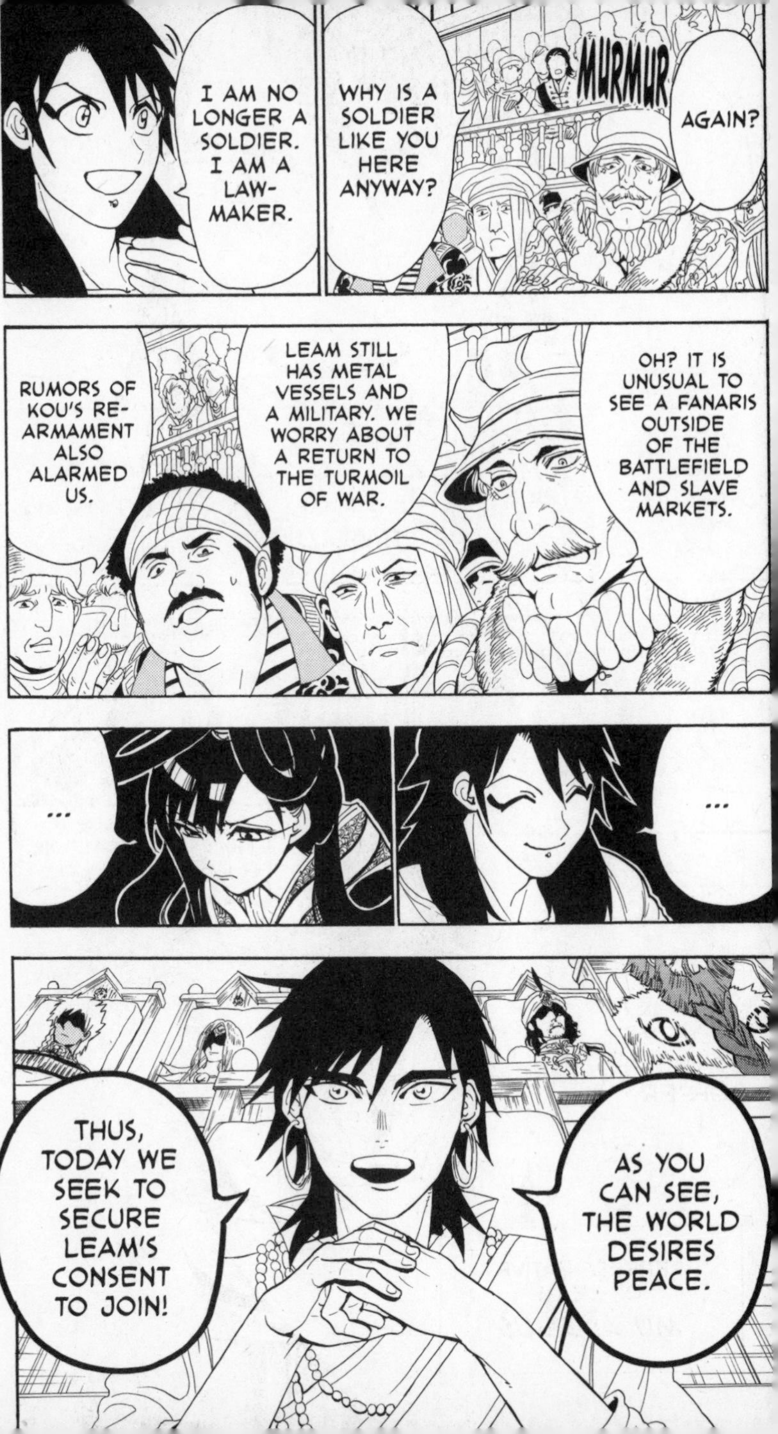
MURMUR
AGAIN?
WHY IS A SOLDIER LIKE YOU HERE ANYWAY?
I AM NO LONGER A SOLDIER. I AM A LAW-MAKER.
OH? IT IS UNUSUAL TO SEE A FANARIS OUTSIDE OF THE BATTLEFIELD AND SLAVE MARKETS.
LEAM STILL HAS METAL VESSELS AND A MILITARY. WE WORRY ABOUT A RETURN TO THE TURMOIL OF WAR.
RUMORS OF KOU'S RE-ARMAMENT ALSO ALARMED US.
...
...
AS YOU CAN SEE, THE WORLD DESIRES PEACE.
THUS, TODAY WE SEEK TO SECURE LEAM'S CONSENT TO JOIN!

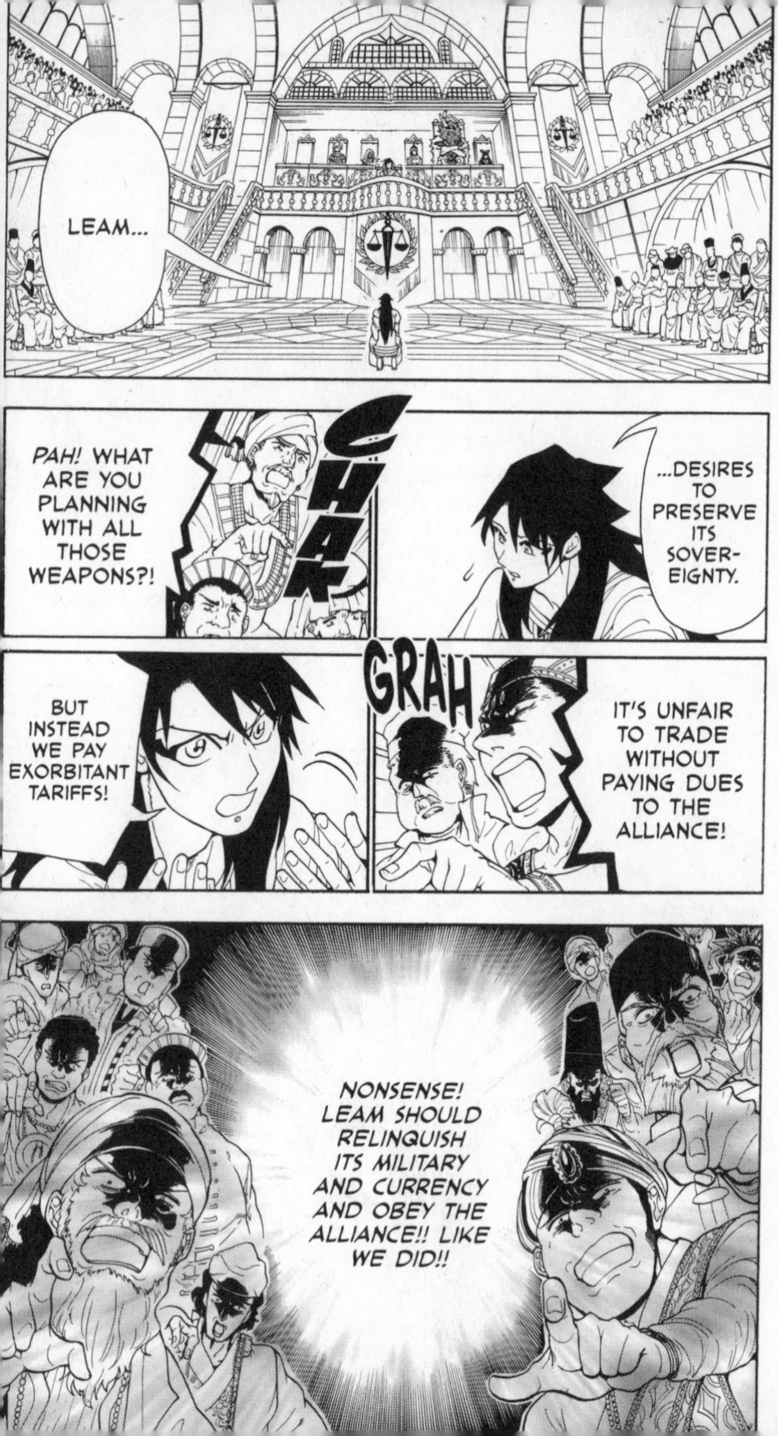
LEAM...
...DESIRES TO PRESERVE ITS SOVEREIGNTY.
CHAK
PAH! WHAT ARE YOU PLANNING WITH ALL THOSE WEAPONS?!
GRAH
IT'S UNFAIR TO TRADE WITHOUT PAYING DUES TO THE ALLIANCE!
BUT INSTEAD WE PAY EXORBITANT TARIFFS!
NONSENSE! LEAM SHOULD RELINQUISH ITS MILITARY AND CURRENCY AND OBEY THE ALLIANCE!! LIKE WE DID!!

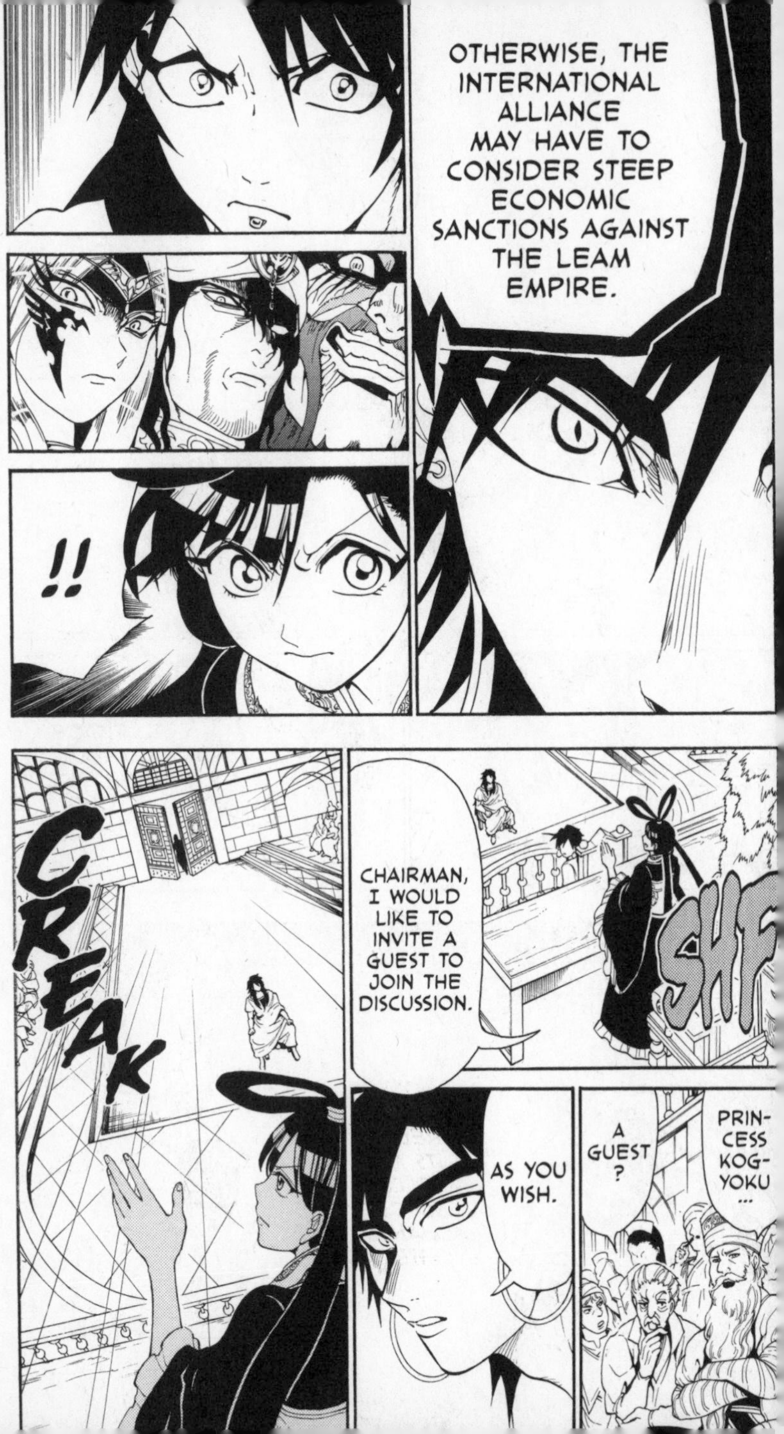
OTHERWISE, THE INTERNATIONAL ALLIANCE MAY HAVE TO CONSIDER STEEP ECONOMIC SANCTIONS AGAINST THE LEAM EMPIRE.
!!
SHF
CHAIRMAN, I WOULD LIKE TO INVITE A GUEST TO JOIN THE DISCUSSION.
CREAK
PRINCESS KOGYOKU...
A GUEST?
AS YOU WISH.

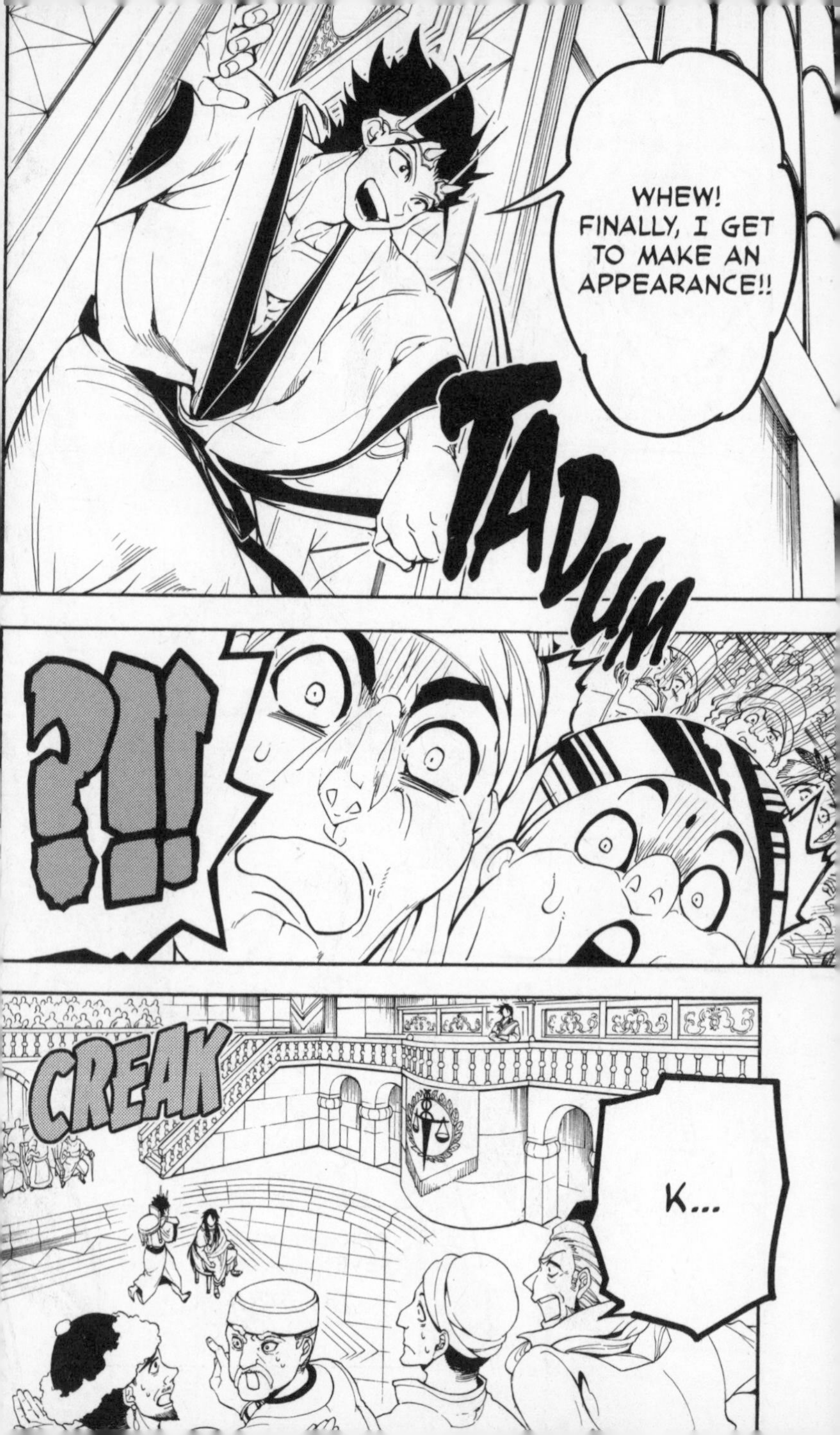
WHEW! FINALLY, I GET TO MAKE AN APPEARANCE!!
TADUM
?!!
CREAK
K...

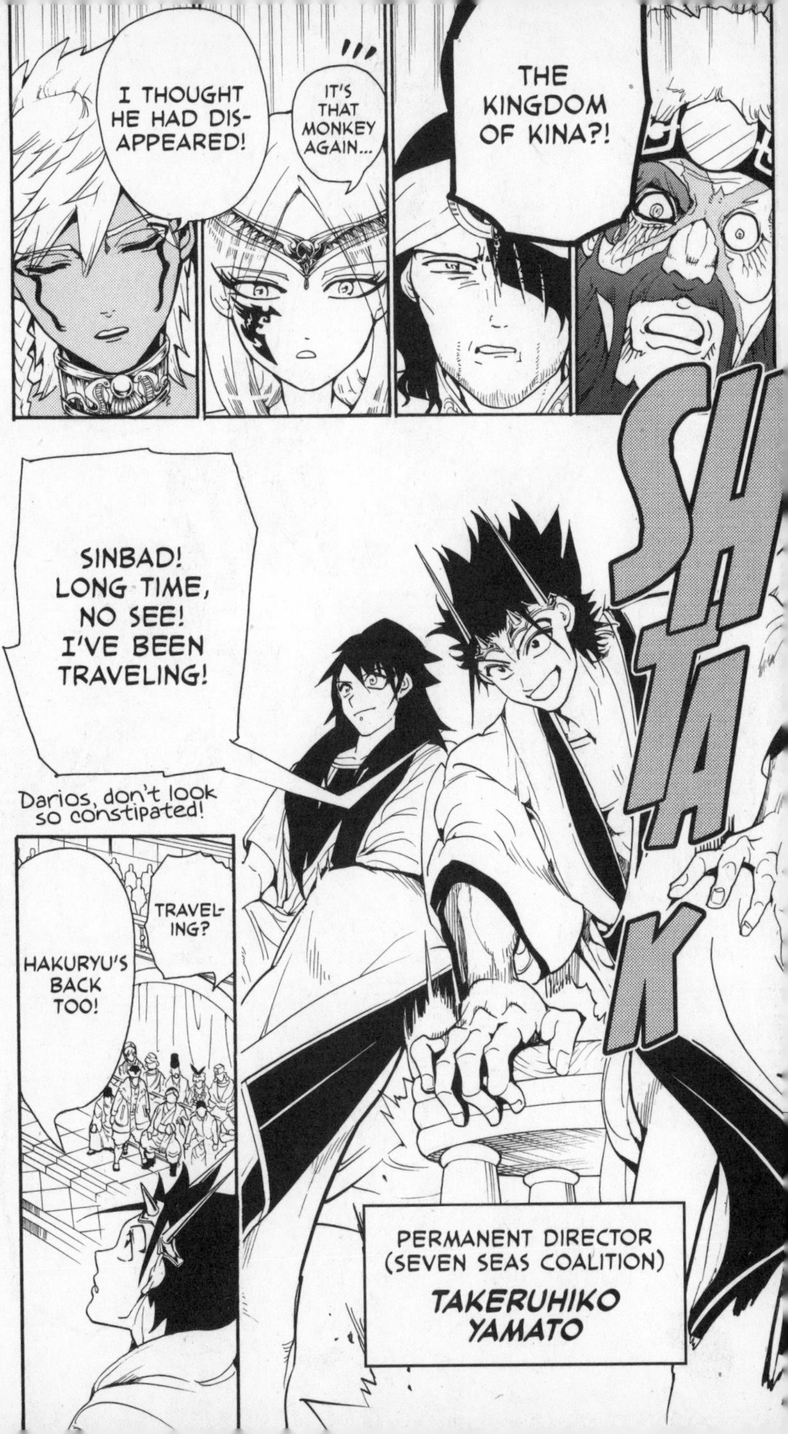
THE KINGDOM OF KINA?!
IT'S THAT MONKEY AGAIN...
I THOUGHT HE HAD DIS-APPEARED!
SHATAK
SINBAD! LONG TIME, NO SEE! I'VE BEEN TRAVELING!
Darios, don't look so constipated!
PERMANENT DIRECTOR (SEVEN SEAS COALITION)
TAKERUHIKO YAMATO
TRAVEL-ING?
HAKURYU'S BACK TOO!

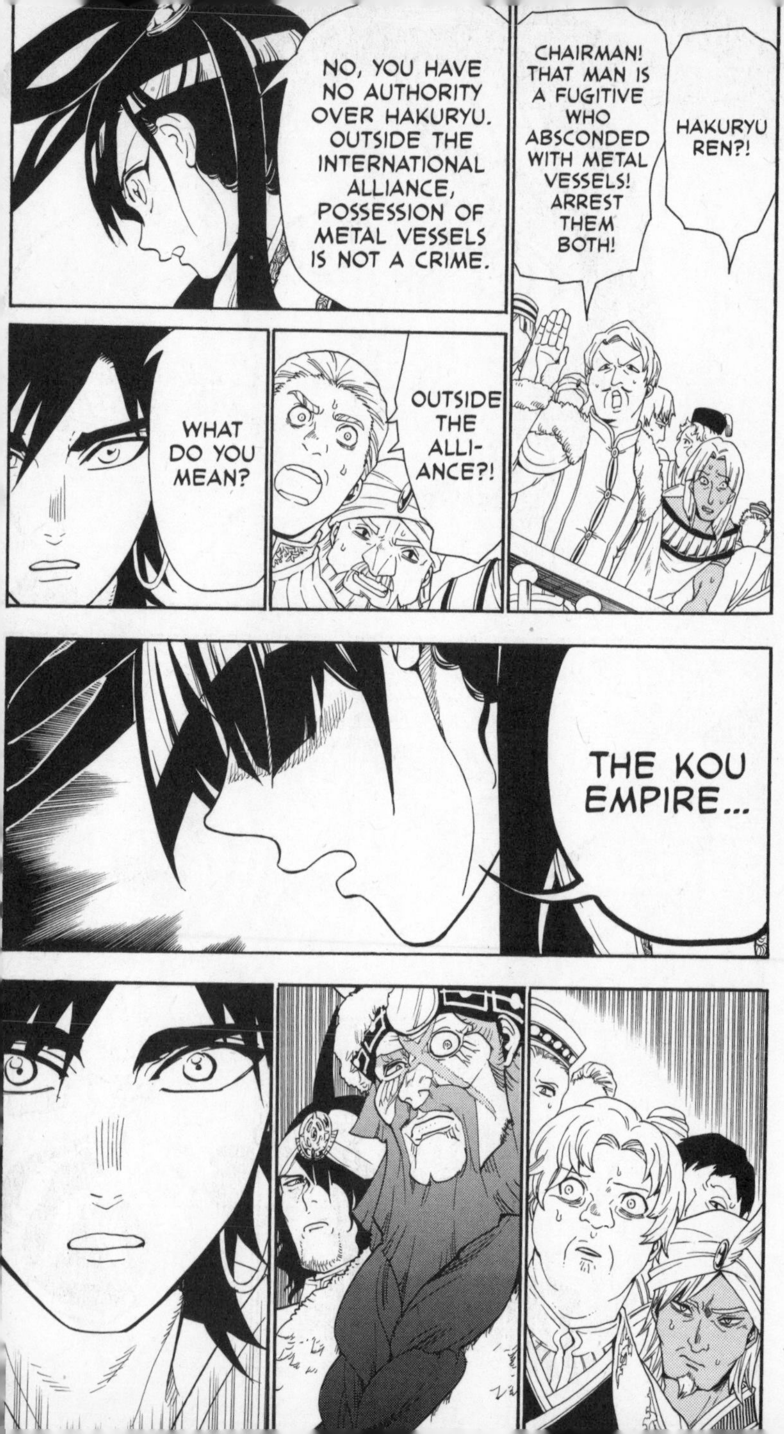
HAKURYU REN?!
CHAIRMAN! THAT MAN IS A FUGITIVE WHO ABSCONDED WITH METAL VESSELS! ARREST THEM BOTH!
NO, YOU HAVE NO AUTHORITY OVER HAKURYU. OUTSIDE THE INTERNATIONAL ALLIANCE, POSSESSION OF METAL VESSELS IS NOT A CRIME.
OUTSIDE THE ALLI-ANCE?!
WHAT DO YOU MEAN?
THE KOU EMPIRE...

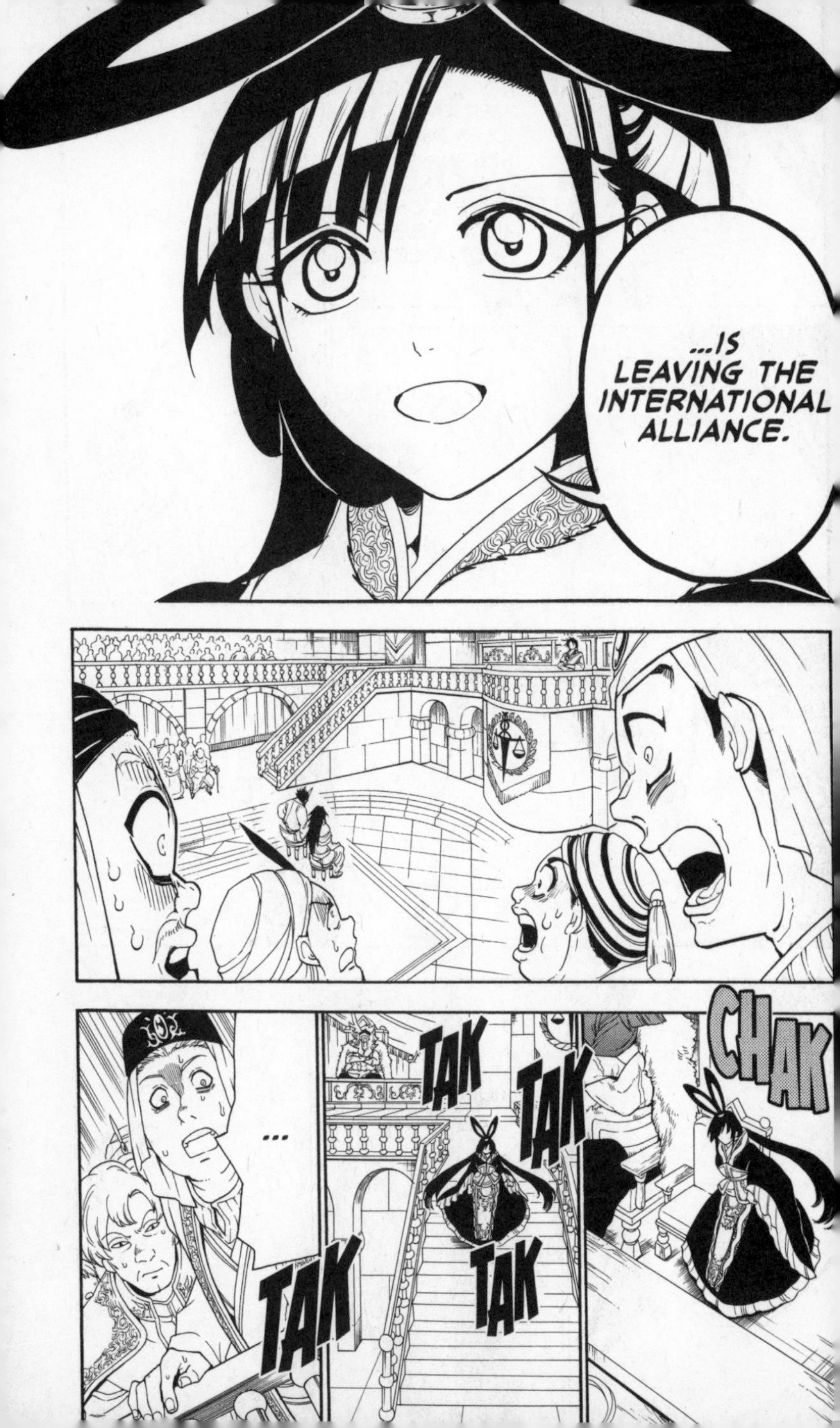
...IS LEAVING THE INTERNATIONAL ALLIANCE.
CHAK
TAK
TAK
TAK
TAK
...

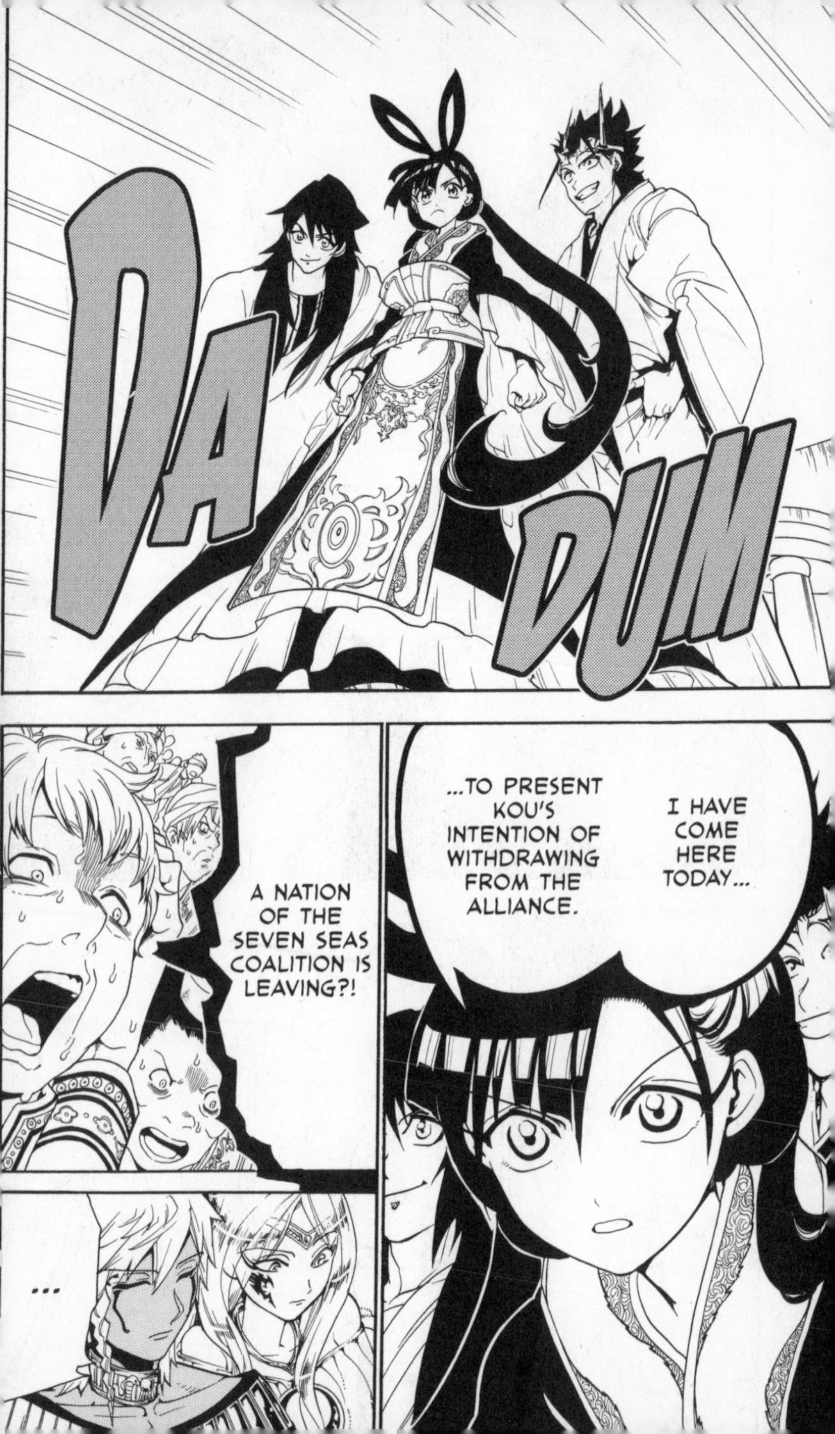
DA
DUM
I HAVE COME HERE TODAY...
...TO PRESENT KOU'S INTENTION OF WITHDRAWING FROM THE ALLIANCE.
A NATION OF THE SEVEN SEAS COALITION IS LEAVING?!
...

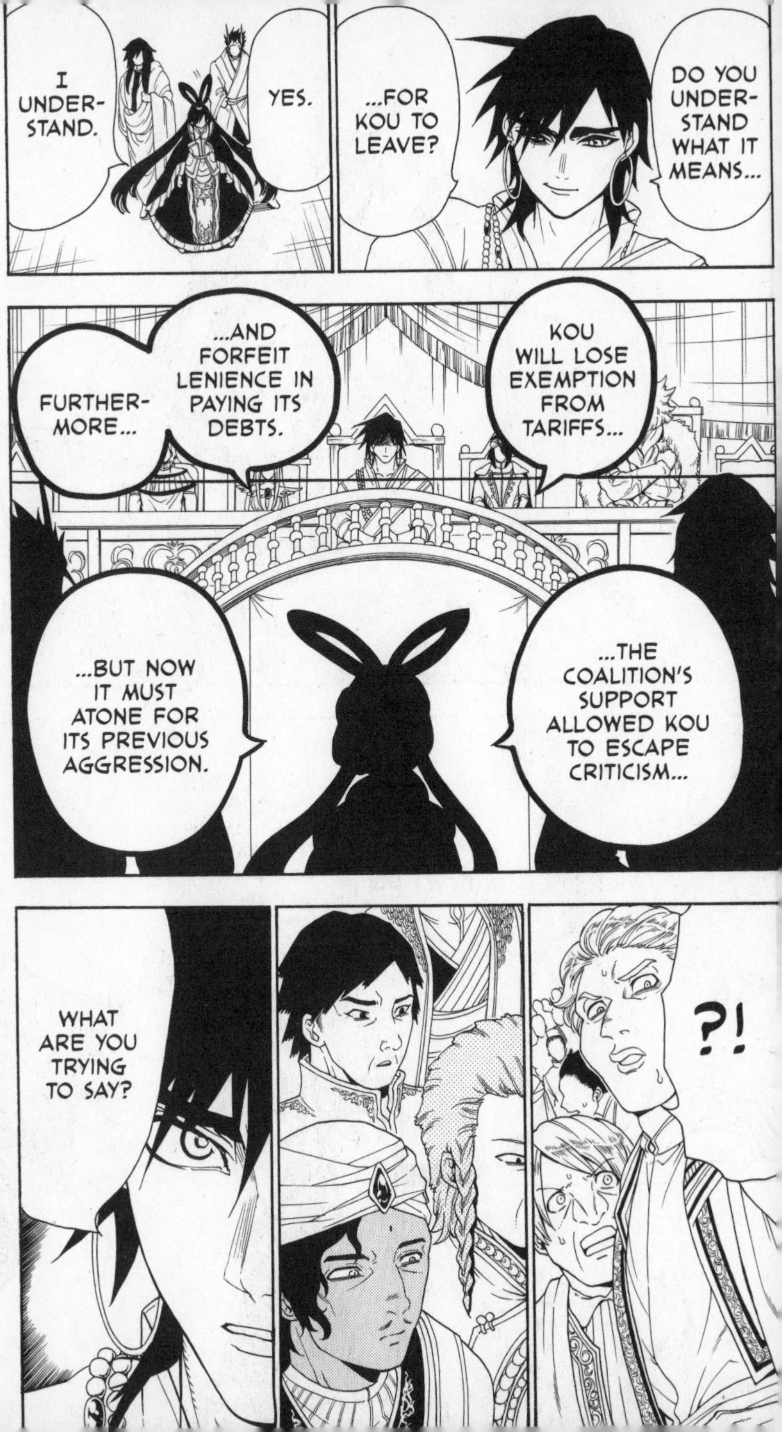
DO YOU UNDER-STAND WHAT IT MEANS...
...FOR KOU TO LEAVE?
YES.
I UNDER-STAND.
KOU WILL LOSE EXEMPTION FROM TARIFFS...
...AND FORFEIT LENIENCE IN PAYING ITS DEBTS.
FURTHER-MORE...
...THE COALITION'S SUPPORT ALLOWED KOU TO ESCAPE CRITICISM...
...BUT NOW IT MUST ATONE FOR ITS PREVIOUS AGGRESSION.
?!
WHAT ARE YOU TRYING TO SAY?

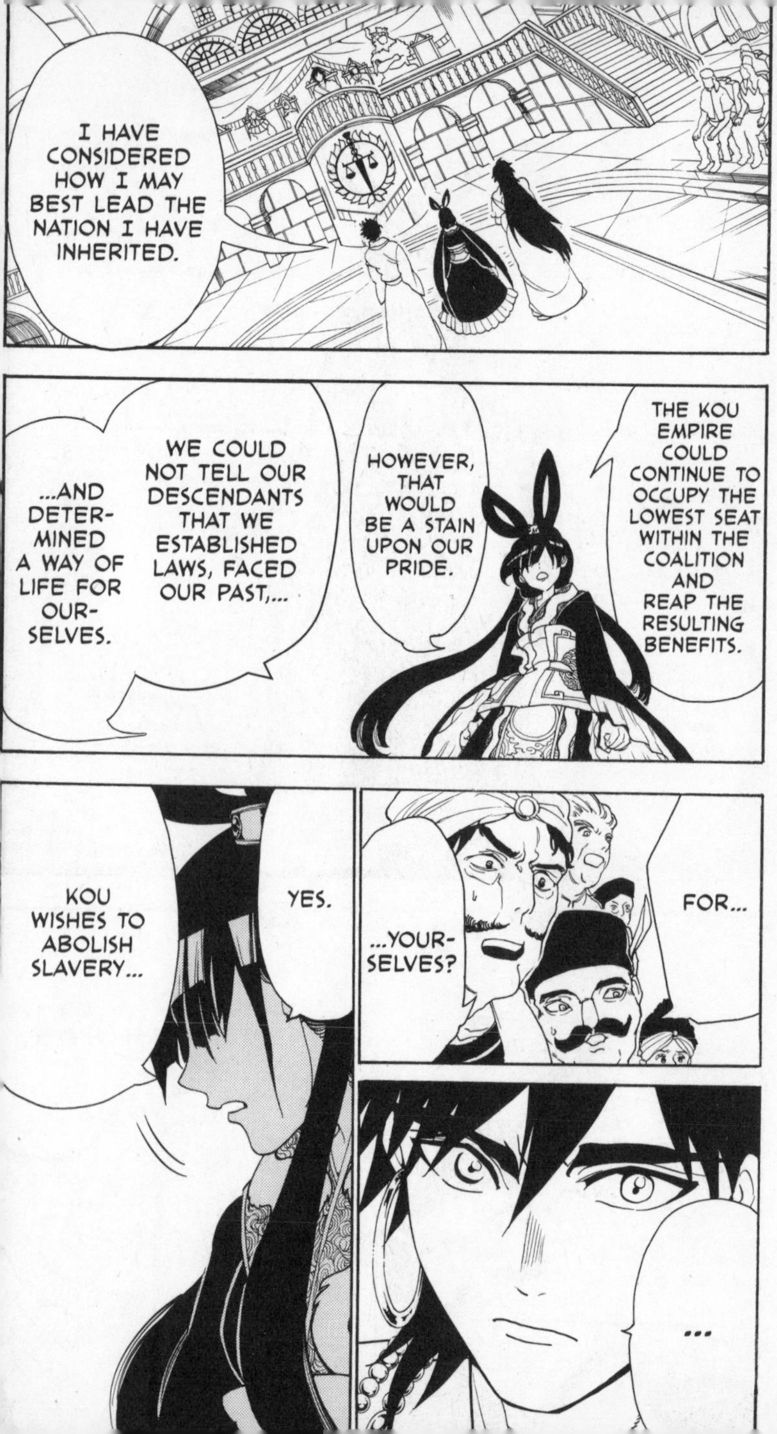
I HAVE CONSIDERED HOW I MAY BEST LEAD THE NATION I HAVE INHERITED.
THE KOU EMPIRE COULD CONTINUE TO OCCUPY THE LOWEST SEAT WITHIN THE COALITION AND REAP THE RESULTING BENEFITS.
HOWEVER, THAT WOULD BE A STAIN UPON OUR PRIDE.
WE COULD NOT TELL OUR DESCENDANTS THAT WE ESTABLISHED LAWS, FACED OUR PAST,...
...AND DETERMINED A WAY OF LIFE FOR OURSELVES.
FOR...
...YOURSELVES?
...
YES.
KOU WISHES TO ABOLISH SLAVERY...

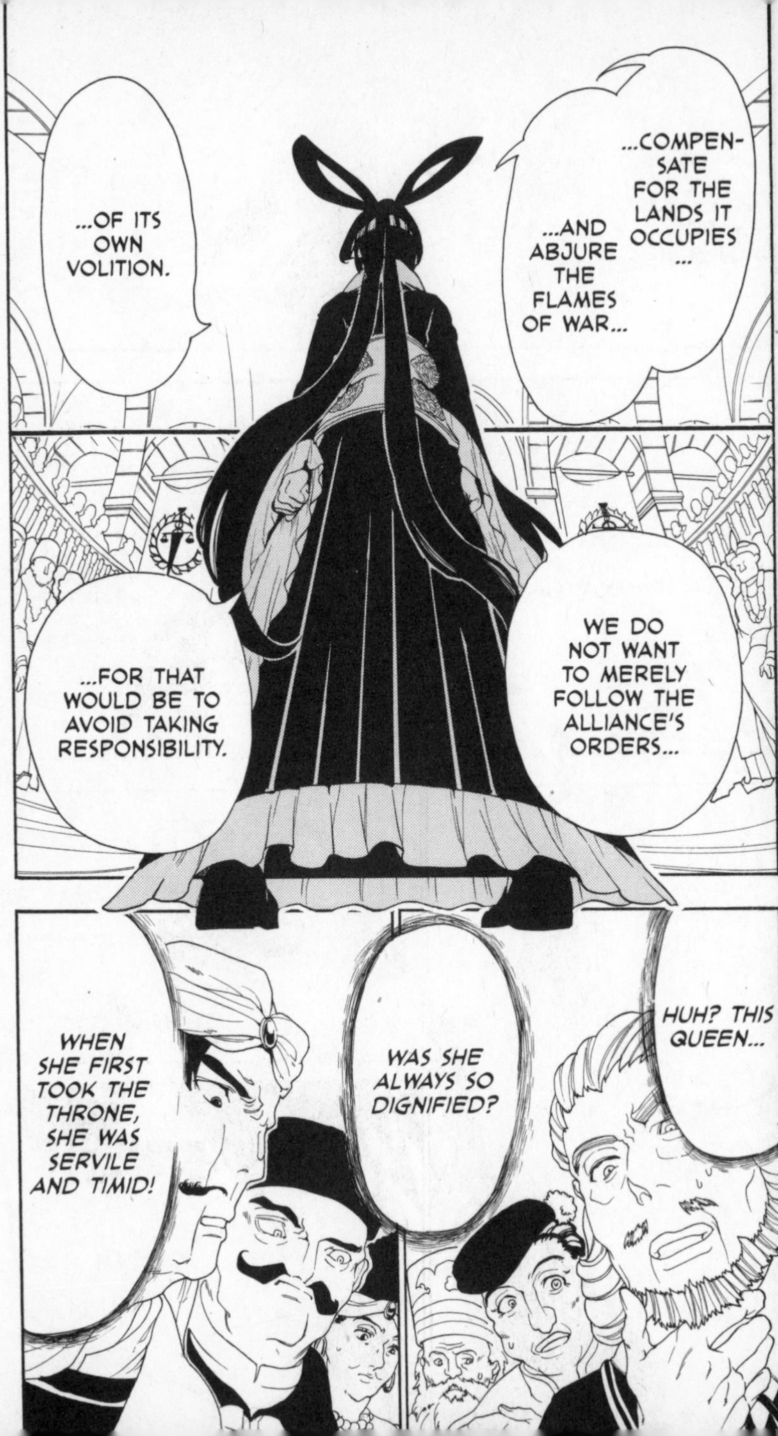
...COMPENSATE FOR THE LANDS IT OCCUPIES...
...AND ABJURE THE FLAMES OF WAR...
...OF ITS OWN VOLITION.
WE DO NOT WANT TO MERELY FOLLOW THE ALLIANCE'S ORDERS...
...FOR THAT WOULD BE TO AVOID TAKING RESPONSIBILITY.
HUH? THIS QUEEN...
WAS SHE ALWAYS SO DIGNIFIED?
WHEN SHE FIRST TOOK THE THRONE, SHE WAS SERVILE AND TIMID!

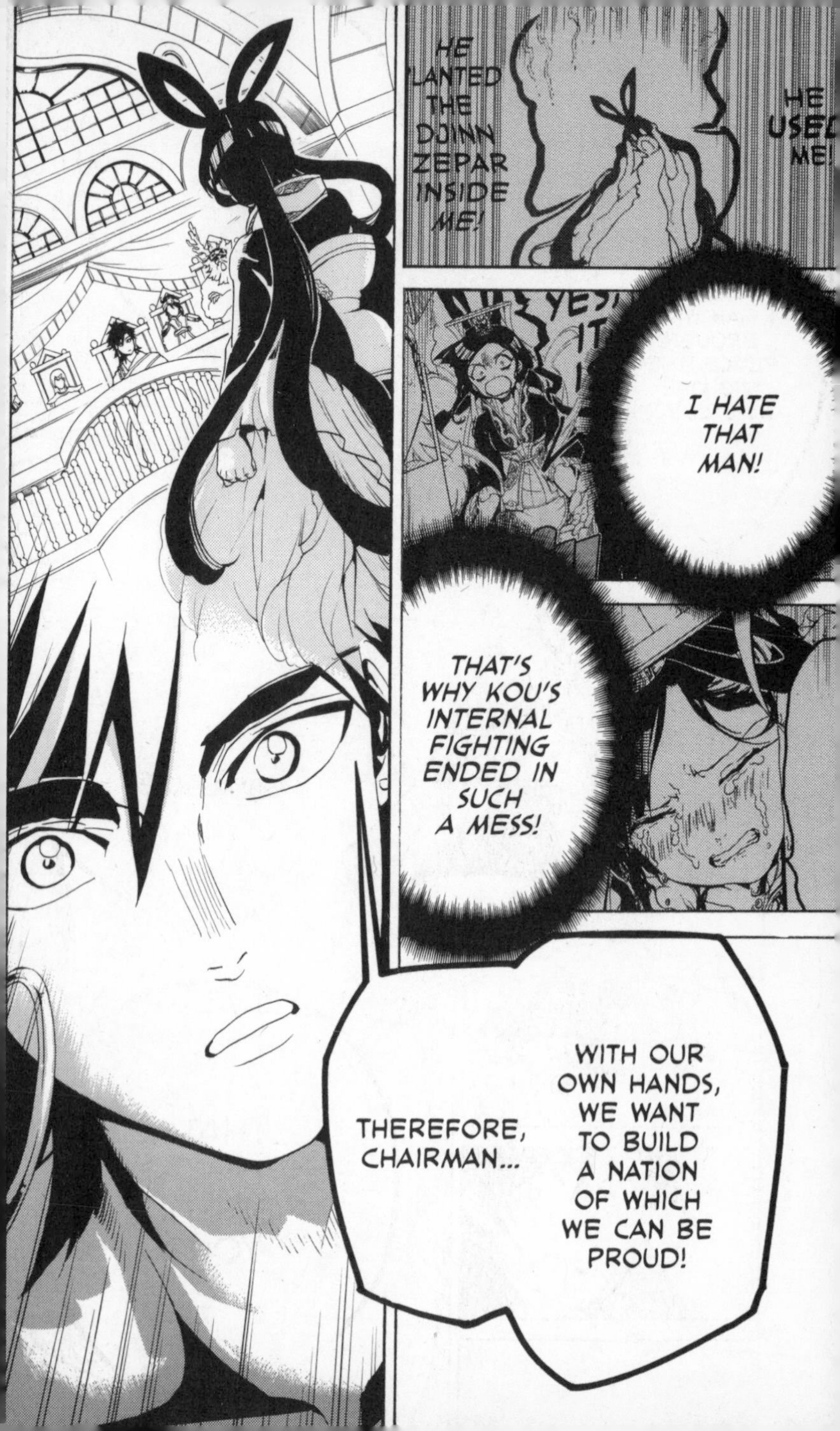
HE USED ME!
HE LANTED THE DJINN ZEPAR INSIDE ME!
YES! IT
I HATE THAT MAN!
THAT'S WHY KOU'S INTERNAL FIGHTING ENDED IN SUCH A MESS!
THEREFORE, CHAIRMAN...
WITH OUR OWN HANDS, WE WANT TO BUILD A NATION OF WHICH WE CAN BE PROUD!

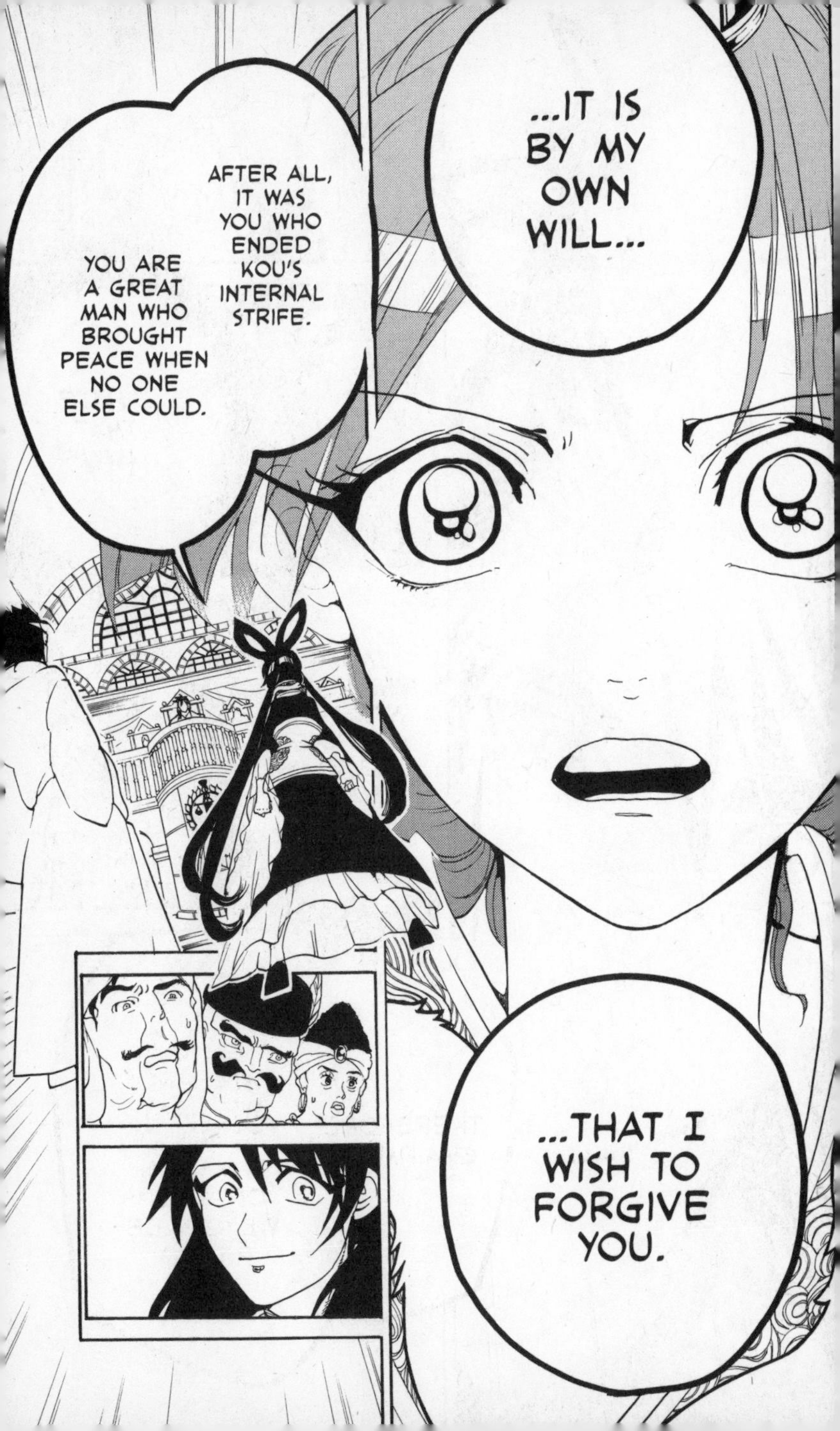
...IT IS BY MY OWN WILL...
AFTER ALL, IT WAS YOU WHO ENDED KOU'S INTERNAL STRIFE.
YOU ARE A GREAT MAN WHO BROUGHT PEACE WHEN NO ONE ELSE COULD.
...THAT I WISH TO FORGIVE YOU.

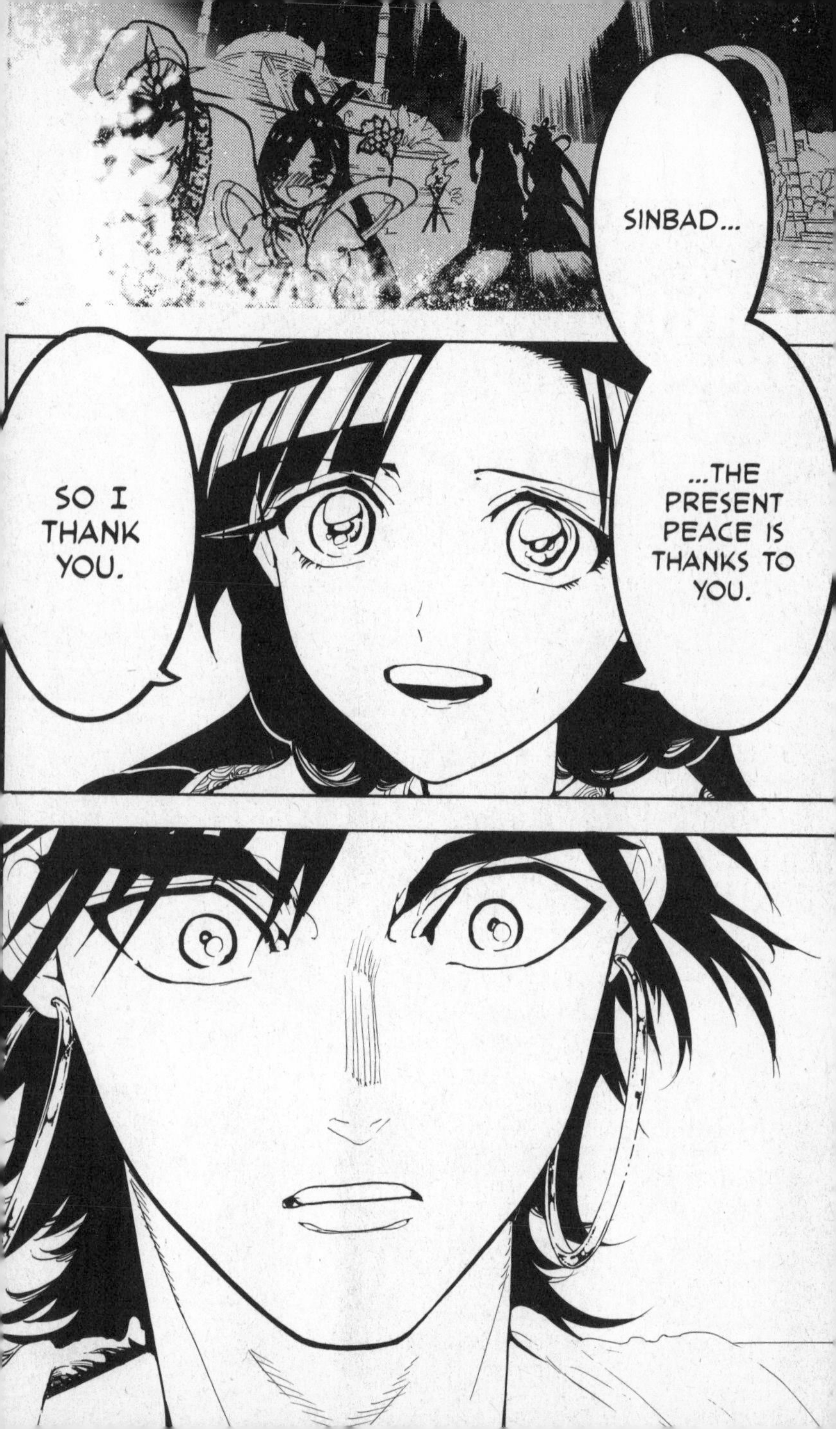
SINBAD...
...THE PRESENT PEACE IS THANKS TO YOU.
SO I THANK YOU.

MAGI
The labyrinth of magic
32

Staff

■ Story & Art
Shinobu Ohtaka

■ Regular Assistants
Hiro Maizima

Yuiko Akiyama

Megi

Aya Umoto

Mami Yoshida

Yuka Otsuji

■ Editors
Kazuaki Ishibashi
Makoto Ishiwata
Katsumasa Ogura

■ Sales & Promotion
Tsunato Imamoto

Yuta Uchiyama

■ Designer
Hajime Tokushige + Bay Bridge Studio

THE LIVES OF YUNAN THE MAGI: TAKE 1 - TAKE 9

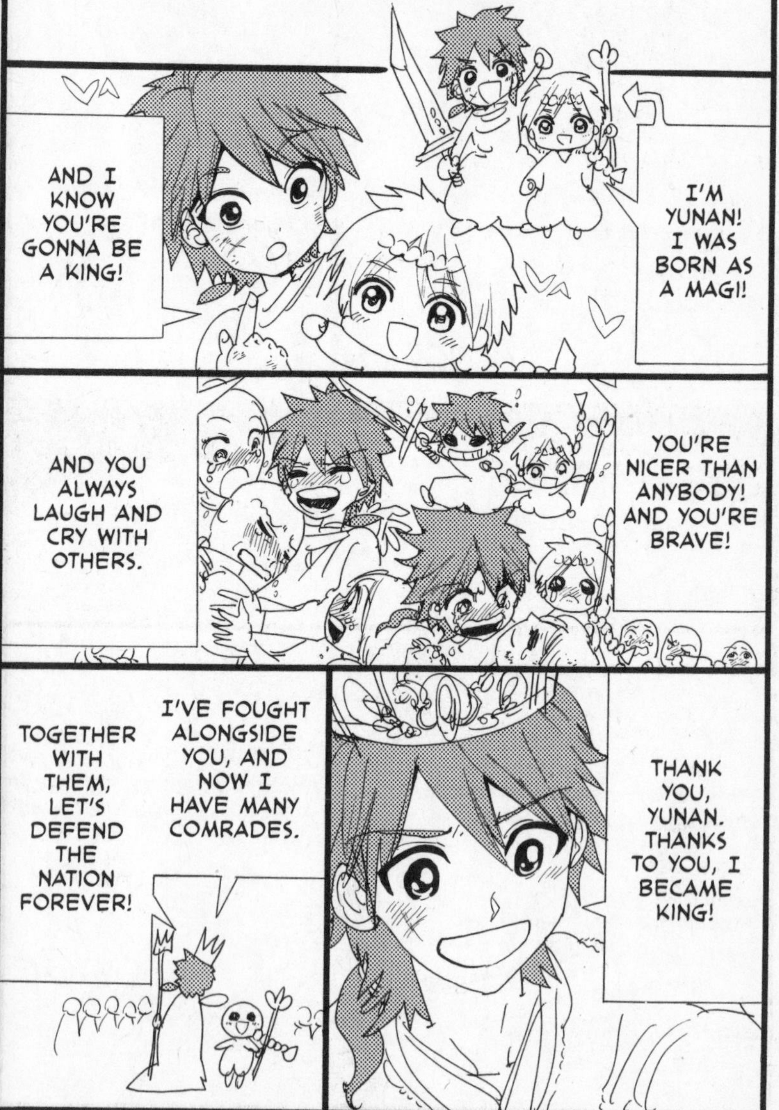

I'M YUNAN! I WAS BORN AS A MAGI!
AND I KNOW YOU'RE GONNA BE A KING!
YOU'RE NICER THAN ANYBODY! AND YOU'RE BRAVE!
AND YOU ALWAYS LAUGH AND CRY WITH OTHERS.
THANK YOU, YUNAN. THANKS TO YOU, I BECAME KING!
I'VE FOUGHT ALONGSIDE YOU, AND NOW I HAVE MANY COMRADES.
TOGETHER WITH THEM, LET'S DEFEND THE NATION FOREVER!

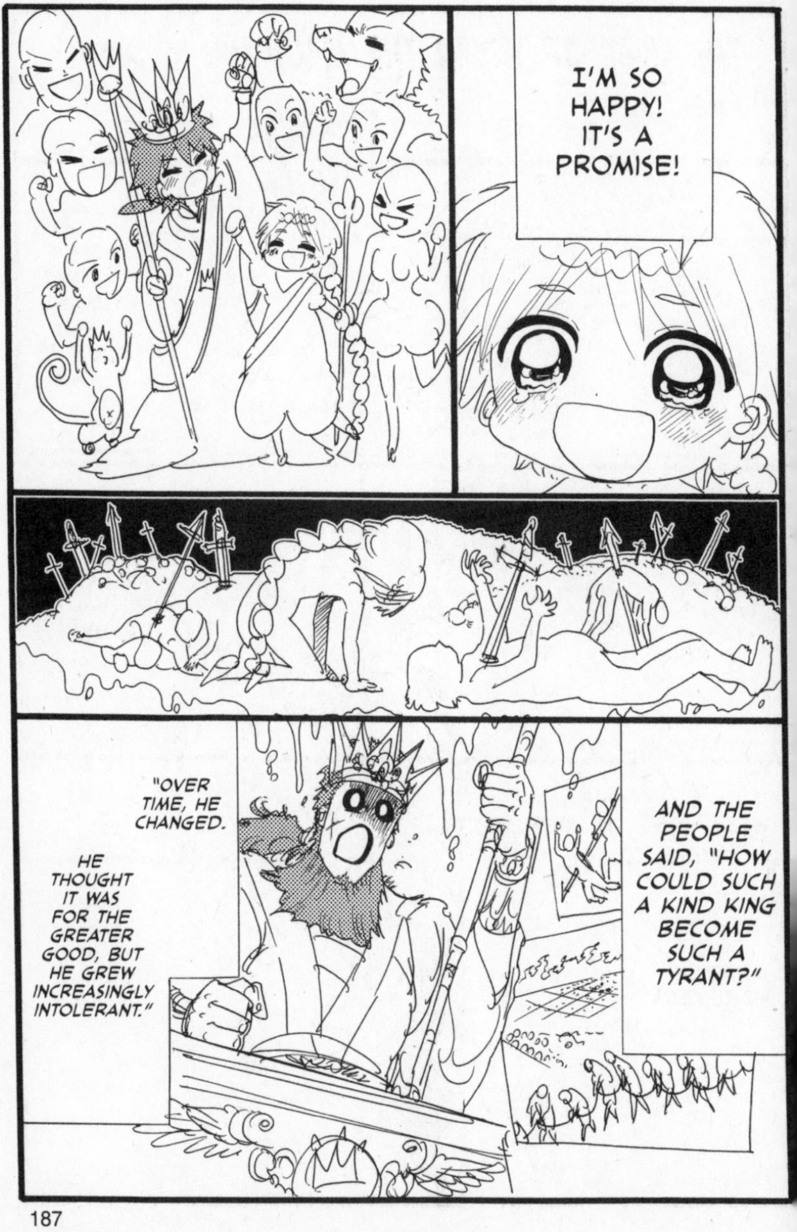
I'M SO HAPPY! IT'S A PROMISE!
AND THE PEOPLE SAID, "HOW COULD SUCH A KIND KING BECOME SUCH A TYRANT?"
"OVER TIME, HE CHANGED.
HE THOUGHT IT WAS FOR THE GREATER GOOD, BUT HE GREW INCREASINGLY INTOLERANT."

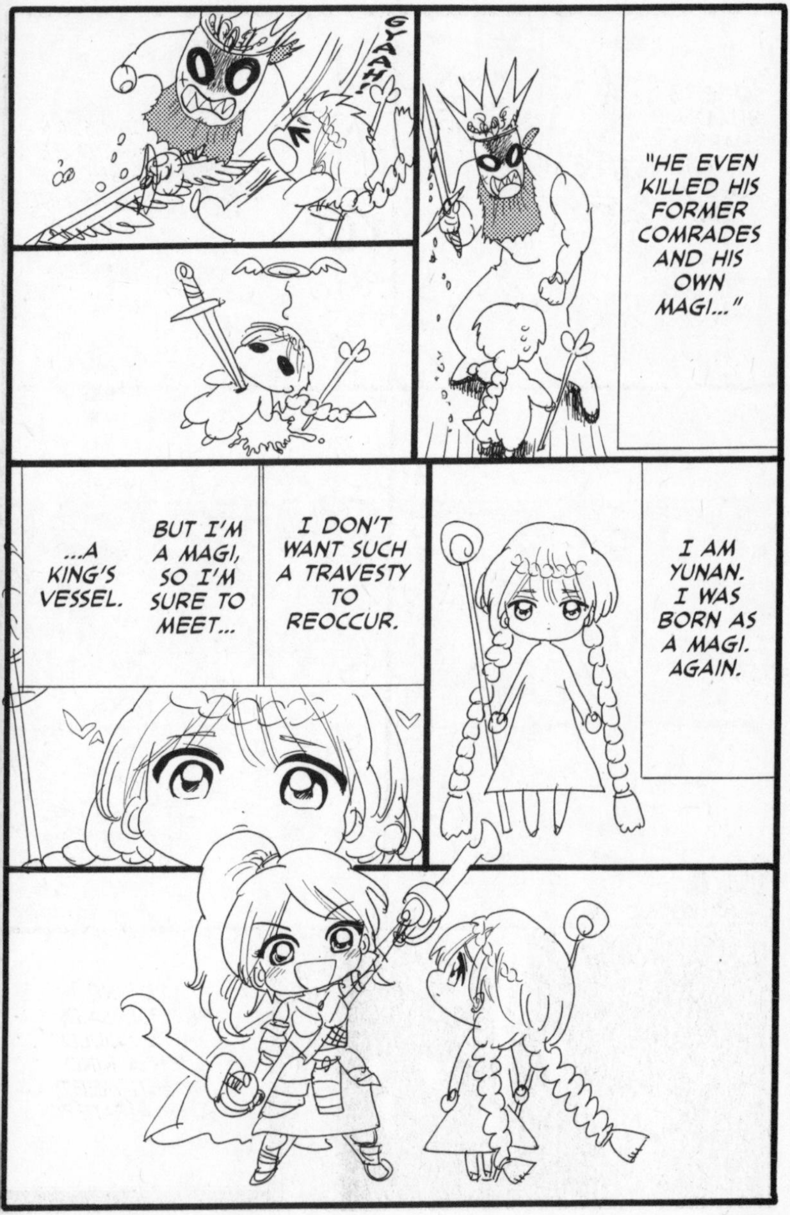
"HE EVEN KILLED HIS FORMER COMRADES AND HIS OWN MAGI..."
GYAAAH!!
I AM YUNAN. I WAS BORN AS A MAGI. AGAIN.
I DON'T WANT SUCH A TRAVESTY TO REOCCUR.
BUT I'M A MAGI, SO I'M SURE TO MEET...
...A KING'S VESSEL.

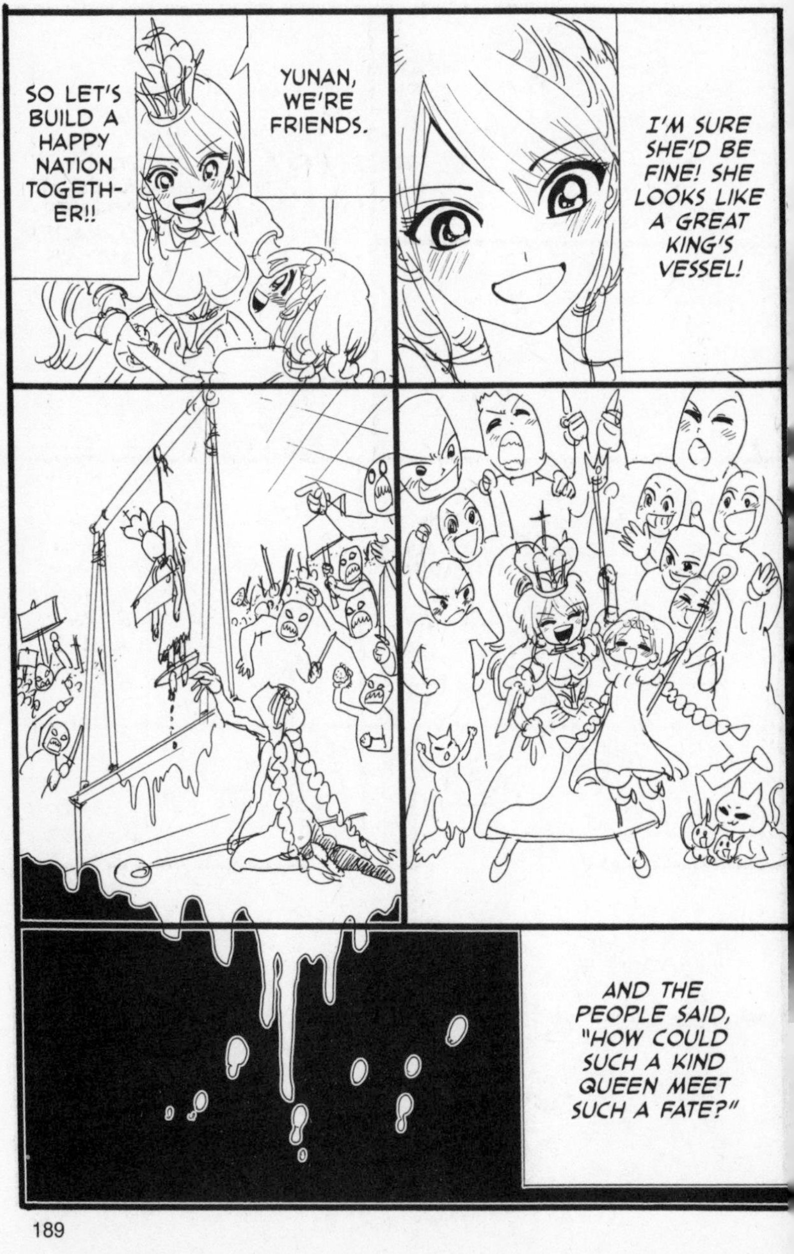
I'M SURE SHE'D BE FINE! SHE LOOKS LIKE A GREAT KING'S VESSEL!
YUNAN, WE'RE FRIENDS.
SO LET'S BUILD A HAPPY NATION TOGETH-ER!!
AND THE PEOPLE SAID, "HOW COULD SUCH A KIND QUEEN MEET SUCH A FATE?"

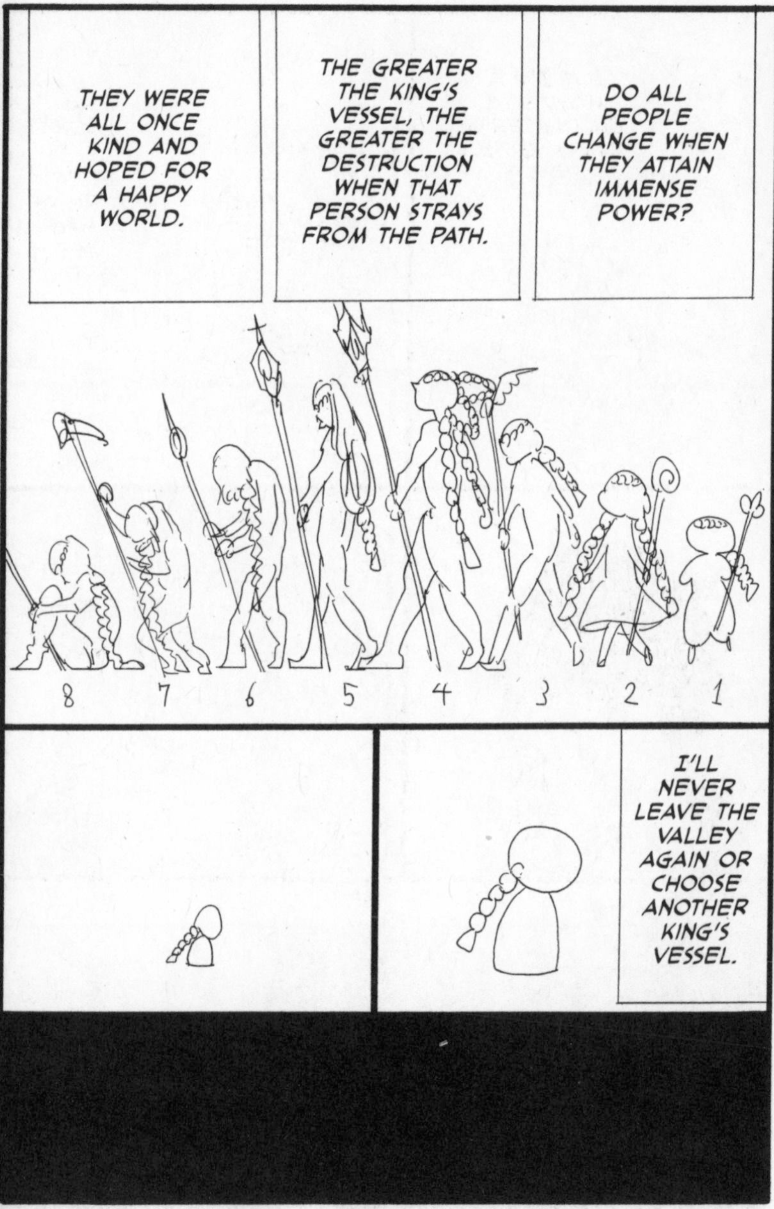
DO ALL PEOPLE CHANGE WHEN THEY ATTAIN IMMENSE POWER?
THE GREATER THE KING'S VESSEL, THE GREATER THE DESTRUCTION WHEN THAT PERSON STRAYS FROM THE PATH.
THEY WERE ALL ONCE KIND AND HOPED FOR A HAPPY WORLD.
1
2
3
4
5
6
7
8
I'LL NEVER LEAVE THE VALLEY AGAIN OR CHOOSE ANOTHER KING'S VESSEL.

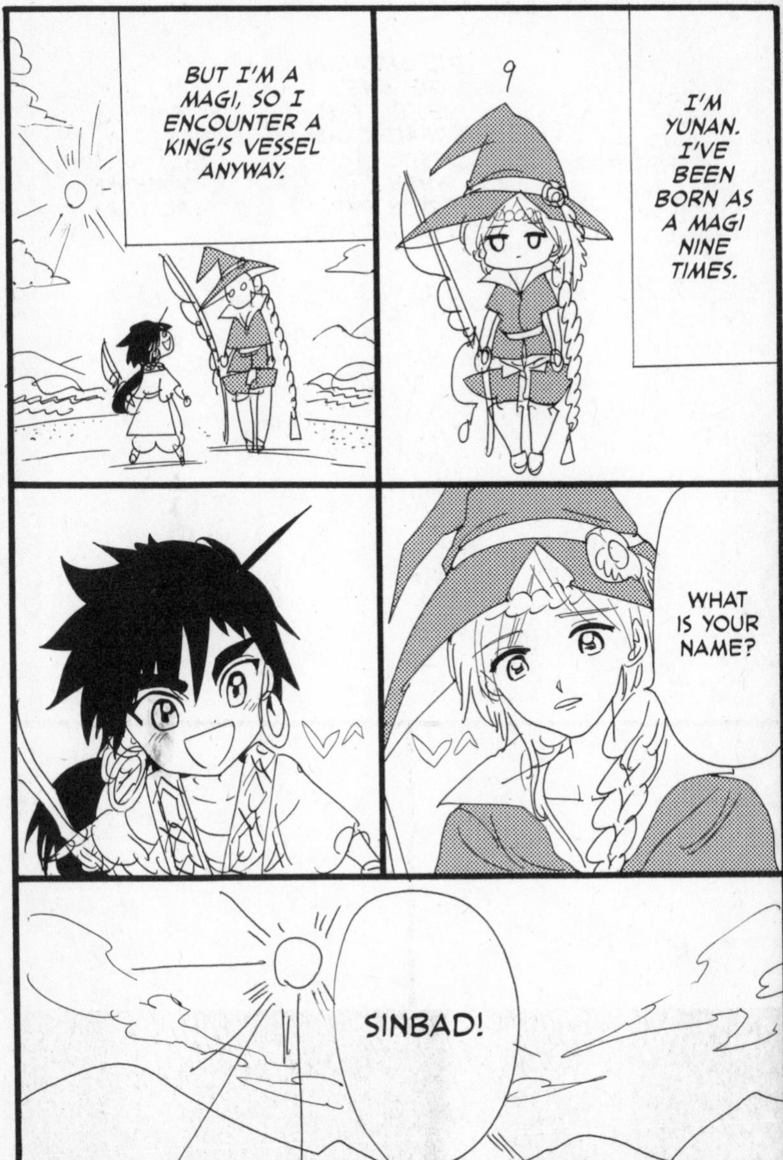
9
I'M YUNAN. I'VE BEEN BORN AS A MAGI NINE TIMES.
BUT I'M A MAGI, SO I ENCOUNTER A KING'S VESSEL ANYWAY.
WHAT IS YOUR NAME?
SINBAD!
The End.

You're reading the WRONG WAY

MAGI reads from right to left, starting in the upper-right corner. Japanese is read from **right** to **left**, meaning that action, sound effects, and word-balloon order are completely reversed from English order.

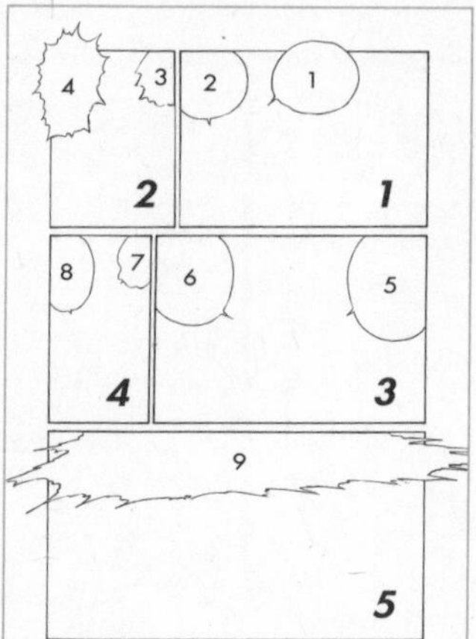
1
1
2
2
3
4
3
5
6
4
7
8
5
9
142

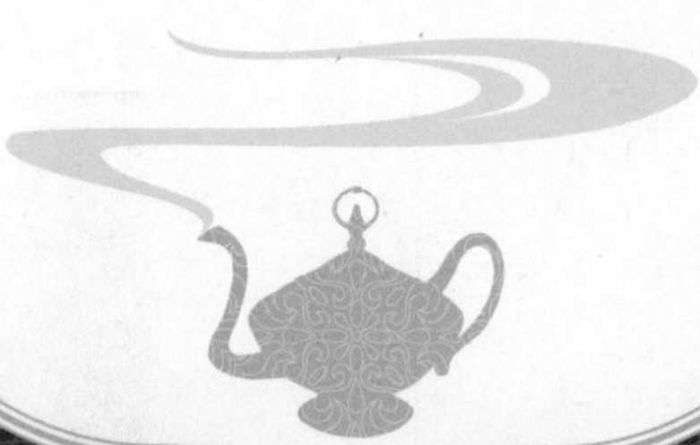